Street by Street

READING, BASINGSTOKE
BRACKNELL
FLEET, HENLEY-ON-THAMES, NEWBURY, WOKINGHAM

Ascot, Goring, Hook, Kingsclere, Odiham, Overton, Pangbourne, Sonning Common, Tadley, Twyford

Ist edition May 2001

© Automobile Association Developments Limited 2001

This product includes map data licensed from Ordnance Survey® with the permission of the Controller of Her Majesty's Stationery Office. © Crown copyright 2000. All rights reserved. Licence No: 399221.

Published by AA Publishing (a trading name of Automobile Association Developments Limited, whose registered office is Norfolk House, Priestley Road, Basingstoke, Hampshire, RG24 9NY. Registered number 1878835).

Mapping produced by the Cartographic Department of The Automobile Association.

A CIP Catalogue record for this book is available from the British Library.

Printed by G. Canale & C. S.P.A., Torino, Italy

The contents of this atlas are believed to be correct at the time of the latest revision. However, the publishers cannot be held responsible for loss occasioned to any person acting or refraining from action as a result of any material in this atlas, nor for any errors, omissions or changes in such material. The publishers would welcome information to correct any errors or omissions and to keep this atlas up to date. Please write to Publishing, The Automobile Association, Fanum House, Basing View, Basingstoke, Hampshire, RG21 4EA.

Ref: MX056

Key to map pages	ii-iii
Key to map symbols	iv-1
Enlarged scale pages	2-15
Street by Street	16-183
Index – towns & villages	184
Index – streets	185-199
Index – featured places	199-201

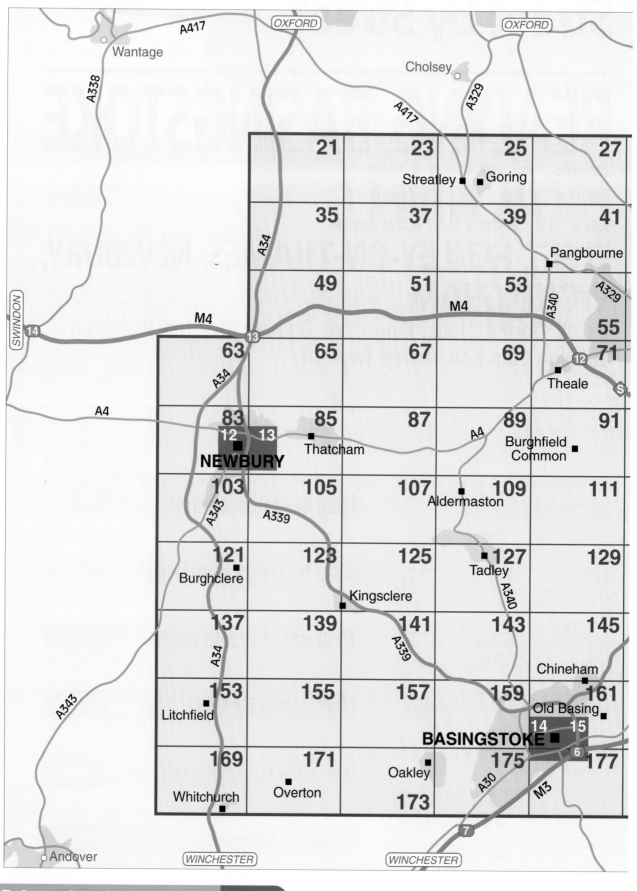

Enlarged scale pages   **1:10,000**   **6.3 inches to 1 mile**

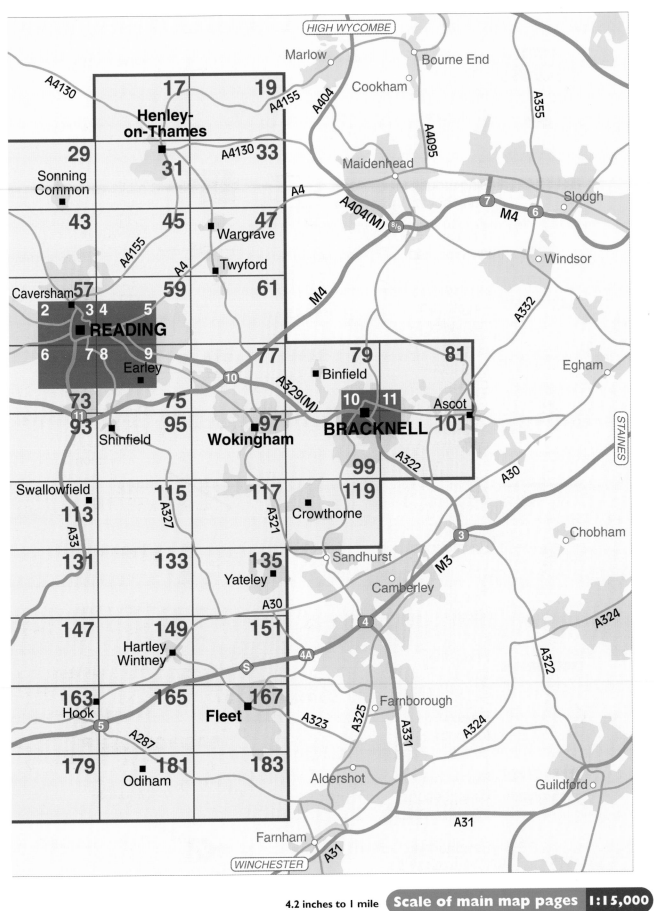

4.2 inches to 1 mile   Scale of main map pages   1:15,000

Symbol	Description
Junction 9	Motorway & junction
Services	Motorway service area
	Primary road single/dual carriageway
Services	Primary road service area
	A road single/dual carriageway
	B road single/dual carriageway
	Other road single/dual carriageway
	Restricted road
	Private road
←	One way street
	Pedestrian street
	Track/footpath
	Road under construction
	Road tunnel
P	Parking
P+	Park & Ride
	Bus/coach station
	Railway & main railway station
	Railway & minor railway station
	Underground station
	Light railway & station
++++++++++	Preserved private railway
LC	Level crossing
•—•—•—•—	Tramway
------------	Ferry route
....	Airport runway
-·-·-·-·	Boundaries-borough/district
▾▾▾▾▾▾▾▾	Mounds
93	Page continuation 1:15,000
7	Page continuation to enlarged scale 1:10,000

River/canal lake, pier			Toilet with disabled facilities
Aqueduct lock, weir			Petrol station
465 Winter Hill	Peak (with height in metres)	PH	Public house
	Beach	PO	Post Office
	Coniferous woodland		Public library
	Broadleaved woodland	i	Tourist Information Centre
	Mixed woodland		Castle
	Park		Historic house/ building
	Cemetery	Wakehurst Place NT	National Trust property
	Built-up area	M	Museum/ art gallery
	Featured building	†	Church/chapel
	City wall		Country park
A&E	Accident & Emergency hospital		Theatre/ performing arts
	Toilet		Cinema

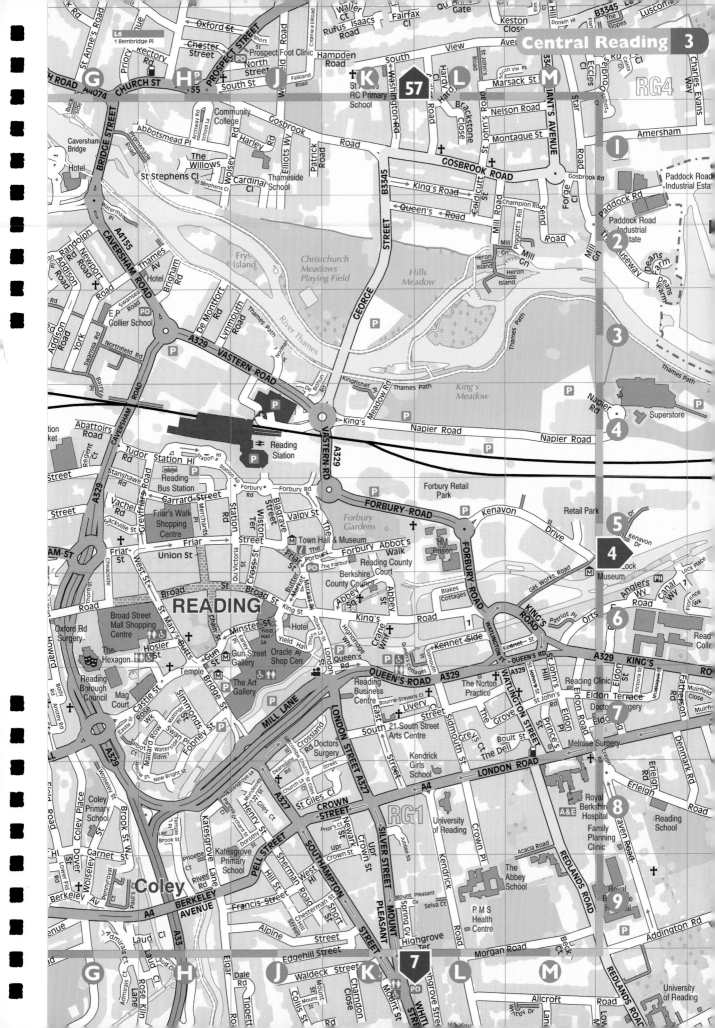

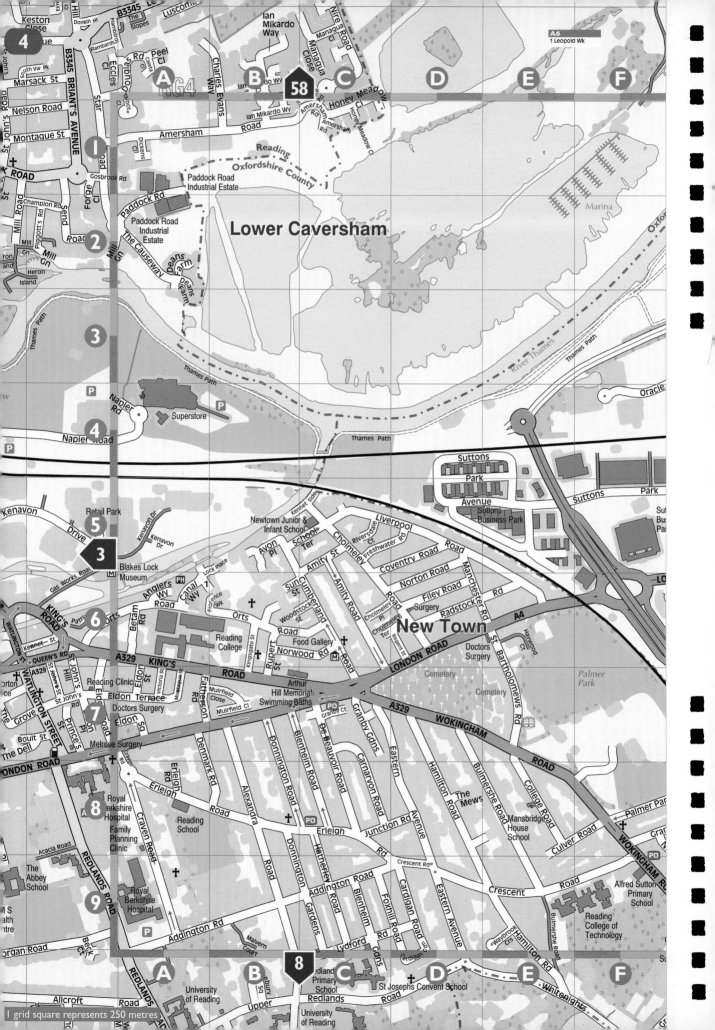

4

6

Delwood Hospital

Jenkins Cl

Dorchester Ct

Amethyst La

Inglewood Ct

Liebenrood Rd

Inglewood

Armadale Court

Road

Trafalgar C

A4

A4155

Benyon Ct

Benyon Court

Berkeley

te Dr

Tazewell

Portway Cl

Epsom Ct

Marborough Ct

oley

Portway Cl

Mansfield Road

Berkeley Av

A **B** **2** **C** **D** **E** **A4** **F**

BATH ROAD **BERKELEY** **AVENUE**

Presentation College

Upavon Dr

Carsdale Close

Carsdale Cl

Shaw Rd

Holybrook Rd

Boston Av

I RG30

Froxfield Av

PO

Wensley Road

Holybrook Rd

Playing Field

Southcote Lane

Southcote Lane

Monks Way

Kenilworth Avenue

Firs Lane

Edenham Crs

Edenham Crs

Barrington Wv

Kimberley Cl

Barrington Wv

Greenlea Ct

Ashley Road

Rembrandt Way

Coley Park Surgery

Coley Park School

Tintern Crs

Road

St Saviour's

Hay Rd

Trelleck Rd

2

Fawley Road

Aldworth Cl

Southcote Lane

Southcote Farm La

St Mary's All Saints C of E Primary School

The Old Lane

Tupsley Rd

Tyberton Pl

St

3

Silchester

Southcote CP School

Southcote Road

Road

Winser Dr

Southcote Farm Lane

Barn Cl

Cowper Wy

Wensley

Wensley Road

Wensley Rd

Lesford Road

Heron Wv

Brookmill

The Old La

Arbour Close

Yew Lane

The Old Lane

Shepley Drive

Restwold

Stanford Rd

Tallis La

Wensley

4

5

72

Southcote Mill

Kennet and Avon Canal

6

Island Rd

Island Road

7

8

Cottage Lane

Island Road

9

Cottage Lane

Kirtons Farm Rd

A **B** **73** **C** **D** **E** **F**

1 grid square represents 250 metres

Way

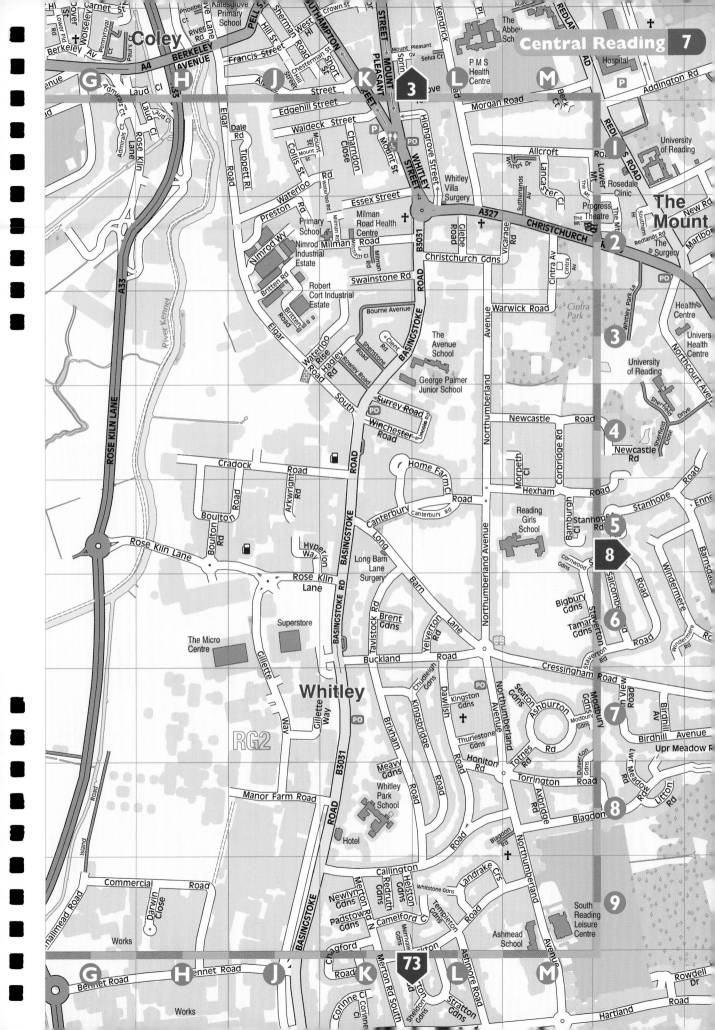

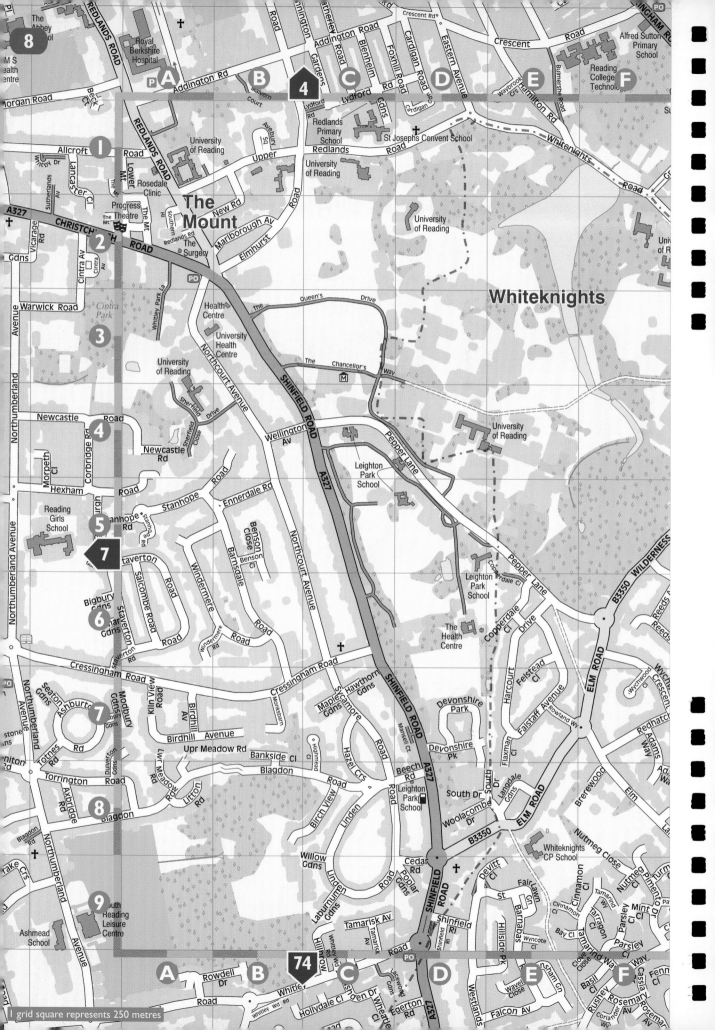

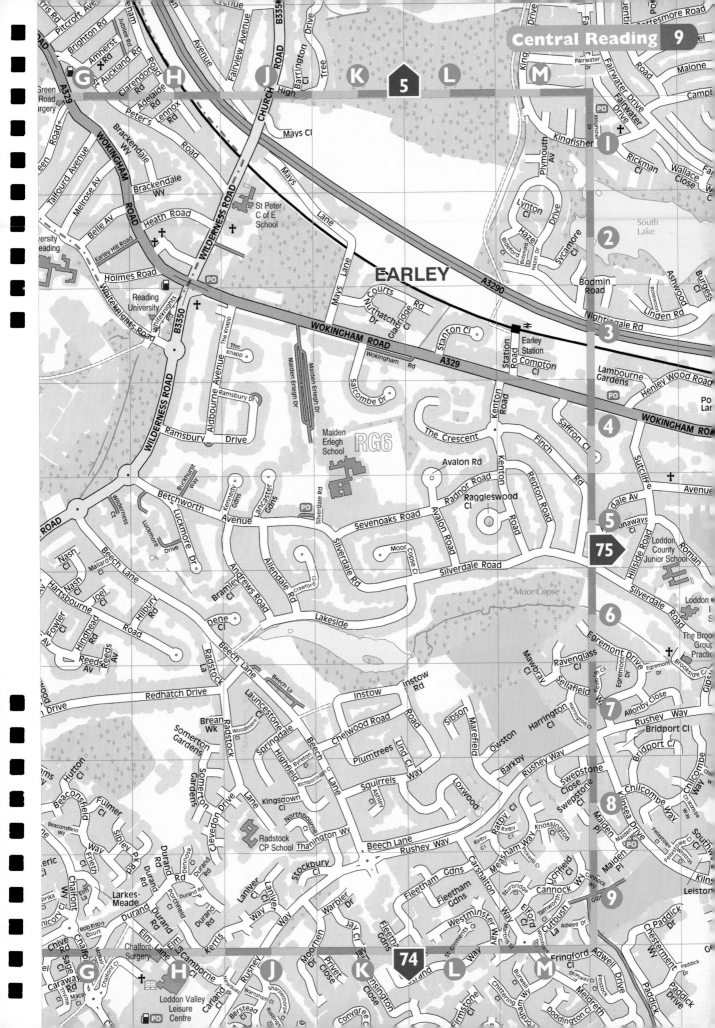

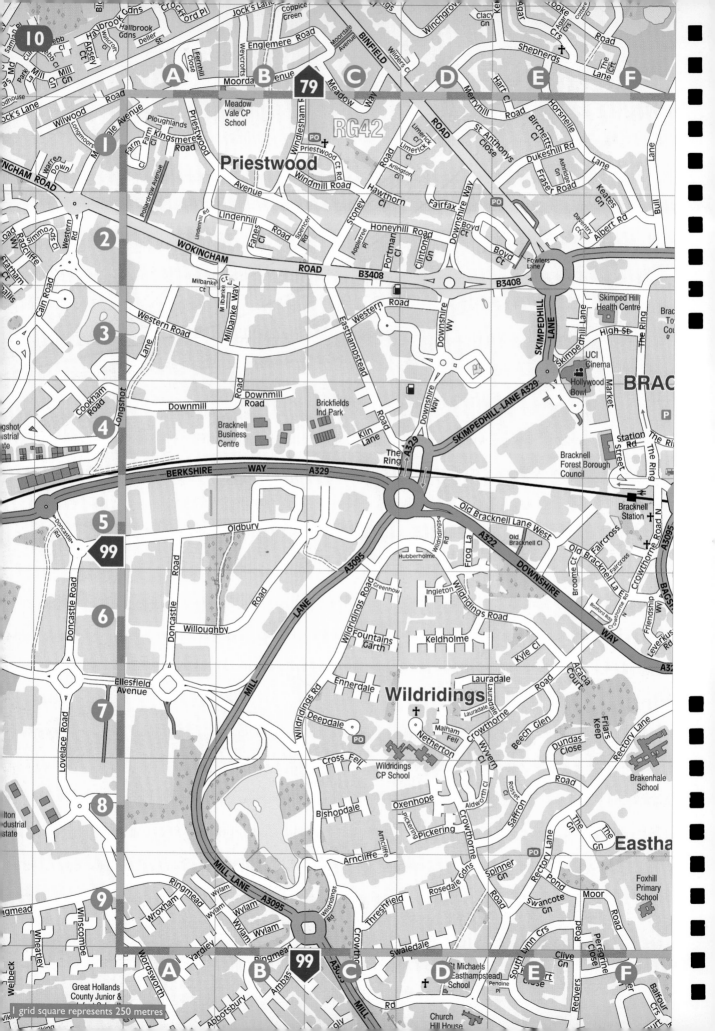

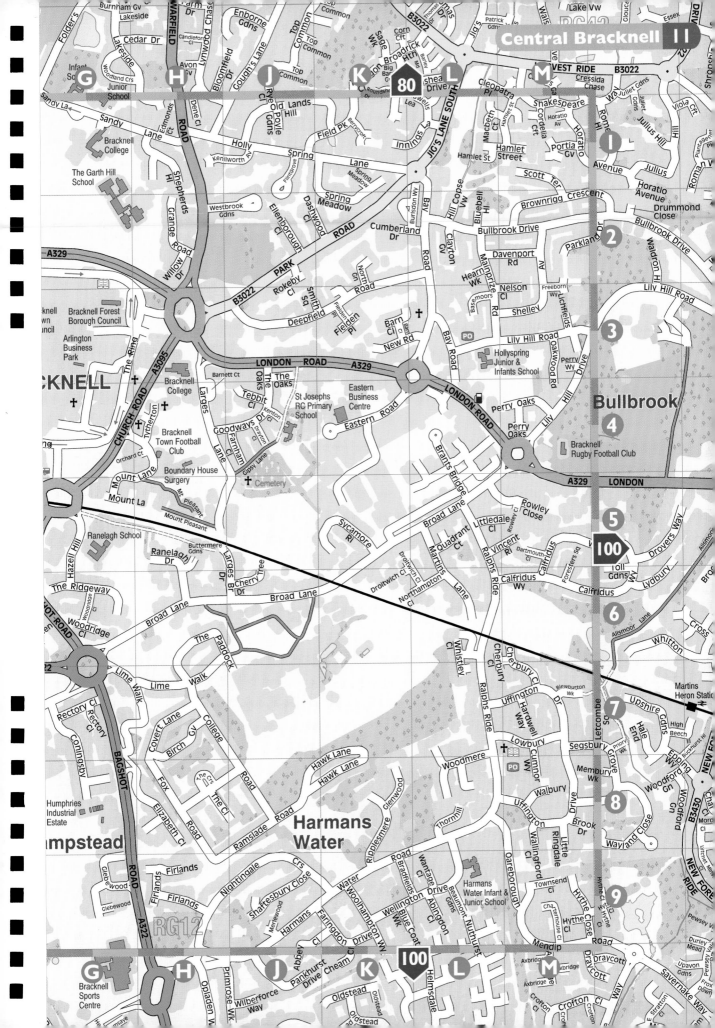

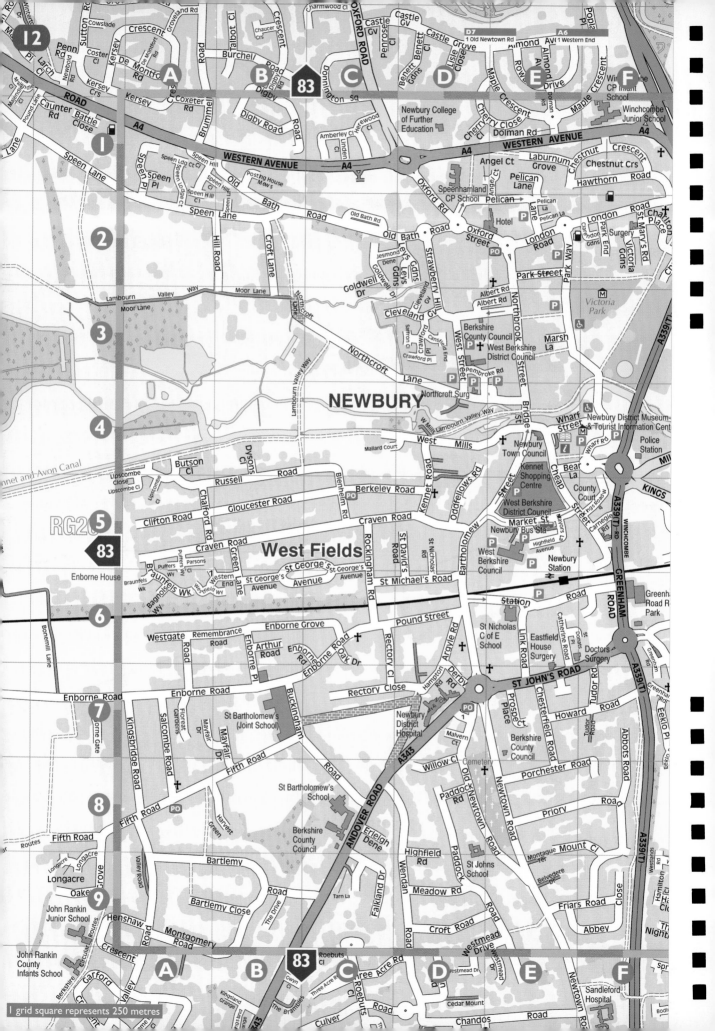

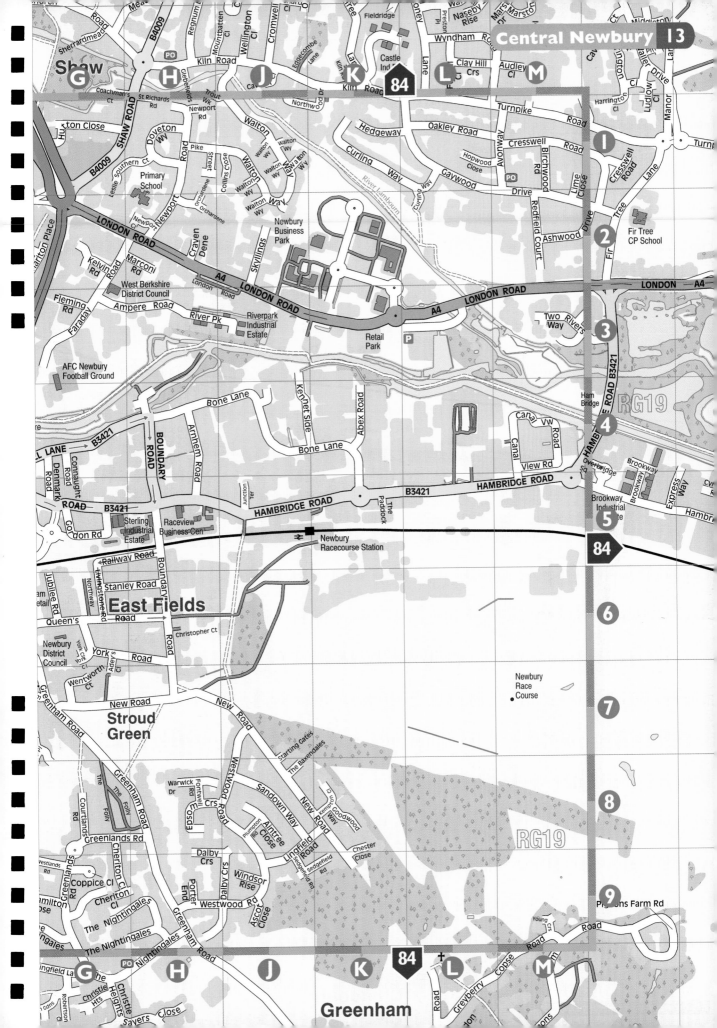

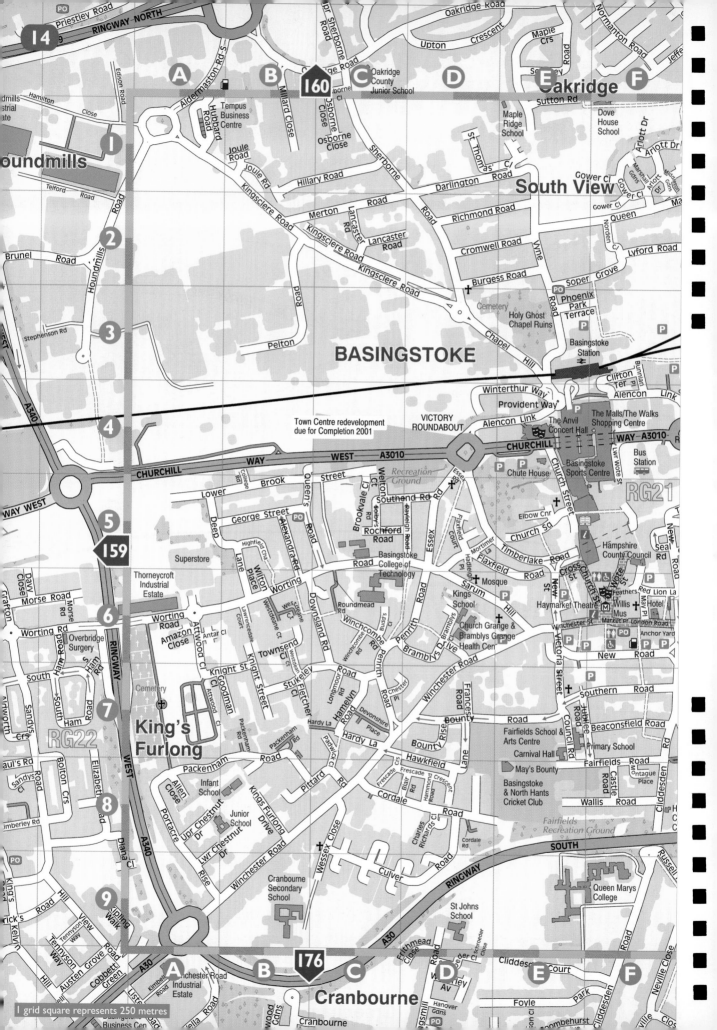

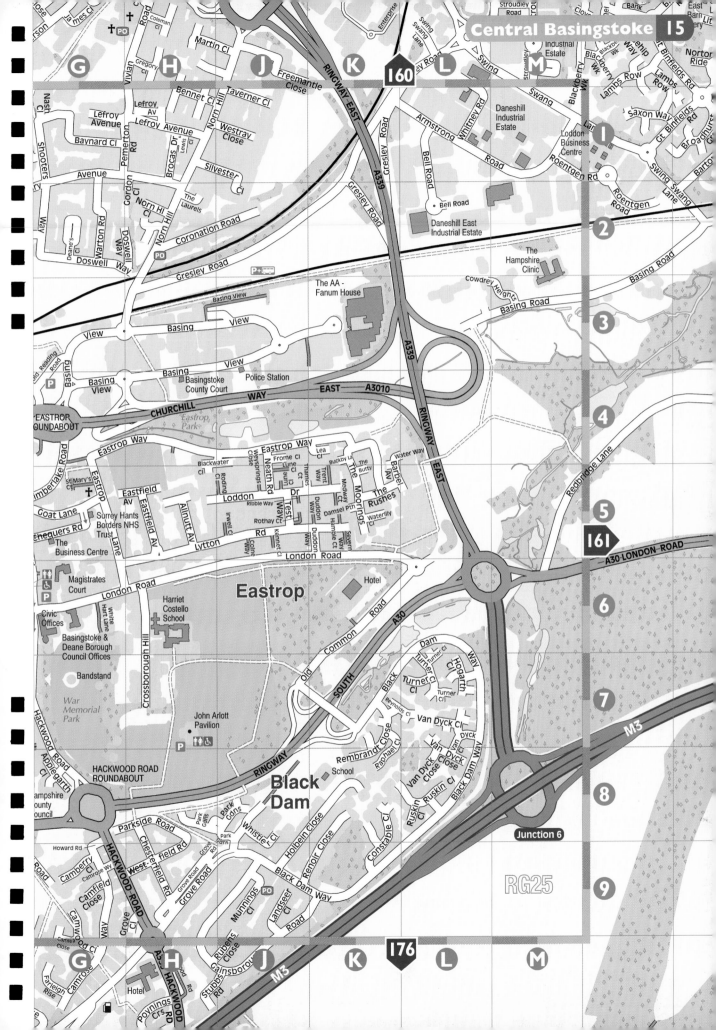

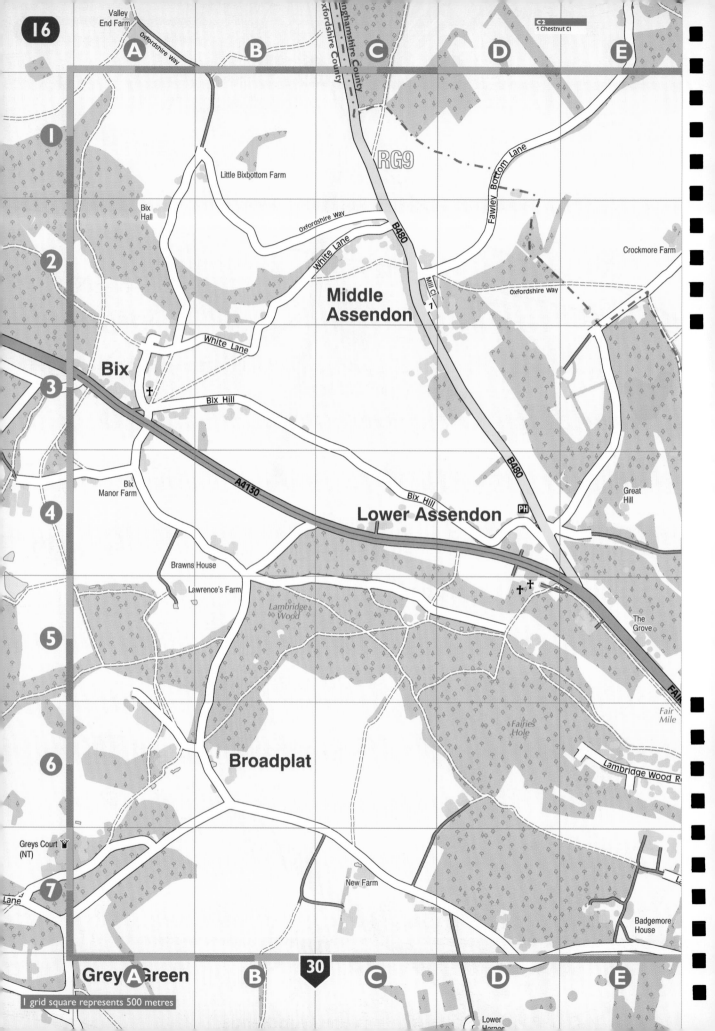

A   B   C   D   E

Manor House

PH

Doctors Surgery

PO

Hambleden

1

Dairy Lane

2

A155

Buckinghamshire County

Wokingham

3

Thames Path

Mill End

Burrow Farm

e Island

4

17

Ferry Lane

Westfield Farm

Remenham Lane

5

Aston Ferry Lane

Aston

Remenham Church Lane

6

Culham Court

River Thames

Thames Path

7

Common Barn

Aston Lane

Lower Culham Farm

Remenham Pla

A   B   **32**   C   D   E

Middle Culham Farm

Remenham Hill

HILL

1 grid square represents 500 metres

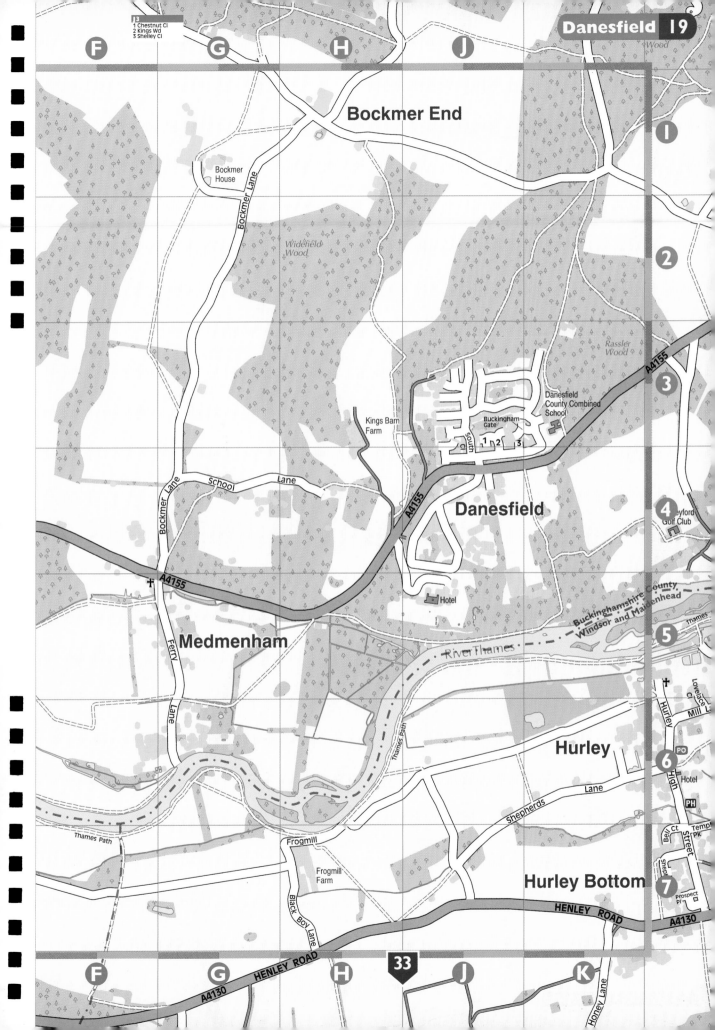

1 Chestnut Cl
2 Kings Wd
3 Shelley Cl

F G H J I

Bockmer End

Bockmer House

Bockmer Lane

Widefield Wood

Rassler Wood

2

A4155

3

Kings Barn Farm

Danesfield County Combined School

Buckingham Gate

South Cl

1 2 3

Danesfield

4

eyford Golf Club

School Lane

Bockmer Lane

A4155

Hotel

Buckinghamshire County
Windsor and Maidenhead

Thames

5

Medmenham

Ferry Lane

River Thames

Thames Path

Lovelace Cl

Mill L

Hurley

PO

6

High

Hotel

Hurley

PH

Lane

Shepherds

Bell Ct

Templ PK

Street

Thames Path

Frogmill

Frogmill Farm

Shep

Prospect Pl

Hurley Bottom

7

HENLEY ROAD

A4130

Black Boy Lane

F G HENLEY ROAD H J K

33

A4130

Honey Lane

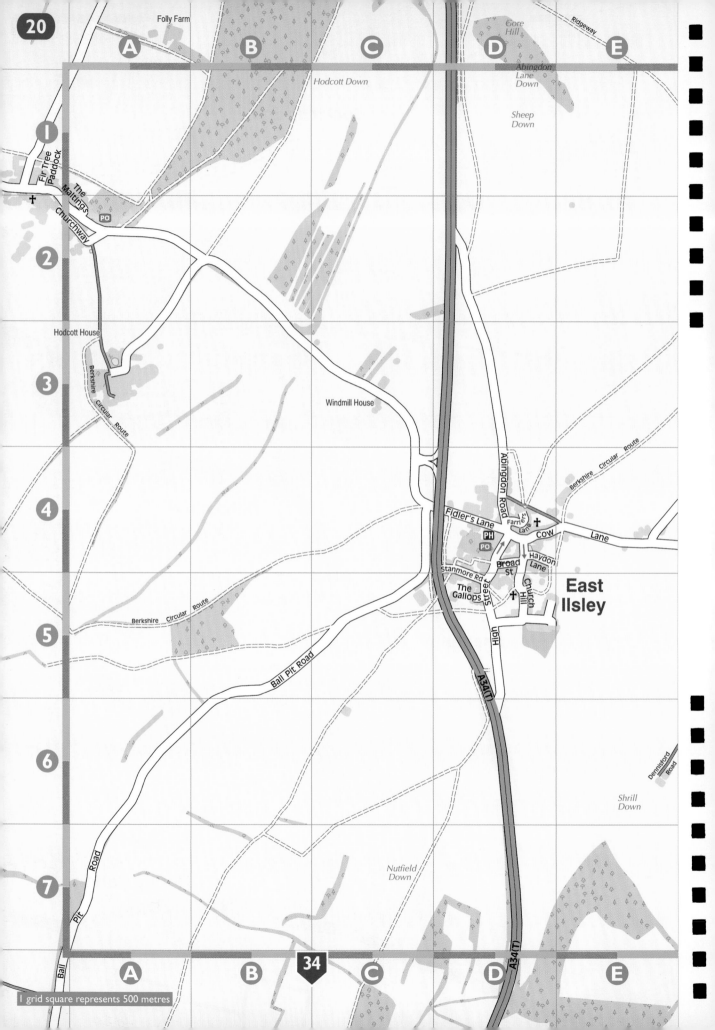

Folly Farm

Hodcott Down

Abingdon Lane Down

Gore Hill

Ridgeway

Sheep Down

A

B

C

D

E

Fir Tree Paddock

The Maltings

Churchway

PO

Hodcott House

Berkshire Circular Route

Windmill House

Berkshire Circular Route

Abingdon Road

Fidler's Lane

Farr... Lane

PH

PO

Cow Lane

Haydon Lane

Broad St

Stanmore Rd

The Gallops

High Street

Church Hill

East Ilsley

Berkshire Circular Route

Ball Pit Road

A34(T)

Dennisford Road

Shrill Down

Nutfield Down

Ball Pit Road

34

A

B

C

D

E

A34(T)

1 grid square represents 500 metres

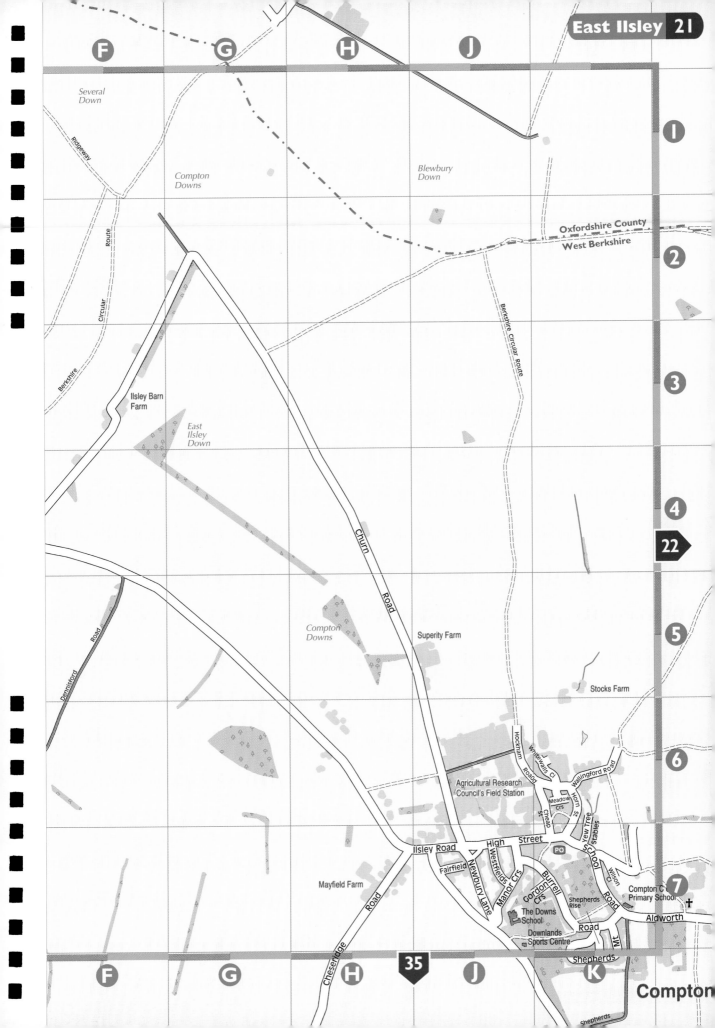

F G H J

Several
Down

Ridgeway

Compton
Downs

Blewbury
Down

Circular

Route

Oxfordshire County

West Berkshire

Berkshire

Berkshire Circular Route

Ilsley Barn
Farm

East
Ilsley
Down

Churn Road

Compton
Downs

Superity Farm

Stocks Farm

Dennisford Road

Hockham Road

Whitewalls Cl

Wallingford Road

Agricultural Research
Council's Field Station

Meadow
Crs

Horn St

Cheap St

Yew Tree Stables

High Street

PO

School

Wilson Cl

Compton C
Primary School

Ilsley Road

Mayfield Farm

Fairfield

Newbury Lane

Westfields

Manor Crs

Gordon
Crs

Burrell

Shepherds
Rise

Road

Aldworth

The Downs
School

Downlands
Sports Centre

School Mt

Cheseridge Road

Shepherds

F G 35 H J K

Compton

Shepherds

1
2
3
4
22
5
6
7

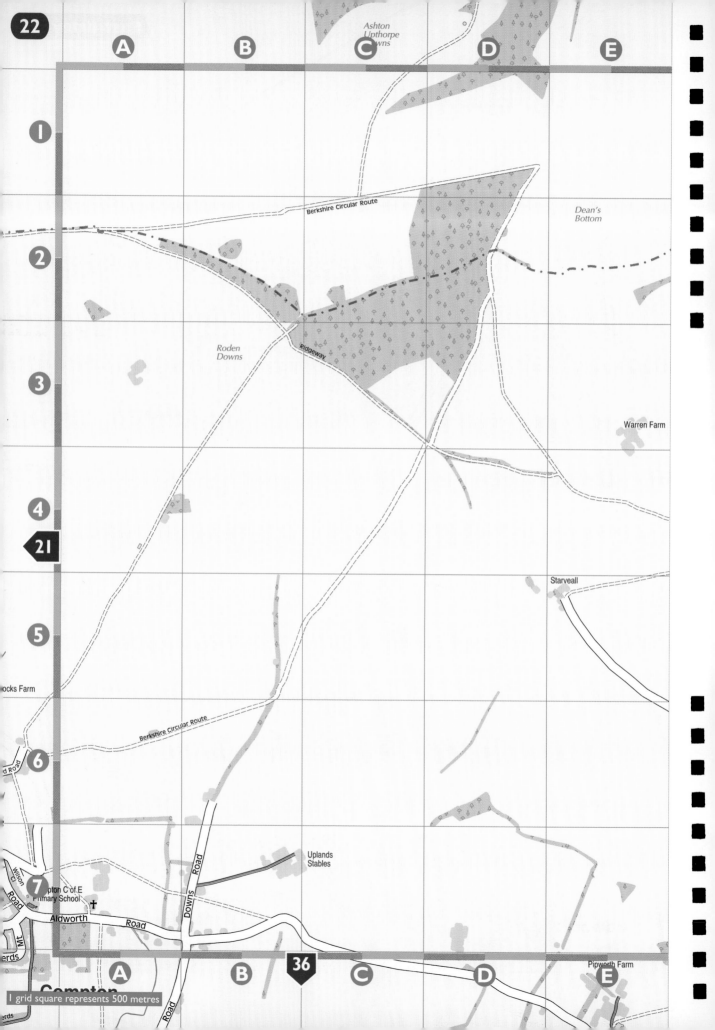

A   B   C   D   E

1

Berkshire Circular Route

Ashton
Upthorpe
Downs

Dean's
Bottom

2

Roden
Downs

Ridgeway

3

Warren Farm

4

21

Starveall

5

...ocks Farm

Berkshire Circular Route

...d Road

6

Uplands
Stables

Wilson
Cl

7

...pton C of E
Primary School

Aldworth   Road

Downs Road

Pipworth Farm

A   B   36   C   D   E

Compton

I grid square represents 500 metres

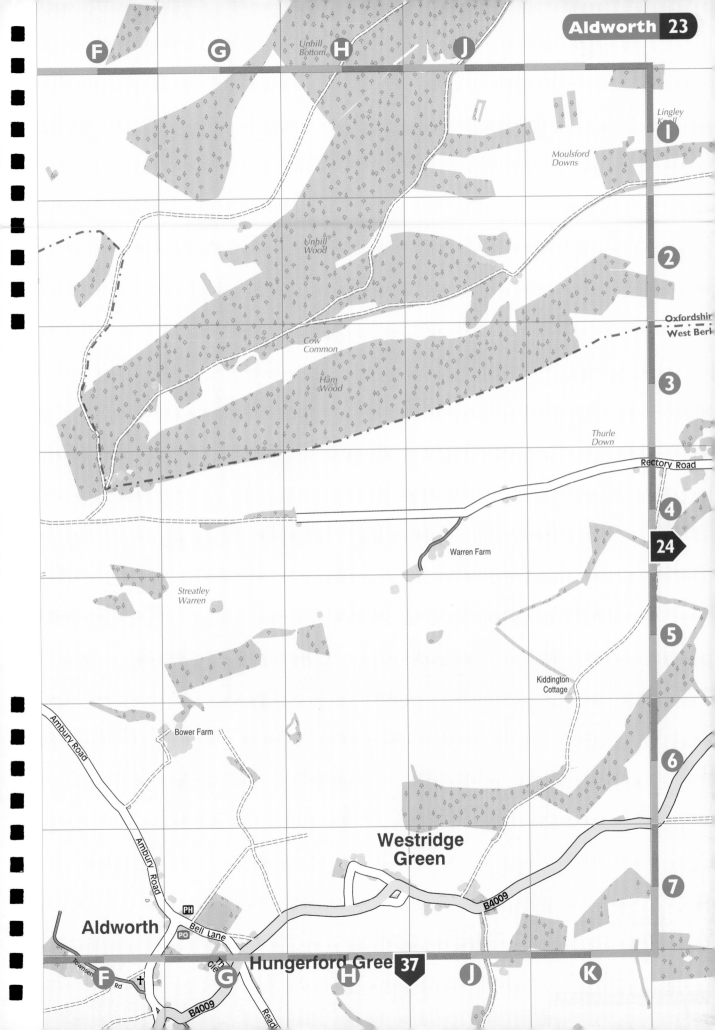

F G *Unhill Bottom* H J

Lingley Knoll

I

Moulsford Downs

2

Oxfordshire West Berk

Unhill Wood

3

Cow Common

Thurle Down

Ham Wood

Rectory Road

4

24

Warren Farm

Streatley Warren

5

Kiddington Cottage

Bower Farm

6

Ambury Road

Westridge Green

B4009

7

Ambury Road

PH

Aldworth

Bell Lane

PO

Hungerford Gree **37**

Townsen

F Rd G H J K

B4009 Read

A B C D E

1

Lingley Knoll

Well Barn

Greenlands Farm

COW Lane

A417

Runsford Hole

A329

2

Oxfordshire County
West Berkshire

Streatley Farm

WANTAGE ROAD

WALLINGFORD ROAD

3

Thurle Grange

Thurle Down

Rectory Road

Goring & Streatley Golf Club

Lough Down

Townsend Road

Three Gables

Lane

4

23

A417

Streatley

Millers

Cleeve Rd

Nun's Acre

Thames Rd

Glebe Ride

Hotel

Boathouse Surgery

PH

Maple Ct

5

STREATLEY HILL

B4009

HIGH STREET

The Bull Meadow

Hill Gardens

The Coombe

Streatley School

READING ROAD

Arcade-Gallery

M

PO

Ferry Lane

Grange Close

Limetree Rd

Manor Road

6

The Beeches

A329

7

Thames path

The Grotto

A B C D E

38

Wood Farm

Stichens Green

F3
1 Springfield End
2 Westway

F4
1 Clevemede
2 Ferne Cl
3 Heron Shaw
4 Mountfield

F5
1 Meadow Cl
2 Red Cross Rd
3 Valley Cl
4 Walnut Tree Ct
5 Yew Tree Ct

F6
1 Elmcroft

F   G   H   J

Grove Farm

Beech Farm

Beech Lane

Beech Lane

Spring Farm

Ridgeway

Oxfordshire County
West Berkshire

Thames Path

The Temple

Wroxhills Wood

Icknield Road

Springhill Road

Cleeve

Icknield Pl

PO

Elvendon Road

Battle Road

Elvendon Priory

Mill Road

Cleeve Rd

Penmylpiece

Goring C of E Primary School

Cleeve Down

Summerfield Rd

Milldown Road

Lycroft Cl

Milldown Av

Elmhurst Rd

Lyndhurst Rd

Fairfield Rd

Lockstile Md

Lockstile Way

Upr Red Cross Rd

Farm Rd

B4526

READING   ROAD   B4526

Park Wood

26

Doctors Surg

Station Rd

GORING
Goring & Streatley Station

Whitehills Gn

Burntwood

Great Chalk Wood

Croft Road

Holmlea Road

Little Cft Rd

Gatehampton Road

Upper Gatehampton Farm

Sta

Gatehampton Manor

Thames Path

River Thames

39

Church Farm

Thames

F   G   H   J   K

A B C D E

1

2

3

4

25

5

6

7

A B 40 C D E

Upper Cadley's

Dean Wood

RED LANE A4074

Tidmore Lane

B471

RED LANE

South Stoke Road

Church Farm

Broad Street Farm

Behoes Lane

South Stoke Road

Health Cen

Reading Road

Woodcote CP School

Woodcote

Secondary School

Beech Farm

Wayside Gn

Walker Cl

Folly Orch Rd

Gap Way

Beech Lane

Beech Lane

Wood La

Beech La

Folly Gn

Chiltern

Whitehouse

The Close

Ashlee Wk

Lackmore Gdns

Elmorepark Wood

GORING ROAD

W Chiltern

Grimmer

Greenmoor

Fox Covert

Bridle Path

Croft Way

Elvendon Lane

Greenmoor Hill

Park Wood

Shirvell's Hill

Potklin Lane

Green La

B471

Eastfield Lane

Flint Ho

Cray's Pond

B4526

Stapnall's Farm

Great Oaks

Cold Harbour

The Oratory Preparatory School

Hill Bottom

Crocketts Cl

Hill Bottom Cl

Checkendon

Checkendon
Court

Checkendon
C of E Aided
Primary School

F

G

H

J

Whitehall Lane

Road

Emmens
Lane

1

Woodcote Farm

Payables Farm

Deer's
Lane

Corker's Farm

Heath
End

2

Beechwood
Farm

The
Oratory
School

Exlade Street

PH

Hookend
Lane

Lower Farm

**Hook
End**

3

Rumerh
Wo

Lane

Laekmore
Wood

4

28

N
G

College
or Abbot's
Wood

Park Lane

5

Common
Wood

6

Long Toll

DEADMAN'S LANE B4526

A4074

Kempwood

7

B4526

Abbotsfield

Deadman's
Lane

Alnut's Hospital

F

G

H

41

J

N**K**ey
Green

C

Goring

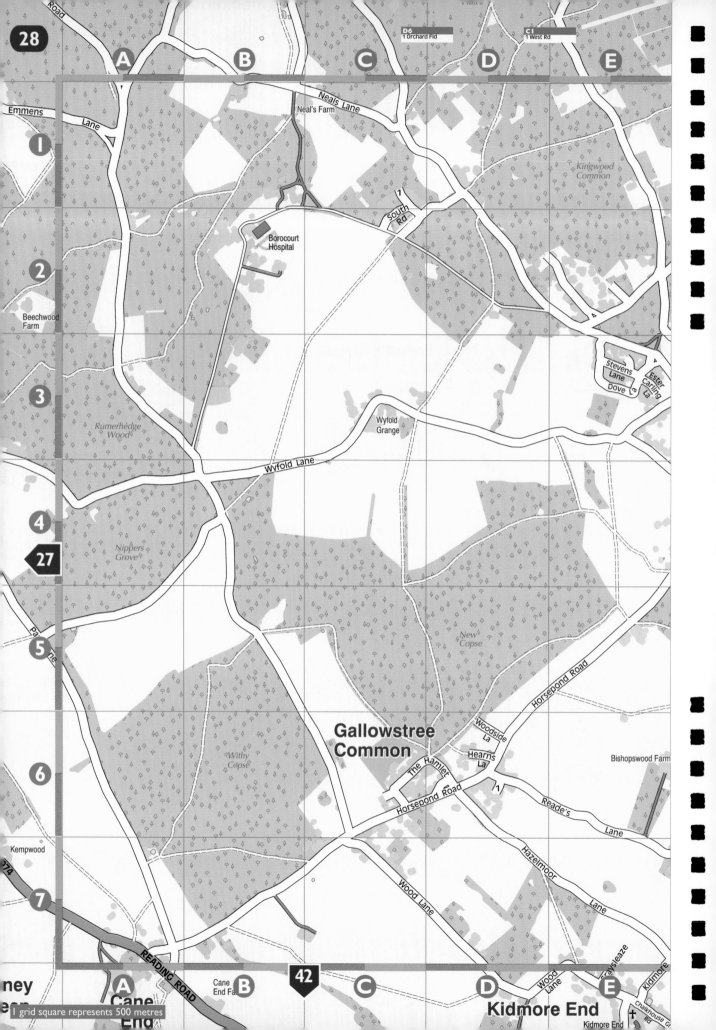

Road

Emmens

Lane

A B C D E

Neals Lane

Neal's Farm

D6
1 Orchard Fld

C1
1 West Rd

Kingwood
Common

1

South
Rd

Borocourt
Hospital

Stevens
Lane

Ester
Carling
La

2

Beechwood
Farm

Dove La

3

Rumerhedge
Wood

Wyfold
Grange

Wyfold Lane

4

Nippers
Grove

27

New
Copse

5

Pa ne

Horsepond Road

Gallowstree
Common

Woodside
La

Hearns
La

Bishopswood Farm

6

Withy
Copse

The Hamlet

Horsepond Road

Reade's

Lane

Kempwood

Hazelmoor

Lane

7

A574

Wood Lane

Wood
Lane

ney

A B C D E

REQADING ROAD

Cane
End

Cane
End Fa

42

Kidmore End

Kidmore End

Chalkhouse Gn
Rd

Craysteaze

Kidmore

1 grid square represents 500 metres

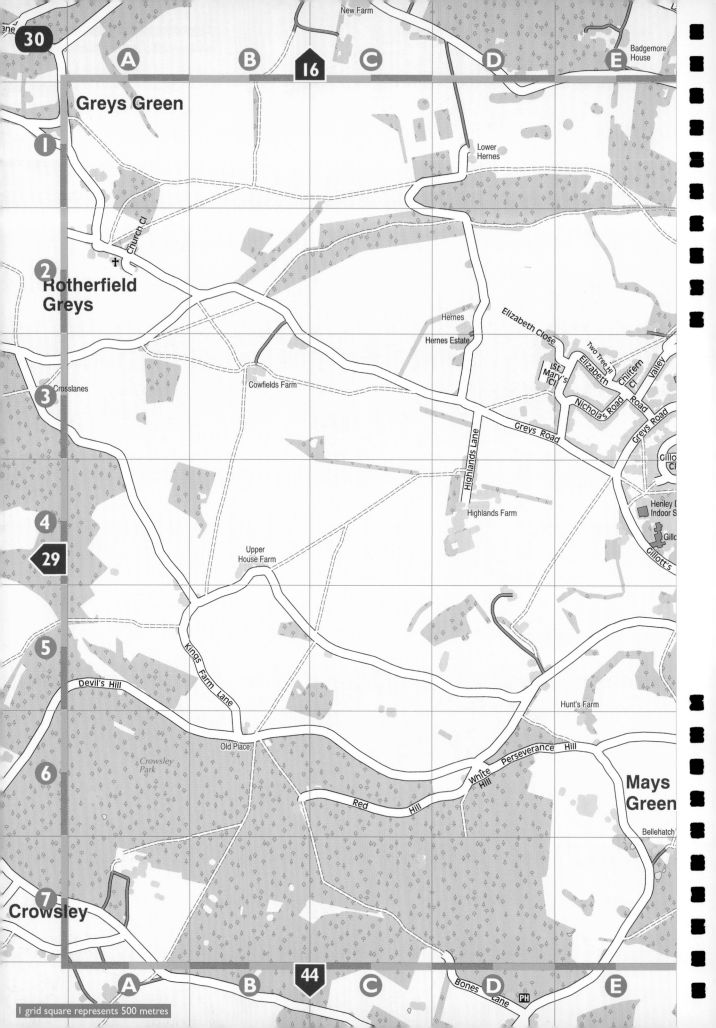

30

A   B   **16**   C   D   E

New Farm

Badgemore
House

Greys Green

1

Lower
Hernes

Church Cl

2
**Rotherfield
Greys**

†

Hernes

Elizabeth Close

Two Tree Hl

Hernes Estate

St
Mary's
Cl

Elizabeth

Chiltern
Cl

Valley

3 Crosslanes

Cowfields Farm

Nichola's Road

Greys Road

Greys Road

Gillo
Cl

Highlands Lane

Henley D
Indoor S

4

Highlands Farm

Gillo

29

Upper
House Farm

Gillott's

5

Hunt's Farm

Kings Farm Lane

Devil's Hill

Perseverance Hill

**Mays
Green**

Old Place

White
Hill

6

*Crowsley
Park*

Red   Hill

Bellehatch

7
Crowsley

Bones Lane

PH

A   B   **44**   C   D   E

1 grid square represents 500 metres

Henley-on-Thames

Woodlands

Newtown

Harpsden

Harpsden Bottom

Harpsden Wood

High Wood

G1
1 Adwell Sq
2 Baronsmead
3 West La

G2
1 Homelands Wy

G3 Street names for this grid square are listed at the back of the index

H2 1 Grove Rd

Cambridge Lane

Dryleas Sports Ground

Badgemore CP School

Townlands Hospital

The Henley College

Clarence Rd
York Rd
Bell Surg
The Hart Surg
The West Street Practice

Paradise Road

Deanfield Av

Leaver Rd

Harcourt Cl
Haywards Cl

Sacred Heart RC School

HENLEY-ON-THAMES

Primary School

Greys Road

Makins Road

itts Lovell Cl

itts School

District Sports Centre

Kenton Theatre

Thames Gallery
Century Galleries Hotel

Police Stn

Art Gallery

Market Pl
Town Hall

Greys Gallery
Bohun Gallery

Primary School

Preparatory School

Trust Cnr

Centenary Business Park

Henley-on-Thames Stn

The River & Rowing Museum at Henley

Fairview Trading Est

Henley Town Football Club

Football Club

Sheephouse Farm

Henley Golf Club

Lower Bolney Farm

Clay House

Upper Bolney House

Northfield Av

Brampton Chase

Park

The Chestnuts

Baskerville

Lower

WHITE HILL
A4130

WARGRAVE ROAD

REMENHAM

Oxfordshire

Thames Path

River Thames

A4155

Woodlands Road

NEW ST
DUKE ST
BELL ST
NORTHFIELD END
Badgemore La
Avenue Road

RIVER Thames

17

32

45

2
3
4
5
6
7

I

32

A   B   **18**   C   D   E

Common Barn

Remenham Place

Middle Culham Farm

Lower Culham Farm

Remenham Hill

1   HILL

A4130

Park Place

2

Upper Culham Farm

3   GRAVE   ROAD

River Thames

Wokingham   Oxfordshire County

Kenton's Lane

Hatchgate House

Cockpole Green

4

31

Worley's Farm

Warren R

Hatch Gate Lane

5

A321

Crazies Hill Primary School

PO

P

Crazies Hill

Bolney Road

Thames Path

Hennerton House

6

Lane

Maple Croft

Highfield Farm

Manor Wd

Gate Nursery

Northfield Av

Trevor Drive

Brampton Chase

Northfield Rd

LC

Basmore Lane

7   Road

Shiplake Station

Lashbrook Road

Willow

Bolney Rd

The Crs

Brocks Way

Oaks Rd

Lowes Close

Westfield Crs

Lashbrook Rd

A   B   **46**   C   D   E

1 grid square represents 500 metres

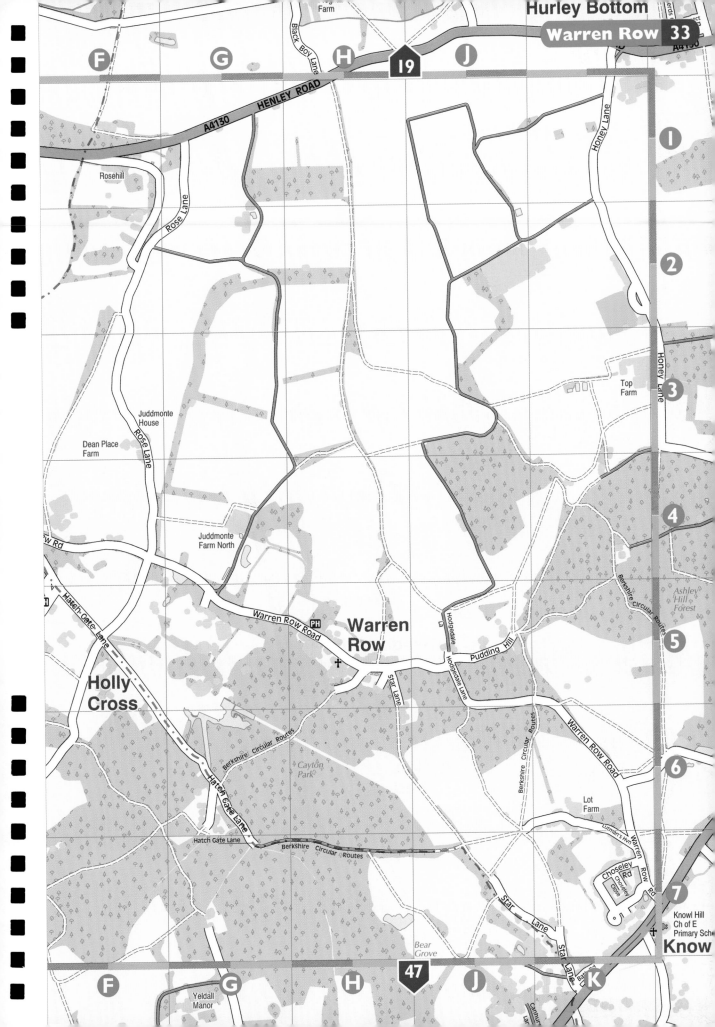

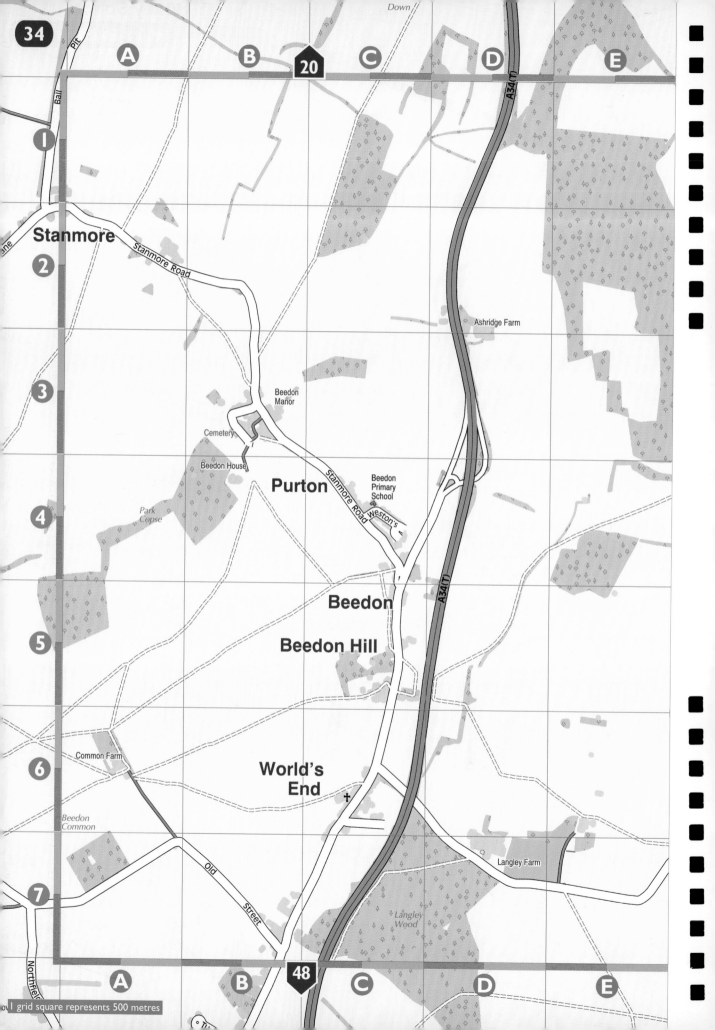

A   B   20   C   D   E

Down

Ball Pit

1

Stanmore

Stanmore Road

2

Beedon Manor

Cemetery

3

Beedon House

Ashridge Farm

Purton

Park Copse

Beedon Primary School

Stanmore Road

Weston's

4

Beedon

Beedon Hill

A34(T)

5

Common Farm

World's End

6

Beedon Common

Langley Farm

Old Street

7

Langley Wood

Northfield

A   B   48   C   D   E

1 grid square represents 500 metres

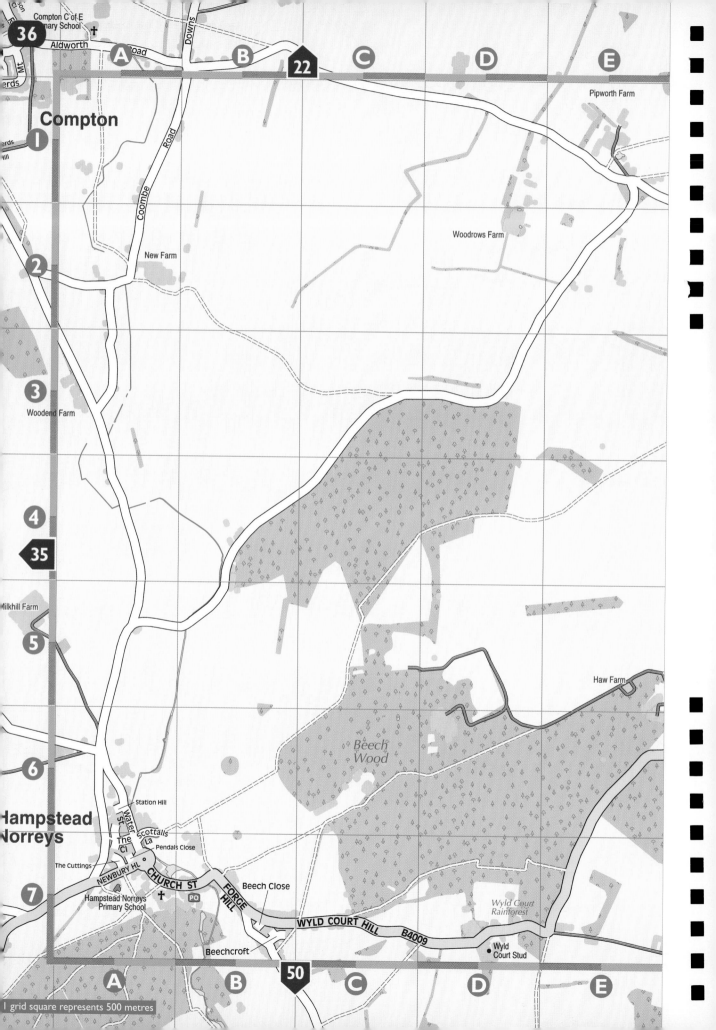

36

Compton C of E
Primary School

Aldworth

A Road

Compton

B Downs

22

C

D

E

Pipworth Farm

1

Coombe Road

Woodrows Farm

2

New Farm

3

Woodend Farm

4

35

Milkhill Farm

5

Haw Farm

6

Station Hill

Beech
Wood

Hampstead
Norreys

Water St

Scottalls La

The Cl

Pendals Close

The Cuttings

NEWBURY HL

CHURCH ST

Beech Close

FORCE HILL

7

Hampstead Norreys
Primary School

PO

Wyld Court
Rainforest

Beechcroft

WYLD COURT HILL B4009

• Wyld
Court Stud

A

B

50

C

D

E

1 grid square represents 500 metres

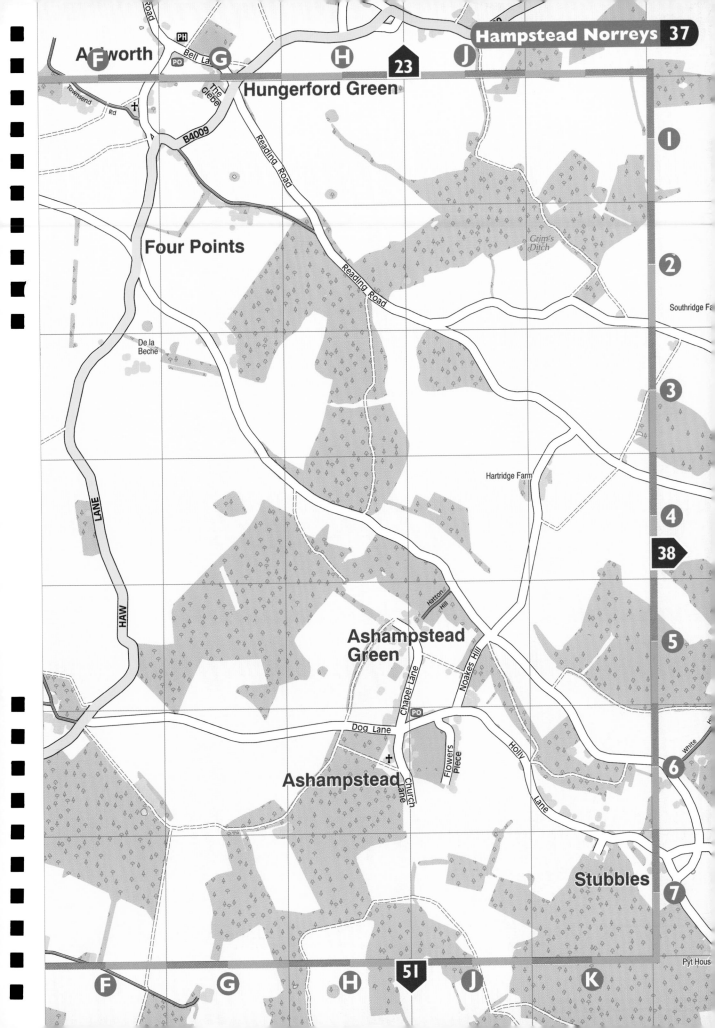

24

37

52

A B C D E

1
2
3
4
5
6
7

The Grotto

A329

Path

Wood Farm

Stichens
Green

Bennet's
Wood

Manor Farm

Southridge Farm

Tomb Farm

Hook
End Farm

Hook End Lane

Park Wall Lane

White Hill

Rushdown Farm

Henwood
Copse

Bethesda Street

Bethesda
Cr

Emery
Acres

Basildon School

Blandy's Lane

Ashampstead Road

Hill
Corner

Whitemoor Lane

Tenaplas Dr

Captains
Gorse

Kiln Ride

Aldworth

Beckfords

Maple
La

Road

Darby La

PH

PO

ubbles

Quick's
Green

Upper Basildon

Pyt House

1 grid square represents 500 metres

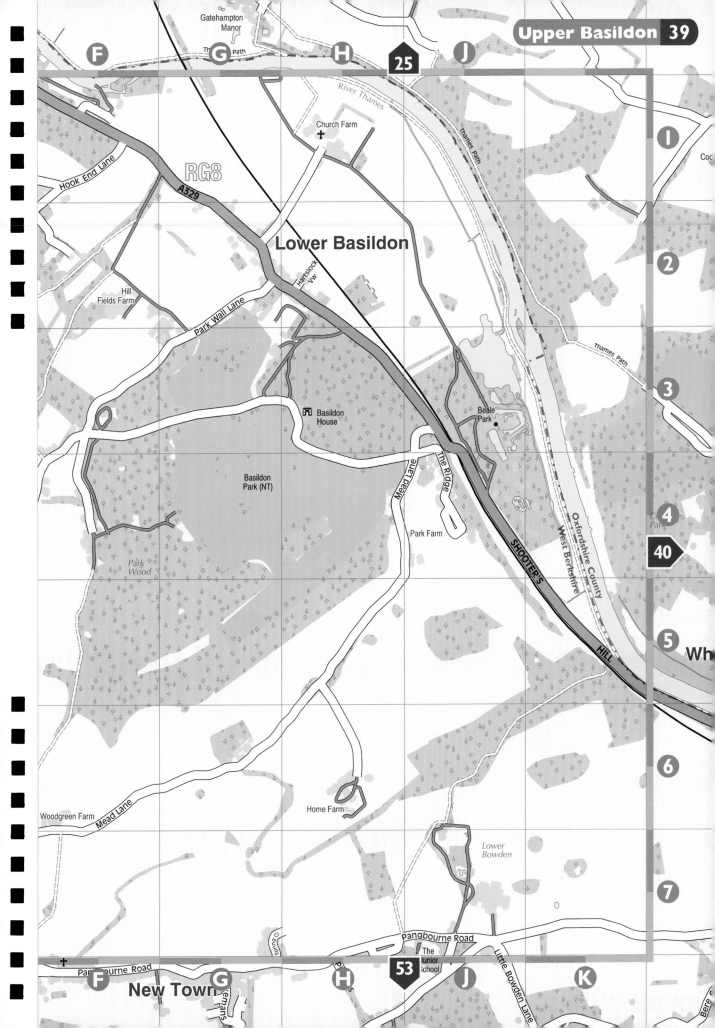

F G H 25 J

River Thames

Church Farm

Thames Path

RG8

Hook End Lane

A329

Lower Basildon

Hartslock Vw

Hill Fields Farm

Park Wall Lane

Thames Path

Basildon House

Beale Park

Basildon Park (NT)

Mead Lane

The Ridge

Park Farm

SHOOTER'S

Oxfordshire County

West Berkshire

Park Wood

HILL

Wh

Woodgreen Farm

Mead Lane

Home Farm

Lower Bowden

Pangbourne Road

The Junior School

Pangbourne Road

F G 53 J K

New Town

1

2

3

4

40

5

6

7

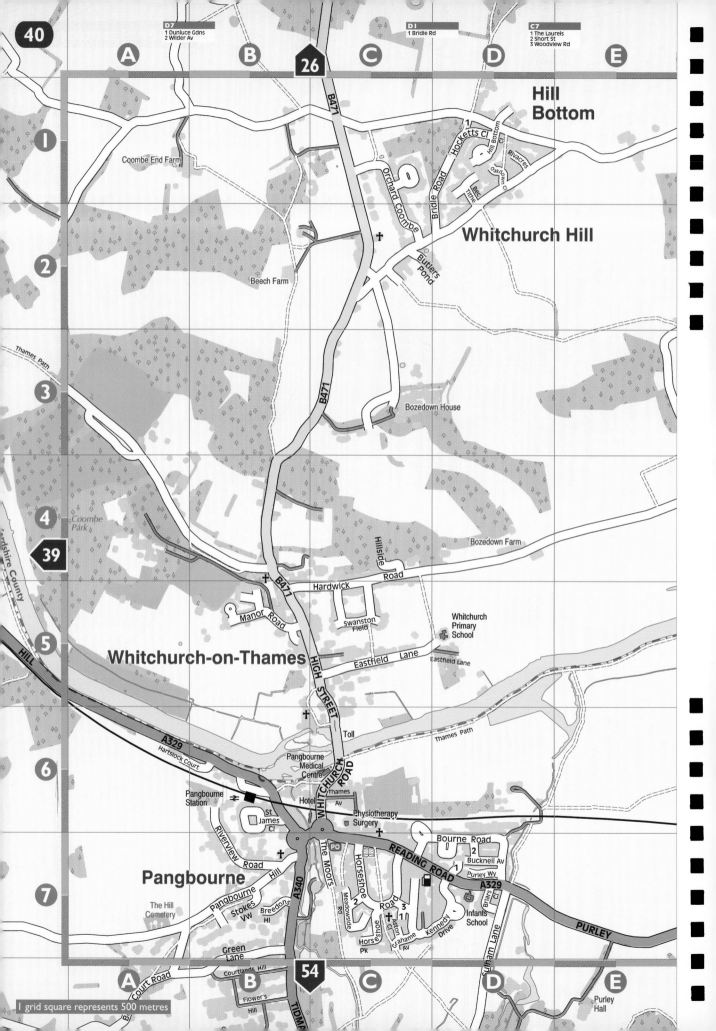

F **G** **H** 27 **J**

G7
1 Bellisle
2 Bryant Pl
3 Elyham

H7
1 Hornbeam Cl
2 Primrose Cl
3 Westridge Av

J7
street names for
this grid square are
listed at the back of
the index

Goring
Heath

Abbotsfield

Alnut's Hospital

Deadman's

Bunce's Lane

Collins
End

Holly
Copse

Whittles Farm

Nuney
Green

Cross La

C

I

2

3

Bottom
Wood

The Baulk

Hardwick
Stud Farm

Bottom Farm

4

42

River Thames

Thames Path

5

Westbury Farm

Mapledurham

6

Watermill

Westbury Lane

Home Farm

Mapledurham
House

Park F

7

School

Glebe Road

PO

Nursery
Gdns

Purley Lane

Purley Village

Lister Ct

Allison
Gdns

Farm
Cl

Thames

Mapledurham

Colyton Way

Wintringham Way

Brading Way

The
Short

Oak Tree

Chestnut
Gv

River Gdns

Thames
Path

RISE

Beech   Road

Herriewood Rise

Bowling Gn
La

Westridge Av

New Hill

St Mary's Avenue

Chiltern
Vw

Watersyde Dr

Thames
Reach

F Purley on Thames **G** **H** 55 **J** **K**

Long Lane
Primary
School

Lane

Cecil Aldin Dr

Highfield
Road

Close

OXF
ROAD

Hazel

Thames Path

Mar

42

A   **B**   **28**   **C**   **D**   **E**

READING ROAD

Cane End Farm

ney een

Cane End

Kidmore End

Kidmore End Primary School

Cemetery

Chalkhouse Rd

Craysleaze

Kidmore

Butlers Orch

Highland Wood

1

Green Dean Wood

2

Wood Lane

Cross Farm

Cross Lanes

Hodmore Farm

GREEN DEAN HILL

Mill Lane

Tokers

3

Lane

Sheepways

ottom Farm

4

Bardolph's Cl

Rokeby Drive

Gaskells End

41

Trench Green

Pithouse Farm

Chazey Heath

A4074

Chazey Cl

Tokers Green

Rosebery Rd

Russe Rd

Beech Rd

Lilley Farm

5

Newell's Lane

Elm Rd

Tokers Gn Lane

Pond Lane

Shepherds Lane

Silverth

Car Ro

6

Rose Farm

Woodcote

Hilltop Rd

Park Farm

Crispin Cl

Gurney Cl

Way

7

Jacksons Lane

Jacksons Lane

Blagrave Farm La

Blagrave Farm

UPPER WOODCOTE ROAD

Knowle Cl

Chazey Wood

New Farm

A   **B**   **56**   **C**   **D**   **E**

Hewett Cl

Avenue

1 grid square represents 500 metres

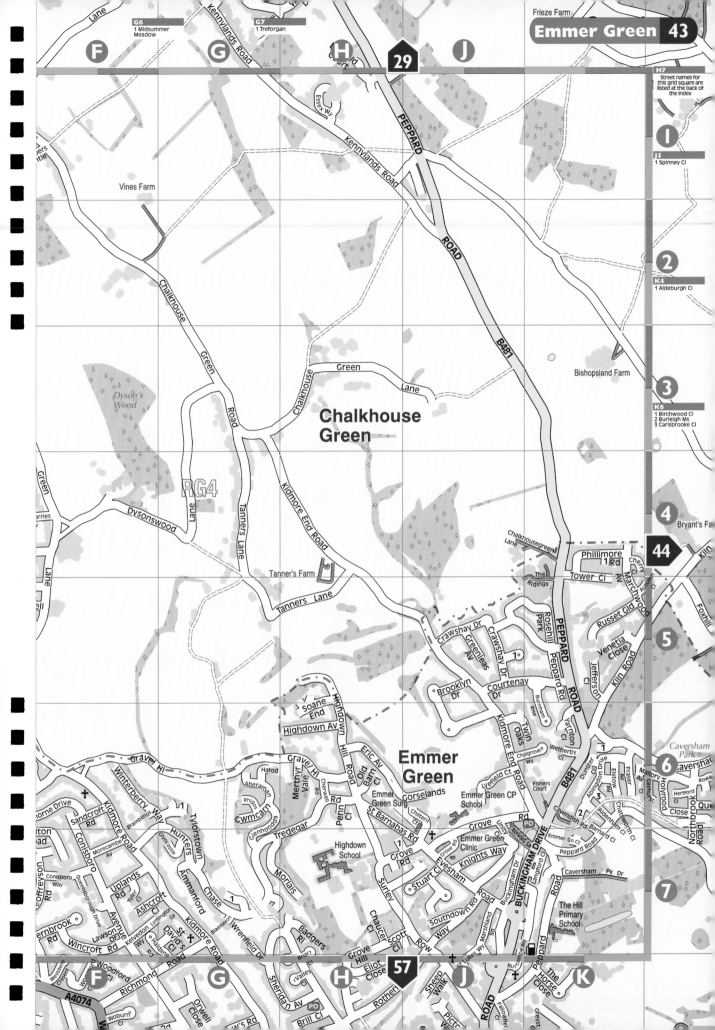

Onsley

A

B6
1 Ilchester Ms
2 Launceston Av
3 Littlestead Cl
4 Melford Gn

B

30

C

A7
1 Shakespeare Cl

D

A6
1 Ragley Ms
2 Thetford Ms
3 Uppingham Gdns

E

1

B7
1 Eynsford Cl
2 Framlingham Dr
3 Gifford Cl
4 Montpelier Dr

Bones Lane

PH

Coppid Hall

Home Farm

2

Comp Farm

Heathfield Av

Heathfield Cl

S
R

3

ishopsland Farm

Gravel

Road

Heath Dr

Green Lane

Binfield Heath

Sandpit

Cork's Farm

Lane

Ham

4

Bryant's Farm

Kiln Road

Row

†

Bint's Farm

43

Phillim

11 k

wer Cl

Marchwood

Russet Gld

Autumn Cl

†

Lane

Foxhill Lane

5

Ven
Clo.

Kiln Road

Jefferson
Cl

Dunsden
Green

A4155

SPAN

Caversham
Park

Road

Primary
Sch

St Martins
RC Primary School

Littlestead
Green

Foxhill Lane

6

Dunster
Cl

Abingdon Drive

stow

ser

Mallory
Cl

Gavhu't

Holyrood
Av

Caversham Park

Queensway

Rowallan

Hertford
Cl

Queensway

Stirling
Cl

Pendennis Av

Netley Cl

Orteley

Kirkham

Whitby Gn

inworth

Kingsway

Foxhill Farm

Henley Road

Spring

Lane

Chatsworth Cl

Aldenham Cl

Barnard Cl

Northbrook
Road

Harlech
Av

Hadleigh Rd

Goodrich

Eltham
Av

Kirkham
Way

Farleigh Ms

Play
Hatch

A4155

d Road

Galsworthy

Dr

Tenby
AV

Ulster
Cl

Quantock

Newton

Repton

otham AV

Kendal

Lomond AV

Peveril

Jordan

Isstone

Highmead

Dumbarton
Way

Caversham Park Road

Foxhill
Cl

A4155

The
Gallery M

B4

7

ill

ersham
Pk Dr

Lowfield Road

PO

B478

PLAYHATCH ROAD

58

A

Lowfield
Road

Cemetery

B

Lowfield
Road

Orchard

GV

nham
Dr
arisfield

led Dacre devo

AV

Corte

Blackwater

58

EY ROAD

A4155

C

D

E

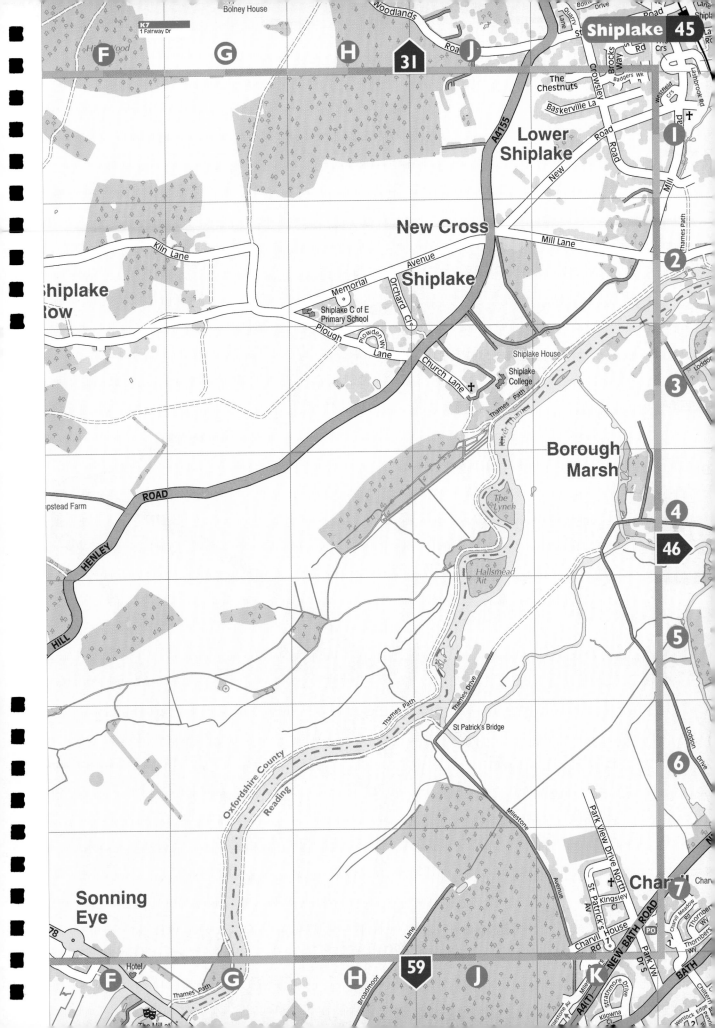

K7
1 Fairway Dr

F G H 31 J

Bolney House

Woodlands Road

The Chestnuts

Baskerville La

Lower
Shiplake

New Road

New Cross

Kiln Lane

Mill Lane

Avenue

Shiplake

Memorial

Orchard Clo

Shiplake C of E
Primary School

Plough

Plowden Wy

Lane

Church Lane

Shiplake House

Shiplake
College

Thames Path

River Thames

Borough
Marsh

ROAD

The
Lynch

apstead Farm

Hallsmead
Ait

HENLEY

HILL

Shiplake
Row

46

Thames Path

Thames Drive

St Patrick's Bridge

Oxfordshire County

Reading

Milestone

Avenue

Sonning
Eye

Thames Path

Broadmoor

Lane

Charvil

St Patrick's
Av

Kingsley
Cl

Charvil
House

Park View Drive North

PO

Loddon Drive

Park View
Dr S

F G H 59 J K

NEW BATH ROAD

BATH

Thornbers
Wy

Strathmore
Drive

Kilowna

Wenlock Edge

Chilterns

The Mill at

I
2
3
4
5
6
7

46

The Crs

Brocks Way

Crowsley Rd

Rd

Westfield Crs

Badgers Wk

Drive

Road

Rd

Road

Mill Road

Lashbrook

Shiplake Station

Lashbrook Rd

Lowes Close

Thames Path

Loddon

Drive

A **B** **32** **C** **D** **E**

C6
1 Kibblewhite Crs
2 Packman Dr

C3
1 Spring Wk

A7
1 Gingells Farm Rd

C7
1 Bell Ct

1

2

D1
1 Dunnock Wy
2 The Spur

D6
1 Southview Cl

3

4

45

E7
1 Milton Wy

5

6

sh

Watermans Wy

Ferry La

Church St

WARGRAVE

Wargrave Station

Station Road

High Street

School St

Backsdeans

McCrae's Wk

Autumn Wk

Road

A321

The Bothy

Wargrave Hill

The Walled Gdns

Hi Lands

Dark Lane

Langhams Wy

Wargrave
Manor

Blakes Rd

The Copse

Rdg Wy

Ryecroft
Cl

Purfield

Fidlers
Walk

Road

East Vw Cl

East Vw

Rd

Newalls

RI

Blakes Road

Highfield
Park

PO

The
Surgery

Victoria

Hamilton Rd

Emma La

Clifton Rl

Beverley

Recreation Rd

SCHOOL LANE

Bayliss Rd

Braybrooke Gdns

Bn

Road

Silverdale Rd

Gdns

B477 SCHOOL HILL

Robert Piggott
C of E
Junior School

Robert Piggott
C of E
Infant School

MUMBERY HILL

B477

A321

Sheeplands Farm

A4(T)

BATH ROAD

The Piggott
Church of England
School

A3032

Loddon
Park Farm

A4(T)

Loddon Drive

NEW

BATH

ROAD

WARGRAVE ROAD

A321

Wargrave Road

New

Road

Malvern
Dr

Badger
Dr

The Willow Way

Carlile
Gdns

Chaseside Av

Yewhurst
Cl

Llewellyn Pk

Longfield
Rd

Amberley
Dr

Willow
Dr

Willow
Dr

Jarvis
Cl

Troutbeck

Cheriton
Cl

Westview
Dr

Hilltop
Road

Heron
Dr

Arbside Cl

St Michael's
Court

Penimfields
Crest Ct

Middlefields

Longfield Road

Kibblewhite
Crs

Junior School

The
Surgery

London

ROAD

St James
Cl

Twyford Health
Centre

Loddon
Hall Rd

Sycamore

Wensley
Rd

Lincoln Gdns

Hermitage Dr

Pine Cl

Polehampton
County Infant
School

Ebony Health
Cen

Cedar
Park School

Charvil

Charvil Farm

New Drive North

Ingsley
Cl

House

Park Vw

BATH

NEW BATH ROAD

PO

Charvil Meadow

Edward
Wy

Thornbers
Rd

Thornbers
Wy

Old Acre Rd

ROAD

A3032

HIGH ST

Old Mill Cl

B3024

St

The

WALTHAM RD

Orchard

Ruscombe Pk

RUSCOMBE LANE

Ruscombe

Walnut
Tree
Close

New
Road

Northbury
Lane

Northbury
Avenue

Northbury Farm

Castle End Rd

WALTHAM ROAD

Church
Lane

Tavistock
Industrial
Estate

Southbury
Lane

TWYFORD

60

Twyford
Business
Park

Wagtail La

Church St

Brook St

Station Rd

Police Stn

WALTHAM RD

Springfield
Rd

Stanlake
Lane

Gas La

A **B** **60** **C** **D** **E**

7

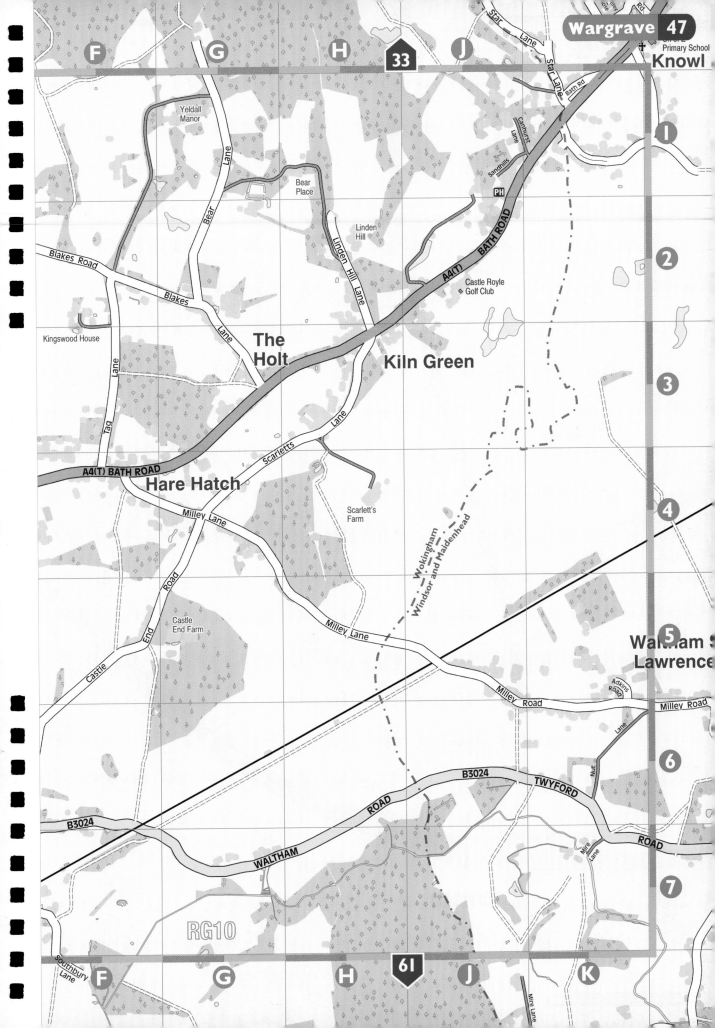

F G H 33 J

Knowl

Yeldall Manor

Bear Place

Linden Hill

Blakes Road

Blakes

Kingswood House

Bear Lane

Linden Hill Lane

Lane

The Holt

Kiln Green

PH

BATH ROAD

A4(T)

Castle Royle Golf Club

Star Lane

Bath Rd

Camhurst Lane

Sandhills

Primary School

I

2

3

Tag Lane

A4(T) BATH ROAD

Hare Hatch

Scarletts

Scarletts Lane

Milley Lane

Scarlett's Farm

Wokingham
Windsor and Maidenhead

4

Castle End Road

Castle End Farm

Castle

Milley Lane

Milley Lane

Milley Road

Milley Road

Adkins Road

Wal...am S Lawrence

5

B3024

WALTHAM

ROAD

B3024

TWYFORD

Lane

Nut

6

Mire Lane

ROAD

7

RG10

Southbury Lane

F G H 61 J K

48

A B **34** C D E

E7
1 Bomford Cl
2 Clough Dr
3 Roy Cl
4 Thompson Cl

A4
1 Hazeldene

A3
1 Pointers Cl

Wood

1

Northfields

ngrove Farm

Tudor Av

Street

A34(T)

Downs
Farm

2
Downend

Bardown

Downend Lane

3 Freshfields
Lane
1

Middle Farm

Chieveley

Bradley
Court

Old   street

4
Manor
Lane

High Street

East
Lane

Oxford Road

Church La
1

PO

eley
ty Primary
ol

Heathfields

1

Priors
Court
School

ool Road

5
Green Lane

Graces   Lane

Horsemoor

A34(T)

Priors Court Road

Priorscourt Farm

Old Street

6
Green Lane

Radnall Farm

Newbury
Showground

M4

Old Street

7

Junction 13

M4

Chieveley Service Area

Crabtree Lane

Crabtree Close

Faircross Quarters

Faircross Quarters

White Cl
7

2

3

Collins Drive
4

A B **64** C D E Faircross
ntn

Woodlands Cl

Kiln   PH

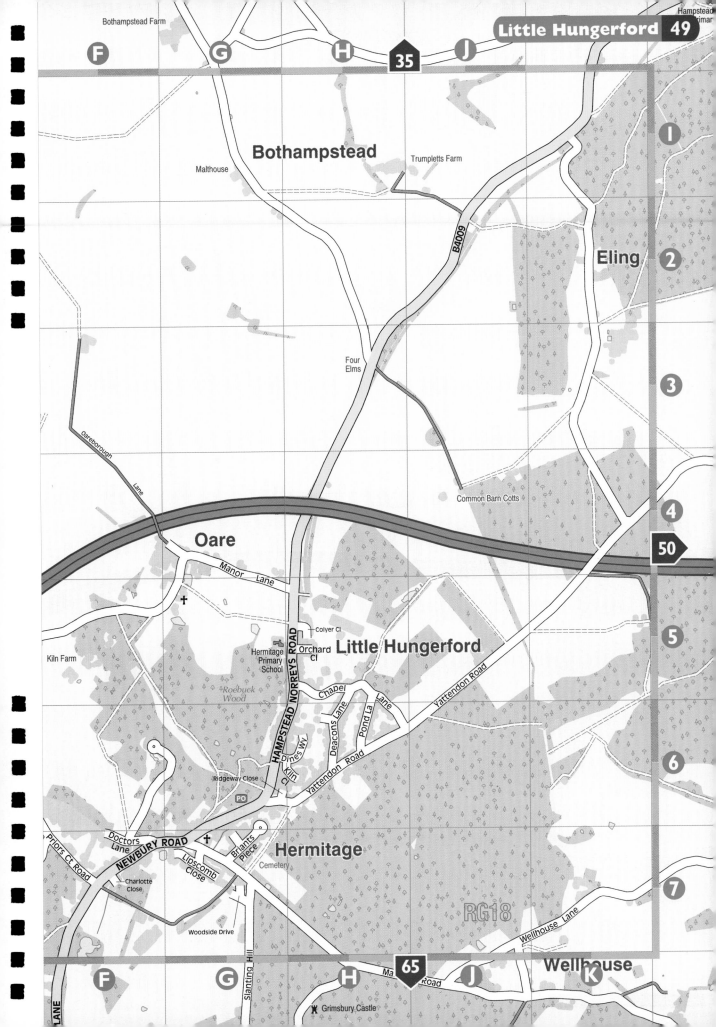

Hampstead
Primar

F G H 35 J

I

Bothampstead Farm

Bothampstead

Malthouse

Trumpletts Farm

B4009

Eling

2

3

Four
Elms

Common Barn Cotts

4

50

Oareborough
Lane

Oare

Manor   Lane

†

Kiln Farm

Colyer Cl

Hermitage
Primary
School

Orchard
Cl

HAMPSTEAD NORREYS ROAD

Little Hungerford

5

Roebuck
Wood

Chapel

Yattendon Road

Dines Wy

Deacons Lane

Pond La

Lane

Yattendon   Road

6

Ridgeway Close

Kiln Cl

PO

Doctors
Lane

NEWBURY ROAD

†

Briants
Piece

Hermitage

Priors Ct Road

Lipscomb
close

Cemetery

RG18

Charlotte
Close

7

Woodside Drive

Wellhouse Lane

LANE

Slanting Hill

F G H 65 Ma Road J Wellhouse K

Grimsbury Castle

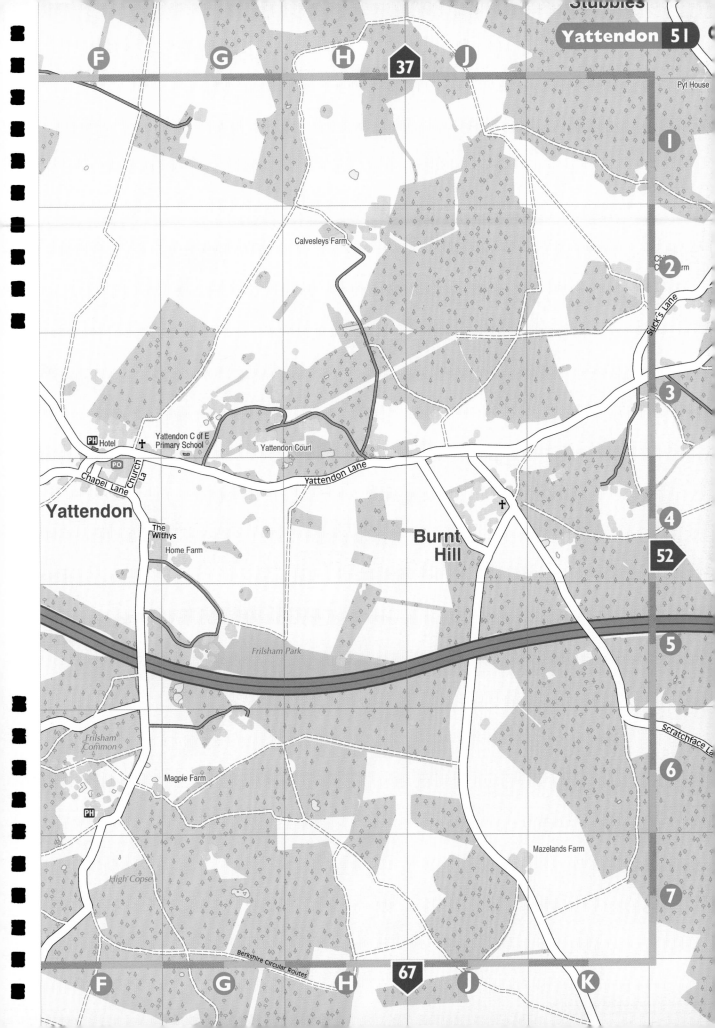

Stubbies

F G H **37** J

Pyt House

I

Calvesleys Farm

Chil
C   rm
2

Suck's Lane

3

PH Hotel
Yattendon C of E
Primary School
Yattendon Court
†

PO
Church La
Chapel Lane
Yattendon Lane
†
4

Yattendon

Burnt
Hill
52

The
Withys
Home Farm

5

Frilsham Park

Scratchface La

Frilsham
Common
6

Magpie Farm

PH

Mazelands Farm

7

High Copse

tubbies

52

A Quick's †
Green

B

38

C

Upp **D** Basildon

E
PO

Kiln Ride

Maple
La
Darby
La
Road

Pyt House

1

Ashampstead
Common

Child's
Court Farm

2

Suck's Lane

3

Slade Gate

Strouds

4

51

Bottomhouse Farm

M4

5

Greathouse
Wood

Scratchface Lane

6

7

Bradfield House

Rushall Farm

A

B

68

C

D

E

Rushall Manor
Farm

1 grid square represents 500 metres

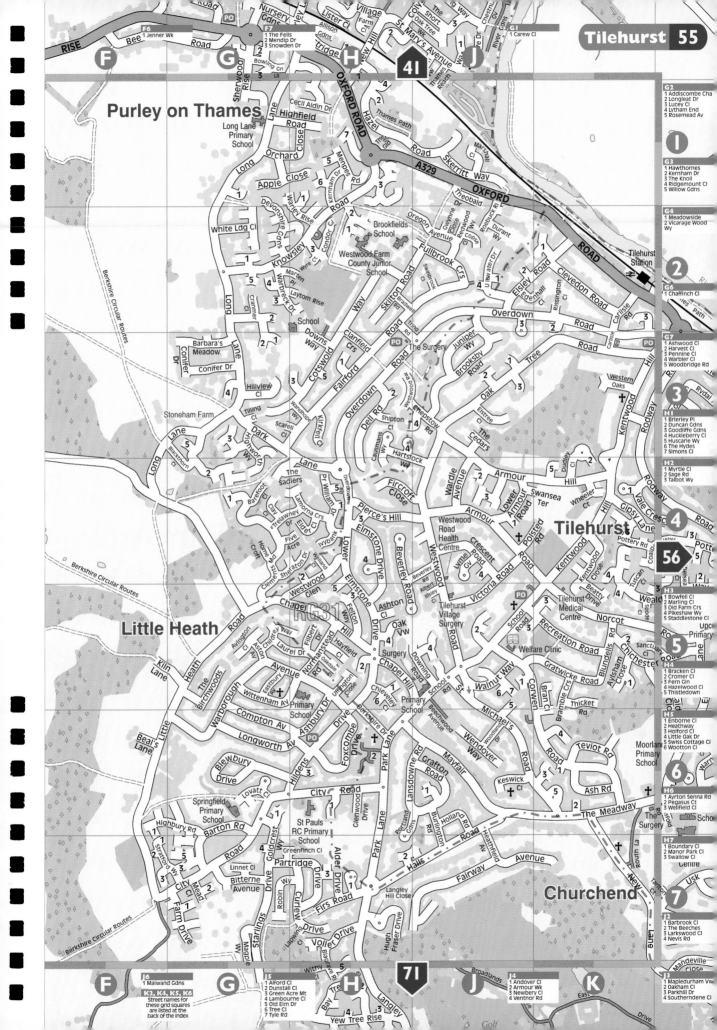

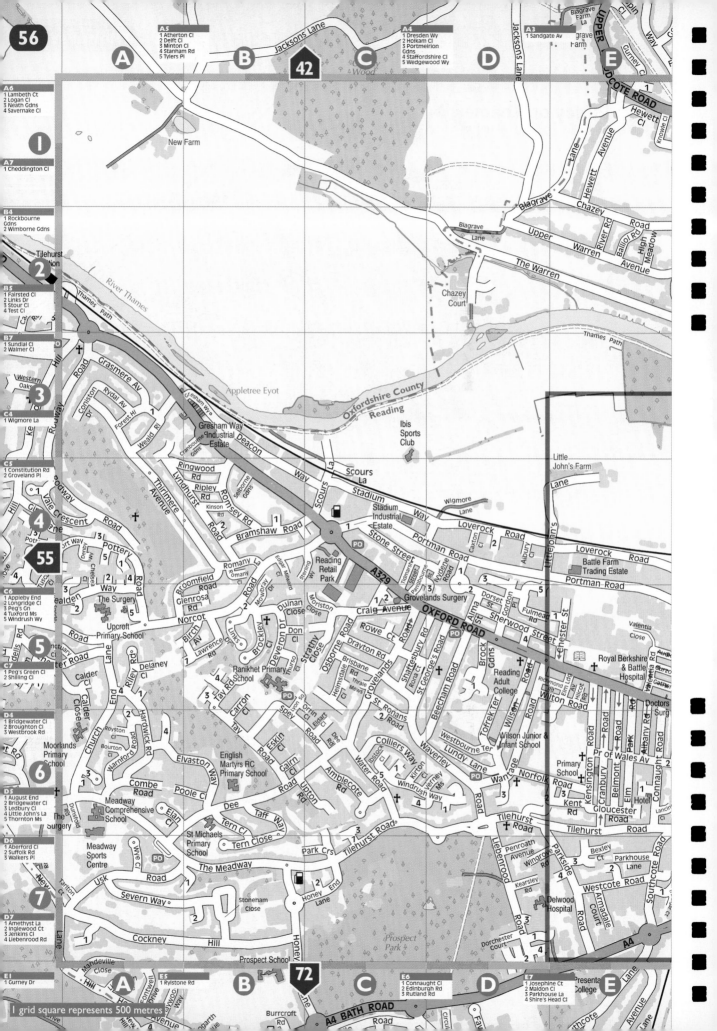

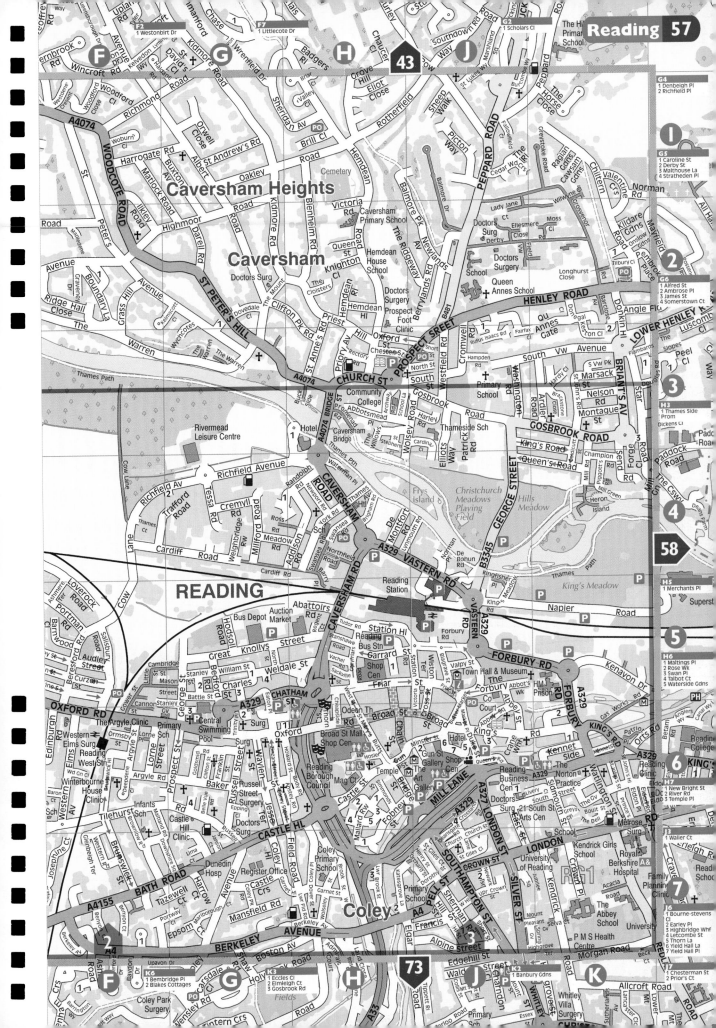

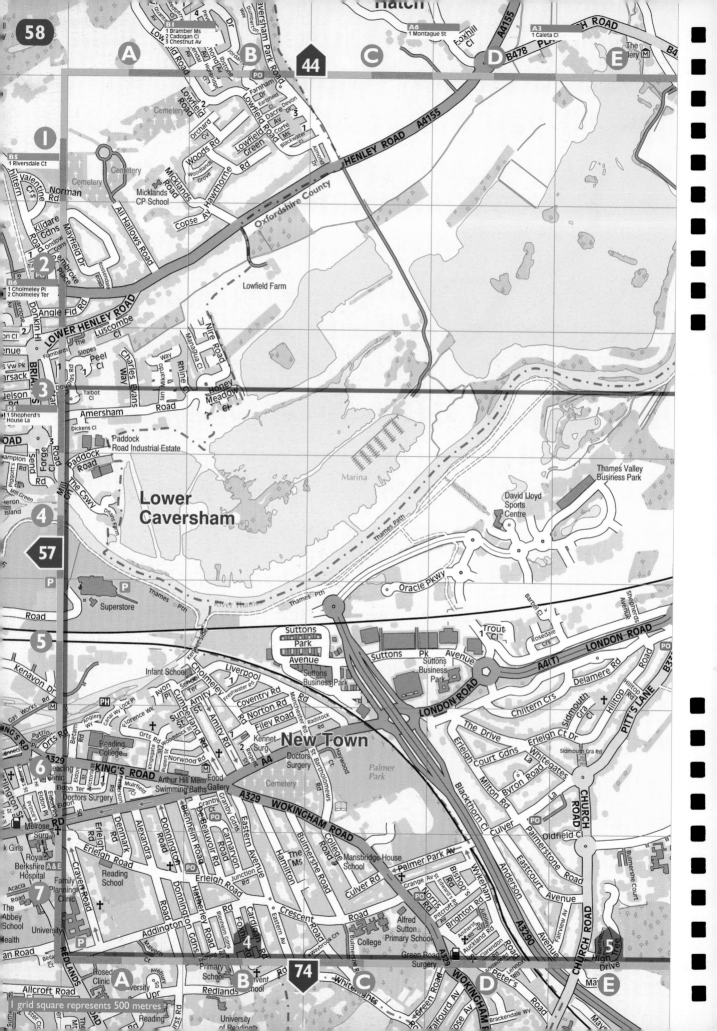

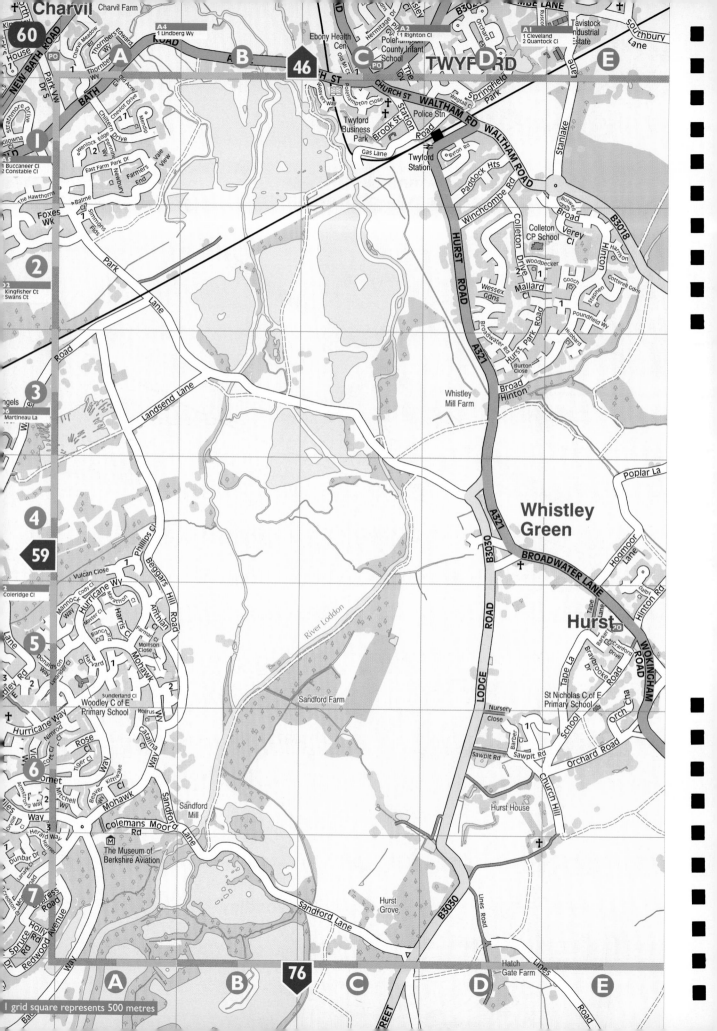

A   B   Borough Hill   C   D   E

Westbrook Farm

Lower Farm

1

Vestbrook

Winterbourne Manor

2

School Lane   Winterbourne Road

Winterbourne Road

Boxford

PH

Boxford Common

3

4

wnham

Lambourn valley way

River Lambourn

Coombesbury Lane

5

Copse Barn

Hunt's Green

Huntsgreen Farm

6

Ba

Lambourn valley way

Woodspeen

Woodspeen Farm

Watermill T & Restaura

7

RG20

Snake Lane

A   B4000   B   82   C   Snake Lane   D   E

Cricketers   Chapel Road

Stockcross School

ROOKSW

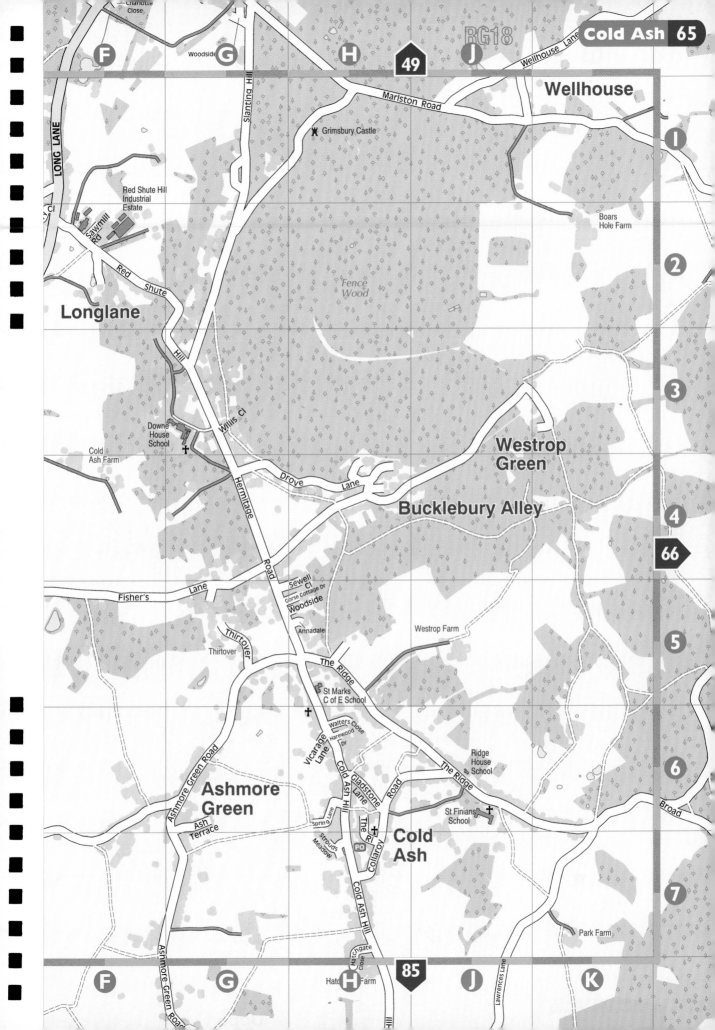

RG18

49

Wellhouse Lane

Wellhouse

Marlston Road

⚔ Grimsbury Castle

I

LONG LANE

Red Shute Hill Industrial Estate

Sawmill Rd

Boars Hole Farm

2

Red Shute

Longlane

Fence Wood

Hill

Willis Cl

Downe House School

Cold Ash Farm

Westrop Green

3

Drove Lane

Hermitage Road

Bucklebury Alley

4

66

Fisher's Lane

Sewell Cl

Gorse Cottage Dr

Woodside

Thirtover

Annadale

Westrop Farm

Thirtover

5

The Ridge

St Marks C of E School

Walters Close

Vicarage Lane

Harewood Dr

Ridge House School

Cold Ash Hill

Gladstone Lane

The Ridge

6

Broad

Ashmore Green

Ashmore Green Road

Ash Terrace

Spring Lane

Strouds Meadow

The Ri

PO

Collaroy Road

St Finians School

Cold Ash

7

Park Farm

Ashmore Green Road

Hatchgate Close

85

Hatc Farm

Lawrences Lane

F   **G**   **H**   **J**   **K**

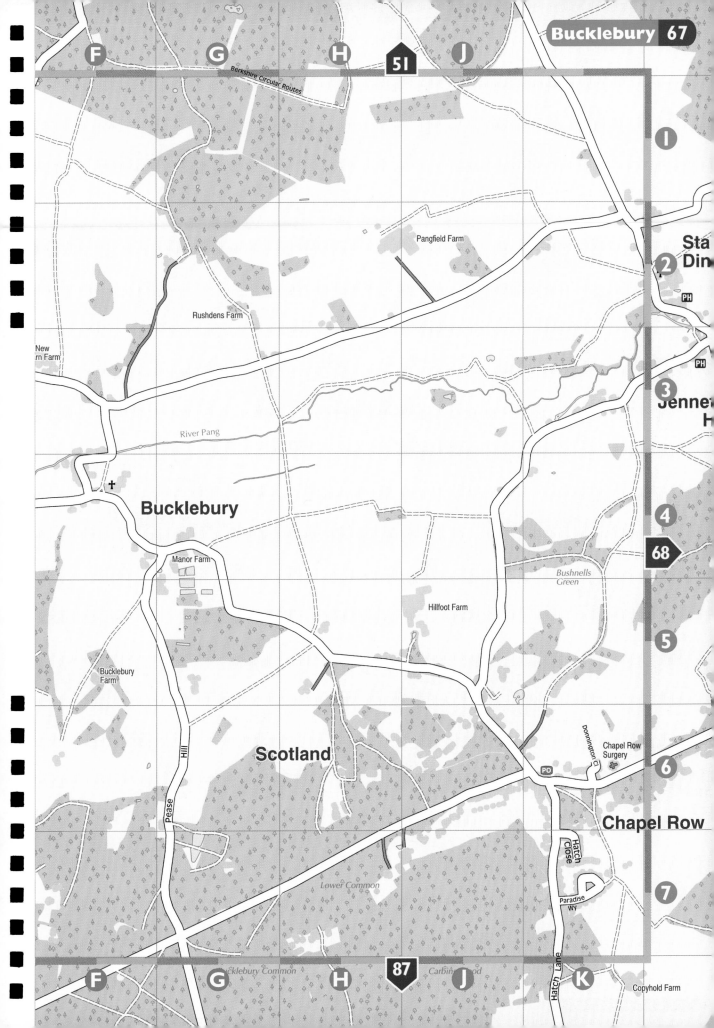

F G H 51 J

I

Pangfield Farm

Sta
Din

2

PH

PH

Rushdens Farm

New
rn Farm

3

Jenne
H

Berkshire Circular Routes

River Pang

†

Bucklebury

4

68

Manor Farm

*Bushnells
Green*

5

Hillfoot Farm

Bucklebury
Farm

Donnington Cl

Chapel Row
Surgery

Hill

Scotland

PO

6

Pease

Chapel Row

Hatch
Close

Lower Common

Paradise
Wy

7

F G *Bucklebury Common* H 87 J *Carbin* od K

Hatch Lane

Copyhold Farm

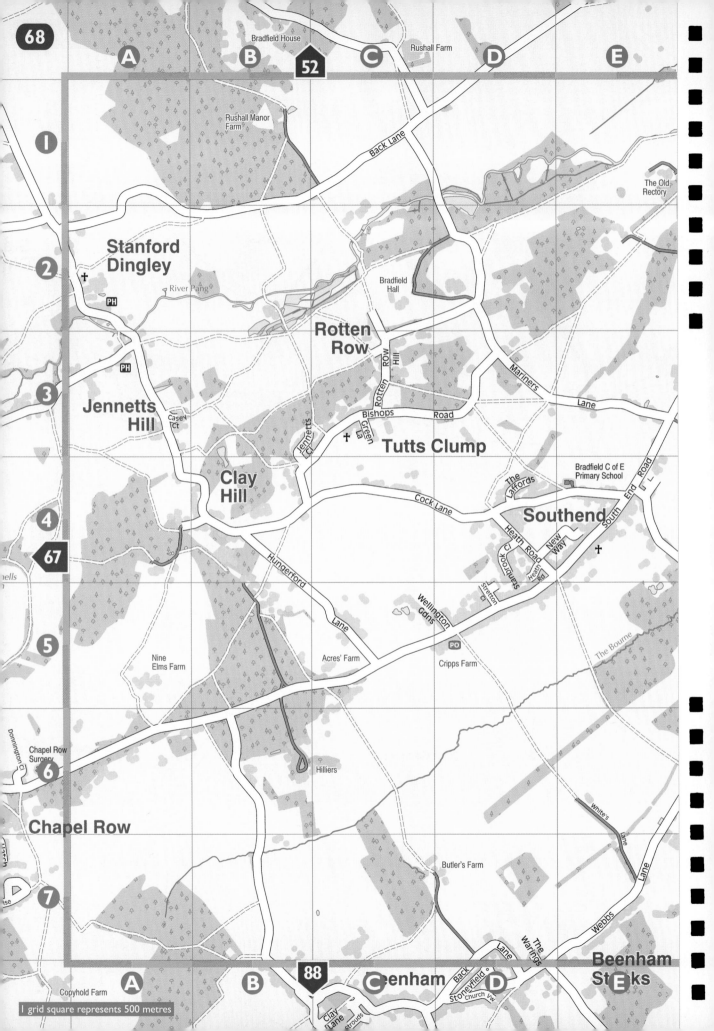

68

A   B   52   C   D   E

I

Stanford Dingley

2   River Pang

Rotten Row

Bradfield House

Rushall Farm

Rushall Manor Farm

Back Lane

Bradfield Hall

The Old Rectory

3   **Jennetts Hill**   Casey Ct

Bishops   Green La   Rotten ROW Hill   Road   Mariners   Lane

Tutts Clump

Jennetts Ct

Bradfield C of E Primary School

4

67

Clay Hill

Cock Lane   The Laffords   **Southend**   South End Road

Heath Road   New Way   Stanbrook Cl   Stretton Cl   Heath Rd

Hungerford   Lane

Wellington Gdns

The Bourne

5   Nine Elms Farm   Acres' Farm   Cripps Farm   PO

Donnington Cl

Chapel Row Surgery

6   Hilliers

Chapel Row

7   Butler's Farm

White's Lane

Webbs Lane

Beenham St Eks

A   B   88   C   Beenham   D   E

Copyhold Farm   Back Lane   Stoneyfield   Church Vw   The Warings   Clay Lane   Strouds

1 grid square represents 500 metres

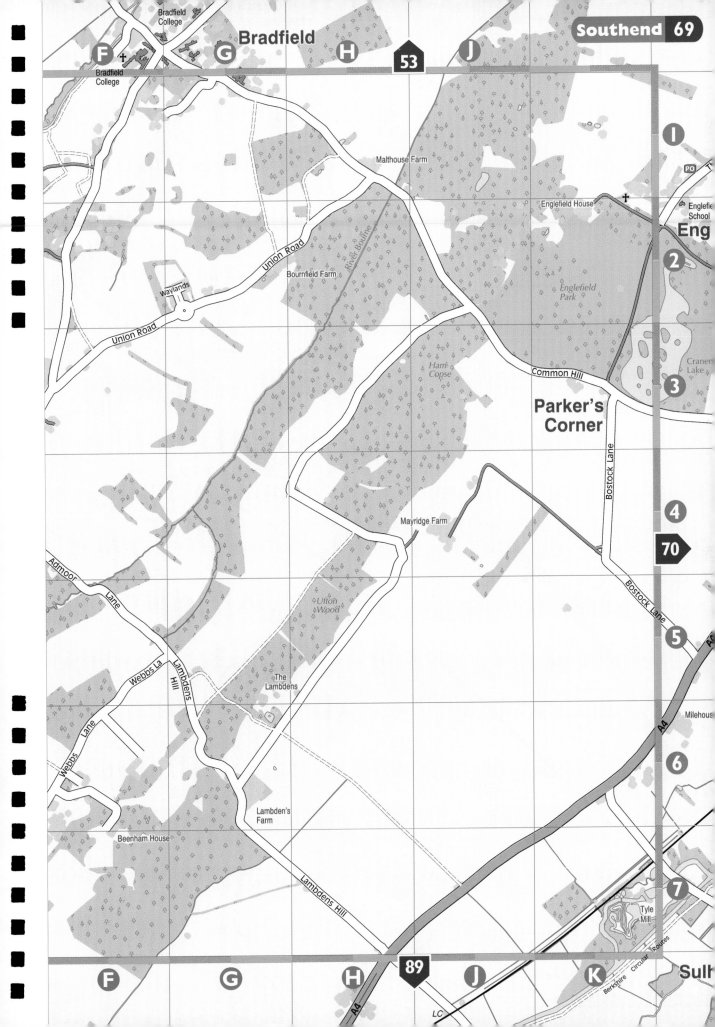

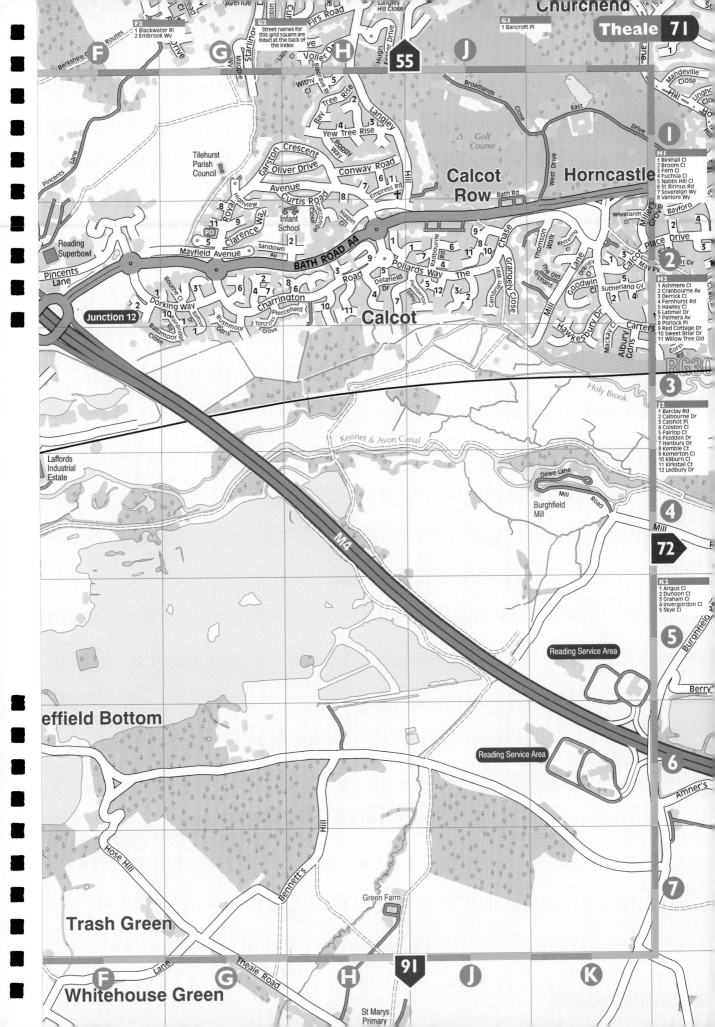

Churchend

F2
1 Blackwater Rl
2 Embrook Wy

G2
Street names for
this grid square are
listed at the back of
the index

G3
1 Bancroft Pl

55

F **G** **H** **J**

Broadlands
Close

Golf
Course

I

H1
1 Birkhall Cl
2 Broom Cl
3 Fern Cl
4 Fuchsia Cl
5 Nabbs Hill Cl
6 St Birinus Rd
7 Sovereign Wy
8 Vaniore Wy

Tilehurst
Parish
Council

**Calcot
Row**

Horncastle

Bath Rd

Wheatlands

Reading
Superbowl

Infant
School

BATH ROAD A4

Calcot

Holy Brook

RG30

H2
1 Ashmere Cl
2 Cranbourne Av
3 Derrick Cl
4 Fernhurst Rd
5 Hawley Cl
6 Latimer Dr
7 Palmera Av
8 Porlock Pl
9 Red Cottage Dr
10 Sweet Briar Dr
11 Willow Tree Gld

2

3

Junction 12

Pincents
Lane

Dorking Way

J2
1 Barclay Rd
2 Calbourne Dr
3 Calshot Pl
4 Colston Cl
5 Fairlop Cl
6 Flodden Dr
7 Hanbury Dr
8 Kemble Ct
9 Kemerton Cl
10 Kilburn Cl
11 Kirkstall Ct
12 Ledbury Dr

Kennet & Avon Canal

Dewe Lane

Burghfield
Mill

Mill Road

4

Laffords
Industrial
Estate

72

Mill

K2
1 Angus Cl
2 Dunoon Cl
3 Graham Cl
4 Invergordon Cl
5 Skye Cl

5

M4

Reading Service Area

Burghfield

effield Bottom

Reading Service Area

6

Berry

Amner

7

Trash Green

Hose Hill

Bennett's

Green Farm

91

F **G** **H** **J** **K**

Whitehouse Green

Theale Road

St Marys
Primary

72

A Cockney Hill B C D E A4

I

orncastle

2

3

Holy Brook

Reading
West Berkshire

4

71

5

6

7

A B C D E

92

Southcote

Manor County School

Kennet Valley Primary School

Burghfield Aqua Sports Club

Searles Farm

Pingewood

Knight's Farm

Amner's Farm

Amner's Farm

M4

Presentation College

Southcote Mill

Kirttons Farm Road

Smallmead Road

Reading Wokingham

Pingewood Road South

Burnthouse

Severn Way

Stoneham Close

Honey Lane

Delwood

Prospect School

Prospect Park

A4 BATH ROAD

Granville Road

Gainsborough Road

Worcester Close

Burrcroft Rd

Virginia Way

Southcote Clinic

Southcote Lane

Southcote

Ashampstead

Hatford

Brunel Road

Circuit Lane

Fawley Road

Aldworth Close

Silchester Road

Southcote CP School

Shepley Dr

Tallis Lane

Monks Way

Kenilworth Avenue

Firs Lane

Winser Drive

Wensley Road

Southcote Farm Lane

RG30

Burghfield Road

Pingewood Road North

Mill Road

Green Lane

Burghfield Road

Berry's Lane

Berrys Lane

1 grid square represents 500 metres

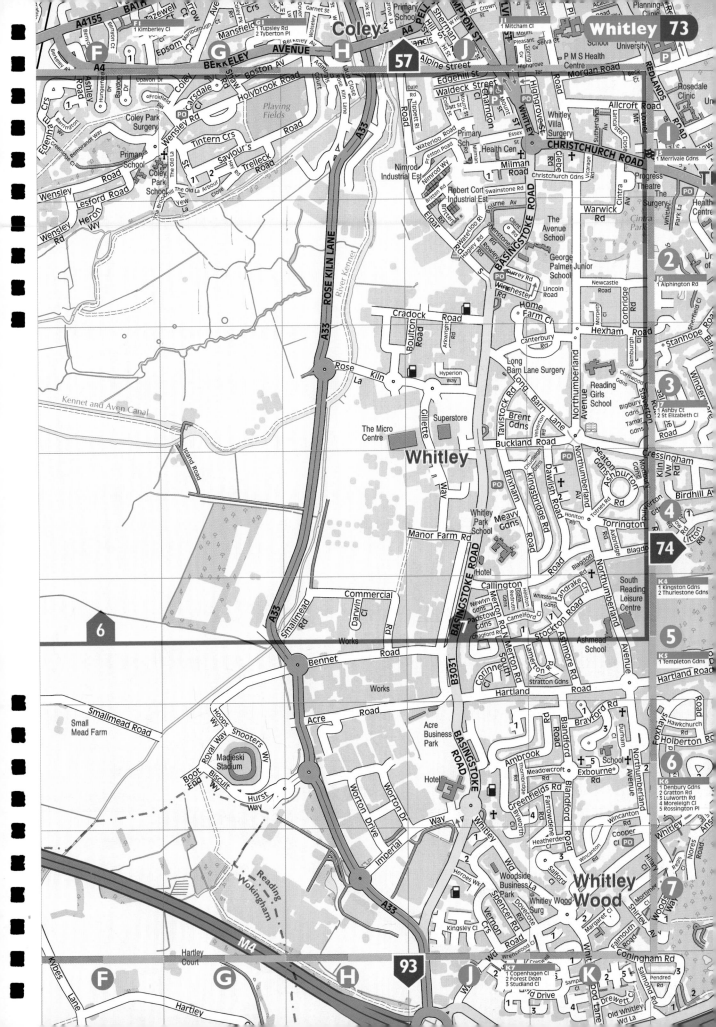

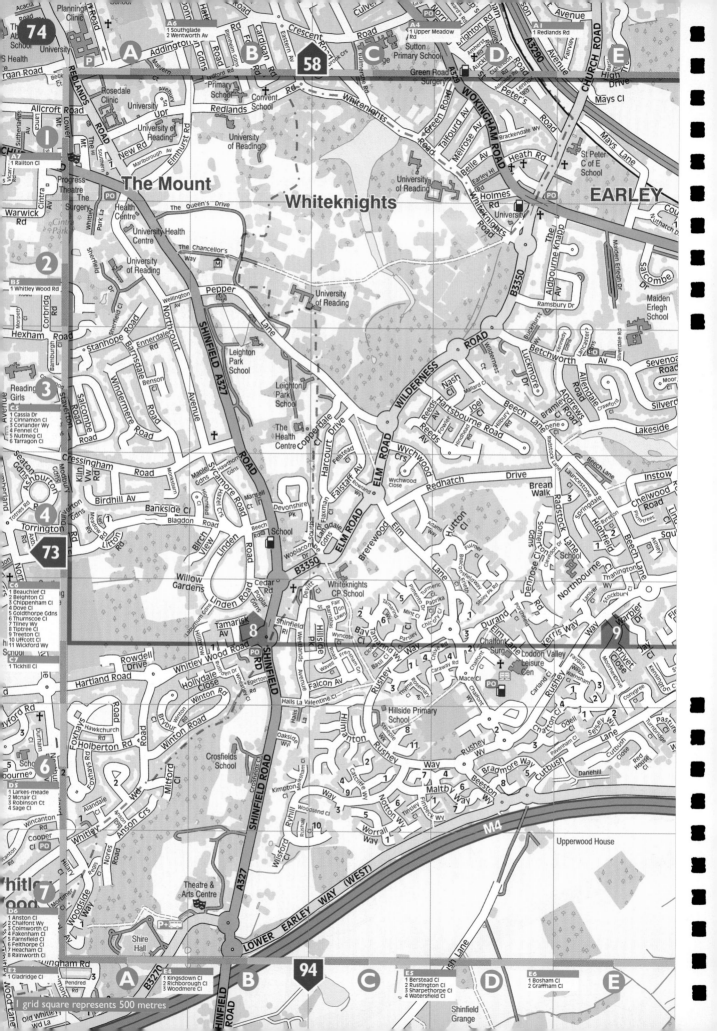

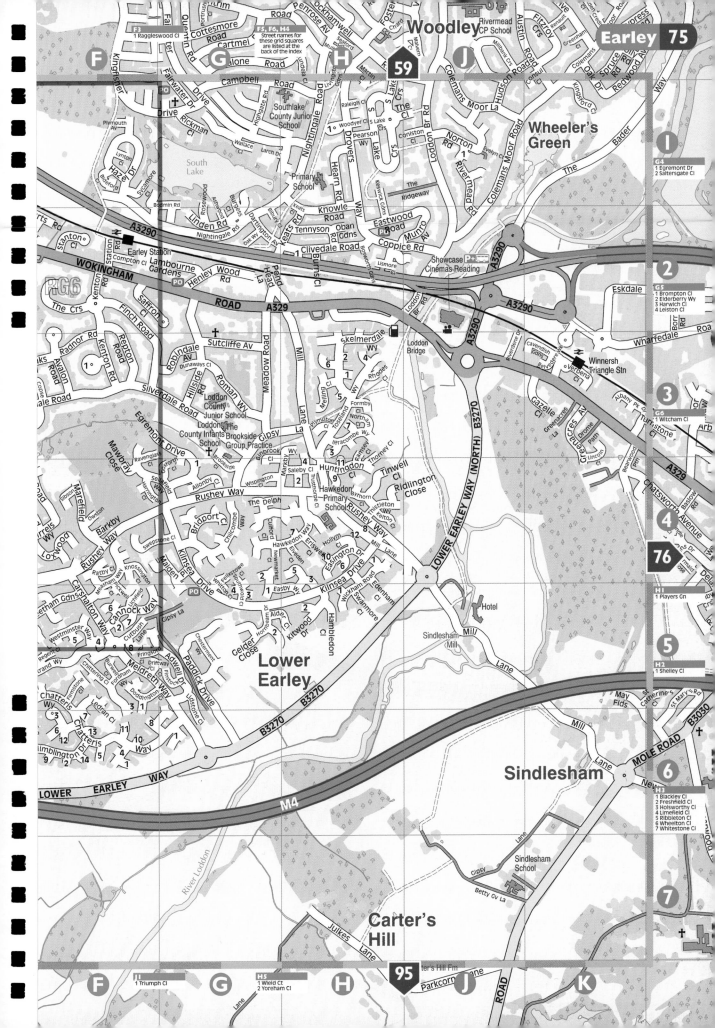

Woodley

Wheeler's Green

Lower Earley

Sindlesham

Carter's Hill

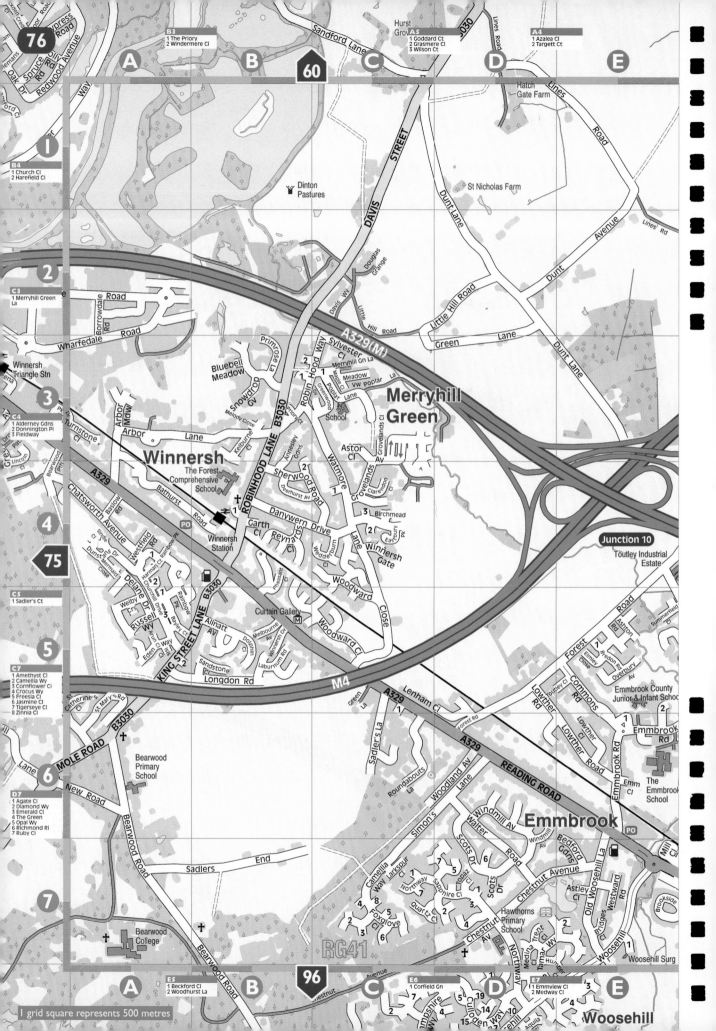

D2
1 Symondson Ms

C4
1 Fisher Gn
2 Horsnape Gdns
3 Randall Mead
4 Wythemede

A7
1 Mower Cl
2 Yarnold Cl

Billingbear Lane

Billingbear Park

Billingbear

CHURCH HILL

CHURCH LANE

1

D3
1 Minchin Gn
2 Thorp Cl
3 Winch Cl

Windsor and Maidenhead
Wokingham

Straight Mile

Carter's Hill

Binfield Park Hospl

Ketcher Green

Wick's Green

Terrace Road North

2

Straight Mile Farm

Carter's Hill

Stevenson Drive

Wordesford

Tilehurst Lane

Tilehurst Lane

D4
1 Caswall Cl
2 Emmets Pk
3 Pitts Cl
4 Wilmot Cl

Terrace Road North

Red Rose

Rose Hill

York Road

Brooke Place

3

E3
1 Arthurstone Birches
2 Pitch Pl

Marchfield House

Binfield Surgery

Chase Gardens

Rosedale

Knox Green

Alben Road

Cheney Close

4

Green Lane

Kingscote

BINFIELD

B3034

PO

Emmets Nest

Hillside Drive

Terrace Road

Roughgrove Copse

Nash Park

Benetfeld Road

Binfield Primary School

Savory Walk

Wiggett Gr

Cressex Cl

Park Farm

Bl

77

E7
1 Blomfield Dl
2 Cloves Farm Wd
3 Jacob Cl
4 Pocket Cl

Binfield Road

Foxley Lane

Angel Place

Murrellhill Lane

Roebuck Estate

Chapel Lane

Woodies Close

Newbold College

5

Bracknell Forest Wokingham

St Mark's Road

Newbold School

Popeswood Road

B3408

Stokes Farm

6

Pavley Drive

Rosebay

Webb

Montague Close

Comfrey Cl

Murrellhill Lane

South

Sampson Pk

Nevelle

Lawrence Grove

PO Hotel

Mutton Oaks

Goldcrest Wood

Fletcher Gdns

Turnpike

Trefoil Cl

Keep Hatch

Clover Cl

Dyer Rd

Springfield Rd

Beehive Lane

Arkwright Dr

Beehive Rd

Cain Rd

7

Charwood Road

De-Vitre Road

Plough Lane

Buttercup Lane

A329(M)

Binfield Road

Popeswood

Milward Gdns

Phoenix Business Park

John Hotel

Nike Wy

LONDON ROAD

B3408

Beehive Road

Amen Corner

Proctors Rd

A329

London Road

1 grid square represents 500 metres

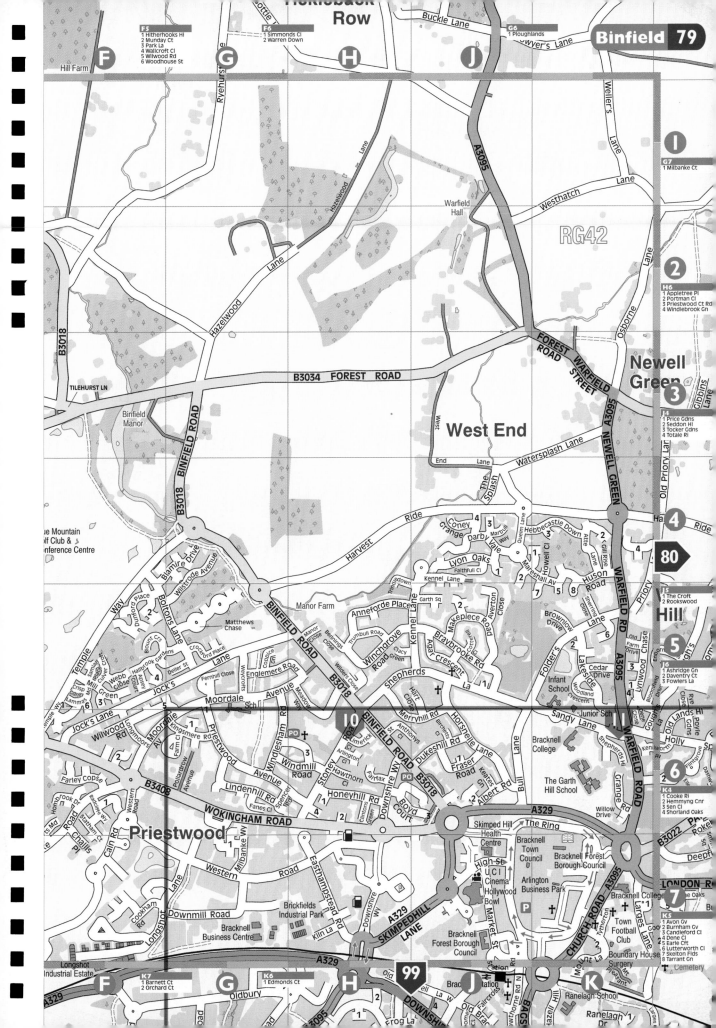

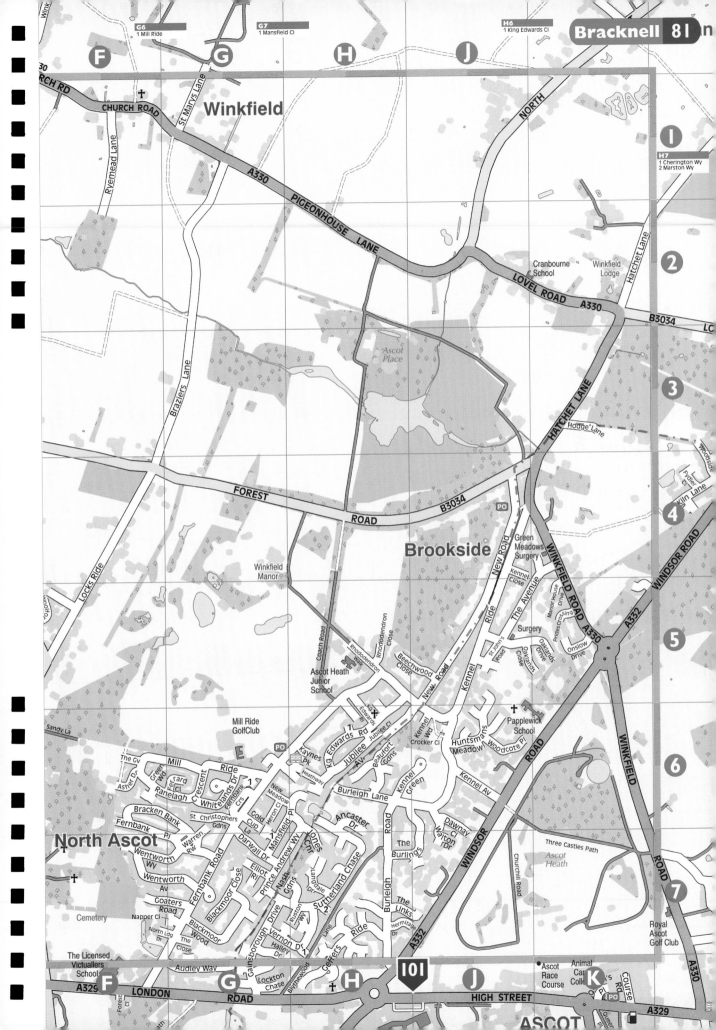

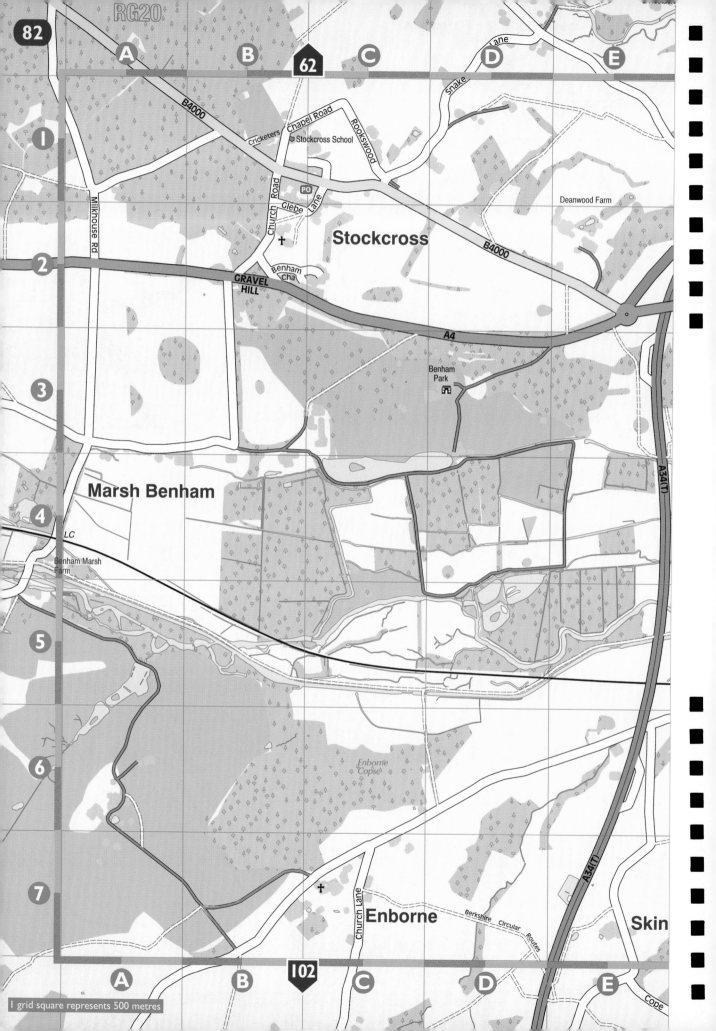

82

A   B   62   C   D   E

I

Milkhouse Rd

B4000

Cricketers   Chapel Road
Stockcross School
Rookswood

Snake Lane

Deanwood Farm

PO
Church Road
Glebe Lane

✝

Stockcross

B4000

2   GRAVEL
HILL
Benham
cha

A4

3   Benham
Park

4   **Marsh Benham**

LC

Benham Marsh
Farm

5

6   *Enborne
Copse*

A34(T)

7   ✝   Church Lane   **Enborne**   Berkshire Circular Routes   **Skin**

A34(T)

A   B   102   C   D   E

Cope

1 grid square represents 500 metres

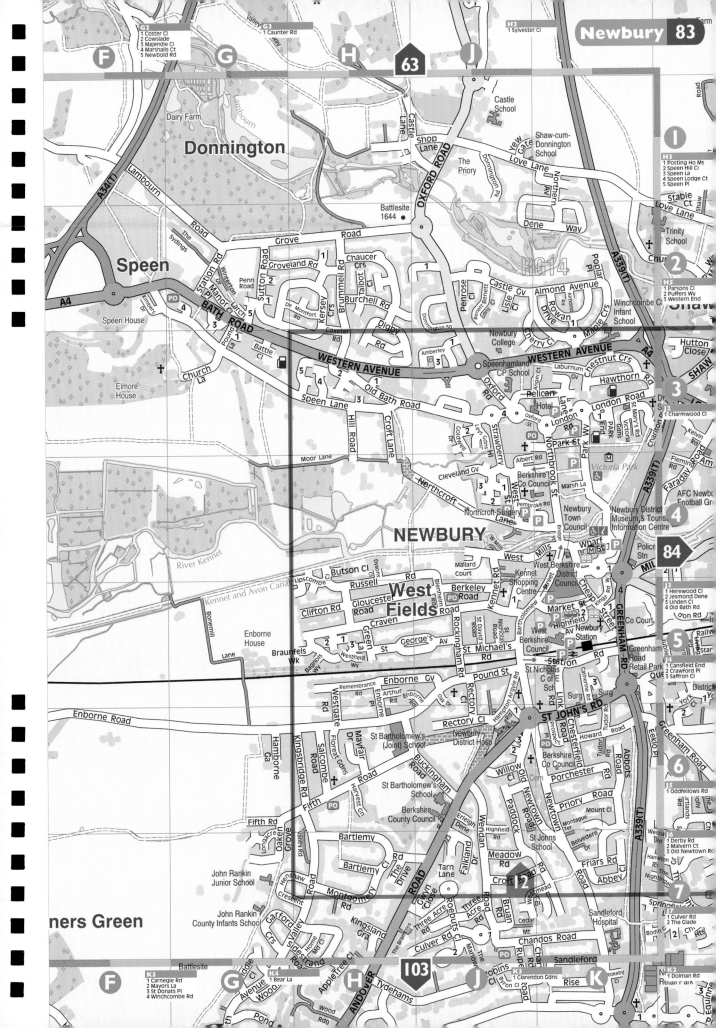

Turner's Green

Green

A5
1 Arrow Smith Wy
2 Bramwell Cl
3 Corderoy Cl
4 Evreux Cl
5 John Hunt Cl
6 Montacute Dr

A4
1 Botany Cl
2 Golding Cl

A3
1 Pimpernel Pl
2 Snowdrop Copse

Farm

1

B4
1 Boscawen Wy
2 Munkle Marsh
3 Poffley Pl

Briff Lane

Roundfield

Broad Lane

Upper
Bucklebury

Heath

Harts Hill Road

PO

Bucklebury
C of E
Primary School

Woodside
Close

Blacklands
Road

Long Grove

Little Lane

2

C1
1 Roundfield

WY

Harts
Hill Farm

Bradley Moore Sq

Blacklands
Copse

3

Hill Road

Floral Way

Trefoil Dro

Larkspur Gdns

Simmons Field

Tamarisk Cct

Ash Ga

King's Farm

Cemetery

Speedwell WY

Broadmeadow End

Poppy Dr

Archangel WY

Celandine Gv

Colthrop Manor

ST   LONDON RD

School

Kennet Secondary School

Siege
Cross Farm

Cox's Lane

4

Skillman drive

Jedburgh Close

Edwin Cl

Wurford Dr

Cholsey Cl

Bolingbroke

Ashman Rd

Wilfred Wy

cropper Cl

Falmouth Way

Way

A4 BATH ROAD

Colthrop

85

Stoney Lane

Domony Close

Scriven's Md

2

1   3

Turners Dr

Hammond Cl

The Martins

Peachey
Drive

Heardman Rd

Rosier Cl

Pavy Cl

Fuller Cl

Pipers

Enterprise Way

Berkshire Drive

Berkshire
Business
Cen

Kennetholme

Longcroft Rd

2

1

PO

Burd
Surger

5

Wheelers Gn

Agricola
Way

Lyon Cl

3

Betteridge Rd

Grassmead

Tokenham

4

6

Colthrop
Wy

Daytona Drive

Station Rd

Webbs Acre

Justice Cl

Mayow Cl

2

Aylesford Wy

Colthrop

Gables

Way

Flag Staff
Square

Buchanan
Square

Pipers
Industrial Est

LC

6

Station Rd

Pipers Lane

LC

Lane

Thatcham
Station

Kennet and Avon Canal

Bury's Bank Road

Thatcham Town
Football Club

Crookham
Manor

River Kennet

7

Mano

1 grid square represents 500 metres

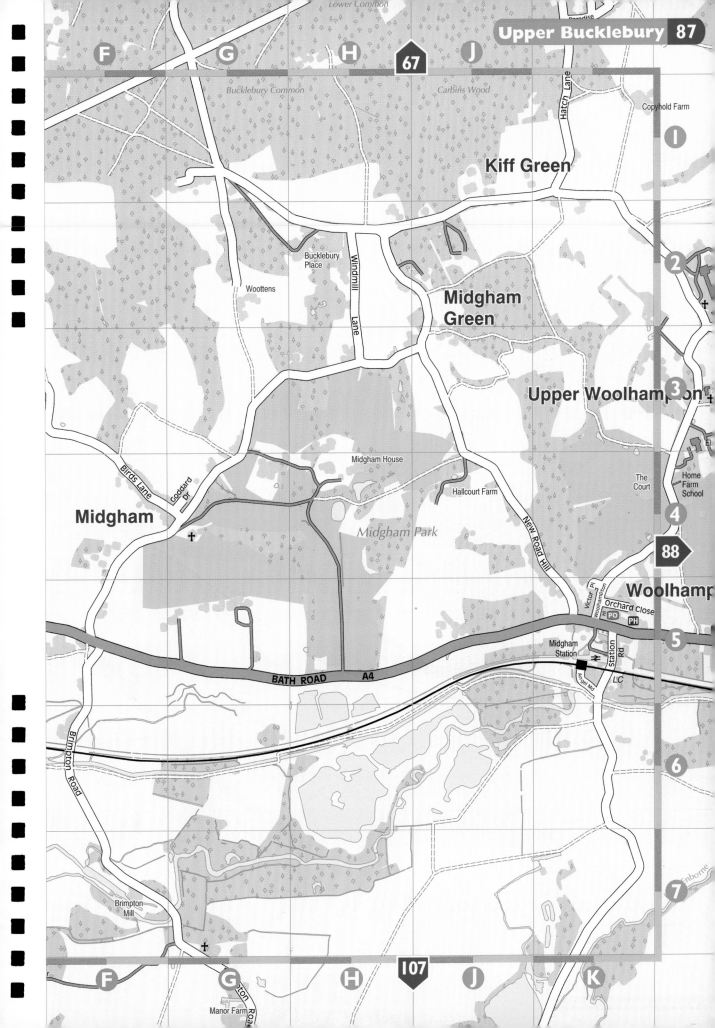

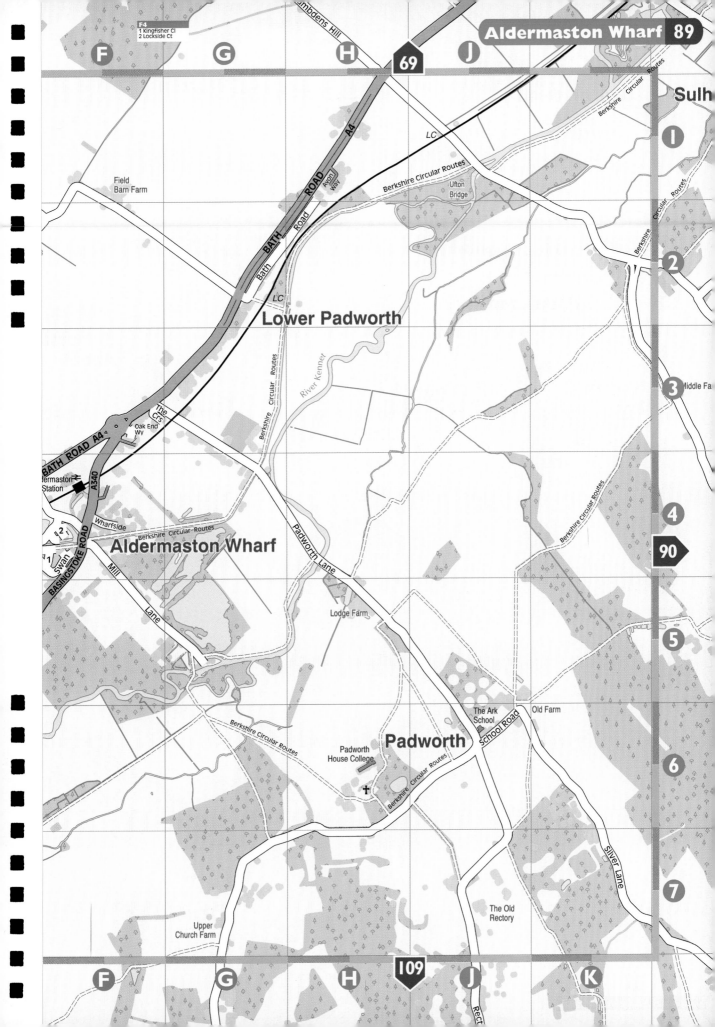

F **F4**
1 Kingfisher Cl
2 Lockside Ct

G

H

69

J

Sulh

I

2

3 Middle Fa

4

90

5

6

7

Field
Barn Farm

BATH ROAD A4

Avon Way

LC

Berkshire Circular Routes

Ufton
Bridge

Lower Padworth

LC

Berkshire Circular Routes

River Kenner

Berkshire Circular Routes

The Crs

Oak End
Wy

BATH ROAD A4

dermaston
Station

A340

Wharfside

Berkshire Circular Routes

Aldermaston Wharf

BASINGSTOKE ROAD

Swan

Mill

Lane

Padworth Lane

Lodge Farm

Berkshire Circular Routes

The Ark
School

Old Farm

School Road

Berkshire Circular Routes

Padworth

Padworth
House College

Berkshire Circular Routes

Silver Lane

Upper
Church Farm

The Old
Rectory

109

F

G

H

J

K

Rect

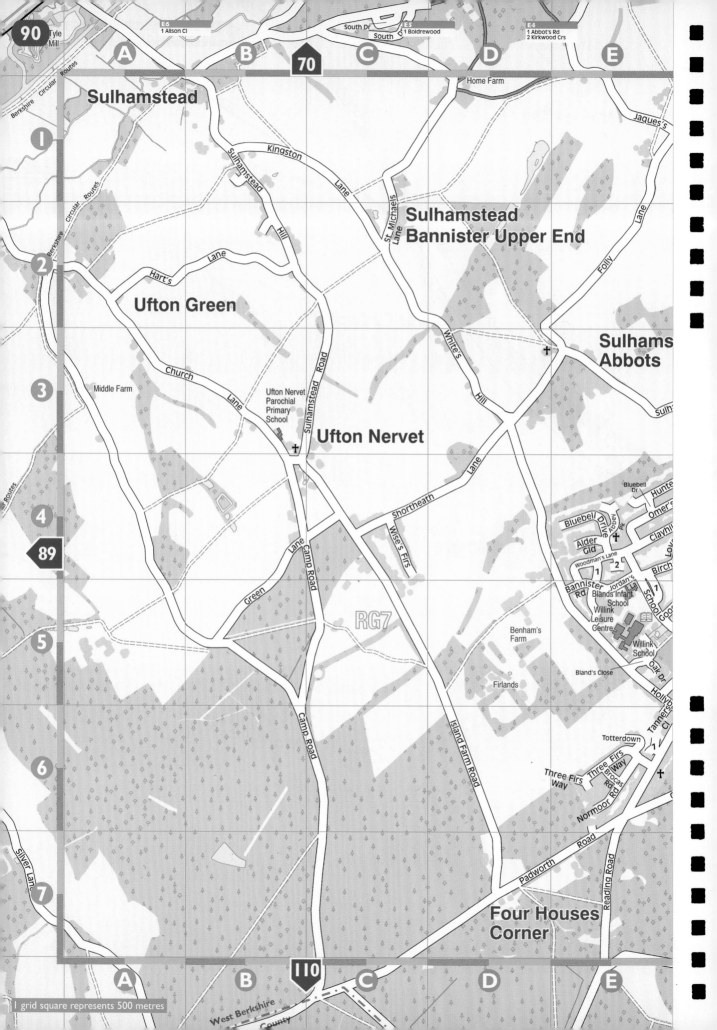

Tyle Mill

E6
1 Allson Cl

South Dr
South

E5
1 Boldrewood

E4
1 Abbot's Rd
2 Kirkwood Crs

A
B
70
C
D
E

Sulhamstead

Berkshire Circular Routes

1

Kingston Lane

Sulhamstead Hill

St Michaels Lane

Home Farm

Jaques's Lane

Sulhamstead
Bannister Upper End

2

Hart's Lane

Ufton Green

Folly

White's Hill

Sulhams
Abbots

Berkshire Circular Routes

3

Church Lane

Middle Farm

Ufton Nervet
Parochial
Primary
School

Sulhamstead Road

Ufton Nervet

Bluebell Dr

Hunter

Bluebell Drive

Abbey Pk

omer's

Clayhill

Woodman's Lane

Alder Gld

1

2

Birch

4

89

Shortneath Lane

Wise's Firs

Green Lane

Camp Road

RG7

Bannister Rd

1

Jordan's La

Blands Infant
School
Willink
Leisure
Centre

School

Goo

7

5

Benham's
Farm

Firlands

Bland's Close

Willink
School

Oak Dr

Hollyb

Tanners Cl

6

Totterdown

Three Firs Way

Three Firs
Way

Three Firs Way

Brocas Rd

Normoor Rd

Island Farm Road

Silver Lane

7

Padworth Road

Reading Road

Four Houses
Corner

A
B
110
C
D
E

West Berkshire County

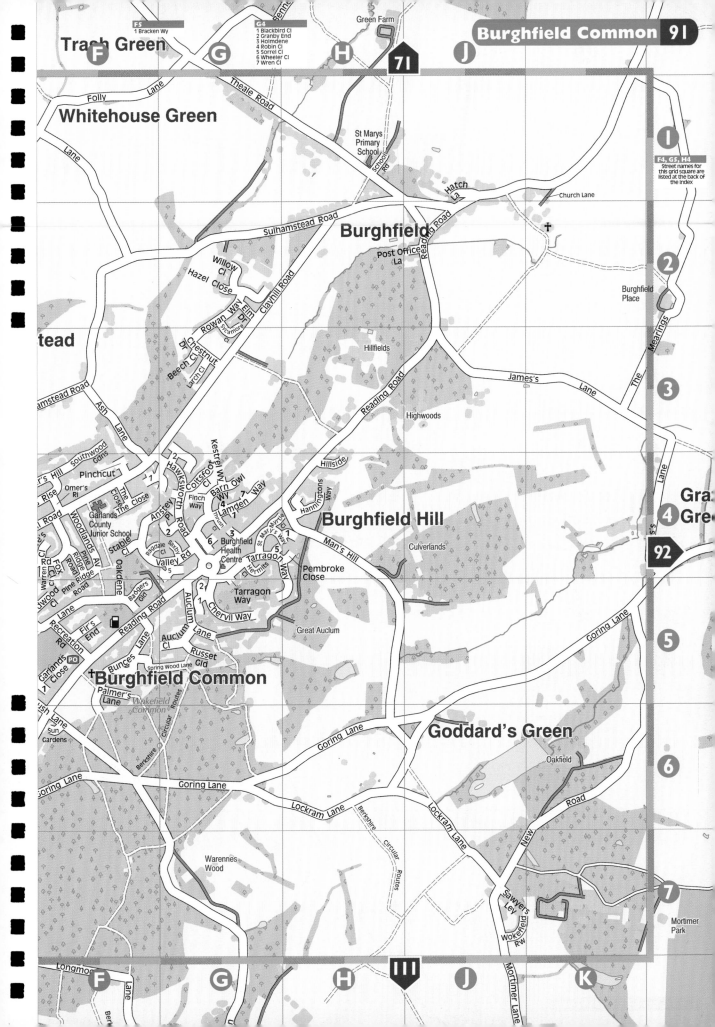

Trash Green

Whitehouse Green

F5
1 Bracken Wy

G4
1 Blackbird Cl
2 Granby End
3 Holmdene
4 Robin Cl
5 Sorrel Cl
6 Wheeler Cl
7 Wren Cl

Green Farm

71

F G H J

1

F4, G5, H4
Street names for
this grid square are
listed at the back of
the index

Folly

Lane

Theale Road

Lane

St Marys
Primary
School

School Rd

Hatch La

Church Lane

2

Sulhamstead Road

Burghfield

Post Office
La

Reading Road

Willow
Cl

Hazel Close

Clayhill Road

Burghfield
Place

Burghfield
Place

The Mearings

Rowan Way

Elm
Dr

Sycamore

Chestnut

Larch Cl

Beech

Hillfields

James's

Lane

The

3

Reading Road

mstead

mstead Road

Ash

Lane

Highwoods

Gra
Gre

southwood
Gdns

Pinchcut

Hawksworth Road

Coltsfoot
Cl

Barn Owl
Wy

Lamden Way

Hillside

Hanningtons Way

Burghfield Hill

James's
La

4

92

's Hill

Omer's
Ri

The Close

Anstey's

Road

Finch
Way

Thrush

St Mary's Way

Man's Hill

Culverlands

Rise

Garlands
County
Junior School

Stable
Cl

Oakdene

Raedale
Cl

Saxby Rd

Valley Rd

Burghfield
Health
Centre

Tarragon
Way

Hermits

Pembroke
Close

Warren
Cl

Fox
Lane

Pine Ridge Road

Badgers
Gld

Reading Road

Bunces Lane

Auclum
Lane

Tarragon
Way

Chervil Way

Great Auclum

Goring Lane

5

Recreation
Rd

Fir's
End

Garlands
Close

PO

Auclum
Cl

Russet
Gld

Spring Wood Lane

Burghfield Common

Goddard's Green

Oakfield

6

Palmer's
Lane

Wakefield
Common

Sun
Gardens

Berkshire

Circular
Routes

Goring Lane

Goring Lane

Goring Lane

Lockram Lane

Lockram Lane

New

Road

7

Longmo

Lane

Warennes
Wood

Berkshire

Circular
Routes

Sawyers
Ley

Wokefield
Rw

Mortimer
Park

Mortimer Lane

F G H J K

A   B   **72**   C   D   E

1

Lane

2

Burghfield
Place

3

Lane

The Mearings

Burnthouse Lane

Pingewood Road South

Hopkiln Farm

West Berkshire
Wokingham

Burnthouse Bridge

Rider's Lane

Fuller's Lane

Manor
Farm

Kybes Lane

Grazeley Court Farm

Poundgreen

4

91

James's Lane

Palmer's Lane

**Grazeley
Green**

Goring Lane

5

Pierce's Farm

Goodboy's Lane

West Berkshire
Wokingham

Pump Lane

Grazeley

6

Thurley Farm

Lambwood
Industrial
Estate

7

Mortimer
Park

Wokefield
Park

Bloomfield
Hatch

Cross Lane

Bloomfieldhatch Lane

Clappers Farm

Foundry Brook

Brook Farm

A   B   **112**   C   D   E   Lane

Crosslane Farm

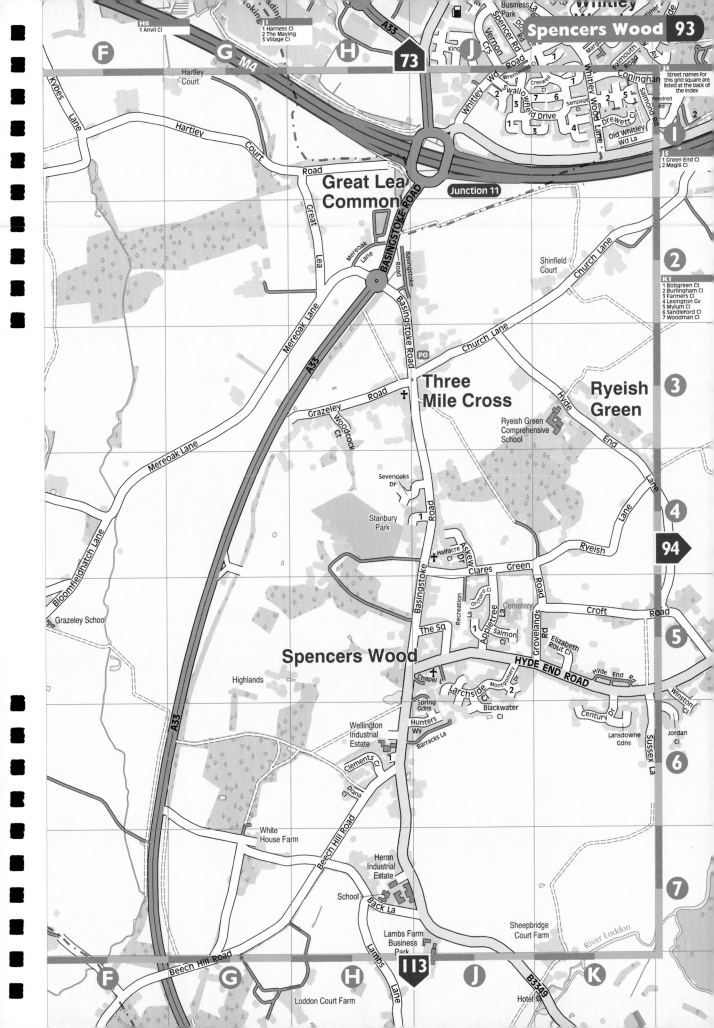

A   B   **LOWER EARLEY WAY**   C   D   E

B2
1 Hirtes Av
2 Milsom Cl

B1
1 Kendal Av
2 Lane End Cl

A1
1 Babbington Rd
2 Longmore Rd
3 Pattinson Rd

intley

Woodside Way

Mortimer Cl

Falmouth Road

Theatre &
Arts Centre

nmire
Hall

Coningham Rd

Salmond Rd

B3270

Pendred Rd

Old

Drewett Cl

C3
1 Wickers Cl

I

1

Cutbush Lane

Shinfield
Grange

M4

Brooker's   Hill

SHINFIELD ROAD

HOLLOW LANE

Cutbush Lane

2

Leyland Gdns

Godard
Av

ROSECROFT

1

Oatlands

Road

RG2

2

Wheatfields Rd

Seymour
Av

Road

Oatlands

SHINFIELD

Ilbury Cl

church

La

Wychelm
Rd

7

Fairmead
Rd

Oatlands

Schoolgreen

School

PO

1

Parrot Farm

ARBORFIELD ROAD   **A327**

Ar

Rye
Green

3

Shinfield
Infant
School

Chestnut Crs

Shinfield
C of E
Junior School

The
Surgery

Millworth
Lane

Bridge Farm

End   Lane

B3349

4

93

High
Copse Farm

Moor
Copse

oft

Road

Winston

5

Hyde
End

de End Rd

Lansdowne
Gdns

Jordan
Cl

Sussex La

6

Nutter's

Lane

Great
Wood

Tanner's Farm

Swallowfield Road

7

Loddon

Swallowfield
Park

Swallowfield Road

Kil

Swall

A   B   C   D   E

1 grid square represents 500 metres

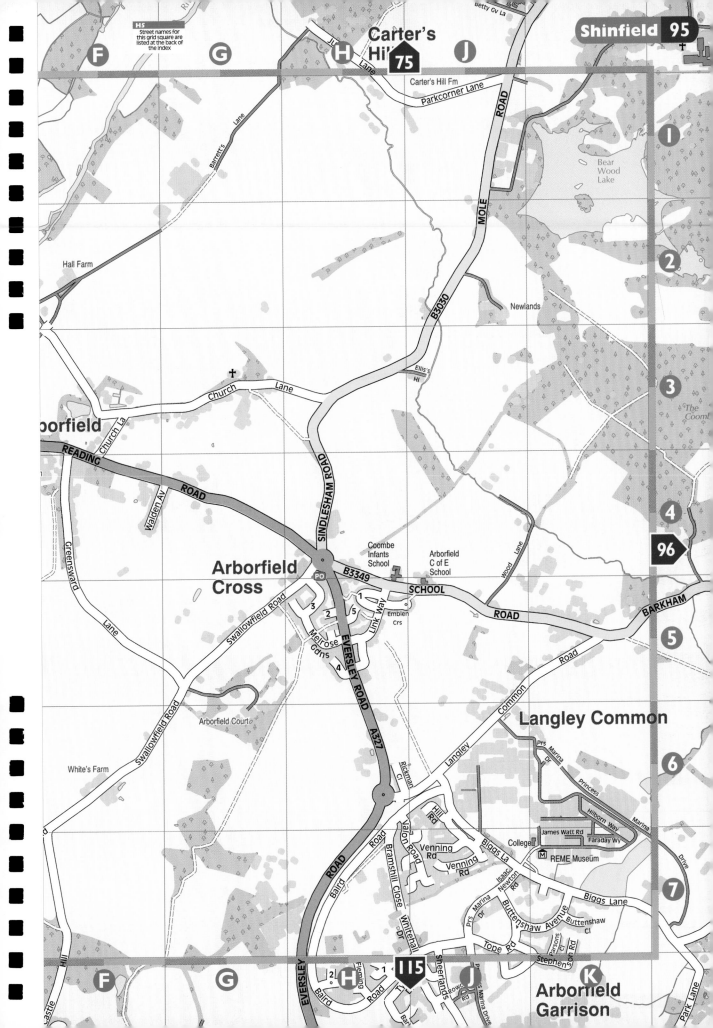

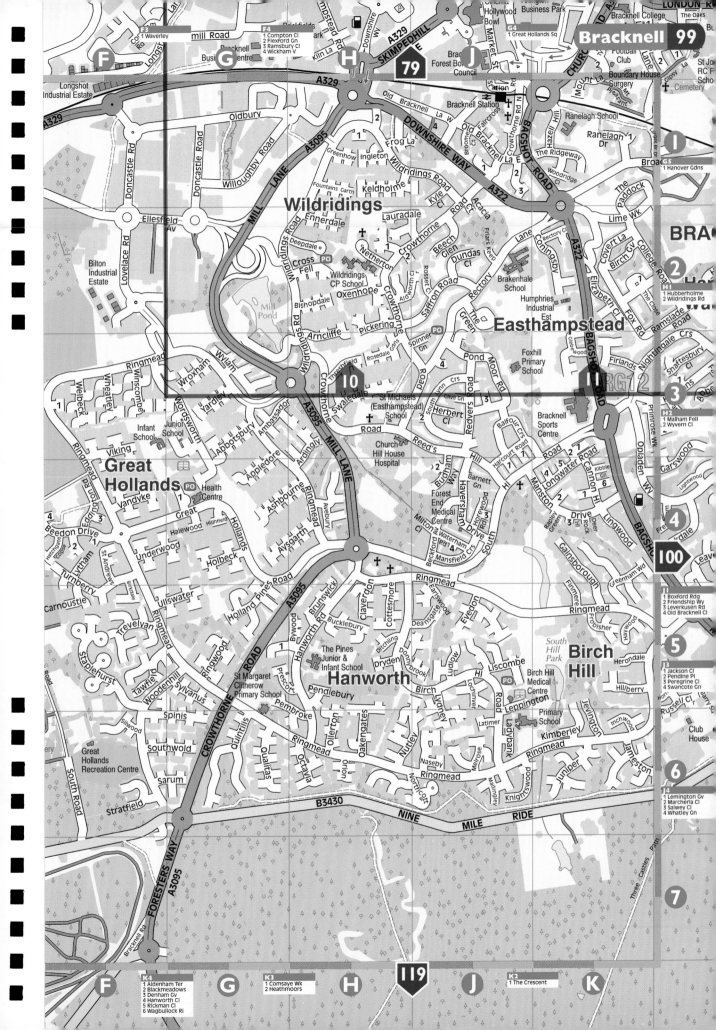

Bracknell

1 grid square represents 500 metres

Bullbrook

BRACKNELL

Harmans Water

Crown Wood

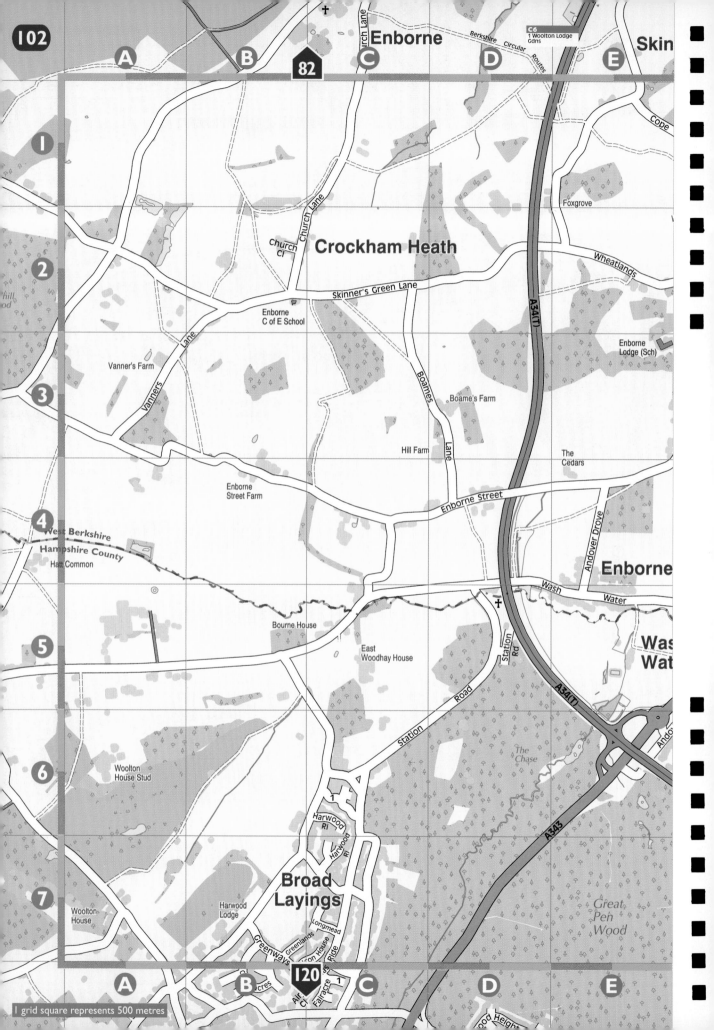

A B 82 C D E Skin

Enborne

† Church Lane Berkshire Circular Routes C6 1 Woolton Lodge Gdns

1

Foxgrove

Church Lane

Church Cl

Crockham Heath

Wheatlands

2

Enborne C of E School

Skinner's Green Lane

A34(T)

Enborne Lodge (Sch)

Vanner's Farm

Vanners Lane

Boames Lane

Boame's Farm

3

Hill Farm

The Cedars

Enborne Street Farm

Enborne Street

Andover Drove

4

West Berkshire Hampshire County

Hatt Common

Enborne

Wash Water

†

Was Wat

Bourne House

East Woodhay House

Station Rd

A34(T)

5

Woolton House Stud

Station Road

The Chase

Ando

6

Harwood Ri

1

A343

Harwood Ri

Broad Layings

Great Pen Wood

7

Woolton House

Harwood Lodge

Longmead

Greenways Greenlands ...son House Ride Acres

A B 120 C D E
Alf Ct Fairacre 1

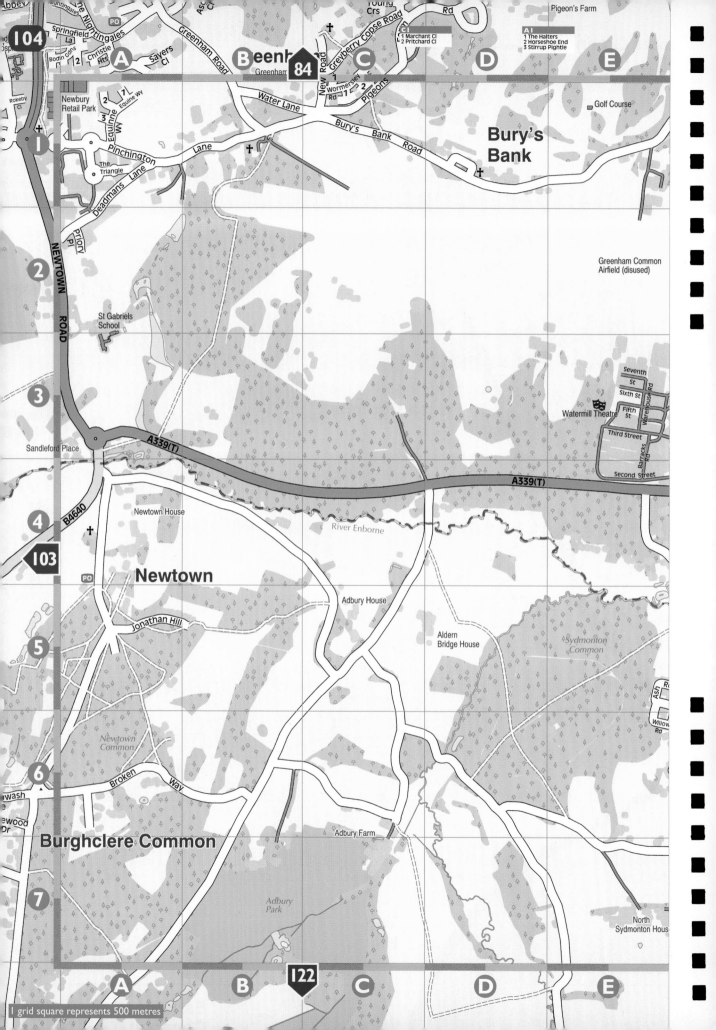

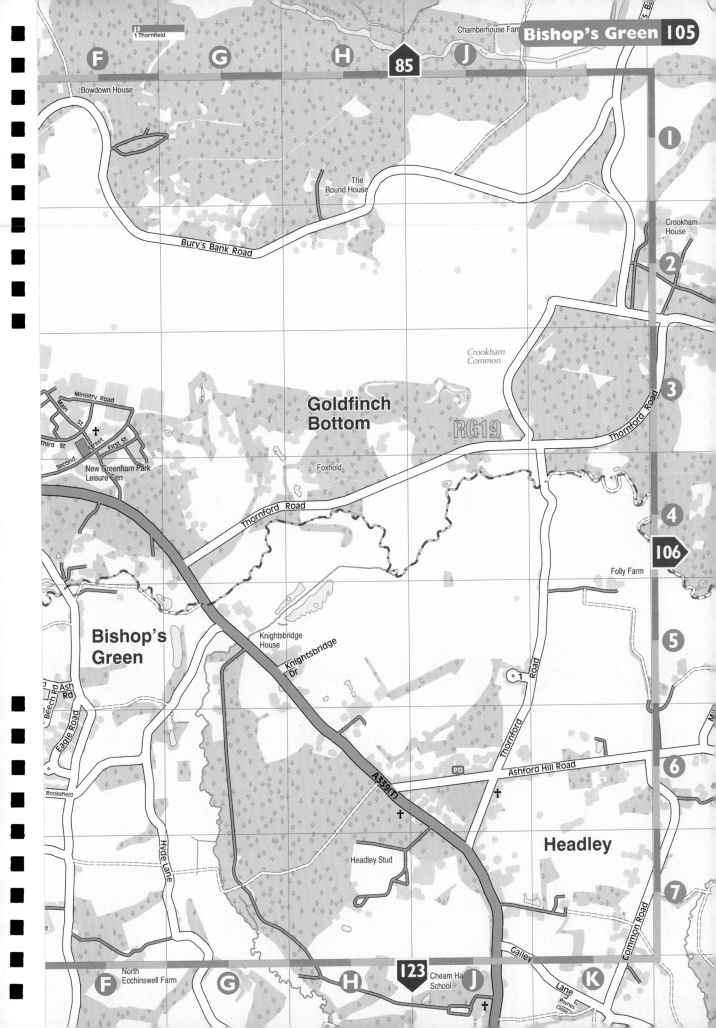

River Kennet

Chamberhouse Farm

F

G

H

85

J

15
1 Thornfield

Bowdown House

I

The
Round House

Crookham
House

2

Bury's Bank Road

Crookham
Common

3

Ministry Road

Goldfinch
Bottom

RG19

Thornford Road

Main St

Third St

Street
First St

†

Second St

New Greenham Park
Leisure Cen

Foxhold

Thornford Road

Folly Farm

4

106

Bishop's
Green

Knightsbridge
House

Knightsbridge
Dr

5

1

Thornford Road

Beech Rd

Ash Rd

Ash
Rd

Eagle Road

PO

Ashford Hill Road

6

Rooksfield

A339(T)

†

†

Headley

Hyde Lane

Headley Stud

7

Galley

North
Ecchinswell Farm

F

G

H

123

Cheam Ha...
School

J

Lane

Paynes
Close

K

†

Common Road

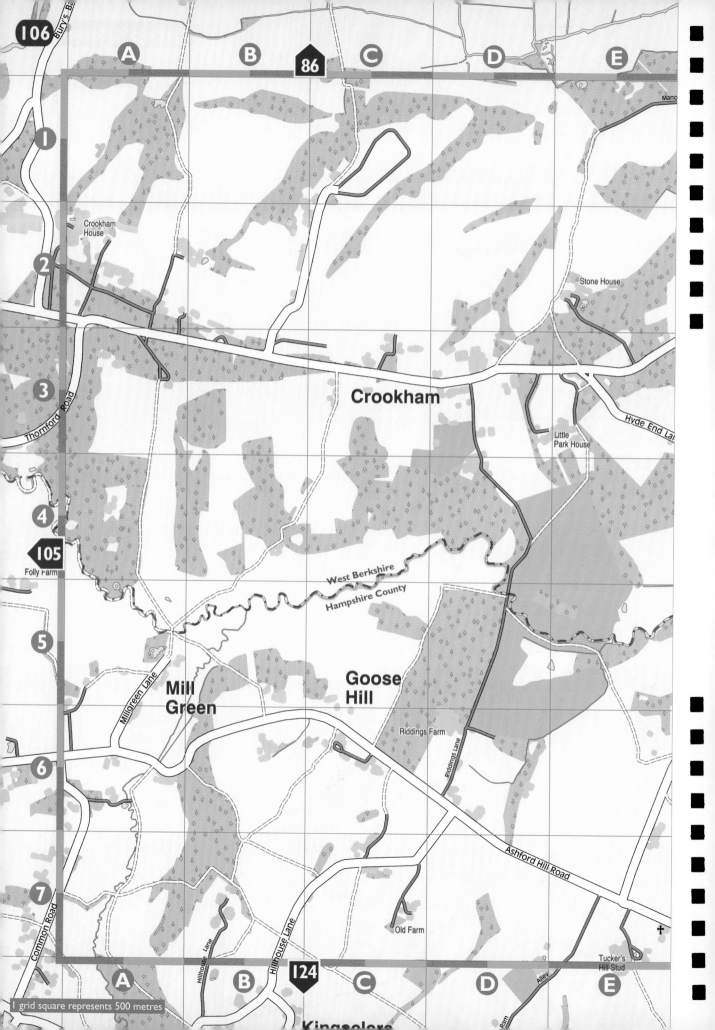

A　　　B　　　86　　　C　　　D　　　E

1

2

Crookham
House

3

Thornford Road

Crookham

Stone House

Hyde End Lane

Little
Park House

4

Folly Farm

West Berkshire
Hampshire County

5

Millgreen Lane

Mill
Green

Goose
Hill

Riddings Farm

Riddings Lane

6

Common Road

7

Hillhouse Lane

Hillhouse Lane

Old Farm

Ashford Hill Road

Tucker's
Hill Stud

A　　　B　　　124　　　C　　　D　　　E

1 grid square represents 500 metres

Kingsclere

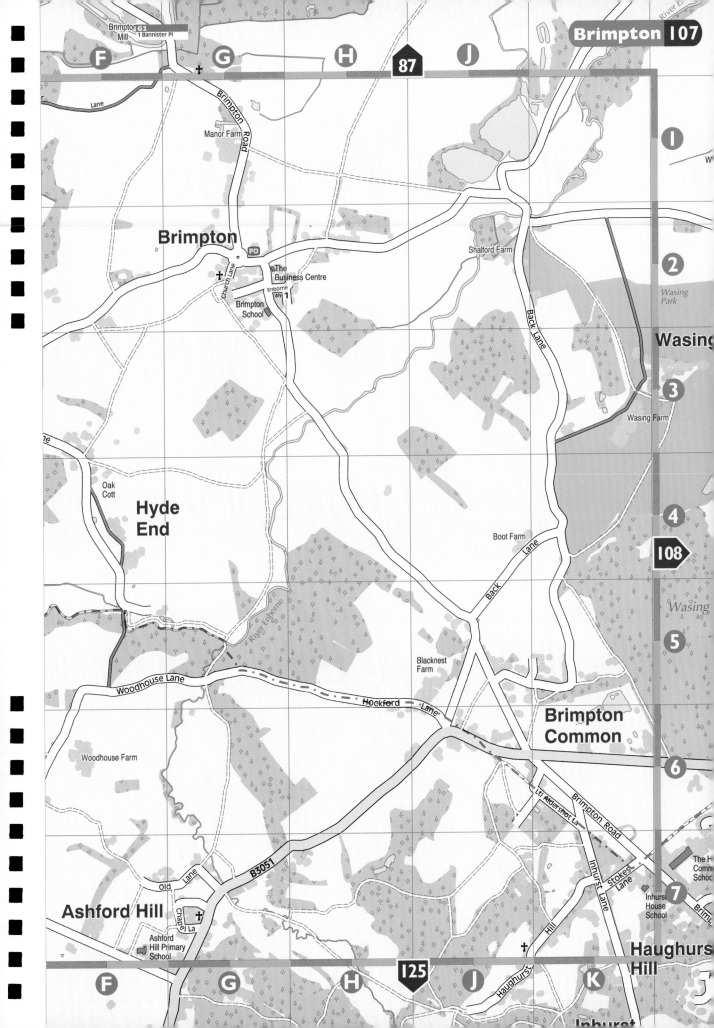

A   B   88   C   D   E

Fisherman's Lane

1

River End

Wasing Lower Farm

Wasing Lane

Aldermaston C of E School

PH

PO

Aldermaston

THE ST

Congreve Close

Cedars School

Church Road

Portland House

2

Wasing Park

Wasing

A340

3

Wasing Farm

4

Youngs Industrial Est

HILL

PAICES

5

Wasing Wood

6

B3051

A340

A340

ALDERMASTON RD

Falcon Fields

A340

PAICES

7

Plantation Rd

Long Gv

Forest Close

Falroak Wy

Conifer Cl

Birch Road

Pinks La

Heather Dr

Furze Road

Burnham Road

O Bee Gardens

Hanger Rd

Almswood Road

Priors Rd

Sarum Rd

Franklin Av

Franklin Avenue

Meon Close

Holmwood Health Centre

Silchester Rd

Silchester

Brick Kiln Industrial Est

Stokes Lane

The Hurst Community School

Woodlands

Portway

PO

Pinewood Close

Mornington Close

Happlewhite Close

Heath End

Shyshack La

Adam Cl

Road

Bishops Wood Road

PO

Heath End

Burnham Copse Junior School

Bishops Cl

Glendale Rd

Turnery Rd

Supa Ardery

Police

MULFORDS HL

Blak

Inhurst House School

Brimpton Road

Wellington Crs

Copper Beech Cl

Sheridan Crs

Heath End

Ash La

Inhurst Wy

Harshill Rd

Wigmore Road

Bishop

Newtown

Newchurch Road

Beavers Cl

Searing Wy

Huntsmoor Road

Sandy Cl

Southdown Road

The Copse

Mount

Newtown

Carrington Rd

Pleasant Hill

Honeybottom Rd

Reynolds Cl

Silverdale Rd

Tadley

Pleasant Cl

Ambrose Rd

Millers Road

Haughurst Hill

A   B   126   C   D   E

Whitedown Road

Huntsmoor Lane

Deainswood Rd

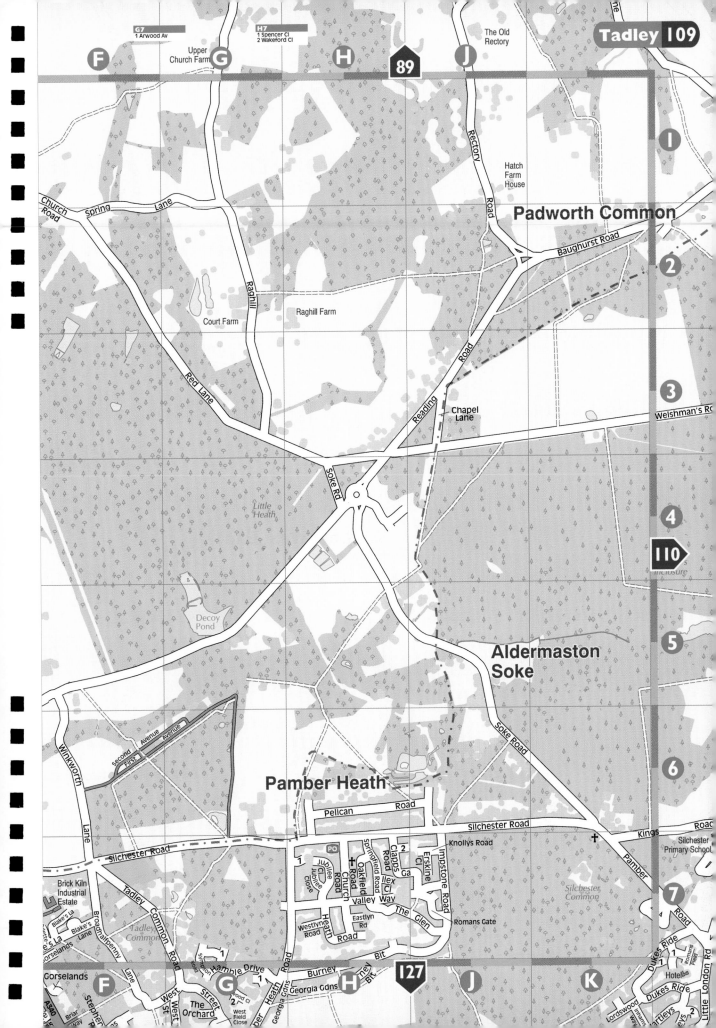

Padworth Common

Aldermaston Soke

Pamber Heath

Gorselands

G7
1 Arwood Av

H7
1 Spencer Cl
2 Wakeford Cl

Upper
Church Farm

The Old
Rectory

Hatch
Farm
House

Church Road

Spring

Lane

Raghill

Red Lane

Court Farm

Raghill Farm

Reading

Road

Rectory

Road

Baughurst Road

Welshman's Rd

Chapel
Lane

Soke Rd

Little
Heath

Decoy
Pond

Enclosure

Soke Road

Silchester Road

Kings Road

Silchester
Primary School

Silchester
Common

Pelican   Road

Knollys Road

Second
Avenue

First

Avenue

Winkworth

Lane

Silchester Road

Tadley

Common

Road

Brick Kiln
Industrial
Estate

Blake's La

Gorselands

Blake's
Lane

Broadhalfpenny

Stephen

PO

Jubilee
Cl
Jubilee
Close

Springfield Road

Oakfield
Road

Church
Road

Clapps
Road

Ga

Ilex
Cl

Erskine
Cl

Impstone Road

Valley Way

The Glen

Eastlyn
Rd

Westlyn
Road

Heath

Road

Bit

Bit

Romans Gate

Pamber

Road

Hamble Drive

Symson
Road

Georgia Gdns

Burney

Bit

Silchester

Pamber

Road

Dukes Ride

Little London Rd

Lordswood

Hartleys

Dukes Ride

Romans
Field

Hotel

West
Street

West St

The
Orchard

West
Field Close

Georgia Gdns

F   G   H   J   K

F   G   H   J

I
2
3
4
5
6
7

89

110

127

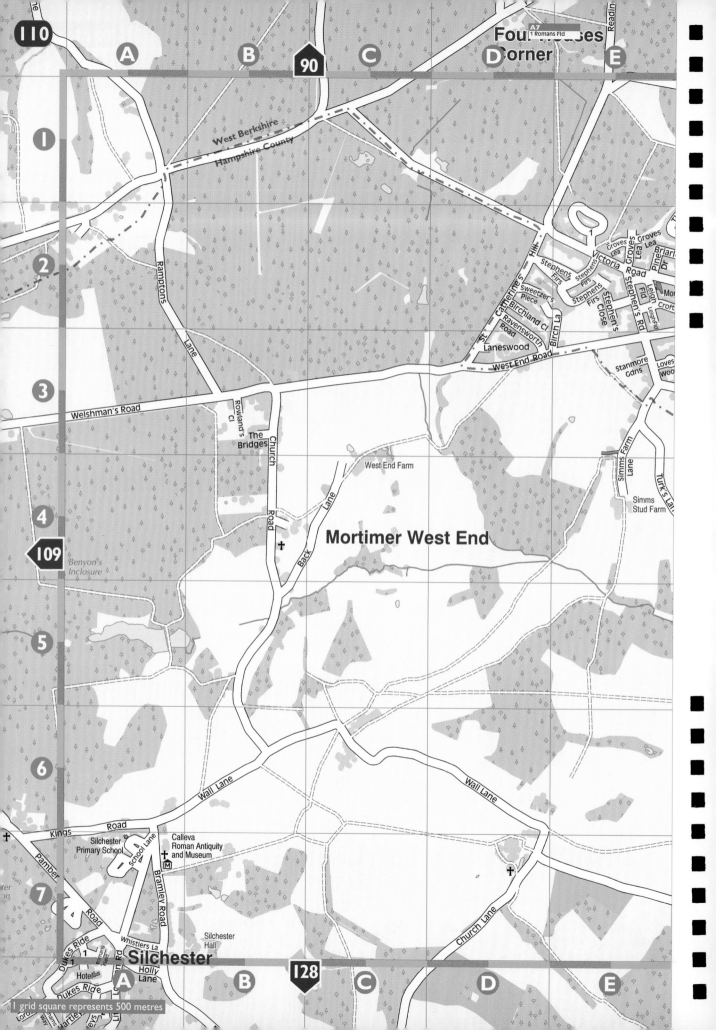

A   B   **90**   C   Fou**r Houses
Corner**   D   E

A7
1 Romans Fld

Readin

I

West Berkshire
Hampshire County

Ramptons Lane

2

Groves Lea
Groves Lea
Stephens Firs
Victoria
Groves Lea
Pine
Briarl
Dr
St Catherine's
Stephens Firs
Road
Stephen's Rd
Sweetzer's Piece
Stephens Firs
Birchland Cl
Stephen's Close
Leigh
Leighfld
Mor
Croft
Ravensworth Road
Birch La
Laneswood
Stanmore Gdns
Loves
Woo
West End Road

3

Welshman's Road

Rowland's Cl
The Bridges

Church Road

West End Farm

Simms Farm Lane
Simms Stud Farm
Turk's La

4

109

Benyon's
Inclosure

Back Lane

Mortimer West End

✝

5

6

Wall Lane

Wall Lane

Kings   Road

Pamber   Road

Silchester Primary School

School Lane

Calleva
Roman Antiquity
and Museum
✝ Ⓜ

✝

Church Lane

✝

7

Dukes Ride

Bramley Road

Whistlers La

Silchester Hall

1
Holly Lane
Hotel
Silchester
Dukes Ride

Lordi
Way
Hartley

Lit
n Rd

A   B   **128**   C   D   E

1 grid square represents 500 metres

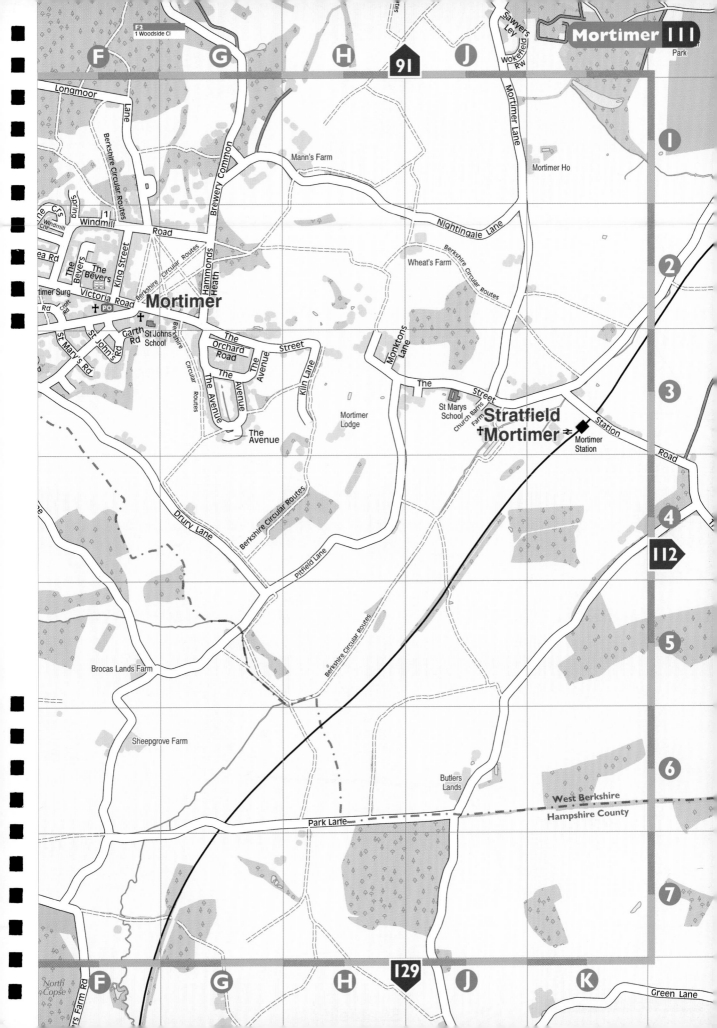

Mortimer Park

F2
1 Woodside Cl

Sawyers Ley

Wokefield Rw

Mortimer Lane

Longmoor Lane

Berkshire Circular Routes

Mann's Farm

Mortimer Ho

Brewery Common

Nightingale Lane

Spring

Windmill Chr

Cfs

1 Windmill

Road

Wheat's Farm

Berkshire Circular Routes

The Bevers

The Bevers

King Street

Berkshire Circular Routes

Hammonds Heath

ea Rd

imer Surg

Victoria Road

Mortimer

Monktons Lane

Rd

St Mary's Rd

St John's Rd

Garth Rd

St Johns School

The Orchard Road

The Avenue

The Avenue

Street

Kiln Lane

The Street

St Marys School

Church Barns Farm

Stratfield Mortimer

Station Road

Mortimer Station

Berkshire Circular Routes

The Avenue

The Avenue

Mortimer Lodge

112

Drury Lane

Berkshire Circular Routes

Pitfield Lane

Berkshire Circular Routes

Brocas Lands Farm

Sheepgrove Farm

Butlers Lands

West Berkshire
Hampshire County

Park Lane

North Copse

s Farm Rd

Green Lane

F   G   H   **129**   J   K

112

Mortimer
Park
Wokefield
Park

Bloomfield
Hatch
Cross Lane

A   **B**   92   **C**   **D**   **E**

Cross Lane

Brook Farm

Crosslane Farm
Cross Lane

I

2

Great
Park Farm

Trunkwell
House

Beech Hill

3

Station
ation

Road

Vale View
Drive

4

The

Forehead
Perrins Farm

Trowe's

Lane

Broad

Way

III

5

Little
Park Farm

Trowe's

Lane

Chequers

6

Park

Lane

Park   Lane

Fair
Cross

Home Farm

7

Wigmore Farm

Forelands

A   **B**   New Stre   130   **C**   **D**   **E**

Green Lane

Stratfield

I grid square represents 500 metres

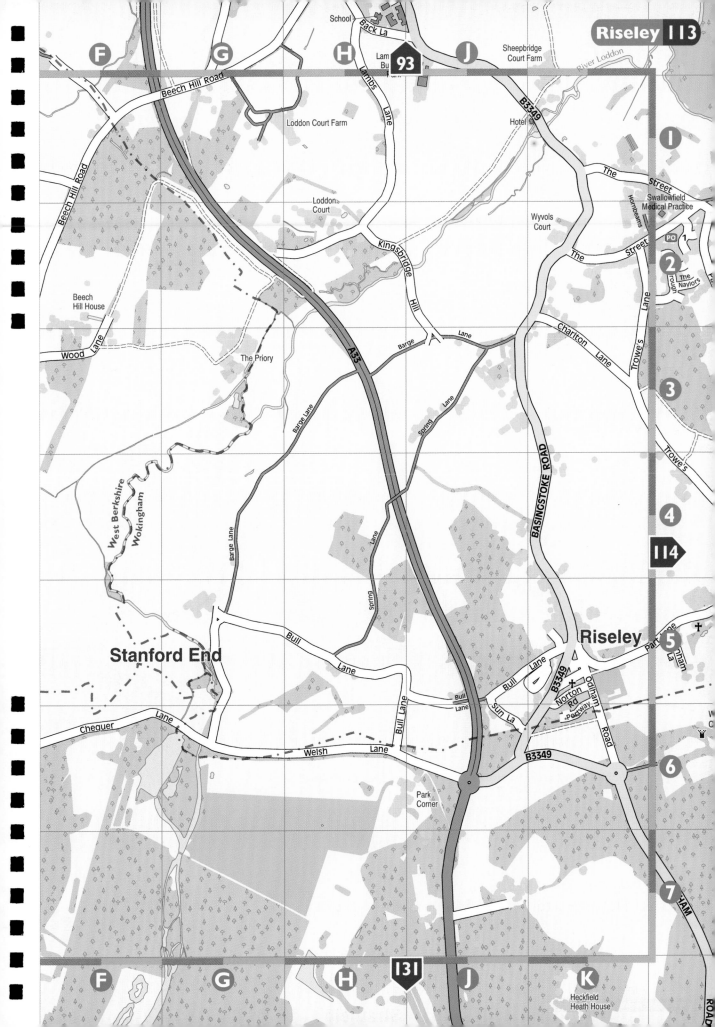

School
Back La
Lam
Bu
93

Sheepbridge
Court Farm

River Loddon

F

Beech Hill Road

G

H

Lambs Lane

J

B3349

Hotel

Loddon Court Farm

Loddon
Court

Wyvols
Court

Kingsbridge

The Street

Swallowfield
Medical Practice

Hornbeams

PO 1

The Naylors

The Street

Trowe's Lane

Barge

Lane

Chariton Lane

I

2

3

Trowe's

Beech Hill House

Wood
Lane

Beech Hill Road

The Priory

Barge Lane

Spring Lane

BASINGSTOKE ROAD

4

114

West Berkshire
Wokingham

A33

Barge Lane

Spring

Lane

Riseley

Park La

Tham
La

5

†

Stanford End

Bull

Lane

Bull Lane

Bull
Lane

Sun La

Bull
Lane

B3349

Norton
Rd

Odiham

Portway

†

Road

Chequer

Lane

Welsh

Lane

B3349

6

Park
Corner

7

HAM

F

G

131

H

J

K

Heckfield
Heath House

ROAD

A B **94** C D E

I

The

Swallowfield
Medical Practice

Swallowfield

Hornbeams

Street

PO 1

Foxborough

The
Naylors

2

Trowe's
Lane

Part Lane

Brookside
Business
Centre

PH

Rowe's Farm

Swallowfield
Road

Swallowfield

Kiln Hill

Road

Bungler's Hill

Lane

3

Trowe's Lane

Part Lane

Cemetery

Nutbean Lane

Sandpit

Lane

Riseley Farm

The Broadwater

4

113

Ford Lane

5

Risel

Part Lane

Benham La

School Lane

School Road

Part Lane

Wokingham
Hampshire County

Cordery's Farm

Well

House

Odiham Av

Road

Wellington
Country Park

6

Riseley
Mill

Ford Lane

7

ODIHAM

Hall's Farm

A B **132** C D E

field
h H l grid square represents 500 metres

Wood

Swallowfield Road

Swall
Park

River Loddon

Ater Farm

River Whitewater

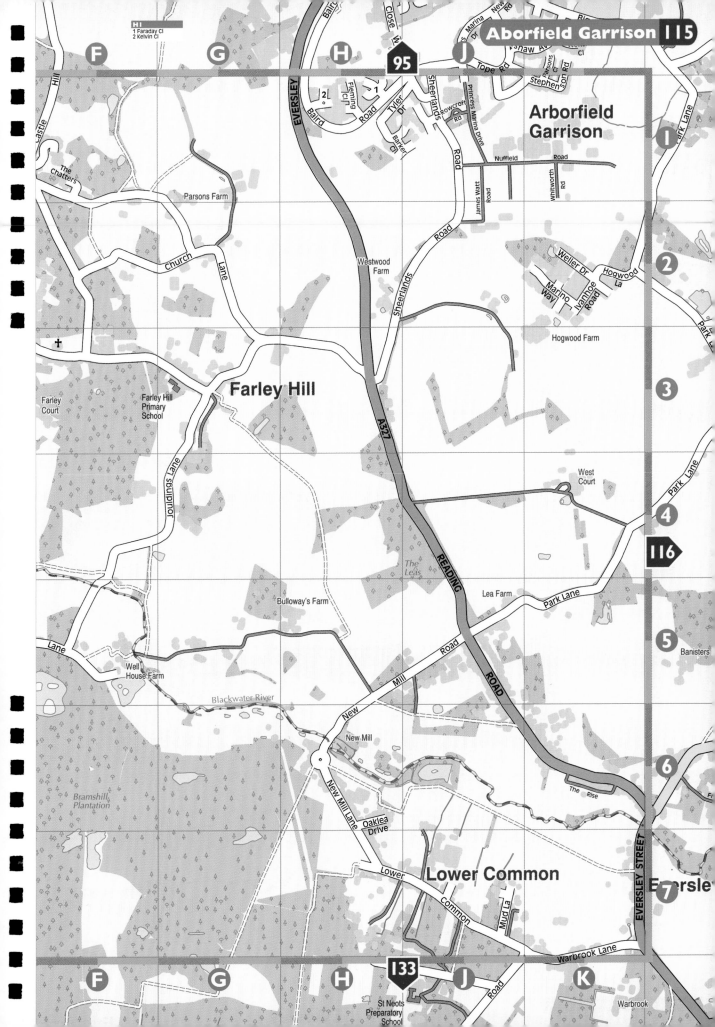

H1
1 Faraday Cl
2 Kelvin Cl

F G H J

95

Aborfield Garrison

Baird

Close W

s Marina Dr

Fleming Cl

Tyler Dr

Barkert Cl

Eversley Road

Baird

Sheerlands

Rowcroft Rd

Princess Marina Drive

Tope Rd

Shaw Av

Parsons

Stephen

New Rd

Ter Cl

1

Nuffield Road

James Watt Road

Whitworth Rd

The Chatters

Castle Hill

Parsons Farm

Church Lane

Westwood Farm

Sheerlands Road

Weller Dr

Marino Way

Ivanhoe Road

Hogwood La

2

Hogwood Farm

Park La

Farley Hill

Farley Court

Farley Hill Primary School

Farley Hill

A327

3

West Court

Park Lane

4

116

Jouldings Lane

The Leas

READING

Lea Farm

Park Lane

Banisters

5

Lane

Well House Farm

Bulloway's Farm

Blackwater River

New Mill Road

ROAD

6

The Rise

Bramshill Plantation

New Mill

New Mill Lane

Oaklea Drive

Eversley Street

Eversle

7

Lower Common

Lower Common

Mud La

Road

Warbrook Lane

Fr

F G H J K

133

St Neots Preparatory School

Warbrook

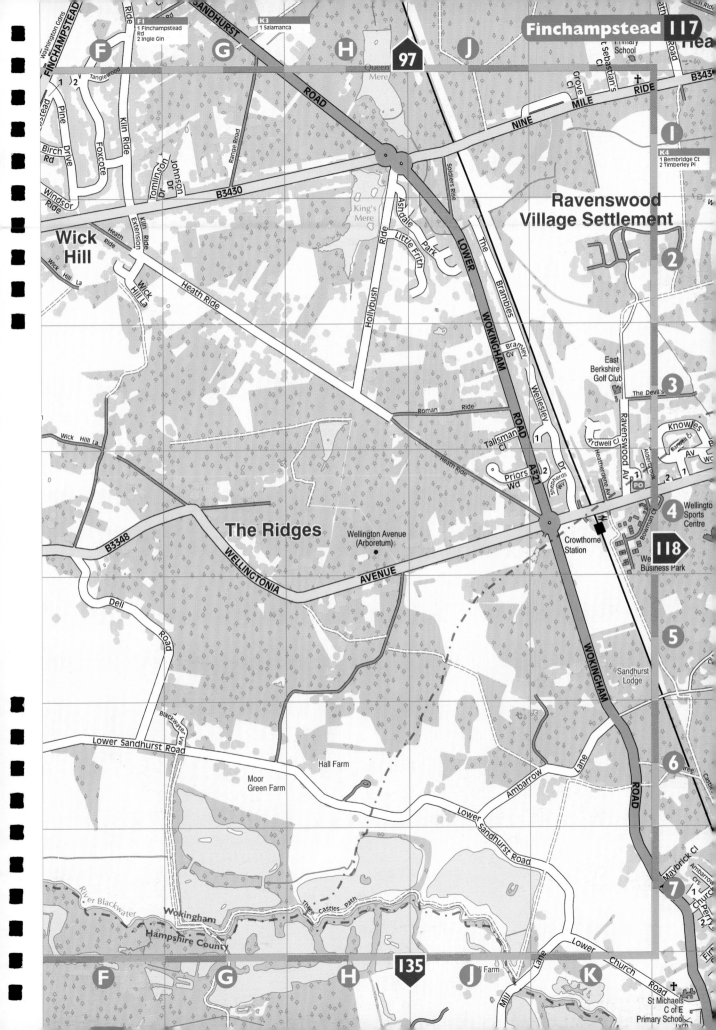

F   G   H   97   J

K3
1 Salamanca

SANDHURST

FINCHAMPSTEAD

1   2

Tanglewood

Pine Ride

Kiln Ride

Birch Rd

Foxcote

Johnson Dr

Tomlinson Dr

Range Road

Windsor Ride

B3430

Kiln Ride Extension

Heath Ride

Wick Hill La

Wick Hill

Wick Hill La

Wick Hill La

Heath Ride

Wick Hill La

ROAD

Queen Mere

King's Mere

Ashdale Park

Hollybush Ride

Little Frith

Soldiers Rise

NINE MILE RIDE

B343

St Sebastian's
Primary School

Grove Cl

I

K4
1 Bembridge Ct
2 Timberley Pl

**Ravenswood
Village Settlement**

2

East Berkshire
Golf Club

The Devil's

3

LOWER

The Brambles

Bramley Gv

Wellesley

Roman Ride

Heath Ride

Talisman Cl

Priors Wd

WOKINGHAM ROAD A321

1

2

Shepherds Dr

WV1

1

Knowles Av

Barwell Cl

Ardwell Cl

Ravenswood Av

Heatherdene Av

Aldernow Cl

1

PO

2

1

4   Wellingto
Sports
Centre

Crowthorne
Station

Bowman Ct

118   We
Business Park

The Ridges

B3348

WELLINGTONIA

Wellington Avenue
(Arboretum)

AVENUE

Dell Road

5

Sandhurst Lodge

WOKINGHAM

ROAD

Blackwater Vw

Lower Sandhurst Road

Hall Farm

Moor
Green Farm

Ambarrow Lane

Lower Sandhurst Road

6

Maybrick Cl

Ambarrow Crs

1

7

River Blackwater

Wokingham

Hampshire County

Three Castles Path

Mill Farm

Mill Lane

Lower Church Road

St Michaels
C of E
Primary School

F   G   H   135   J   K

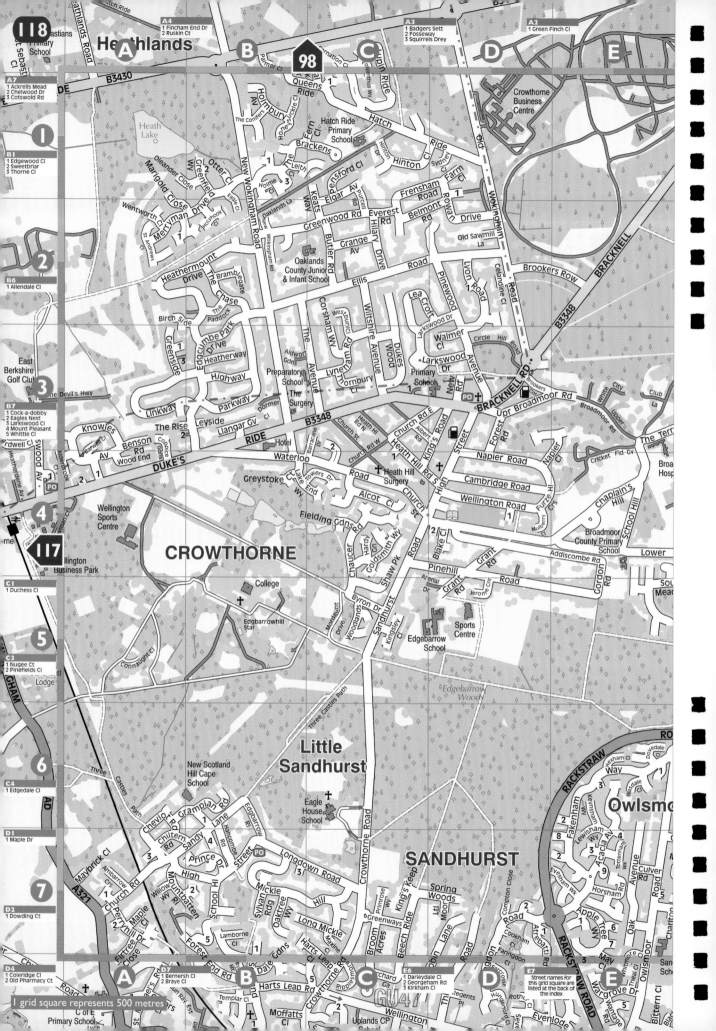

F6
1 Barkis Mead
2 Frodsham Wy
3 Peggotty Pl
4 Steerforth Copse
5 Trotwood Cl

F7
1 Crown Pl
2 Grantham Cl
3 Rugby Cl

F G H 99 J

1

2

3

4

5

6

7

ROAD

A3095 FORESTERS WAY

Crowthorne Wood

RG45

Kentigern

Drive

...ace

...dmoor
...ital

Broadmoor Road

Eastern Lane

Three Castles Path

Three Castles Path

Broadmoor Farm

FORESTERS WAY

A3095

...uth
...dow

South Road

A3095

Copperfield Av

1 3 4
5

Magdalene Road

...moor

Rookwood Av

Durham Rd

Oxford Rd

Keble Wy

Merton Cl

Yale Cl

Peterhouse Ct

Union Cl

Church Road

Cambridge Road

Millins Cl

3

Victoria Rd

1

2

PO

Yeovil

The Surgery

Brook

Owlsmoor Primary School

Birkbeck Pl

Trinity

Nuffield Dr

Balliol Wy

Girton

Hanard Rd

Wadham

Woodlands Ct

College Town

...dhurst
...ool

Hallmark Cl

...kbird

...kcap Pl

Cannon Close

Range VW

Windsor Ride

Epsom Cl

Matthews Rd

King's Crs

Queen Elizabeth Road

King's Ride

Everest Rd

Goodwood Road

F G H J K

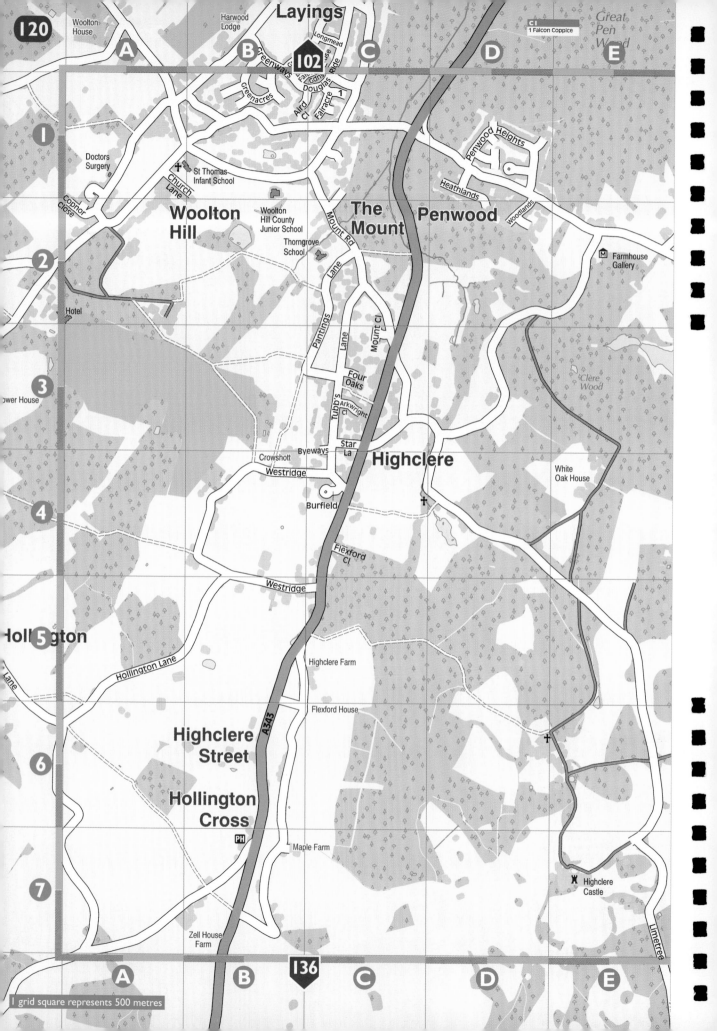

Layings

A   B   C   D   E

102

C1
1 Falcon Coppice

Great
Pen
Wood

1

Woolton
House

Harwood
Lodge

Longmead

Greenways

Greenacres

Aird Cl

Douglas

Fairacre

Fairacre Gdns

Falcon Ride

1

Penwood Heights

Doctors
Surgery

Copnor
Close

St Thomas
Infant School

Church
Lane

Heathlands

Woodlands

2

Woolton
Hill

Woolton
Hill County
Junior School

Thorngrove
School

Mount Rd

Lane

The
Mount

Penwood

Farmhouse
Gallery

M

2

Hotel

Pantings

Lane

Mount Cl

'Clère
Wood

ower House

3

3

Four
Oaks

Tubbs

Arkwright
Cl

White
Oak House

Byeways

Crowshott

Westridge

Star
La

Highclere

†

4

Burfield

4

Flexford
Cl

Westridge

Holl gton

5

Hollington Lane

Highclere Farm

5

Lane

Flexford House

A343

†

Highclere
Street

6

6

Hollington
Cross

PH

Maple Farm

7

7

Highclere
Castle

Zell House
Farm

Limetree

A   B   C   D   E

136

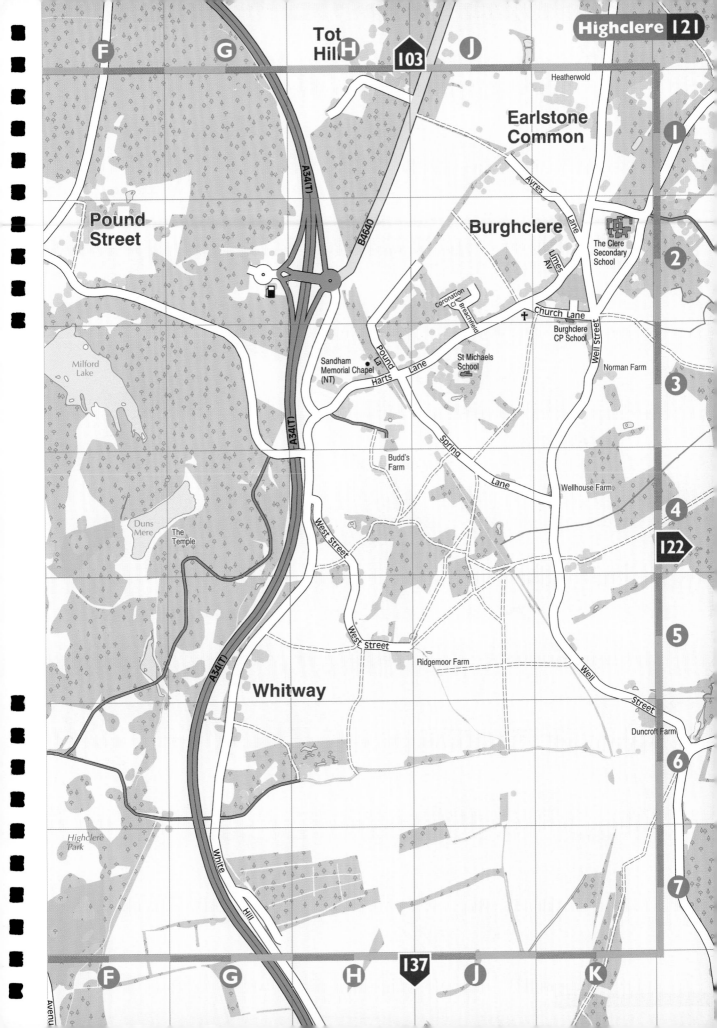

122

I

A   B   **104**   C   D   E

The Clere
Secondary
School

2

Palmer's Hill
House

Frith
Copse

Adbury
Park

North
Sydmonton Hous

Whitehouse Farm

Well Street

Norman Farm

3

4

121

Earlstone Manor

Woodside
Farm

5

Cowhouse Farm

Oakfields
Close

White Hill

Street

Duncroft Farm

6

Watership
Farm

7

A   B   **138**   C   D   E

Nuth   Farm

I grid square represents 500 metres

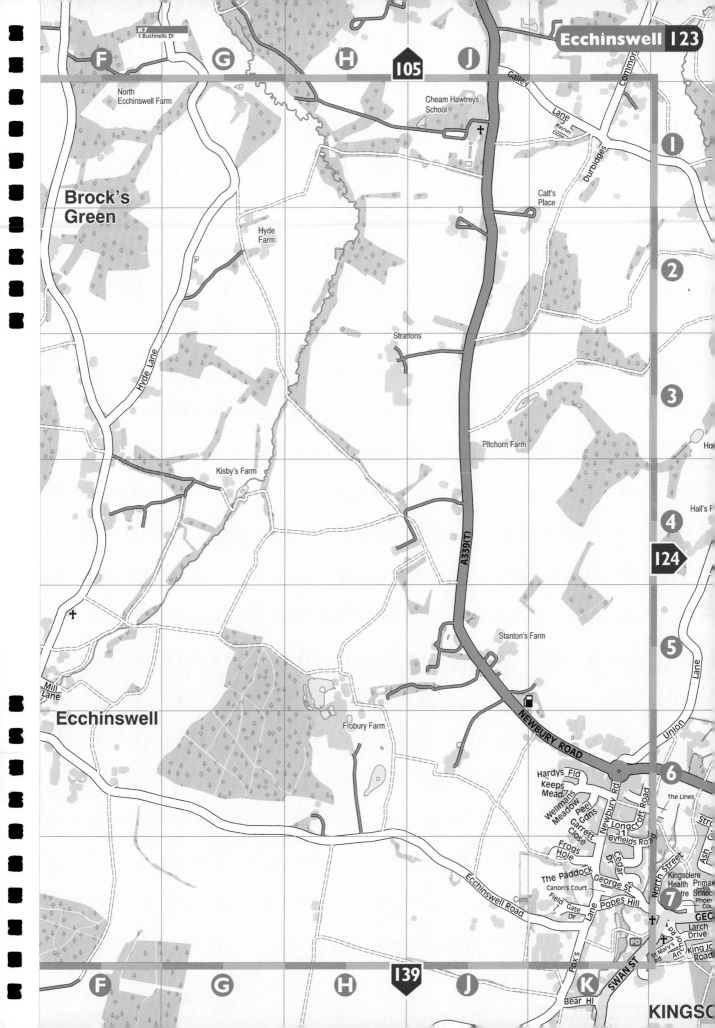

K7
1 Bushnells Dr

F G H 105 J

I

2

3

4

124

5

6

7

North Echinswell Farm

Brock's Green

Hyde Farm

Cheam Hawtreys School

Galley Lane

Paynes Close

Catt's Place

Durbidges

Commor

Hyde Lane

Strattons

Pitchorn Farm

Hall's F

Ho

Kisby's Farm

A339(T)

Stanton's Farm

Mill Lane

Ecchinswell

Frobury Farm

NEWBURY ROAD

Union Lane

Hardys Fld
Keeps Mead
Wellmans Meadow
Peel Gdns
Garrett Close
Frogs Hole

The Paddock

Canon's Court

The Lines

Longc
Byfields Rd
Cedar Dr

George St
Popes Hill

Field Gate Dr

Kingsclere Health Centre

North Street

Ash

Stro

Primar Schoo

Phoer Cou

GEO

Larch Drive

King Jo Road

Cem

Ecchinswell Road

Fox's

St Mary's Ar
PO

Bear Hl

SWAN ST

K

KINGSC

F G H 139 J

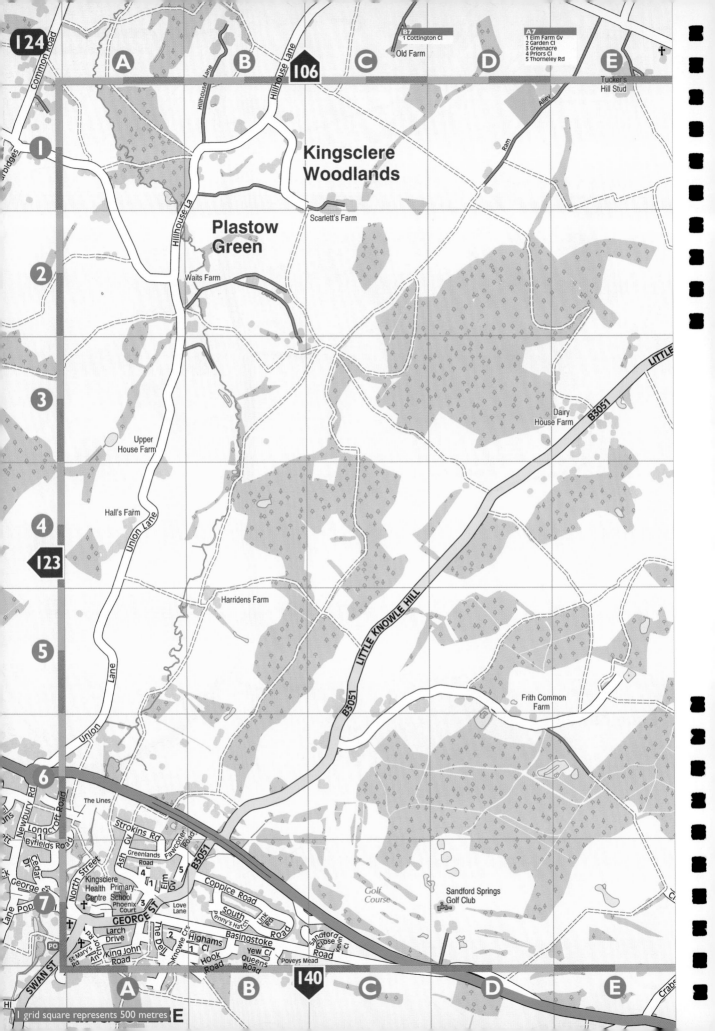

124

A **B** Hillhouse Lane **106** **C** Old Farm **D** **E**

Tucker's
Hill Stud

1

Kingsclere
Woodlands

Ram Alley

Hillhouse La

Scarlett's Farm

**Plastow
Green**

2 Waits Farm

LITTLE

Dairy
House Farm B3051

3

Upper
House Farm

4

123 Hall's Farm

Union Lane

Harridens Farm

LITTLE KNOWLE HILL

5

B3051

Frith Common
Farm

Union Lane

6

The Lines

Newbury Rd
Longcroft Road

Byfields Road

Strokins Rd

Greenlands Road

Ash Gv

Fawconer Road

B3051

Coppice Road

North Street

Kingsclere
Health
Centre

Kingsclere
Primary
School

Phoenix Court

Elm Gv

Love
Lane

4
1

3

5

Golf
Course

Sandford Springs
Golf Club

7

George

PO

St Mary's Rd

GEORGE ST

Larch Drive

The Dell

Knowle Crs

King John Road

Hook Road

Highams Cl

South

Penny's Hatch

Basingstoke

Yew Cl
Queens Road

Link Rd

Sandford Close

Poveys Mead

Kevin Cl

Road

Crabs

SWAN ST

HI

A **B** **140** **C** **D** **E**

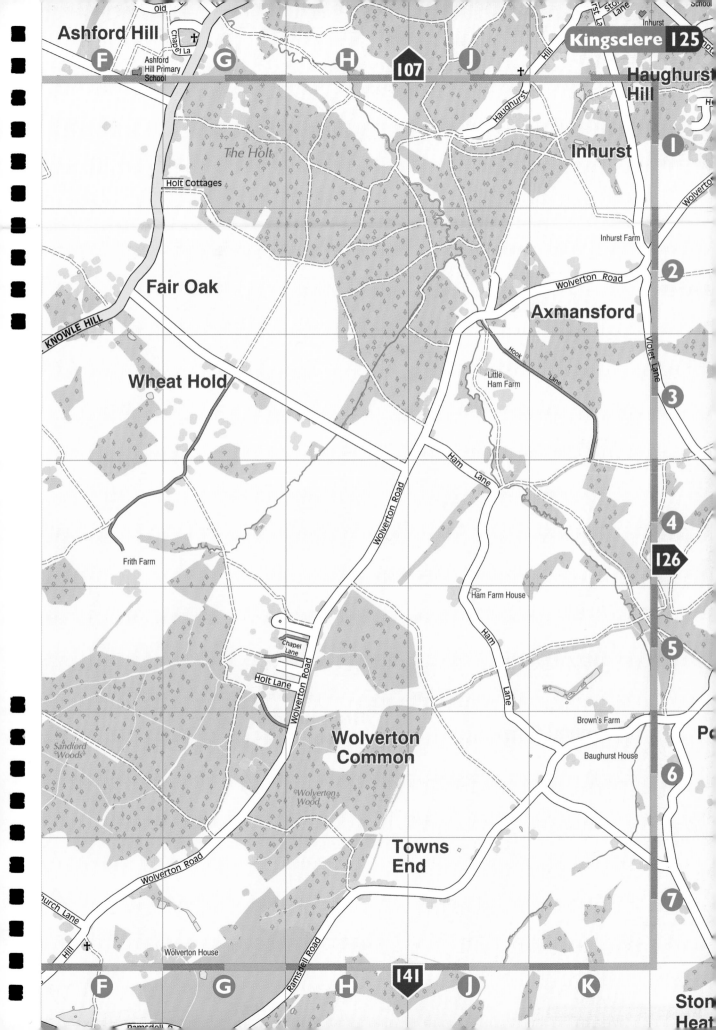

Ashford Hill

F   G   H   **107**   J

Old

Chapel La

Ashford Hill Primary School

The Holt

Holt Cottages

Haughurst Hill

Inhurst

J

I

Inhurst Farm

2

Fair Oak

Wolverton Road

Axmansford

KNOWLE HILL

Wheat Hold

Little Ham Farm

Hook Lane

3

Violet Lane

Frith Farm

Ham Lane

Wolverton Road

4

126

Ham Farm House

Chapel Lane

Holt Lane

Wolverton Road

Ham Lane

5

Sandford Woods

Brown's Farm

Wolverton Common

Baughurst House

Po

Wolverton Wood

6

Towns End

7

Wolverton Road

Church Lane

Hill

Wolverton House

Ramsdell Road

F   G   **141**   H   J   K

Ston Heat

Ramsdell R

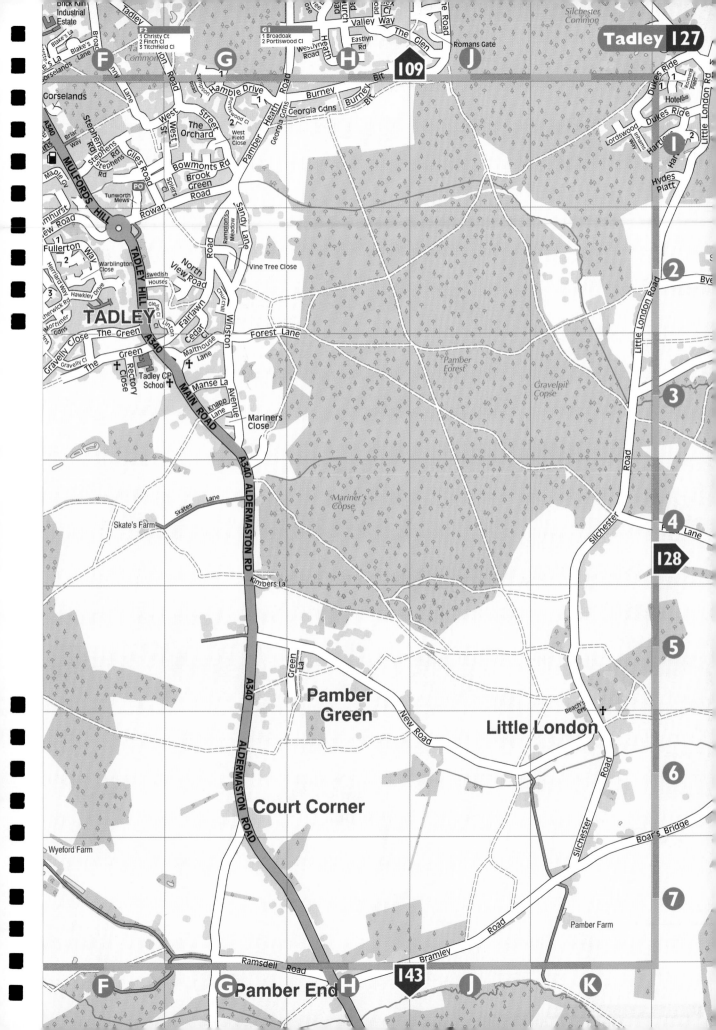

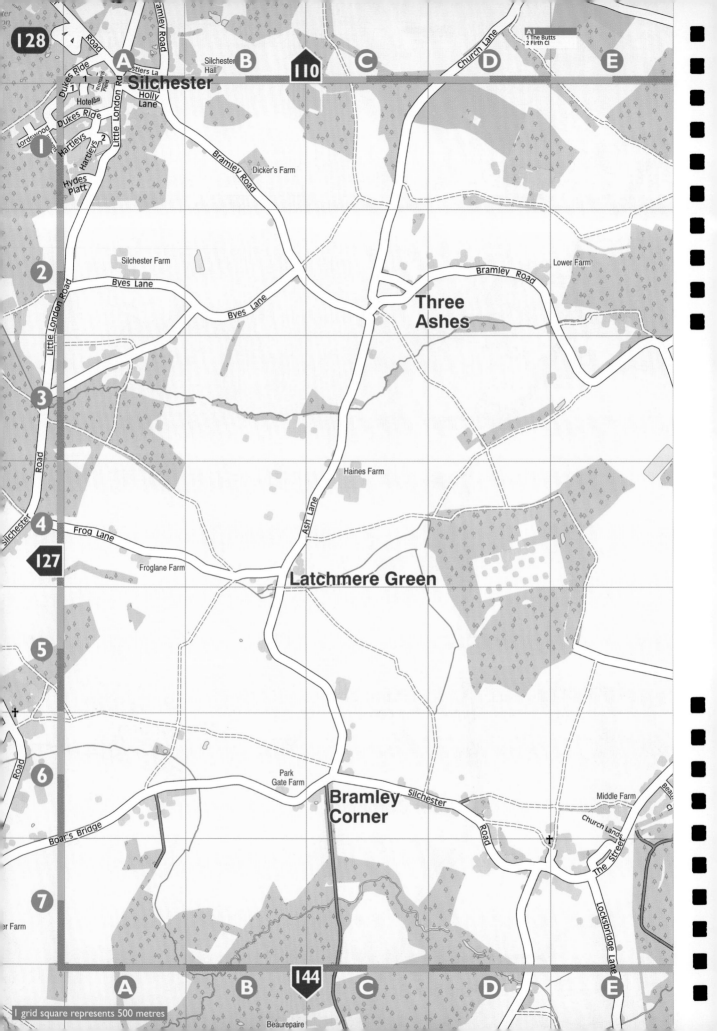

128

A Silchester
Dukes Ride
Romans Field
1
Hotel
Dukes Ride
Lordswood
Hartleys
Hydes Platt
Holly Lane

Astlers La
Silchester Hall

B

110

C

Church Lane

D

A1
1 The Butts
2 Firth Cl

E

Bramley Road
Little London Rd
Dicker's Farm

Lower Farm
Bramley Road

1

2 Silchester Farm
Little London Road
Byes Lane
Byes Lane

Three Ashes

3 Silchester Road

Haines Farm

Ash Lane

4 Frog Lane
127
Froglane Farm

Latchmere Green

5 †

Road

6 Park Gate Farm
Bramley Corner
Silchester Road
Middle Farm
Church Lands
†
The Street

7 Boar's Bridge
er Farm

Locksbridge Lane

A

B

144

C

D

E

Beaurepaire

1 grid square represents 500 metres

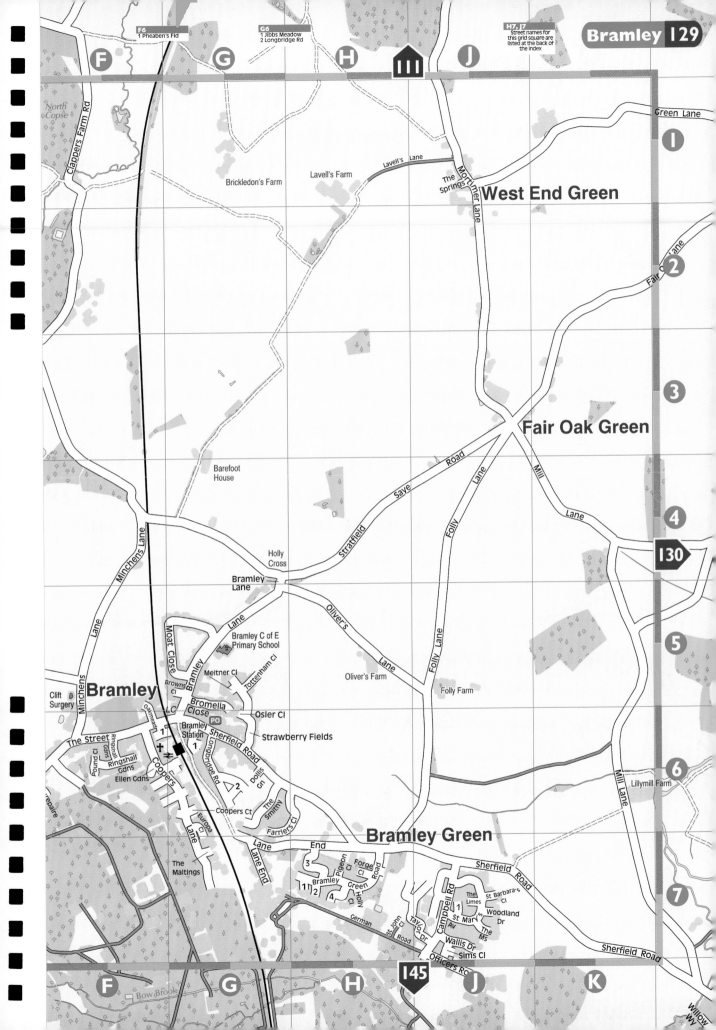

F6
1 Pheaben's Fld

G6
1 Jibbs Meadow
2 Longbridge Rd

H7, J7
Street names for this grid square are listed at the back of the index

F **G** **H** **J**

I

Green Lane

2

Fair Oak Lane

North Copse

Clappers Farm Rd

F6
1 Pheaben's Fld

Brickledon's Farm

Lavell's Farm

Lavell's Lane

Mortimer Lane

The springs

West End Green

3

Fair Oak Green

Barefoot House

Save

Stratfield

Road

Lane

Folly

Mill

Lane

4

130

Minchens Lane

Holly Cross

Bramley Lane

Lane

Oliver's

Lane

Oliver's Farm

Folly Lane

Folly Farm

5

Bramley C of E Primary School

Meitner Cl

Tottenham Cl

Lane

Browns Cl

Moat Close

Bramley

Clift Surgery

Bramley

Minchens Lane

Oakmead

Bromelia Close

PO

Osler Cl

Strawberry Fields

Sherfield Road

The Street

Ringshall Gdns

Pound Cl

Ringshall Gdns

Ellen Gdns

Coopers

Bramley Station

1

Longbridge Rd

Dollis Gn

2

Lillymill Farm

6

Mill Lane

Repaire

Europa Cl

Lane

Coopers Ct

The Smithy

Farriers Cl

Lane End

Bramley Green

Sherfield Road

The Maltings

End

3

Pigeon Cl

Forge Cl

Green Rd

Holly

Bramley

1

2

4

German

St John Road

Taylor Dr

Campbell Rd

St Mary's

1 The Limes Cl

The Ms

St Barbara's Cl

Woodland Dr

Wallis Dr

Sims Cl

Officers Rd

Sherfield Road

F **G** **H** **145** **J** **K**

Bow Brook

Willow Wy

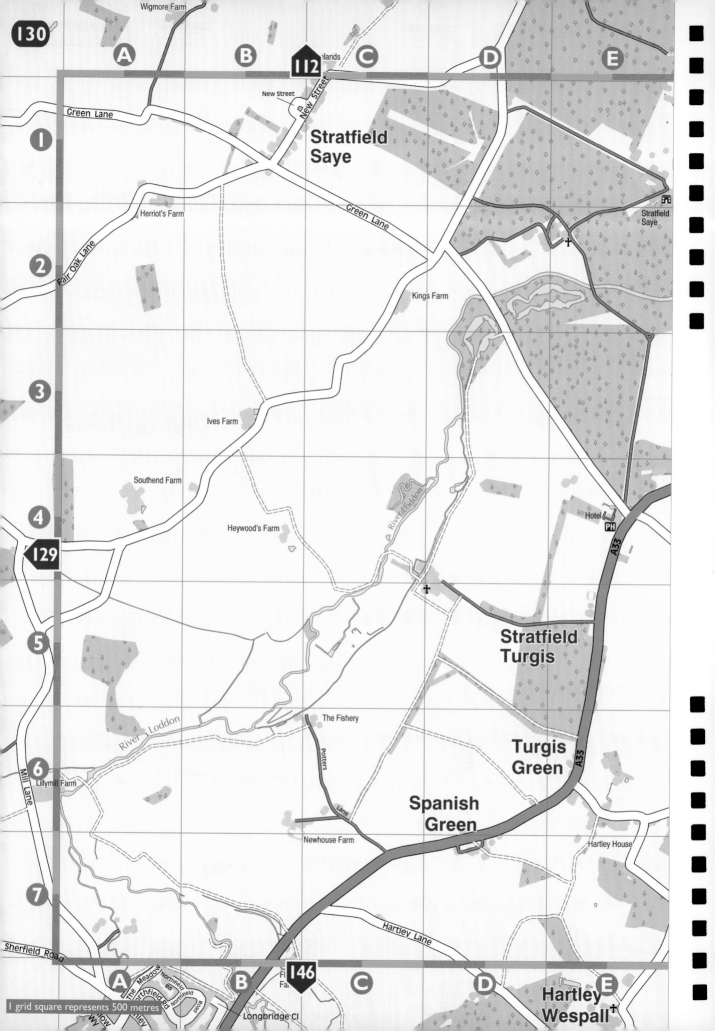

130

112

129

146

A B C D E

1 **2** **3** **4** **5** **6** **7**

Wigmore Farm

Green Lane

New Street

New Street

**Stratfield
Saye**

Green Lane

Herriot's Farm

Fair Oak Lane

Kings Farm

Stratfield
Saye

†

Ives Farm

Southend Farm

River Loddon

Heywood's Farm

Hotel
PH

A33

†

**Stratfield
Turgis**

River Loddon

The Fishery

**Turgis
Green**

A33

Mill Lane

Lillymill Farm

Potters
Lane

**Spanish
Green**

Newhouse Farm

Hartley House

Sherfield Road

Hartley Lane

The Meadow
Northfield Rd
Northfield
Road

Longbridge Cl

Fi
Fa

**Hartley
Wespall** †

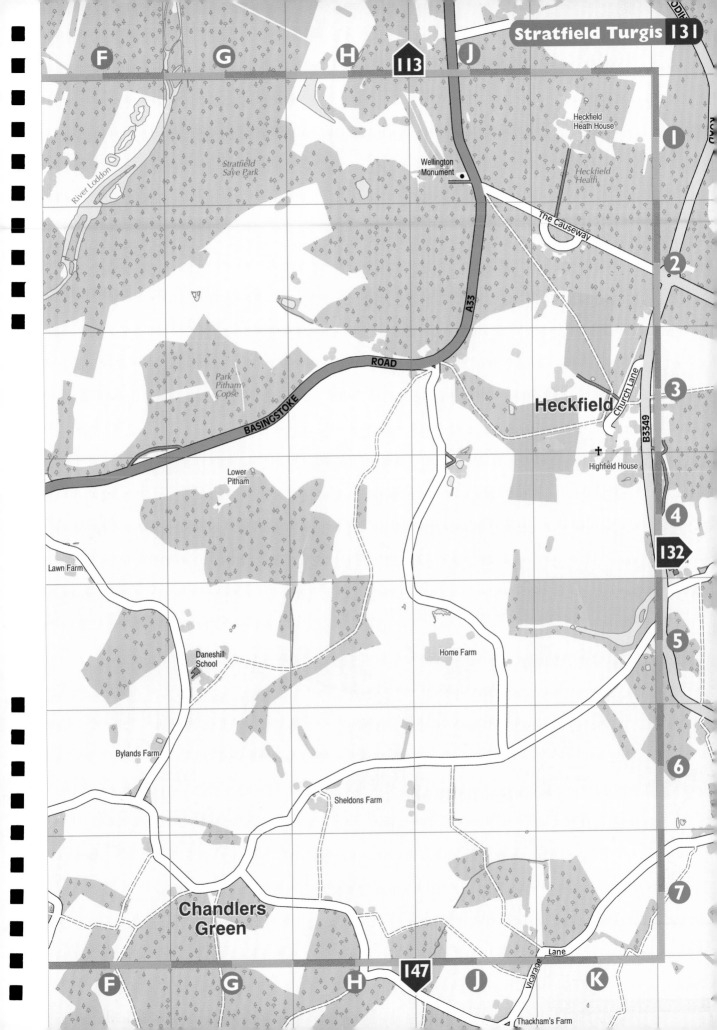

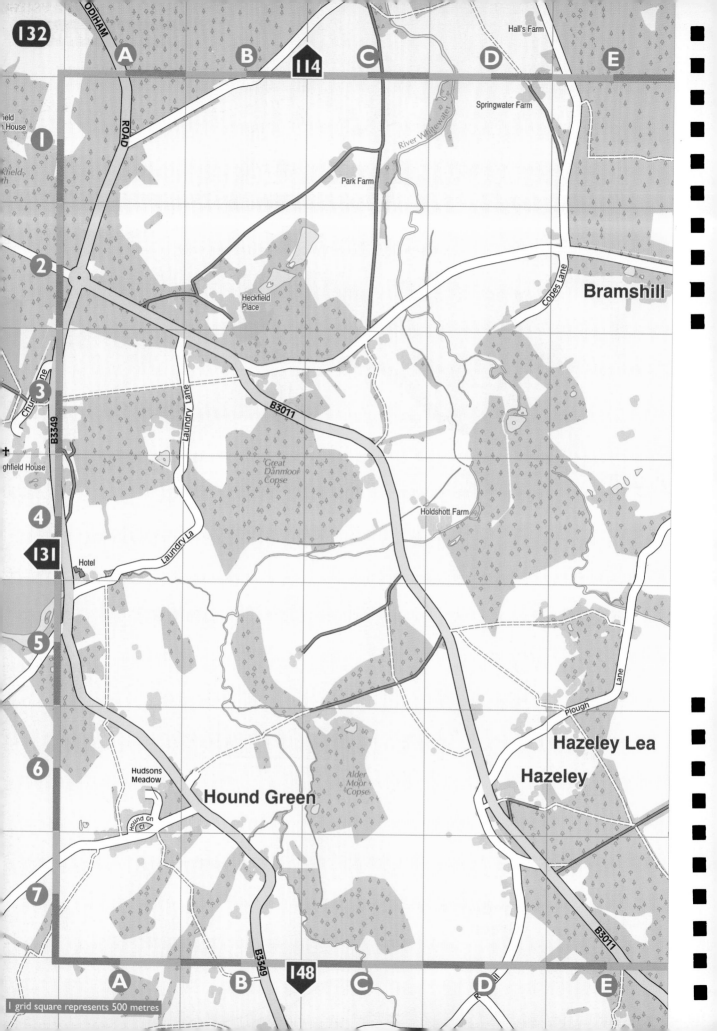

132

A   B   **114**   C   D   E

1

2

3

4

131

5

6

7

A   B   **148**   C   D   E

Hall's Farm

Springwater Farm

River Whitewater

Park Farm

Heckfield Place

Copes Lane

Bramshill

ODIHAM ROAD

Church Lane

B3349

B3011

Laundry Lane

Laundry La

Hotel

Great Danmoor Copse

Holdshott Farm

Plough Lane

Hazeley Lea

Hazeley

Hudsons Meadow

Hound Green

Hound Gn Cl

Alder Moor Copse

B3349

B3011

field n House

khfield th

ghfield House

1 grid square represents 500 metres

F
G
H
115
J

Warbrook Lane

St Neots Preparatory School

St Neot's Road

Warbrook

1

2

Common

Mud La

Heath Warren

3

Plough Lane

Three Castles Path

4

134

Lakeside Dr

Lower Pool Road

Mansion Drive

Bramshill Park

Warren Heath

5

Three Castles Path

6

River Hart

7

Hazeley Heath

Hulford's Copse

F
G
H
149
J
K

Purdies Farm

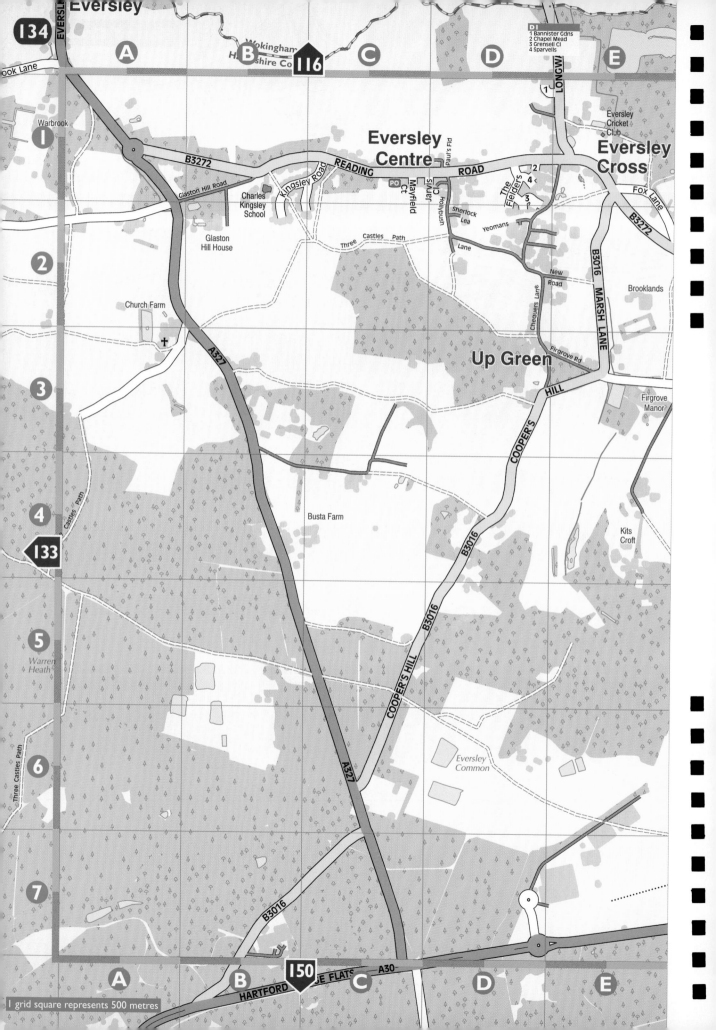

134

A   B   116   C   D   E

Eversley

Wokingham
shire Co

D1
1 Bannister Gdns
2 Chapel Mead
3 Grensell Cl
4 Sparvells

1

Warbrook

Eversley
Cricket
Club

B3272

**Eversley
Centre**

Paul's Fld

READING   ROAD

**Eversley
Cross**

Glaston Hill Road

Kingsley Road

PO

Mayfield
Ct

Jarvis Cl

Holtybush

sherlock
Lea

The Fielders
2
4
3

Fox Lane

Charles
Kingsley
School

Yeomans

B3272

2

Three Castles Path

Lane

New
Road

Chequers Lane

B3016   MARSH LANE

Brooklands

Glaston
Hill House

Church Farm

✝

A327

Up Green

Firgrove Rd

3

COOPER'S   HILL

Firgrove
Manor

4

Busta Farm

B3016

Kits
Croft

133

5

Warren
Heath

COOPER'S HILL

B3016

*Eversley
Common*

6

Three Castles Path

A327

7

B3016

A   B   150   C   A30   D   E

HARTFORD   FLATS

A B **120** C D E

Zell House Farm

Limetree

Highclere Castle

1

Wayfarer's Walk

2

Cross Lane

Three Legs House

Wayfarer's Walk

A343

HILL

3

Grotto Copse

Highclere St

RED

4

Mopper's Barn

rux Easton

Upper Woodcott Down

5 †

Wayfarer's Walk

6

Beech Hanger Copse

Hook Copse

7

152 Woodcott

A B † C D E

1 grid square represents 500 metres

Wood

Lower Woodcott Farm

F G H **121** J

I

2

3

4

138

5

6

7

Old Burghclere

Hill

Ivory Farm

262
▲
Beacon
Hill

Lower
Woodcott
Down

Great
Litchfield
Down

Wayfarer's Walk

Avenue

ud

F G H **153** J K

138

122

A   B   C   D   E

Nuthanger Farm

Wergs Farm

Fossicks

1

Sydmonton Court

† **Sydmonton**

2

3

Watership Down

234
▲
Ladle
Hill

137

Wayfarer's Walk

4

5

*Great
Litchfield
Down*

6

Ashley Warren Farm

7

A   B   154   C are Warren arm   D   E

F G H **123** J

EO

St Mary's Phoer
Rd Art Cou
King Jo
Road

KINGSC

Bear HI

Hollowshot Lane

1

2

Park House Stables

Field Barn Farm

B3051

3

WINCHESTER ROAD

SWAN ST

FOX'S

Ropes Hill

Field

Cem

iswell Road

Centre Schoo
ch

4

140

ington's

23

5

Freem

WHITE HILL

Cannon Heath Down

Wayfarer's Walk

Wayfarer's Walk

6

Cannon Heath Farm

Walkeridge Fa

7

Meadham Lane

F G H **155** J K

B3

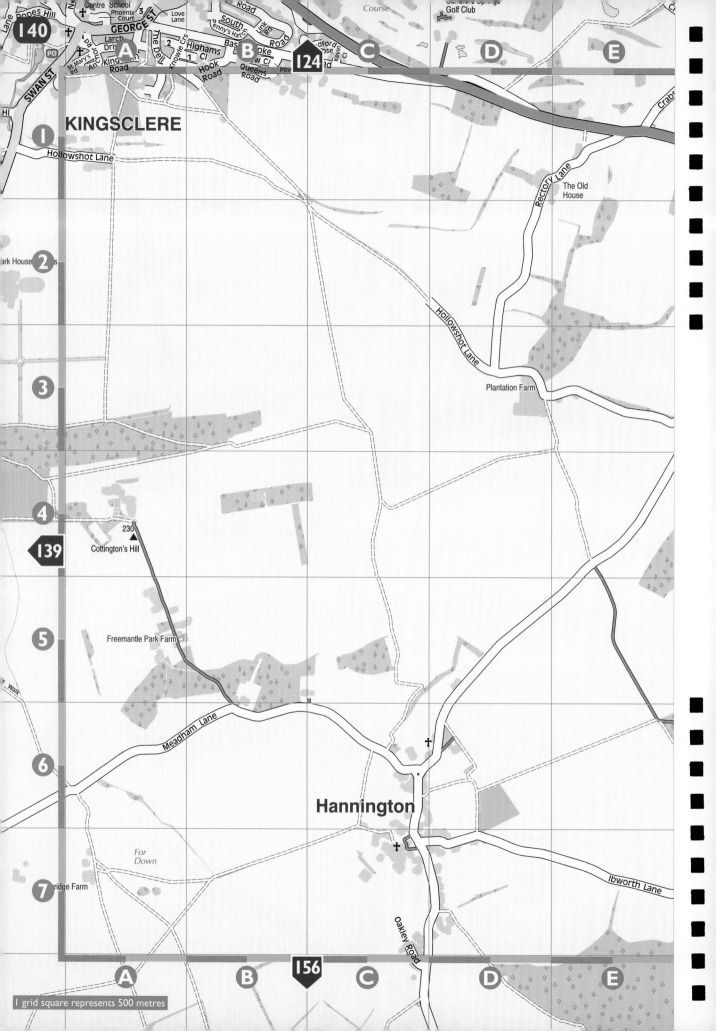

Stony
Heath

Povey's Farm

The Firs

Baughurst Road

Old Vyne Lane

Ho__sh Lane

West
Heath

White Hart Lane

PH †

Sherborne Road

Charter
Alley

Monk †

Beal's Pightle

Ewhurst Road

Skyer's Farm

Ramsdell

RG26

Ewhurst Park

Sheepwash Lane

Skyer's
Wood

Privett
Copse

Lloyd's Lane

Basingstoke Road

Lower Farm

Woodgarston Farm

Upper
Wootton

Field Barn Farm

Basingstoke Road

A339(T)   KINGSCLERE ROAD

1 grid square represents 500 metres

F G H 127 J

Ramsdell Road

Pamber End

I

The Priory
Primary
School

Priory
Farm

A340

Salters Heath

2

Hill End Farm

Tubb's

La

Rawlins Farm

ALDERMASTON ROAD

Cranes
Copse

3

Salters Heath Road

4

144

Monk Sherborne

The Ct

Kiln Lane

Kiln
Green

5

Salters Heath Rd

West End

Weybrook Ct

Manor Farm

6

Vyne Meadow

Cranesfield

Cranesfield

Cem

Sherborne
St John
Primary School

Vyne Road

Cranes Spring Rd

Cranes Spring Ct

Bourne Fld

Sherborne St John

Spring Ct

The Severals

PO

Dark La

Dancers Meadow

7

Kiln R

Tyfield

Elm Road

159

Manor Road

F G H J K

ALDER

Elm Road

A B **128** C D E

1

Beaurepaire
House

Hill
End Farm

Vyne Road

Baker's
Farm

2

Beaurepaire
Farm

Vyne
Lodge Farm

3

Morgaston Road

143

Morgaston
Wood

Vyne
Park

The Vyne (NT) ✝

4

Vyne Farm

Vyne Road

5

6

Vyne Meadow

Vyne Road

Sherborne
St John
Primary School ✝

Spier's
Copse

Mari's Lane

em

Dancer's Meadow

Dark La

PO

Elm Road

Kiln Road

7

Carpenters
Down Wood

A B **160** C Jersey Cl D E

Guernse Cl

Down

Tasm

1 grid square represents 500 metres

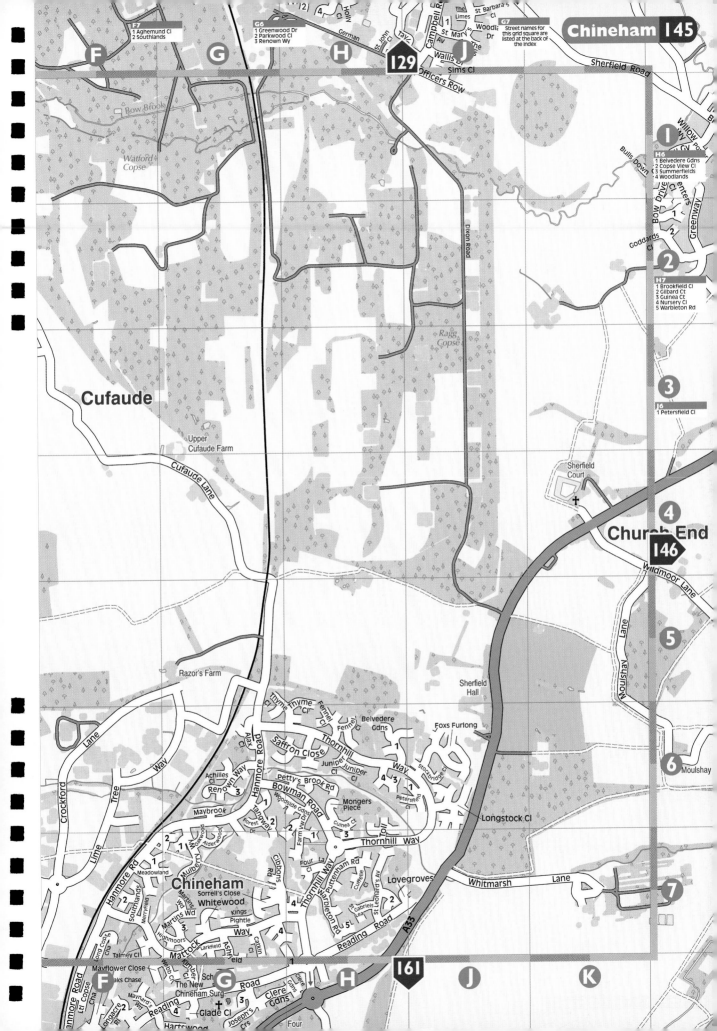

129

Sherfield Road

I

2

3

4

5

6

7

146

Church End

Sherfield Court

Sherfield Hall

Foxs Furlong

Moulshay

Cufaude

Watford Copse

Bow Brook

Ragg Copse

Upper Cufaude Farm

Cufaude Lane

Dixon Road

St John

German

Holly

Campbell Rd

The Limes

St Barbara's

St Mary

Woodla Dr

St Man Av

Wallis Dr

Sims Cl

Officers Row

Bulls Down

Willow

Bow Drive

Goddards Cl

Greenway

Wildmoor Lane

Moulshay Lane

Whitmarsh Lane

Longstock Cl

Lovegroves

Razor's Farm

Crockford Lane

Lime Tree Way

Hanmore Rd

Renown Way

Achilles Cl

Maybrook

Tangway

Forest Dr

Oakwood

Alderwood

Mulberry Cl

Meadowland

Southlands

Merryfield

Martins Wa

Martins Wd

Highmoors

Talmey Cl

Long Copse Cha

Kimber Cl

Webb Cl

Catkin

Larkfield

Ashfield

Kings Pightle Way

Whitewood

Sorrell's Close

Chineham

Thyme Cl

Thyme Cl

Fennel Cl

Fennel

Belvedere Gdns

Thornhill Way

Saffron Close

Alax Cl

Juniper Juniper Cl

Petersfield Cl

Stockbridge

Petty's Brook Rd

Bowman Road

Woodside Gdns

Farm Vw Dr

Mongers Piece

Guinea Ct

Four La

Clibbons Rd

Thornhill Way

Putenham Rd

Toll

Gabriels Lea

St Leonard's Av

Curfelle

Warbleton Rd

Reading Road

A33

Mattock

Mayflower Close

Oaks Chase

Reading Road

Clere Gdns

The New Chineham Surg

Glade Cl

Joseph's Crs

Hartswood

Maynard's

Longacre Wy

Clere Copse

Four

Sch

129

161

146

F

G

H

I

J

K

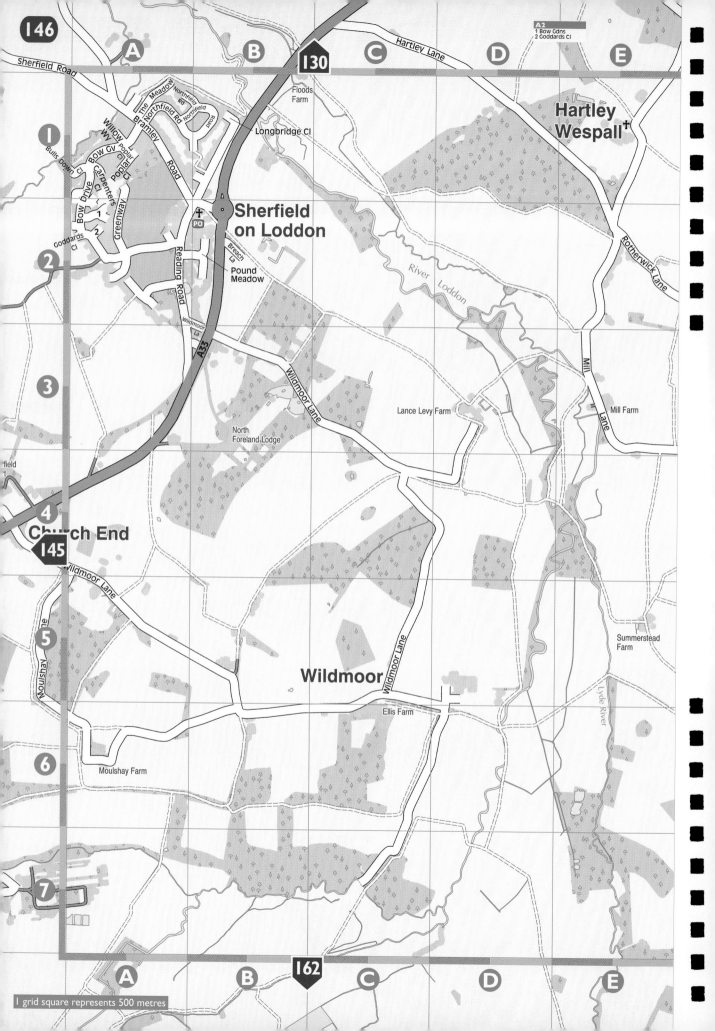

A B 130 C Hartley Lane D E

A2
1 Bow Gdns
2 Goddards Cl

Sherfield Road

Floods
Farm

Hartley
Wespall †

The Meadow
Northfield Rd
Northfield Road

Willow Wy
Bramley

Longbridge Cl

1

Bow Gv
Poplar Cl
Poplar
Bulls Down Cl

Bow Drive
Carpenter's Cl
1
2

Greenway
Reading Road

† PO

Sherfield
on Loddon

Rotherwick Lane

2

Goddards Cl

Breach La

Pound
Meadow

River Loddon

Mill Lane

3

A33

Wildmoor La

Lance Levy Farm

Mill Farm

North
Foreland Lodge

Wildmoor Lane

4

Church End

145

Wildmoor Lane

Wildmoor Lane

5

Moulshay La

Summerstead
Farm

Wildmoor

Lyde River

6

Moulshay Farm

Ellis Farm

7

A B 162 C D E

1 grid square represents 500 metres

Chandlers
Green

F   G   H   131   J

131

Lane

Vicarage

Thackham's Farm

I

Blue
House Farm

Bottle Lane   2

Rotherwick   Lane

3

Black
Wood

Frog Lane

Lyde Green   Wedman's Lane

Mill Lane

Lampards
Cl

Cowfold Lane   4

148

Rotherwick   +   Street End
Copse

Whitewater
C of E (Controlled)
Primary School   Readon
Pond

+   The   Street   Hook   5

Post

Road

The Old
House   6

Horn

Tylney Park
Golf Club   Lane

7

Hotel

Tylney House   B3349

F   G   H   163   J   K

CRIFFIN

John Morgan L

John
Morgan
Cl

Reading Rd

Ashlea
Wood

Coppice   Oak

Sheldons   Oak Tree

Reading Road

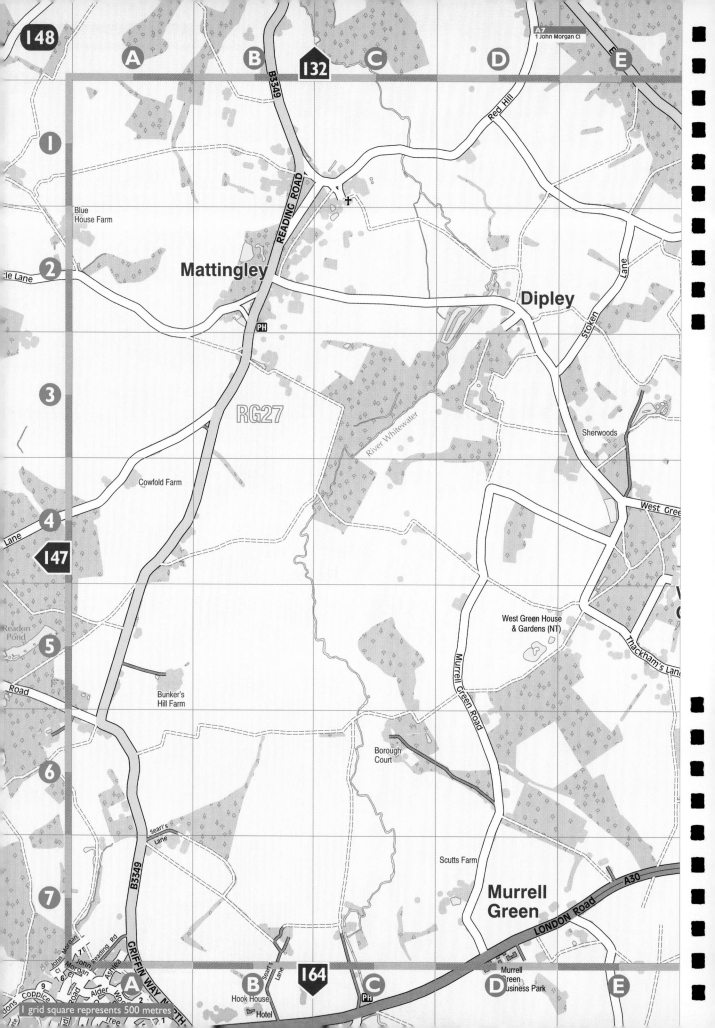

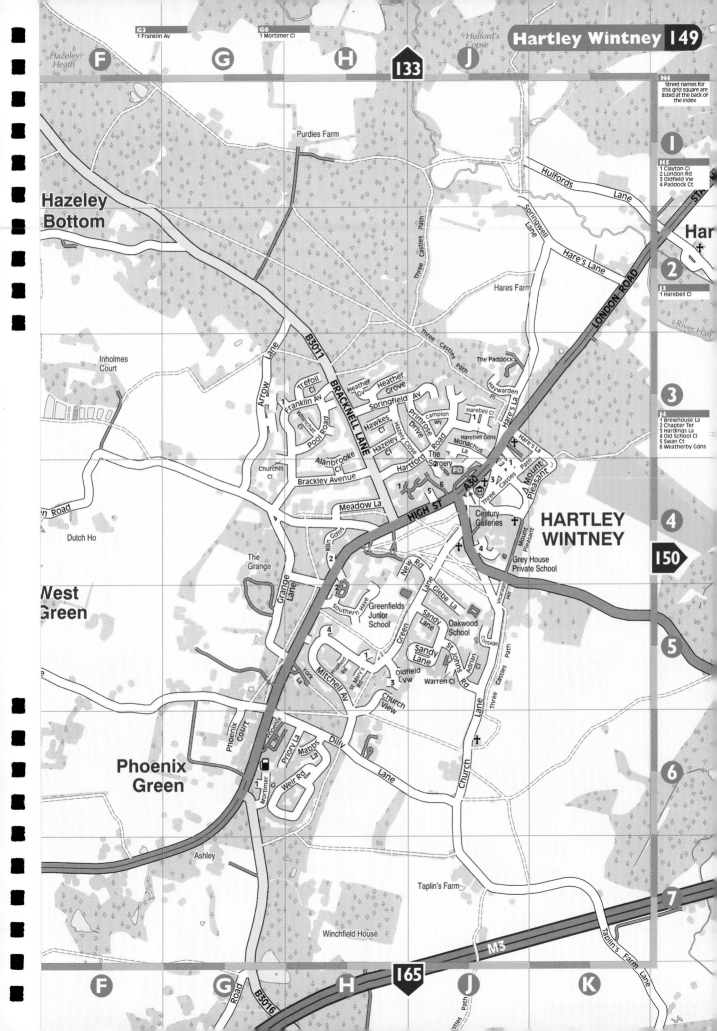

F

G

H

J

Hazeley Heath

1 Mortimer Cl

Hulford's Copse

I

Purdies Farm

Hulfords Lane

Har

Springwell Lane

Hare's Lane

2

Hazeley Bottom

Hares Farm

River Hart

The Paddock

3

Three Castles Path

Haywarden Pl

Inholmes Court

B3011

Arrow Lane

Trefoil Cl

Heather Gv

Heather Grove

Springfield Av

Harebell Cl

LONDON ROAD

Franklin Av

BRACKNELL LANE

Campion Wy

Harebell Gdns

Hare's La

Whinchat Ct

Pool Road

Hawkes Cl

Primrose Drive

Monachus La

Mount Pleasant

Churchill Cl

Hazeley Close

Hartford Road

The Surgery

PO

Alanbrooke Cl

Brackley Avenue

M

4

Three Castles Path

150

Meadow La

HIGH ST

A30

Century Galleries

HARTLEY WINTNEY

West Green

Dutch Ho

Kiln Gdns

The Grange

New Rd

Lane

Clebe La

Grey House Private School

Mount Pleasant

5

Grange Lane

Greenfields Junior School

Green

Southern Haye

Sandy Lane

Oakwood School

St Johns Rd

St Adrian Ct

Cottage

Vicarage Hill

Three Castles Path

Hopfield Rd

St Mary's Rd

Sandy Lane

Oldfield Vw

Warren Cl

York

Mitchell Av

Church View

Church Lane

6

Phoenix Court

Phoenix Ter

Priory La

Mabbs La

Dilly Lane

Phoenix Green

Mortimer

Welr Rd

Ashley

Taplin's Farm

7

Winchfield House

M3

Taplin's Farm Lane

F

G

Road

B3016

H

165

J

K

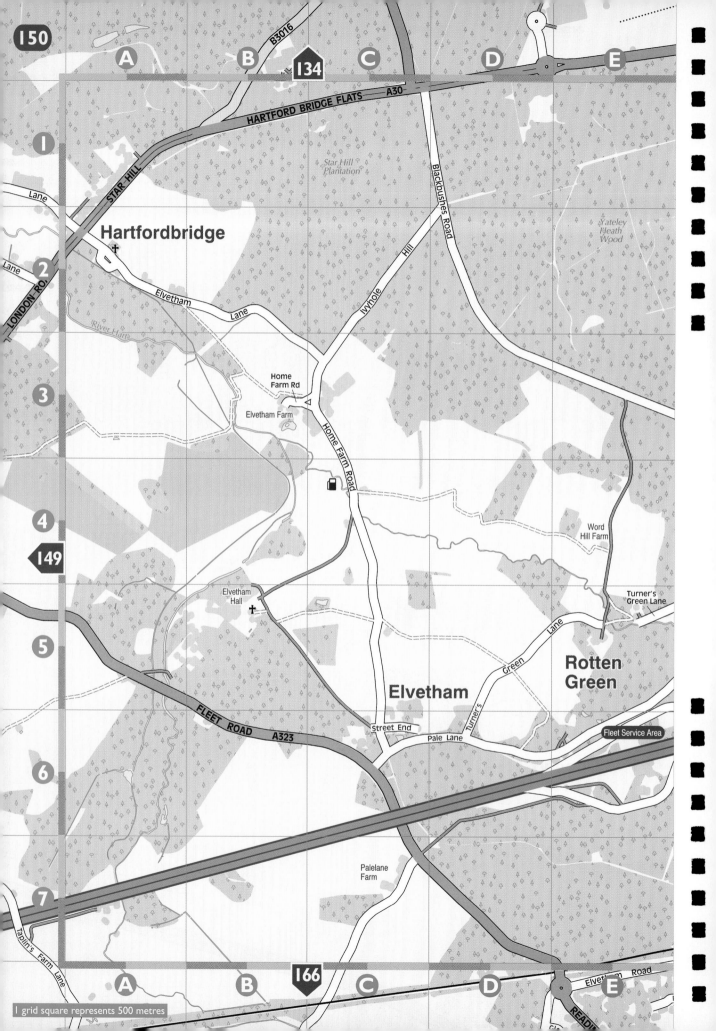

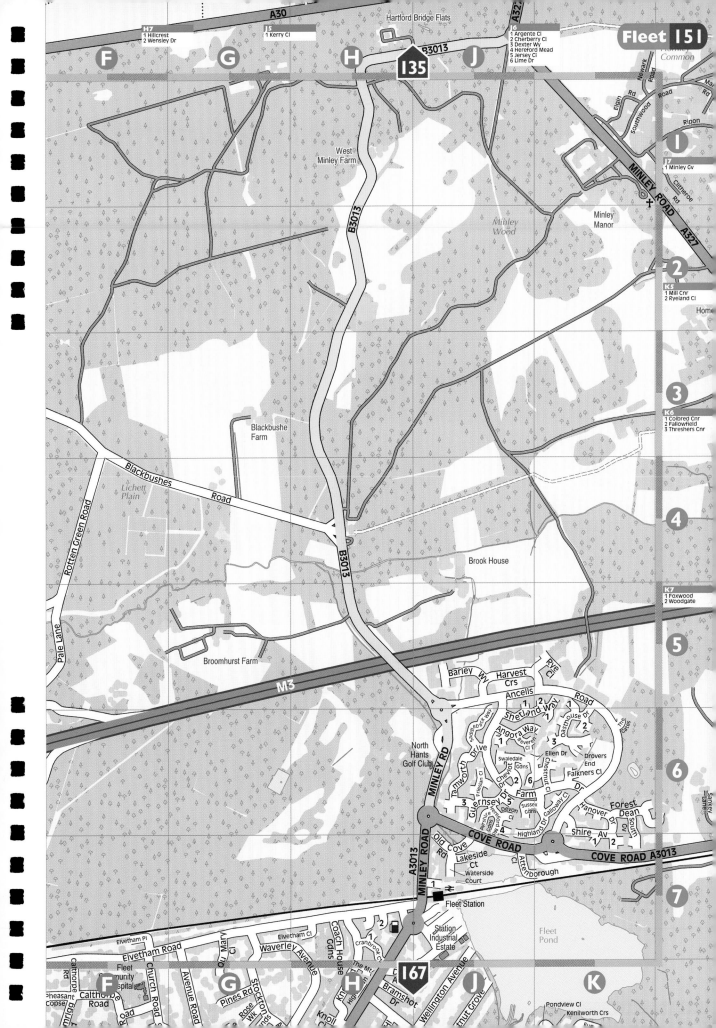

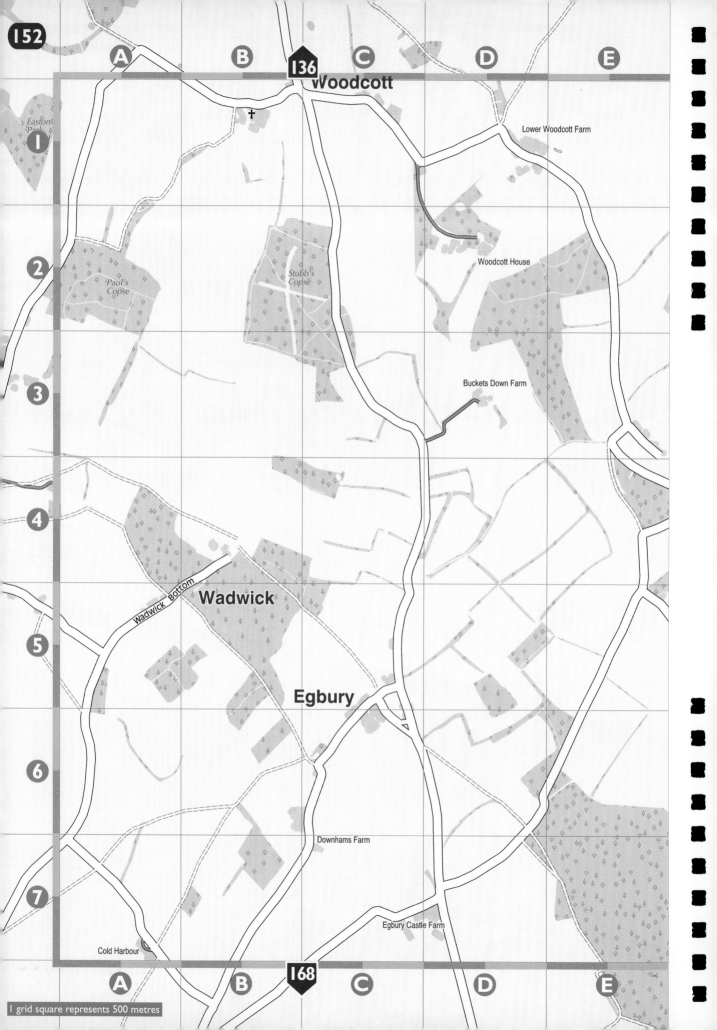

A   B   138   C   D   E

1

Hare Warren
Farm

2

3

Wormley
Copse

*Caesar's
Belt*

4

153

Ridgeway Farm

5

6

Twinley Manor

7

Whitnal

A   B   170   C   D   E   Ne n

1 grid square represents 500 metres

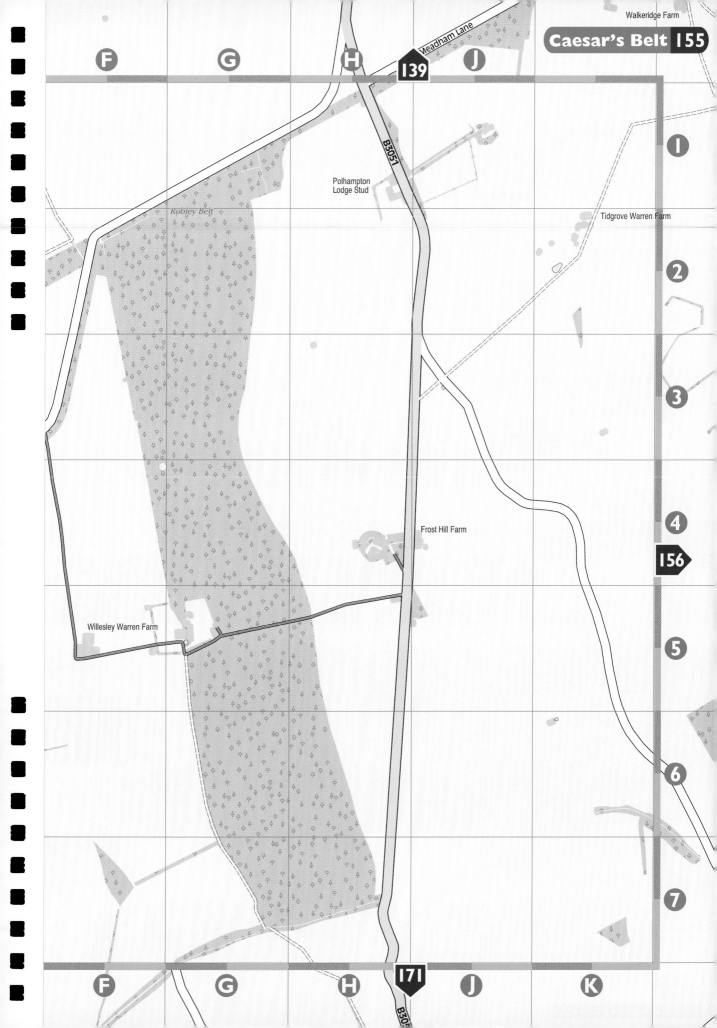

F G H J

Walkeridge Farm

139

Meadham Lane

I

B3051

Polhampton
Lodge Stud

Tidgrove Warren Farm

Robley Belt

2

3

4

Frost Hill Farm

156

Willesley Warren Farm

5

6

7

F G H J K

171

B30

Walkeridge Farm

A   B   140   C   D   E

Oakley Road

Ibworth Lane

I

Tidgrove Warren Farm

Wayfarer's Walk

2

North
Oakley

3

Wayfarer's Walk

Freemantle Farm

4

155

Frith
Wood

5

6

7

Ashe
Warren Ho

A   B   172   C   D   E

1 grid square represents 500 metres

F
G
H 141
J

Balstone Farm

Ibworth

I
2
3
4
158
5
6
7

Warren Bottom Copse

Hay Wood

Hook Lane

Shear Down Farm

Malshangar House

White Lane

Wayfarer's Walk

Great Deane Wood

Summer Down Lane

Little Deane Wood

Summer Down Farm

F
G 173
H
J
K

A   B   142 ston Farm   C   D   Basingstoke Road   Field Barn Farm   E

Upper
Wootton

A339(T)   KINGSCLERE ROAD

1

2

Whitedown

3

157

Tangier

PO

Wootton
St Lawrence

4

5

6

Worting House

7

B3400   WORTING   ROAD

RG23

Newfound   A   B   174   C   D   E

F7
1 Kempshott Gv

G5
1 Hillcrest Ct
2 Kenilworth Rd

F

G

H

143

J

I
G6
1 Pembroke Rd

2
G7
1 Cairngorm Cl
2 Charnwood Cl

3
Hotel
H4
1 Claudius Dr
2 Hadrians Wy

4

160

H6
1 Caernarvon Cl

5

6

7

A339(T)
KINGSCLERE ROAD

ALDERMASTON ROAD A340

Elm Road

Elm Bottom Cross

Rooksdown Lane

Priestley Road

Nightingale Gdns
Florence Wy
Gillies Dr
Burton Cl
Gander Dr
Rooksdown Av
Julius Cl
Mill Rd
Vespasian Gdns

Saxonwood
School for the
Handicapped

A&E

North
Hampshire
Hospital

Vickers
Business Cen

PO
Priestley

RINGWAY NORTH

Hamilton Close

Aldermaston

Edison Rd

Worting Wood Farm

Kingsclere
Rd
Roman Rd
Augustus Cl
Tiberius Cl
Waterloo Av
Rose Hodson Pl
PO
Arundel Gdns
Dunsford Crs
Wellington Terrace
Napoleon Dr
Way
Beech
Elmwood
Firs Wy
Oaklands Way
Hawthorn
Cedar Way
Willow Wy
Laburnum Wy
Sycamore Wy
Watson Wy
Winklebury Way
Watson Wy
Wilmott Wy
Hazelwood Dr
Hazelwood Cl

Houndmills

Houndmills
Industrial
Estate

Telford Road

RINGWAY WEST

Brunel Road

Stephenson
Rd

A340

Restormel Carlisle Cl
Kenilworth Rd
Blackthorn Way
Fort Hill
School
Pendennis Cl
Pendennis Ct
Tintagel Way
Warwick Rd
Warwick Rd
Coppice Ms
Carisbrooke Cl
Warwick Rd
Lilac Way
Sycamore Wy
Infant
School
Wilmott
Willoughby Wy
Junior
School
Woolford Wy

Winklebury

Kenilworth Rd
Kenilworth Rd
Kenilworth Rd
2 1
Forthill
Surgery
Winklebury
Medical Centre
Caernarvon Close
June Dr
Dudley
Junior
School
Winklebury Way
Porway Pl
Pembroke Rd
Tiverton Rd
Hereford Rd
Greenbury Cl
Harlech Close
Bury Rd
Dover Cl
Woolford Wy
Winklebury Way
Ludlow Cl
Ludlow Gdns

Euskirchen Way
Milestones
Museum

**West
Ham**

CHURCHILL-WAY

Wayside Rd
Tiverton Rd
Basingstoke
Ice Rink
Wessex
Bowl
Euskirchen Way
Euskirchen Wy
B3400 CHURCHILL WAY WEST
Superstore
Thorneycroft
Industrial Est

Worting

Roman Way
Beckett Cl
Cabonel Cl
Tiverton
Roman Road
Aylings Cl
Dorchester Cl
Hastings Cl
Wykeham Drive
Church La
Glebe Lane

West Ham Lane
PO
Grafton Way
W Ham Cl
Grafton Way
Grafton Way
Morse Rd
Davy Rd
Worting Rd
Worting Road
Overbridge
Surgery
Worting Rd

B3400 WORTING ROAD
B3400 WORTING ROAD

Cotswold Cl
Cotswold Way
Tweeds Cl
Mourne Cl
Campsie Way
Cairngorm Way
Edgemill Cl
Butler Cl
Butler Cl
St
Brewer Cl
Burnaby Rd
Fiske Cl
Mercer Cl
Mercer
Old Worting Road
Salisbury Gdns
Orchard Rd
Bardwell
St Peter's
St Nicholas Ct
Worting
Road
Margaret Rd
Charles St
Aldworth
Sandys Cl
Ringway
Amazon
Attwood
Attwood Cl

Worting County
Infant School
Junior
School
Buckskin
Hampshire Cl
Alpine Cl
Wicklow
Webb Cl
Ochil Cl
Rodmin Cl
Exmoor Cl
Dibley
Claythorpe
Grampian Way
Cheviot
Alliston
Branton Cl
Pentland Cl
Chiltern
Highlands Rd
Kempshott

175

Limington
House
School

South

St Andrews Rd
St Paul's
Kimberley Rd
King's Rd
Bolton
Elizabeth Cl
Portacre
Packenham
Infant
Allen Cl

King's Furlong

Cem

F

G

H

J

K

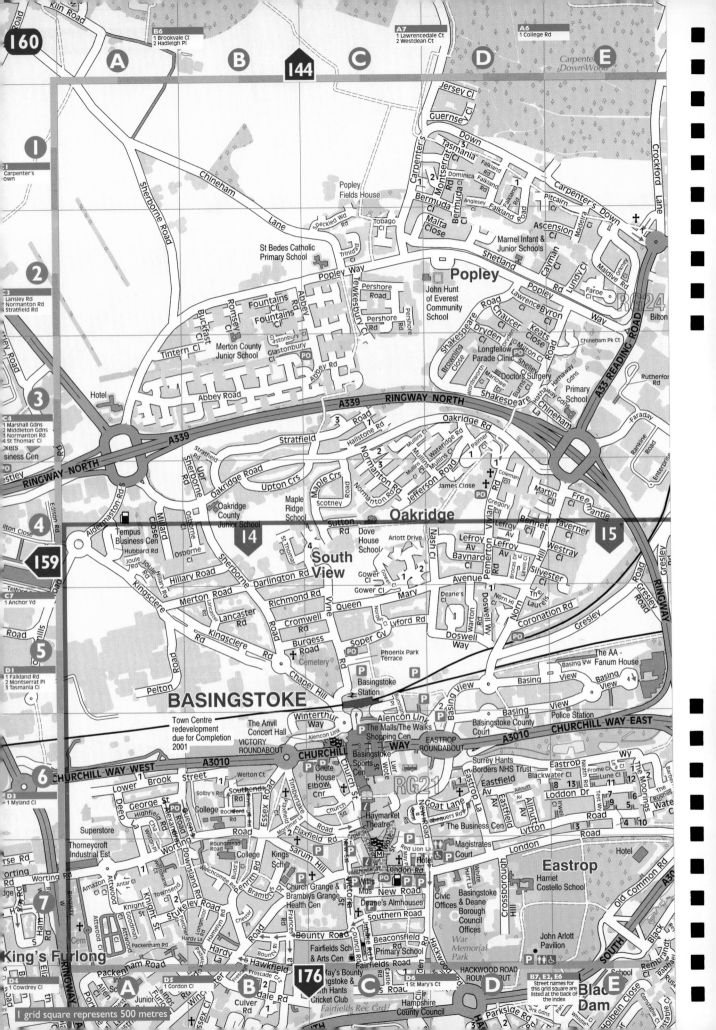

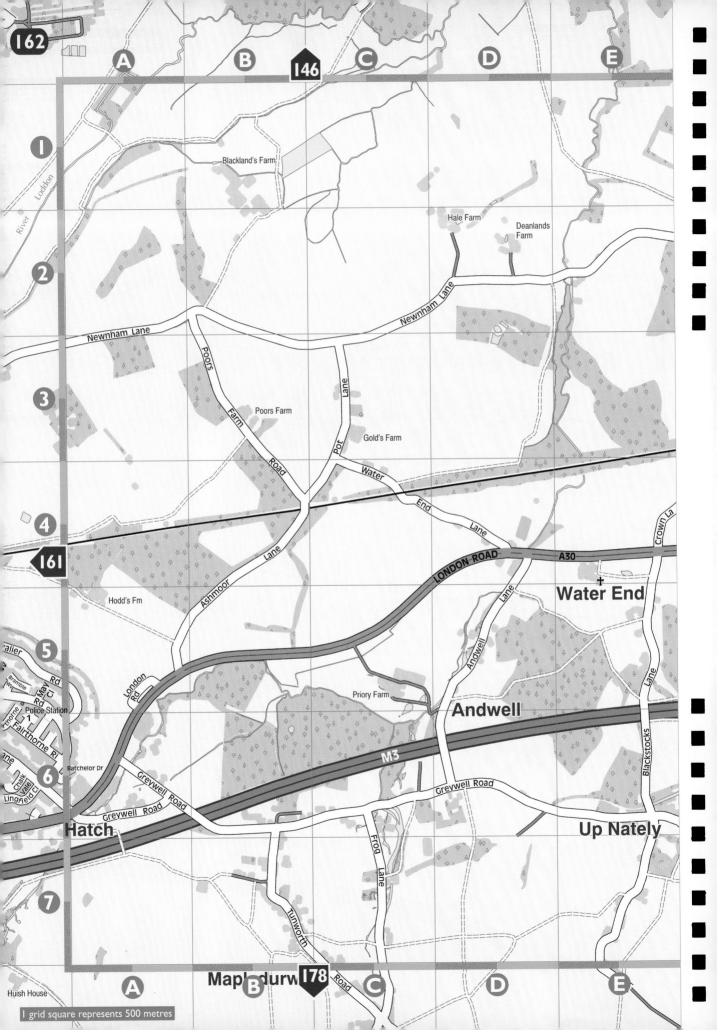

162

A   B   146   C   D   E

1

Blackland's Farm

River Loddon

Hale Farm

Deanlands Farm

2

Newnham Lane

Newnham Lane

Poors Farm Road

Pot Lane

3

Poors Farm

Gold's Farm

Water

4

End

161

Lane

A30

Crown La

London Road

Water End

Ashmoor Lane

Hodd's Fm

Andwell Lane

5

allier

May Rd

Bramble

Police Station

Fairthorne Rd

Priory Farm

Andwell

London Rd

M3

6

Batchelor Dr

Chalk Vale

Lingfield Cl

Greywell Road

Greywell Road

Greywell Road

Up Nately

Frog Lane

Hatch

Blackstocks Lane

7

Huish House

A   Maplҽdurw   178   B   C   D   E

1 grid square represents 500 metres

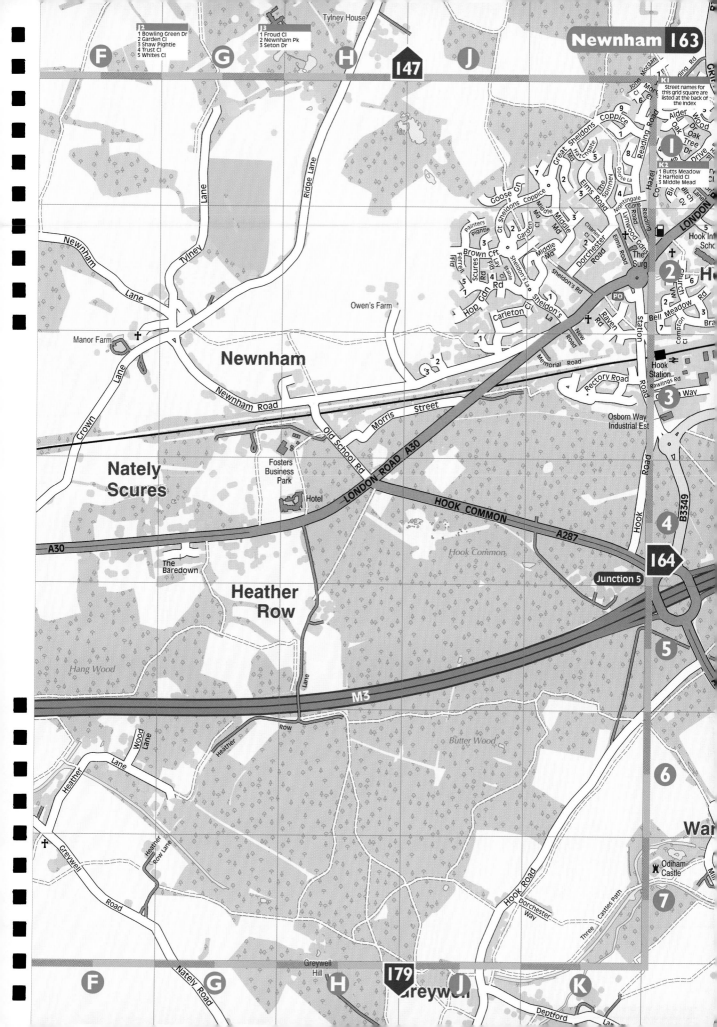

F G H J

147

K1
Street names for this grid square are listed at the back of the index

I

K2
1 Butts Meadow
2 Harfield Cl
3 Middle Mead

J2
1 Bowling Green Dr
2 Garden Cl
3 Shaw Pightle
4 Trust Cl
5 Whites Cl

J3
1 Froud Cl
2 Newnham Pk
3 Seton Dr

Tylney House

LONDON RD

Hook Inf
Sch

2

Great Sheldons
Hatchgate
Coppice
The Spinney
Goose La
Nightingale
Gdns
Charles
Cl
Dorchester
Road
Elms Road
Lynwood Gdns
Reading Road
The
Surg
PO

Coppice
Alder
Wood
Oak
Tree
Dr
Oak
Drive
Birch Gv
Hazel
Lane

Church La
Comp'ton Way
Bell Meadow

Goose Gn
Gt Sheldons Coppice
Garden
Cl
Middle
Md
Middle
Md
Middle
Md
Sheldon's La
Sheldon's Rd
Sheldon's
La
Elms Road

Painters
Pightle
Brown Cft
Ferrell
Fld
Scures
Rd
Lav
Stable
Hop Gdn
Carleton Cl

New
Road
Raven
Rd

Station
Road

Memorial Road

Rectory Road

Hook
Station

Rawlings Rd

Osborn Way
Industrial Est

Hook
Road

B3349

3

Way

4

164

Junction 5

5

Newnham Lane
Tylney
Lane
Ridge Lane

Manor Farm

Newnham

Newnham Road

Owen's Farm

Crown
Lane

Morris Street

Old School Rd

LONDON ROAD A30

HOOK COMMON A287

Hook Common

A30

**Nately
Scures**

Fosters
Business
Park

Hotel

The
Baredown

**Heather
Row**

Hang Wood

Lane

Row

M3

Heather

Butter Wood

6

Wa

Wood Lane

Heather
Lane

Heather
Row Lane

Greywell
Road

Greywell
Hill

Hook Road

Dorchester
Way

Three Castles Path

Odiham
Castle

7

Deptford

Greywell
Nately Road

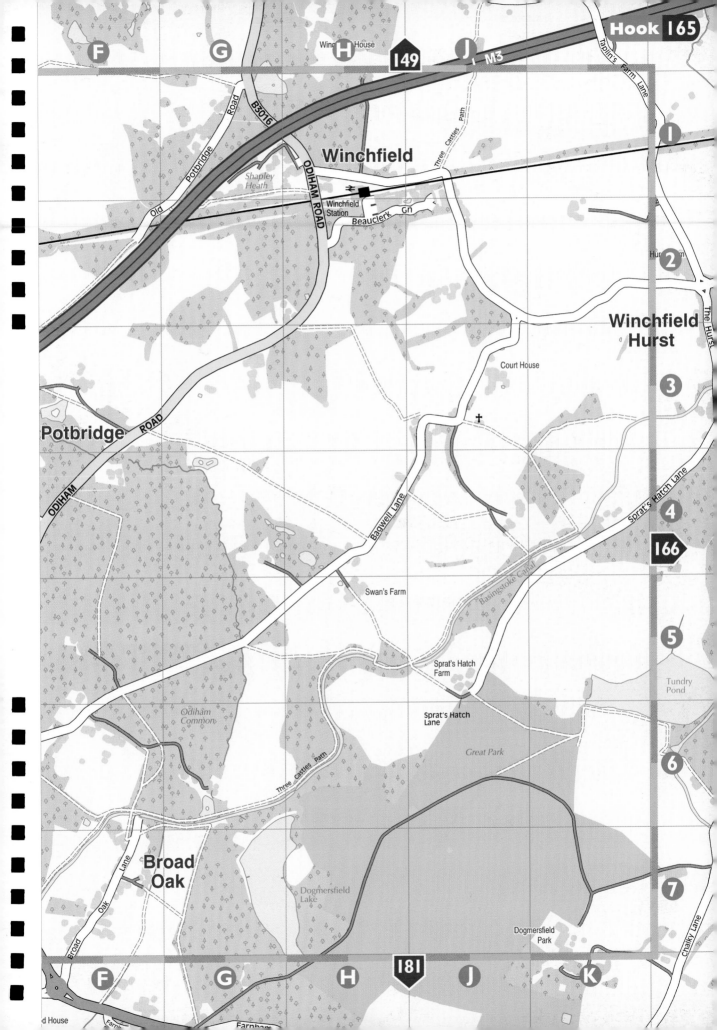

F G H **149** J M3

Wind House

I

B3016

ODIHAM ROAD

Potbridge Road

Old

Winchfield

Three Castles Path

Taplin's Farm Lane

Shapley Heath

Winchfield Station

Beauclerk

Gn

2

Winchfield Hurst

The Hurst

Court House

3

ODIHAM ROAD

Potbridge

Sprat's Hatch Lane

4

166

Bagwell Lane

Basingstoke Canal

Swan's Farm

5

Tundry Pond

Sprat's Hatch Farm

Sprat's Hatch Lane

Great Park

6

Odiham Common

Three Castles Path

Broad Oak

Broad Oak Lane

Dogmersfield Lake

Dogmersfield Park

Chalky Lane

7

F G H **181** J K

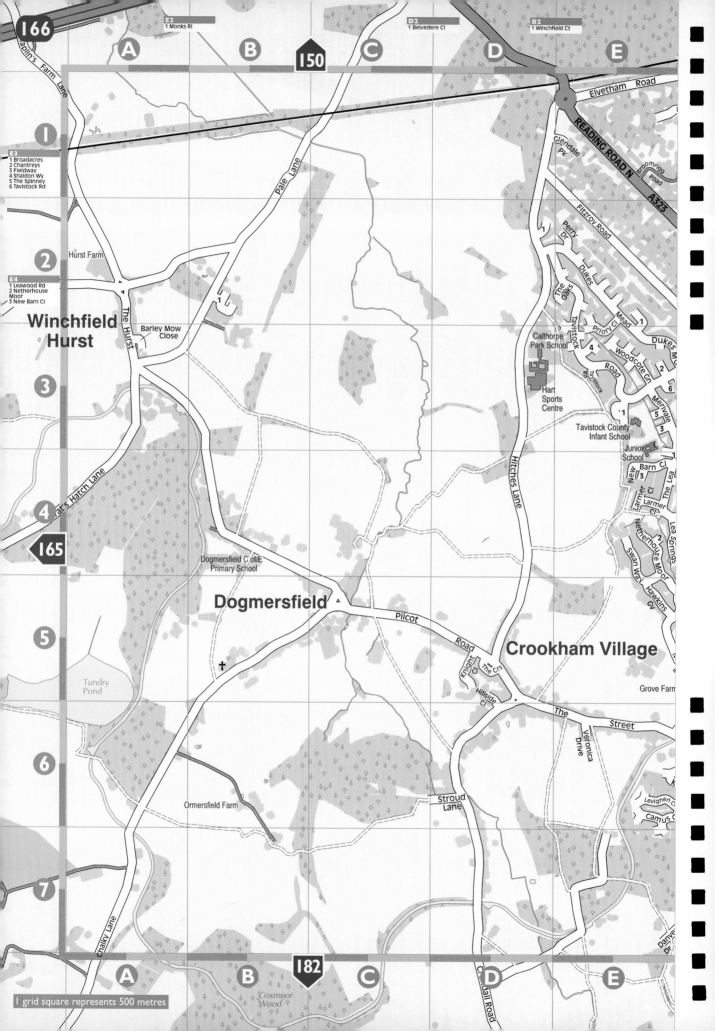

A   B   150   C   D   E

1

Elvetham   Road

E3
1 Broadacres
2 Chantreys
3 Fieldway
4 Shaldon Wy
5 The Spinney
6 Tavistock Rd

READING ROAD N   A323

Glendale Pk

Broomrigg Road

2

Hurst Farm

Fitzroy Road

E4
1 Leawood Rd
2 Netherhouse Moor
3 New Barn Cl

Perry Dr

Dukes

Mead

Priory Cl

**Winchfield
Hurst**

The Hurst

Barley Mow
Close

The Oaks

Tavistock Road

Woodcote Gn

Dukes Mo

Calthorpe
Park School

3

Merivale

Hart
Sports
Centre

Tavistock Rd

Tavistock County
Infant School

Sat's Hatch Lane

4

Junior
School

New Barn Cl

165

Dogmersfield C of E
Primary School

Larmer Cl

Larmer Cl

Netherhouse Moor

Lea Springs

The Lea

Dogmersfield

Pilcot

5

Tundry
Pond

Pilcot
Road

Crookham Village

Knight

The Crs

Grove Farm

Hillside
Cl

Swan Way

Hawkins Gv

The   Street

Veronica
Drive

6

Ormersfield Farm

Stroud
Lane

Levignen Cl

Camus Cl

7

Chalky Lane

A   B   182   C   Jail Road   D   E

Danver Dr

1 grid square represents 500 metres

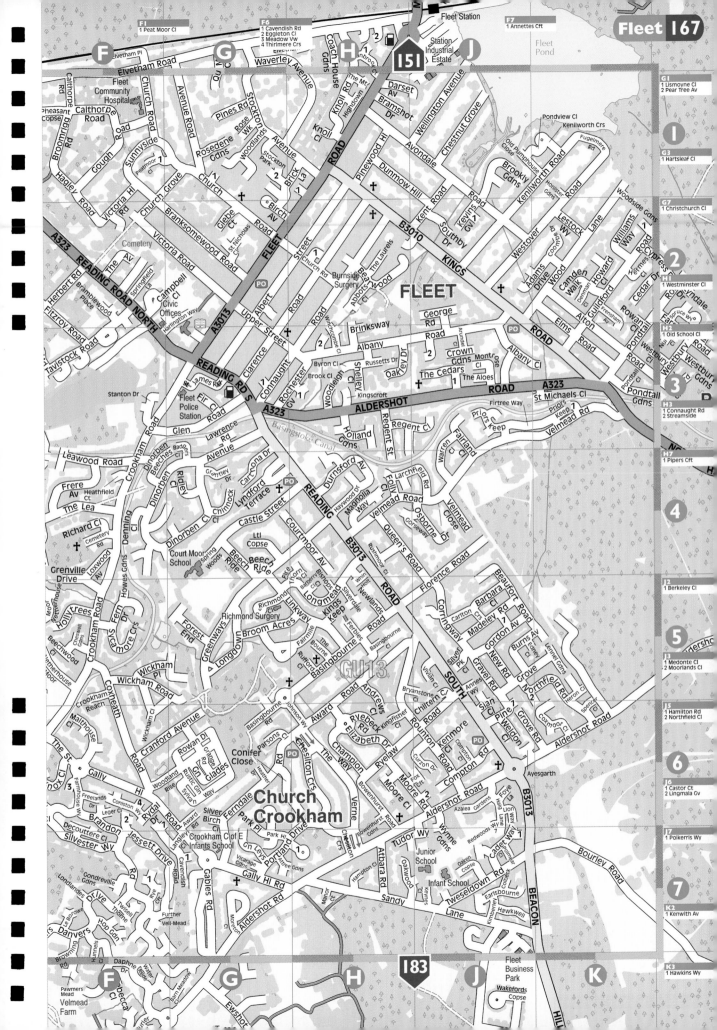

FLEET

Church Crookham

GU13

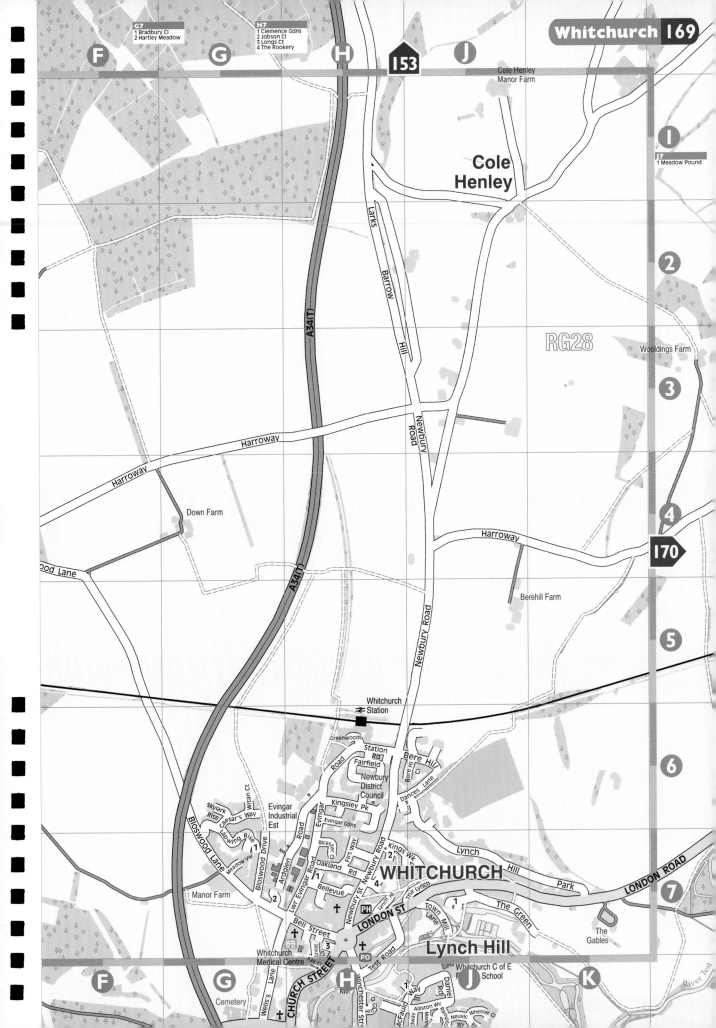

F **G** **H** **153** **J**

I

Cole Henley Manor Farm

2

Cole Henley

Larks

RG28

Barrow Hill

Wooldings Farm

3

A34(T)

Newbury Road

Harroway

Harroway

Down Farm

4

170

Harroway

A34(T)

od Lane

Berehill Farm

5

Whitchurch Station

6

Greenwoods

Bere Hill

Station Rd

Fairfield

Bere Cl

Dances Lane

Newbury District Council

Skylark Rise

Witan Ct

Evingar Industrial Est

Kingsley Pk

Evingar Gdns

Caesar's Way

Lapwing Rise

Evingar Road

Kings Wk

Bicester Cl

Firs Way

Meadow Vw

Bloswood Drive

Ardglen

Oakland Rd

Bellevue

Lynch Hill Park

Newbury St

Newbury Road

WHITCHURCH

Manor Farm

Bloswood Lane

Lwr Evingar Road

The Lynch

Lynch Hl

Kings Wk

London Road

7

Bell Street

Great

Fair Cl

London St

LONDON ST

Test Road

Lynch Hl Lane

Town Mill

The Green

The Gables

Whitchurch Medical Centre

PH

PO

Lynch Hill

River Test

F **G** **H** **J** **K**

Cemetery

Wells's Lane

CHURCH STREET

Manchester Str

Test Road

Mill

Whitchurch C of E P School

Daniel Rd

McFauld Way

Alliston Wy

Hides Cl

Neuvic Wy

Wheeler Cl

bamboo

A   B   154   C   Whitnal   D   E

D6
1 Marsden Ct

New Barn

1

2

Wooldings Farm

3
The
Orchards

Watch Lane

4

169

Priory Lane

Watch Lane

S Vw Cottages

5
Home Farm

Laverstoke Ho

6
Freefolk
Priory Farm
PH
Way
Colne Valley
LONDON ROAD
ROTTEN HILL
Laverstoke

B3400
DON ROAD

Laverstoke Lane

Colne Valley
Way

Florence Portal
Cl

7
DON ROAD

The
Gables

River

A   B   C   D   E

1 grid square represents 500 metres

155

1 Waltham Ct

F G H J K

Court Drove

B3051

Overton Station

Foxdown 2

Hilltop Road

Hill Meadow

Elm Rd
Beech Cl
Copse

Station Road

Station Hill

Quidhampton 3

KINGSCLERE ROAD B3051

Primary School

Court Farm

Court Drove Lane

Glebe Meadow

Church Road

Waltham Rd

Overton Surgery

Riverside Close

Station Road

4

172

Lynch

The Lynch

Silk Mill

Mill Lane

Lordsfield Gdns

Bridge St

White Hart Gallery

Overton Gallery

LONDON ROAD B3400

Berrydown

Southington Close

Southington La

HIGH ST

King's Meadow

Red Lion Lane

Poyntz Rd

The Orchard

PO

Battens Avenue

The Green

Two Ga Meadow

Gate Lane

Berrydown Lane

Harveys Fld

Oak Close

Woodlands

Lion Cl

Winchester Street

1

Nightingale Rise

OVERTON

5

Berrydown Farm

Southington

Vinns Lane

Dellands Lane

Kerchers Fld

Dellands

Greyhound La

Alexander Road

Two Sydes

Papermill

Mede Close

Pound Road

Waltham Road

B3400

ROTTEN HILL

Charledown Cl
Close

Crawts Road

Charledown Road

Poultons Road

Poultons Cl

Sapley Lane

6

Pond Close

Turrill Hill Farm

Sapley Farm House

7

F G H J K

156

A
B
C
D
E

I

oxd⊙n 2

Polhampton Farm

3

Deane

✝

Ashe
✝

Source of
the River Test

4

171

B3400

ANDOVER ROAD
PH

Cheesedown Farm

Berrydown Court

Ashe
Park

5

Berrydown
Farm

down Lane

6

Burley
Wood

Burley Lane

7

Waltham Lane

A
B
C
D
E

Steventon

Waltham

Ashe
Warren Ho

Harrow W

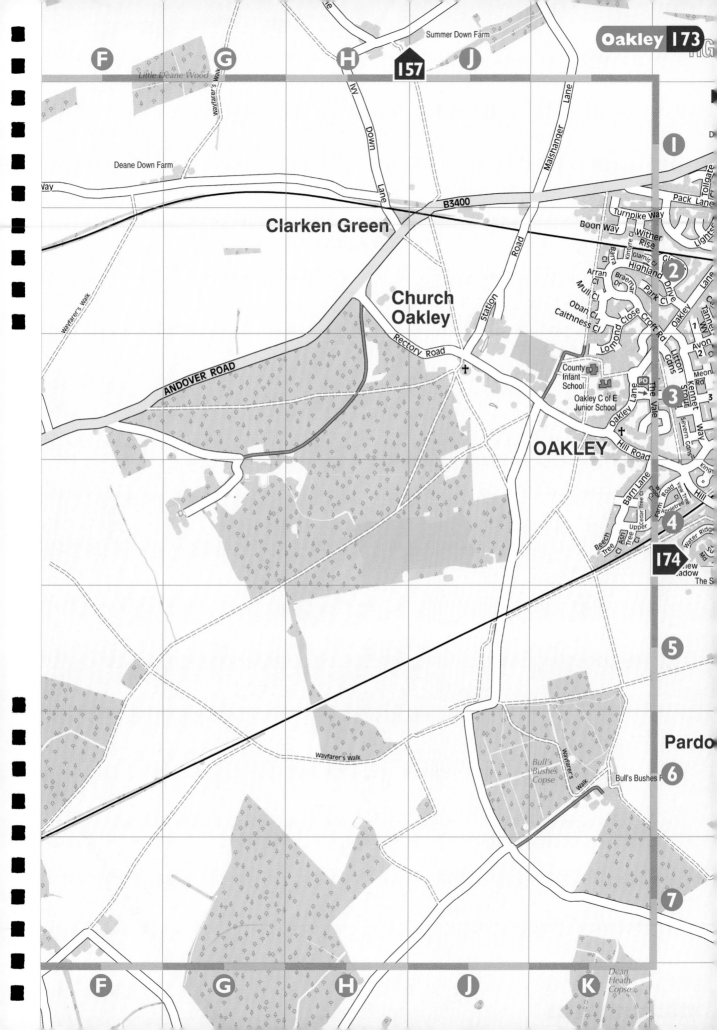

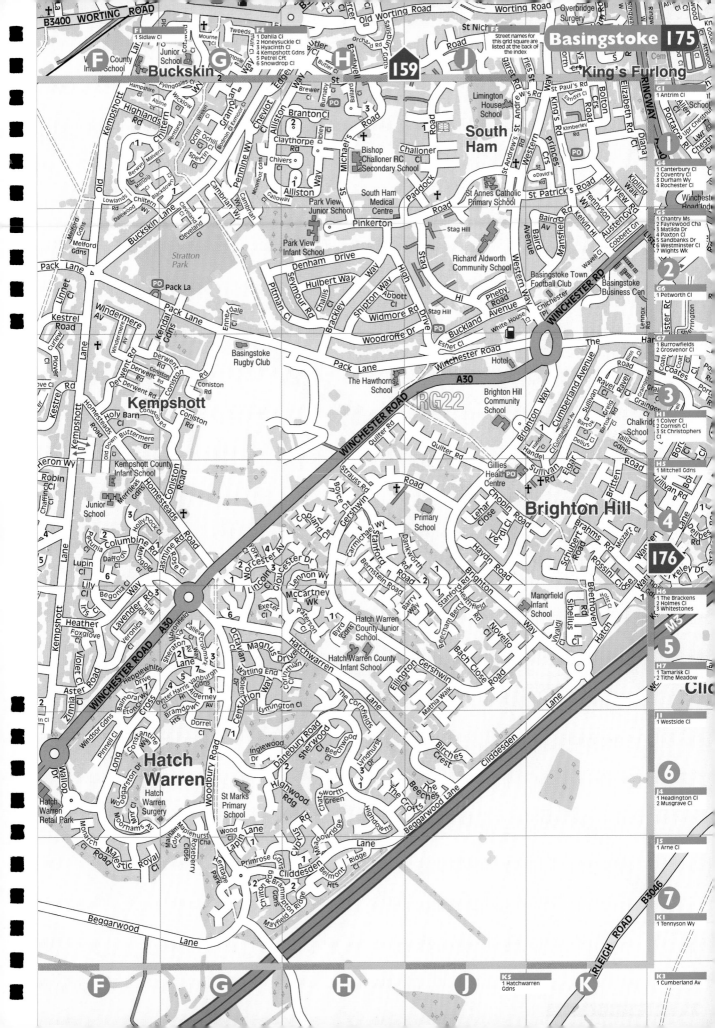

A   B   162   C   D   E

Mapledurwell

1

Gray's Farm

Hungry Lodge

2

Tunworth Road

Down Lane

3

Castles Path

Three

Five Lanes End

4

177

Tunworth House

Down Farm

Three Castles Path

5

Cleves Lane

6

Tunworth

Upton Grey House

7

Upton Grey

Cemetery Lane

PO

Bidden Rd

The Dower House

Limbrew

A   B   C   D   E

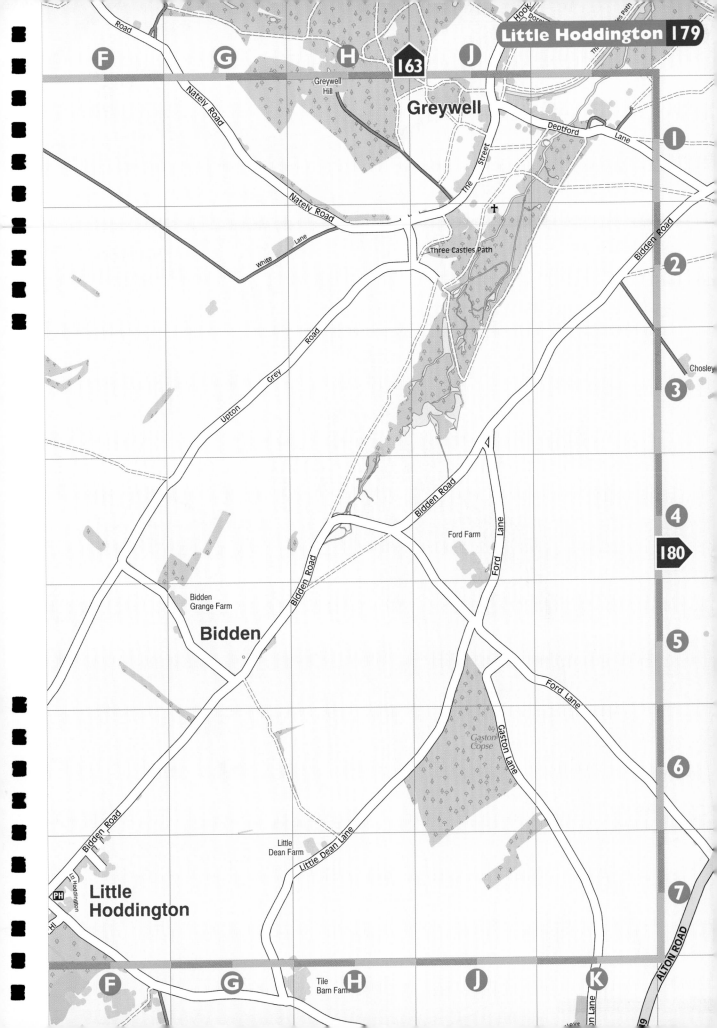

163

Greywell
Greywell
Hill

Deptford Lane

Nately Road

The Street

Three Castles Path

Chosley

Nately Road

White Lane

Upton Grey Road

Bidden Road

Ford Farm

Ford Lane

180

Bidden Road

Bidden
Grange Farm

Bidden

Gaston Copse

Gaston Lane

Ford Lane

Bidden Road

Little
Dean Farm

Little Dean Lane

PH

Bidden Road

Lt Hoddington Hl

**Little
Hoddington**

Tile
Barn Farm

ALTON ROAD

F G H J K

F G H J

I

2

3

4

5

6

7

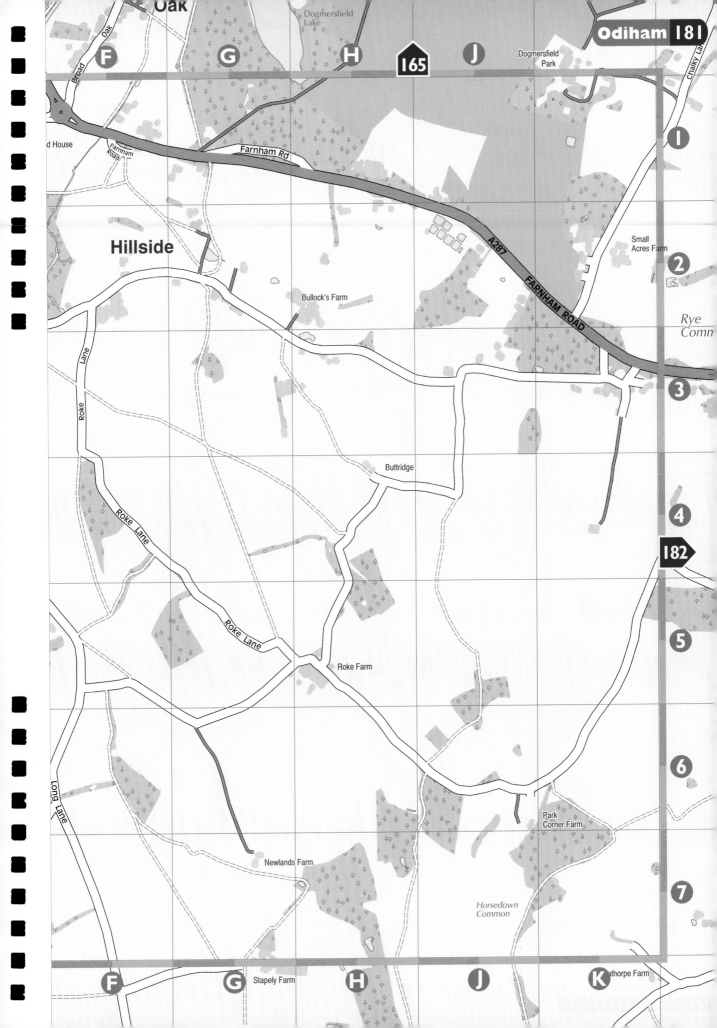

F G H 165 J

Dogmersfield Lake

Dogmersfield Park

Chalky Lane

1

d House

Farnham Road

Farnham Rd

A287

Small Acres Farm

2

Hillside

FARNHAM ROAD

Rye Comn

Bullock's Farm

3

Roke Lane

Buttridge

4

182

Roke Lane

5

Roke Lane

Roke Farm

6

Long Lane

Park Corner Farm

Newlands Farm

7

Horsedown Common

F G Stapely Farm H J K athorpe Farm

166

E7
1 Ravelin Cl

D6
1 Hannam's Farm

A **B** **C** **D** **E**

Chalky Lane

Crondall Road

Danve
Dr

I

Coxmoor
Wood

Hancock's Farm

Bowenhurst La

Small
Acres Farm

2

Coxmoor
Farm Light
Industrial Estate

Finns
Industrial
Park

Rye
Common

**Mill
Lane**

3

A287

Downsland House

Marsh Farm
Business
Centre

Bowling Alley

4

Hannam's
Copse

Eastbridge

181

Lefroy's
Fld

Lane

Handcroft
Cl

Hyde

Green springs

The Surgery

Itchel
Home Farm

Ashley Cl

Ashley Cl se

Street

Redlands La

5

Pankridge

Crondall

Itchel

Penn
Croft Farm

Lane

6

Road

The Borough

PO

Dippenhall

Well

Church Street

Lane

Glebe
Rd

Heath
La

Croft

Crondall CP
School

St Cross
Rd

Street

7

Farm La

Chaundlers
Cl

nthorpe Farm

A **B** **C** **D** **E**

1 grid square represents 500 metres

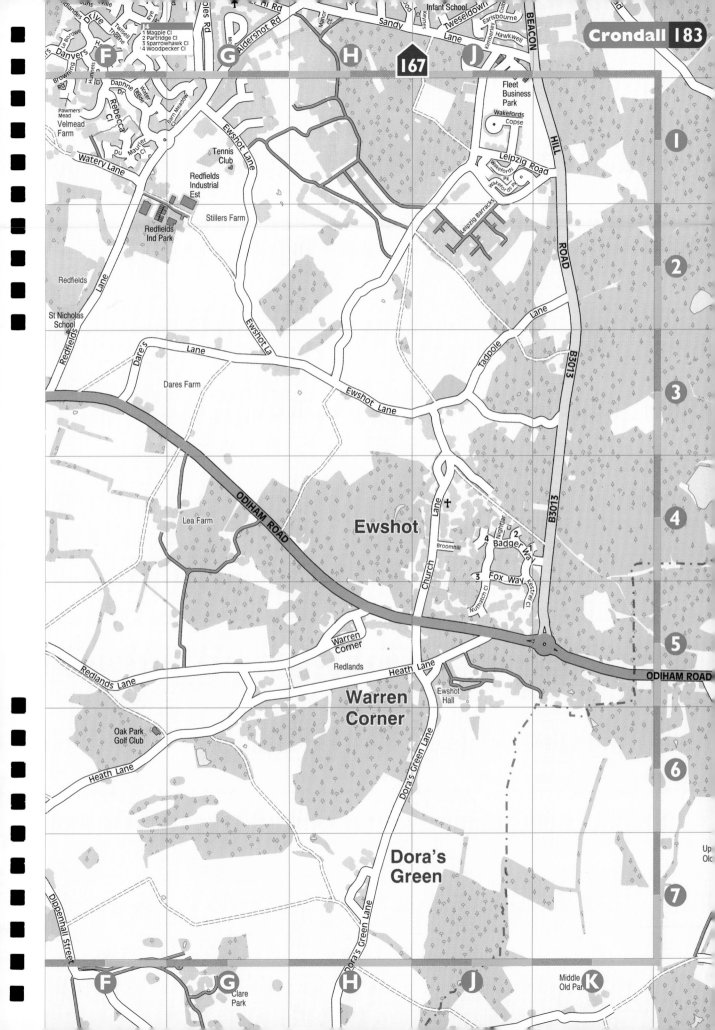

Aldermaston 108 C1
Aldermaston Soke 109 J5
Aldermaston Wharf 89 F4
Aldworth 23 F7
Amen Corner 98 C1
Andwell 162 D6
Arborfield 94 E3
Arborfield Cross 95 G4
Arborfield Garrison 115 K1
Ascot 101 J1
Ashampstead 37 G6
Ashampstead Green 37 H5
Ashe 172 B4
Ashford Hill 107 F7
Ashmore Green 65 G6
Aston 18 B5
Axmansford 125 K2
Bagnor 62 E6
Barkham 96 A5
Basingstoke 14 C3
Baughurst 126 A2
Beech Hill 112 D3
Beedon 34 C5
Beedon Hill 34 B5
Beenham 88 C1
Beenham Stocks 88 E1
Bidden 179 G5
Binfield 78 C4
Binfield Heath 44 D3
Birch Hill 99 K5
Bishop's Green 105 F5
Bix 16 A3
Black Dam 15 J8
Bockmer End 19 H1
Borough Marsh 45 K4
Bothampstead 49 G1
Bowling Alley 182 D4
Boxford 62 A3
Bracknell 10 F4
Bradfield 53 G7
Bramley 129 F5
Bramley Corner 128 C6
Bramley Green 129 H7
Bramshill 132 E2
Brighton Hill 175 J4
Brimpton 107 F2
Brimpton Common 107 K6
Broad Layings 102 B7
Broad Oak 165 F7
Broadplat 16 B6
Brock's Green 123 F1
Brookside 81 H4
Browninghill Green 126 C6
Bucklebury 67 F4
Bucklebury Alley 65 H4
Buckskin 159 F7
Bullbrook 80 C7
Burghclere 121 J2
Burghclere Common 103 K7
Burghfield 91 H2
Burghfield Common 91 F5
Burghfield Hill 91 H4
Burnt Hill 51 J4
Bury's Bank 104 D1
Calcot 71 H2
Calcot Row 71 J1
Cane End 42 A1
Carter's Hill 75 H7
Caversham 57 G2
Caversham Heights 57 G1
Chalkhouse Green 43 H3
Chandlers Green 131 G7
Chapel Row 67 K6
Charter Alley 142 E2
Charvil 45 K7
Chavey Down 80 E7
Chazey Heath 42 D5
Chieveley 48 A3
Chineham 145 G7
Church Crookham 167 G6
Churchend 55 K7
Church End 145 K4
Church Oakley 173 H2
Clarken Green 173 G2
Clay Hill 68 B4
Cleeve 25 F3
Cliddesden 176 A5
Cockpole Green 32 E3
Cold Ash 65 H7
Cold Harbour 26 A7
Cole Henley 169 J1
Coley 3 G9
Collins End 41 G2
Colt Hill 180 E1

Colthrop 86 C4
Compton 21 J6
Compton 35 K1
Court Corner 127 G6
Cranbourne 176 A2
Cray's Pond 26 C5
Crazies Hill 32 D5
Cricket Hill 135 K4
Crockham Heath 102 C2
Crondall 182 D5
Crookham 106 C3
Crookham Village 166 D5
Cross Lanes 41 K3
Crown Wood 100 A4
Crowsley 29 K7
Crowthorne 118 A4
Cufaude 145 F3
Curridge 64 C1
Danesfield 19 J4
Daneshill 161 F3
Deane 172 D3
Dipley 148 D2
Dogmersfield 166 B5
Donnington 83 G1
Dora's Green 183 H7
Dowlesgreen 77 H6
Dunley 153 F3
Dunsden Green 44 C5
Earley 9 K2
Earlstone Common 121 J1
East Fields 13 G6
Easthampstead 10 F8
Eastheath 97 F4
East Ilsley 20 E5
East Oakley 174 B2
Eastrop 15 J6
Ecchinswell 123 F6
Egbury 152 B5
Eling 49 K2
Elvetham 150 C5
Emmbrook 76 D6
Emmer Green 43 H6
Enborne 82 C7
Enborne Row 102 E4
Englefield 70 A2
Eversley 116 A7
Eversley Centre 134 C1
Eversley Cross 134 E1
Ewshot 183 H4
Exlade Street 27 G3
Fair Oak 125 F2
Fair Oak Green 129 J3
Farley Hill 115 G3
Finchampstead 116 C5
Fleet 167 H2
Four Houses Corner 90 D7
Four Points 37 F2
Foxdown 171 K2
Freefolk 170 A6
Frilsham 50 D6
Gallowstree Common 28 C6
Gardeners Green 97 K5
Goddard's Green 91 J6
Goldfinch Bottom 105 H3
Goose Hill 106 C5
Goring 25 F5
Goring Heath 41 F1
Grazeley 92 E5
Grazeley Green 92 A4
Great Hollands 99 F4
Great Lea Common 93 H1
Greenham 84 B7
Greenlands 17 K2
Greys Green 30 A1
Greywell 179 H1
Hambleden 18 A1
Hampstead Norreys 35 K6
Hannington 140 C6
Hanworth 99 H5
Hare Hatch 47 F4
Harmans Water 11 J8
Harpsden 31 H5
Harpsden Bottom 31 F5
Hartfordbridge 150 A2
Hartley Wespall 146 D1
Hartley Wintney 149 K4
Hatch 161 K6
Hatch Warren 175 F6
Haughurst Hill 107 K7
Hazeley 132 D6
Hazeley Bottom 149 F1
Hazeley Lea 132 E6
Headley 105 K7
Heath End 108 C7

Heather Row 163 G5
Heathlands 98 A7
Heckfield 131 K3
Henley-on-Thames 31 G2
Hermitage 49 G7
Highclere 120 C4
Highclere Street 120 A6
Hill Bottom 40 D1
Hillside 181 F7
Hollington Cross 120 A6
Holly Cross 33 F5
Holme Green 98 A4
Holt 164 C2
The Holt 47 G3
Honey Hill 98 B6
Hook 164 A2
Hook End 27 J3
Hopgoods Green 66 D6
Horncastle 71 K1
Hound Green 132 B6
Houndmills 159 K4
Hungerford 61 J3
Hungerford Green 37 G1
Hunt's Green 62 A5
Hurley 19 K6
Hurley Bottom 19 J7
Hurst 60 E5
Hyde End 107 F4
Ibworth 157 J1
Inhurst 125 K1
Jennetts Hill 68 A3
Kempshott 175 F3
Kidmore End 42 D1
Kiff Green 87 J1
Kiln Green 47 H3
Kingsclere 139 K1
Kingsclere Woodlands 124 B1
King's Furlong 14 A7
Langley Common 95 J6
Latchmere Green 128 B4
Laverstoke 170 D7
Limmerhill 96 D2
Litchfield 153 H3
Little Heath 55 F5
Little Hoddington 179 F7
Little Hungerford 49 H5
Little London 127 J6
Little Sandhurst 118 B6
Littlestead Green 44 B6
Longlane 65 F2
Lower Assendon 16 C4
Lower Basildon 39 G2
Lower Caversham 4 B2
Lower Common 115 J7
Lower Earley 75 G5
Lower Padworth 89 G2
Lower Shiplake 45 J1
Lyde Green 147 H3
Lynch 171 F4
Lynch Hill 169 J7
Malpas 54 C7
Mapledurham 41 K6
Mapledurwell 178 B1
Marsh Benham 82 A4
Matthewsgreen 77 F7
Mattingley 148 A2
Mays Green 30 E6
Medmenham 19 G5
Merryhill Green 76 C3
Middle Assendon 16 C2
Midgham 87 F4
Midgham Green 87 J2
Miles's Green 66 D7
Mill End 18 B3
Mill Green 106 A5
Mill Lane 182 B3
Monk Sherborne 143 G4
Mortimer 111 F2
Mortimer West End 110 C4
The Mount 8 A7
The Mount 120 C2
Murrell Green 148 D7
Nately Scures 163 F4
Newbury 12 C4
New Cross 45 H2
Newell Green 79 K3
Newfound 174 A1
Newnham 163 G3
New Town 4 D6
New Town 53 F1
Newtown 31 H3
Newtown 104 A4
North Ascot 81 F7
North Oakley 156 B2

North Street 70 C1
North Warnborough 164 B7
Nuney Green 41 K1
Oakley 173 K3
Oakridge 160 C4
Oare 49 G6
Odiham 180 D2
Old Basing 161 H5
Old Burghclere 137 H2
Overton 171 J5
Owlsmoor 118 E6
Padworth 89 H6
Padworth Common 109 J2
Pamber End 143 G1
Pamber Green 127 H5
Pamber Heath 109 G6
Pangbourne 40 A7
Pardown 174 A6
Parker's Corner 69 K3
Penwood 120 C2
Pheonix Green 149 F6
Pingewood 72 D6
Plastow Green 124 B2
Play Hatch 44 C7
Popeswood 78 C6
Popley 160 D2
Potbridge 165 F3
Poundgreen 92 D4
Pound Green 126 A6
Pound Street 121 F2
Priestwood 10 B1
Purley on Thames 55 F1
Purton 34 B4
Pyott's Hill 161 H2
Quick's Green 38 A7
Quidhampton 171 J3
Ramsdell 142 D3
Ravenswood
  Village Settlement 117 K2
Reading 3 H6
Remenham 17 K5
Remenham Hill 32 B1
The Ridges 117 G4
Riseley 113 K5
Rotherfield Greys 29 K2
Rotherfield Peppard 29 G4
Rotherwick 147 H4
Rotten Green 150 E5
Rotten Row 68 C3
Ruscombe 46 D7
Ryeish Green 93 K3
Salters Heath 143 J2
Sandhurst 118 C7
Schoolgreen 94 A3
Scotland 67 G6
Sheffield Bottom 70 E6
Sherborne St John 143 J7
Sherfield on Loddon 146 B2
Shinfield 94 A2
Shiplake 45 H2
Shiplake Bottom 29 F5
Shiplake Row 44 E2
Silchester 128 A1
Sindlesham 75 J6
Skinners Green 82 E7
The Slade 66 B6
Sonning 59 G1
Sonning Common 29 G5
Sonning Eye 45 F7
South Ascot 101 K4
Southcote 72 C2
Southend 68 D4
South Ham 175 J1
Southington 171 G5
South View 14 E1
Spanish Green 130 C6
Speen 83 F2
Spencers Wood 93 G5
Stanford Dingley 68 A2
Stanford End 113 F5
Stockcross 82 C2
Stony Heath 142 A1
Stratfield Mortimer 111 J3
Stratfield Saye 130 C1
Stratfield Turgis 130 D5
Streatley 24 D4
Stroud Green 13 G7
Stubbles 37 K7
Sulham 54 D4
Sulhampstead Abbots 90 E3
Sulhampstead
  Bannister Upper End 90 C2
Sulhamstead 90 A1

Swallowfield 114 A2
Sydmonton 138 C2
Tadley 127 F2
Thatcham 85 H3
Theale 70 C3
Three Ashes 128 C2
Three Mile Cross 93 J3
The Throat 97 F6
Tidmarsh 54 A3
Tilehurst 55 K4
Tokers Green 42 E5
Tot Hill 103 H7
Towns End 125 H7
Trash Green 71 F7
Trench Green 42 B5
Tunworth 177 K6
Turgis Green 130 D6
Turner's Green 66 C7
Tutts Clump 68 C3
Twyford 46 D7
Ufton Green 90 A2
Ufton Nervet 90 C3
Up Green 134 D3
Up Nately 162 E7
Upper Basildon 38 D7
Upper Bucklebury 86 D1
Upper Woolhampton 87 J3
Upper Wootton 158 B1
Upton Grey 178 D7
Wadwick 152 B5
Waltham St Lawrence 47 K5
Warfield 80 B1
Wargrave 46 B3
Warnborough Green 164 A6
Warren Corner 183 H5
Warren Row 33 H5
Wash Common 103 G3
Wash Water 102 E5
Wasing 108 A3
Water End 162 E5
Wellhouse 65 K1
West End 61 K1
West End Green 129 J1
West Fields 12 B5
West Green 148 E5
West Ham 159 J6
West Heath 142 D1
Westridge Green 23 H7
Westrop Green 65 J3
Wheat Hold 125 F3
Wheeler's Green 75 K1
Whistley Green 60 D4
Whitchurch 169 H7
Whitchurch Hill 40 D2
Whitchurch-on-Thames 40 A5
Whitehall 164 E5
Whitehouse Green 91 F1
Whiteknights 8 E3
Whitley 7 J7
Whitley Wood 73 K7
Whitway 121 G5
Wick Hill 80 A5
Wick Hill 117 F2
Wildmoor 146 B5
Wildridings 10 C7
Winchfield 165 H1
Winchfield Hurst 165 K3
Winkfield 81 G1
Winkfield Row 80 D5
Winklebury 159 G5
Winnersh 76 A4
Winslade 177 G7
Winterbourne 63 F1
Wokingham 97 J1
Wolverton 141 G1
Wolverton Common 125 H6
Woodcote 26 D3
Woodcott 152 C1
Woodlands 31 H1
Woodley 59 J7
Woodley Green 59 J6
Woodspeen 62 D7
Woolhampton 87 K5
Woolton Hill 120 A7
Woose Hill 96 E1
Wootton St Lawrence 158 C4
World's End 34 B6
Worting 159 F6
Yateley 135 J3
Yattendon 51 F4

USING THE STREET INDEX

Street names are listed alphabetically. Each street name is followed by its postal town or area locality, the Postcode District, the page number, and the reference to the square in which the name is found.

Example: **Abbots CI** *GOR/PANG* RG8......................26 E3 🔢

Some entries are followed by a number in a blue box. This number indicates the location of the street within the referenced grid square. The full street name is listed at the side of the map page.

GENERAL ABBREVIATIONS

ACC......ACCESS	CHYD......CHURCHYARD	CTS......COURTS	FK......FORK	HGR......HIGHER	
ALY......ALLEY	CIR......CIRCLE	CTYD......COURTYARD	FLD......FIELD	HL......HILL	
AP......APPROACH	CIRC......CIRCUS	CUTT......CUTTINGS	FLDS......FIELDS	HLS......HILLS	
AR......ARCADE	CL......CLOSE	CV......COVE	FLS......FALLS	HO......HOUSE	
ASS......ASSOCIATION	CLFS......CLIFFS	CYN......CANYON	FLS......FLATS	HOL......HOLLOW	
AV......AVENUE	CMP......CAMP	DEPT......DEPARTMENT	FM......FARM	HOSP......HOSPITAL	
BCH......BEACH	CNR......CORNER	DL......DALE	FT......FORT	HRB......HARBOUR	
BLDS......BUILDINGS	CO......COUNTY	DM......DAM	FWY......FREEWAY	HTH......HEATH	
BND......BEND	COLL......COLLEGE	DR......DRIVE	FY......FERRY	HTS......HEIGHTS	
BNK......BANK	COM......COMMON	DRO......DROVE	GA......GATE	HVN......HAVEN	
BR......BRIDGE	COMM......COMMISSION	DRY......DRIVEWAY	GAL......GALLERY	HWY......HIGHWAY	
BRK......BROOK	CON......CONVENT	DWGS......DWELLINGS	GDN......GARDEN	IMP......IMPERIAL	
BTM......BOTTOM	COT......COTTAGE	E......EAST	GDNS......GARDENS	IN......INLET	
BUS......BUSINESS	COTS......COTTAGES	EMB......EMBANKMENT	GLD......GLADE	IND EST......INDUSTRIAL ESTATE	
BVD......BOULEVARD	CP......CAPE	EMBY......EMBASSY	GLN......GLEN	INF......INFIRMARY	
BY......BYPASS	CPS......COPSE	ESP......ESPLANADE	GN......GREEN	INFO......INFORMATION	
CATH......CATHEDRAL	CR......CREEK	EST......ESTATE	GND......GROUND	INT......INTERCHANGE	
CEM......CEMETERY	CREM......CREMATORIUM	EX......EXCHANGE	GRA......GRANGE	IS......ISLAND	
CEN......CENTRE	CRS......CRESCENT	EXPY......EXPRESSWAY	GRG......GARAGE	JCT......JUNCTION	
CFT......CROFT	CSWY......CAUSEWAY	EXT......EXTENSION	GT......GREAT	JTY......JETTY	
CH......CHURCH	CT......COURT	F/O......FLYOVER	GTWY......GATEWAY	KG......KING	
CHA......CHASE	CTRL......CENTRAL	FC......FOOTBALL CLUB	GV......GROVE	KNL......KNOLL	

L ...LAKE	MTS ...MOUNTAINS	PREC ...PRECINCT	SCH ...SCHOOL	TRL ...TRAIL
LA ...LANE	MUS ...MUSEUM	PREP ...PREPARATORY	SE ...SOUTH EAST	TWR ...TOWER
LDG ...LODGE	MWY ...MOTORWAY	PRIM ...PRIMARY	SER ...SERVICE AREA	U/P ...UNDERPASS
LGT ...LIGHT	N ...NORTH	PROM ...PROMENADE	SH ...SHORE	UNI ...UNIVERSITY
LK ...LOCK	NE ...NORTH EAST	PRS ...PRINCESS	SHOP ...SHOPPING	UPR ...UPPER
LKS ...LAKES	NW ...NORTH WEST	PRT ...PORT	SKWY ...SKYWAY	V ...VALE
LNDG ...LANDING	O/P ...OVERPASS	PT ...POINT	SMT ...SUMMIT	VA ...VALLEY
LTL ...LITTLE	OFF ...OFFICE	PTH ...PATH	SOC ...SOCIETY	VIAD ...VIADUCT
LWR ...LOWER	ORCH ...ORCHARD	PZ ...PIAZZA	SP ...SPUR	VIL ...VILLA
MAG ...MAGISTRATE	OV ...OVAL	QD ...QUADRANT	SPR ...SPRING	VIS ...VISTA
MAN ...MANSIONS	PAL ...PALACE	QU ...QUEEN	SQ ...SQUARE	VLG ...VILLAGE
MD ...MEAD	PAS ...PASSAGE	QY ...QUAY	ST ...STREET	VLS ...VILLAS
MDW ...MEADOWS	PAV ...PAVILION	R ...RIVER	STN ...STATION	VW ...VIEW
MEM ...MEMORIAL	PDE ...PARADE	RBT ...ROUNDABOUT	STR ...STREAM	W ...WEST
MKT ...MARKET	PH ...PUBLIC HOUSE	RD ...ROAD	STRD ...STRAND	WD ...WOOD
MKTS ...MARKETS	PK ...PARK	RDG ...RIDGE	SW ...SOUTH WEST	WHF ...WHARF
ML ...MALL	PKWY ...PARKWAY	REP ...REPUBLIC	TDG ...TRADING	WK ...WALK
ML ...MILL	PL ...PLACE	RES ...RESERVOIR	TER ...TERRACE	WKS ...WALKS
MNR ...MANOR	PLN ...PLAIN	RFC ...RUGBY FOOTBALL CLUB	THWY ...THROUGHWAY	WLS ...WELLS
MS ...MEWS	PLNS ...PLAINS	RI ...RISE	TNL ...TUNNEL	WY ...WAY
MSN ...MISSION	PLZ ...PLAZA	RP ...RAMP	TOLL ...TOLLWAY	YD ...YARD
MT ...MOUNT	POL ...POLICE STATION	RW ...ROW	TPK ...TURNPIKE	YHA ...YOUTH HOSTEL
MTN ...MOUNTAIN	PR ...PRINCE	S ...SOUTH	TR ...TRACK	

POSTCODE TOWNS AND AREA ABBREVIATIONS

ASC ...Ascot	CWTH ...Crowthorne	HTWY ...Hartley Wintney	RAND ...Rural Andover	WAR/TWY ...Wargrave/Twyford
BFOR ...Bracknell Forest/Windlesham	DEAN ...Deane/Oakley	KEMP ...Kempshott	RDGW ...Reading west	WDSR ...Windsor
BLKW ...Blackwater	DID ...Didcot	KSCL ...Kingsclere/Rural Newbury	READ ...Reading	WGFD ...Wallingford
BNFD ...Binfield	EARL ...Earley	MDHD ...Maidenhead	RFNM ...Rural Farnham	WHCH ...Whitchurch
BRAK ...Bracknell	EWKG ...Wokingham east	MLW ...Marlow	SHST ...Sandhurst	WHIT ...Whitley/Arborfield
BSTK ...Basingstoke	FARN ...Farnborough	NTHA ...Thatcham north	STHA ...Thatcham south	WODY ...Woodley
CAV/SC ...Caversham/Sonning Common	FLET ...Fleet	NWBY ...Newbury	TADY ...Tadley	WWKG ...Wokingham west
CBLY ...Camberley	GOR/PANG ...Goring/Pangbourne	ODIM ...Odiham	THLE ...Theale/Rural Reading	YTLY ...Yateley
CHIN ...Chineham	HEN ...Henley-on-Thames	OVTN ...Overton/Rural Basingstoke	TLHT ...Tilehurst	

Index - streets

A

Abattoirs Rd *READ* RG1 .... 3 G4
Abbey Cl *BRAK* RG12 .... 100 A3
EWKG RG40 .... 77 H7
NWBY RG14 .... 12 F9
Abbey Pk *THLE* RG7 .... 90 E4
Abbey Rd *CHAM* RG24 .... 160 B2
Abbey Sq *READ* RG1 .... 3 K6
Abbey St *READ* RG1 .... 3 K6
Abbotsbury *BRAK* RG12 .... 99 C3
Abbots Cl *FLET* GU13 .... 167 H2
GOR/PANG RG8 .... 26 E5
Abbotsmead Pl *READ* RG1 .... 3 G1
Abbots Rd *NWBY* RG14 .... 12 F7
THLE RG7 .... 90 E4
Abbot's Wk *READ* RG1 .... 3 K5
Abbott Cl *KEMP* RG22 .... 175 J1
Abbottswood Cl *TADY* RG26 .... 126 E2
Aberaman *CAV/SC* RG4 .... 43 G6
Aberford Cl *TLHT* RG30 .... 56 D6
Abex Rd *NWBY* RG14 .... 13 K4
Abingdon Cl *BRAK* RG12 .... 11 L9
Abingdon Dr *CAV/SC* RG4 .... 43 K6
Abingdon Rd *KSCL* RG20 .... 20 D4
Abrahams La *HEN* RG9 .... 17 F7
Acacia Av *SHST* GU47 .... 118 E7
Acacia Ct *BRAK* RG12 .... 10 E6
Acacia Rd *READ* RG1 .... 3 M9
Achilles Cl *CHAM* RG24 .... 145 G6
Ackrells Md *SHST* GU47 .... 118 A7
Acorn Dr *EWKG* RG40 .... 77 H7
NTHA RG18 .... 85 J2
Acre Rd *WHIT* RG2 .... 73 H6
Adam Cl *TADY* RG26 .... 108 B7
Adam Ct *HEN* RG9 .... 31 G1
Adams Dr *FLET* GU13 .... 167 J2
Adams Wy *EARL* RG6 .... 8 F7
Addington Rd *READ* RG1 .... 4 A9
Addiscombe Cha *CALC* RG31 .... 55 G2
Addiscombe Rd *CWTH* RG45 .... 118 D4
Addison Gdns *ODIM* RG29 .... 180 D1
Addison Rd *READ* RG1 .... 3 C3
Adelaide Rd *EARL* RG6 .... 9 H1
Adey's Cl *NWBY* RG14 .... 13 G7
Adkins Rd *WAR/TWY* RG10 .... 47 K5
Admirals Ct *WHIT* RG2 .... 3 G9
WHIT RG2 .... 7 G1
Admoor La *THLE* RG7 .... 69 F4
Adrian Cl *HTWY* RG27 .... 149 J5
Adwell Dr *EARL* RG6 .... 9 M9
EARL RG6 .... 75 G5
Adwell Sq *HEN* RG9 .... 31 G1
Adwood Ct *STHA* RG19 .... 85 K4
Agar Crs *BNFD* RG42 .... 79 C3
Agate Cl *READ* RG1 .... 76 D7
Aggisters La *WWKG* RG41 .... 96 B4
Aghemund Cl *CHAM* RG24 .... 145 F7
Agincourt Cl *WWKG* RG41 .... 96 D1
Agricola Wy *STHA* RG19 .... 86 A5
Ainsdale Crs *TLHT* RG30 .... 72 B2
Aintree Cl *NWBY* RG14 .... 13 J8
Aird Cl *KSCL* RG20 .... 120 B1
Ajax Cl *CHAM* RG24 .... 145 G6
Alanbrooke Cl *HTWY* RG27 .... 149 H4
Alandale Cl *WHIT* RG2 .... 74 A6
Albany Cl *FLET* GU13 .... 167 J3
Albany Park Dr *WWKG* RG41 .... 75 G3
Albany Rd *FLET* GU13 .... 167 H3
TLHT RG30 .... 2 B6
Alben Rd *BNFD* RG42 .... 78 D3
Albert Illsley Cl *CALC* RG31 .... 55 J5
Albert Rd *BNFD* RG42 .... 10 F2
CAV/SC RG4 .... 57 C1
CWTH RG45 .... 118 C3
EWKG RG40 .... 97 C2
HEN RG9 .... 31 H2
NWBY RG14 .... 12 D3
Albert St *FLET* GU13 .... 167 C2
Albury Cl *TLHT* RG30 .... 56 D4
Albury Gdns *CALC* RG31 .... 71 K3
Alcot Cl *CWTH* RG45 .... 118 C4
Aldbourne Av *EARL* RG6 .... 9 H4
Aldeburgh Cl *CAV/SC* RG4 .... 43 K4

Aldenham Cl *CAV/SC* RG4 .... 43 K6
Aldenham Ter *BRAK* RG12 .... 99 K4
Alderbrook Cl *CWTH* RG45 .... 117 K4
Alder Cl *EARL* RG6 .... 75 C5
Alder Dr *CALC* RG31 .... 55 H7
Alderfield Cl *THLE* RG7 .... 70 E2
Alder Gld *THLE* RG7 .... 90 E4
Alder Gv *YTLY* GU46 .... 135 H4
Alderley Cl *WODY* RG5 .... 59 J4
Alderman Willey Cl
EWKG RG40 .... 97 G1
Aldermaston Rd *TADY* RG26 .... 108 D6
TADY RG26 .... 127 G4
Aldermaston Rd South
BSTK RG21 .... 14 A1
Alderney Av *KEMP* RG22 .... 175 G5
Alderney Gdns *WWKG* RG41 .... 76 C4
Aldershot Rd *FLET* GU13 .... 167 K6
The Alders *NTHA* RG18 .... 85 J3
Alderwood *CHAM* RG24 .... 145 G7
Alder Wood Dr *HTWY* RG27 .... 164 A1
Aldridge Pk *BNFD* RG42 .... 80 E4
Aldworth Cl *BRAK* RG12 .... 10 D8
TLHT RG30 .... 72 D1
Aldworth Crs *KEMP* RG22 .... 159 K7
Aldworth Gdns *CWTH* RG45 .... 118 B3
Aldworth Rd *GOR/PANG* RG8 .... 38 D6
KSCL RG20 .... 21 K7
Alexander Rd *OVTN* RG25 .... 171 H5
STHA RG19 .... 85 K5
Alexandra Ct *EWKG* RG40 .... 97 H2
Alexandra Rd *BSTK* RG21 .... 14 B5
READ RG1 .... 8 B1
Alford Cl *TLHT* RG30 .... 55 J5
Alfred St *READ* RG1 .... 2 F6
Alison Cl *THLE* RG7 .... 90 E6
Allcroft Rd *READ* RG1 .... 7 M1
Allen Cl *BSTK* RG21 .... 14 A8
Allendale Cl *SHST* GU47 .... 118 B6
Allendale Rd *EARL* RG6 .... 9 M9
All Hallows Rd *CAV/SC* RG4 .... 58 A2
Allison Gdns *GOR/PANG* RG8 .... 41 H7
Alliston Wy *KEMP* RG22 .... 175 H1
Allnatt Av *WWKG* RG41 .... 97 H4
Allnutt Av *BSTK* RG21 .... 15 H5
Allonby Cl *EARL* RG6 .... 75 G4
All Saints Ri *BNFD* RG42 .... 80 B5
Allsmoor La *BRAK* RG12 .... 100 C1
All Souls' Rd *ASC* SL5 .... 101 K3
Alma St *TLHT* RG30 .... 56 D5
Almond Av *NWBY* RG14 .... 83 K2
Almond Cl *CHAM* RG24 .... 161 H5
WWKG RG41 .... 96 B3
Almond Dr *CAV/SC* RG4 .... 58 C1
NTHA RG18 .... 85 J3
Almswood Rd *TADY* RG26 .... 108 D6
Alphington Rd *WHIT* RG2 .... 73 J6
Alpine Ct *KEMP* RG22 .... 175 F1
Alpine St *READ* RG1 .... 3 J9
Alston Ms *STHA* RG19 .... 85 H5
Alton Rd *FLET* GU13 .... 167 K2
ODIM RG29 .... 180 C3
Amazon Cl *BSTK* RG21 .... 14 A6
Ambarrow Crs *SHST* GU47 .... 118 A7
Ambarrow La *CWTH* RG45 .... 117 J6
Ambassador *BRAK* RG12 .... 99 G3
Amberley Cl *NWBY* RG14 .... 12 C1
Amberley Dr *WAR/TWY* RG10 .... 46 C6
Amblecote Rd *TLHT* RG30 .... 56 C6
Ambleside Cl *WODY* RG5 .... 59 H6
Ambrook Rd *WHIT* RG2 .... 73 J6
Ambrose Pl *READ* RG1 .... 2 F6
Ambrose Rd *TADY* RG26 .... 126 E1
Ambury Rd *GOR/PANG* RG8 .... 23 F6
Amersham Rd *CAV/SC* RG4 .... 4 A1
Amethyst Cl *WWKG* RG41 .... 76 C7
Amethyst La *TLHT* RG30 .... 56 D7
Amherst Rd *EARL* RG6 .... 5 C9
Amity Rd *READ* RG1 .... 4 C6
Amity St *READ* RG1 .... 4 C5
Ammanford *CAV/SC* RG4 .... 43 G7
Amners Farm Rd *TLHT* RG30 .... 72 A6
Ampere Rd *NWBY* RG14 .... 13 G3

Amport Cl *CHAM* RG24 .... 161 H3
Ancaster Dr *ASC* SL5 .... 81 H6
Ancastle Gn *HEN* RG9 .... 31 F2
Ancells Rd *FARN* GU14 .... 151 J5
Anchor Rd *KSCL* RG20 .... 124 A7
Anchor Yd *BSTK* RG21 .... 14 F6
Anderson Av *EARL* RG6 .... 9 H4
Anderson Crs *WHIT* RG2 .... 95 H5
Andover Cl *CALC* RG31 .... 55 J4
Andover Dro *KSCL* RG20 .... 102 E4
Andover Rd *DEAN* RG23 .... 173 G3
KSCL RG20 .... 102 E6
NWBY RG14 .... 103 H1
OVTN RG25 .... 172 D4
Andrew Cl *EWKG* RG40 .... 97 K2
Andrews Cl *FLET* GU13 .... 167 H5
THLE RG7 .... 70 D3
Andrews Rd *EARL* RG6 .... 9 J5
Andwell La *HTWY* RG27 .... 162 D5
Angel Ct *NWBY* RG14 .... 12 E2
Angel Md *THLE* RG7 .... 87 K5
Angel Mdw *ODIM* RG29 .... 180 D1
Angel Pl *BNFD* RG42 .... 78 D4
Angle Field Rd *CAV/SC* RG4 .... 57 K2
Anglers Wy *READ* RG1 .... 4 A6
Anglesey Cl *CHAM* RG24 .... 160 D1
Angora Wy *FARN* GU14 .... 151 J6
Angus Cl *CALC* RG31 .... 71 K2
Annadale *NTHA* RG18 .... 65 H5
Anneforde Pl *BNFD* RG42 .... 79 H5
Annesley Gdns *WWKG* RG41 .... 76 B3
Annes Wy *FLET* GU13 .... 167 F7
Annettes Cft *FLET* GU13 .... 167 F7
Anson Crs *WHIT* RG2 .... 74 A7
Anstey Cl *BSTK* RG21 .... 176 B2
Anstey Pl *THLE* RG7 .... 91 F4
Anstey Rd *READ* RG1 .... 3 G7
Anston Cl *EARL* RG6 .... 74 D6
Antar Cl *BSTK* RG21 .... 14 A8
Antares Cl *WWKG* RG41 .... 96 E1
Anthian Cl *WODY* RG5 .... 60 A5
Anton Cl *DEAN* RG23 .... 174 A3
Antrim Cl *KEMP* RG22 .... 175 G1
Antrim Rd *WODY* RG5 .... 59 G7
Anvil Cl *THLE* RG7 .... 93 H6
Appelford Cl *STHA* RG19 .... 85 J5
Appleby End *TLHT* RG30 .... 56 C6
Apple Cl *CALC* RG31 .... 55 G1
WWKG RG41 .... 96 E2
Appledore *BRAK* RG12 .... 99 G4
Appleford Rd *TLHT* RG30 .... 72 B2
Applegarth Cl *BSTK* RG21 .... 15 G8
Apple Tree Cl *NWBY* RG14 .... 103 H1
Appletree Cl *CAV/SC* RG4 .... 29 F5
DEAN RG23 .... 174 A4
Appletree La *THLE* RG7 .... 93 J5
Appletree Pl *BNFD* RG42 .... 10 C2
Apple Tree Wy *SHST* GU47 .... 118 E7
Apple Wy *CHAM* RG24 .... 161 J6
Apsey Ct *BNFD* RG42 .... 79 F5
Aquila Cl *WWKG* RG41 .... 96 D1
Arborfield Rd *WHIT* RG2 .... 94 C3
Arbor La *WWKG* RG41 .... 76 A3
Arbor Mdw *WWKG* RG41 .... 76 A3
Arbour Cl *READ* RG1 .... 6 A2
Archangel Wy *NTHA* RG18 .... 86 A3
Archery Flds *ODIM* RG29 .... 180 E1
Archway Rd *READ* RG1 .... 3 H1
Arden Cl *BRAK* RG12 .... 80 D7
Ardglen Rd *WHCH* RG28 .... 169 G7
Ardingly *BRAK* RG12 .... 99 H4
Ardwell Cl *CWTH* RG45 .... 117 K3
Arenal Dr *CWTH* RG45 .... 118 C3
Argente Cl *FARN* GU14 .... 151 J6
Argyle Rd *NWBY* RG14 .... 12 D6
READ RG1 .... 2 D7
Argyle St *READ* RG1 .... 2 D6
Arkle Av *STHA* RG19 .... 84 E4
Arkwright Cl *KSCL* RG20 .... 120 C3
Arkwright Dr *BNFD* RG42 .... 78 C4
Arkwright Rd *WHIT* RG2 .... 7 J5
Arlington Cl *BNFD* RG42 .... 10 C1
Arlott Dr *BSTK* RG21 .... 14 F1
Armadale Ct *TLHT* RG30 .... 2 A9
Armour Hl *CALC* RG31 .... 55 J4
Armour Rd *CALC* RG31 .... 55 J4

Armour Wk *CALC* RG31 .... 55 J4
Armstrong Rd *CHAM* RG24 .... 15 L1
Armstrong Wy *WODY* RG5 .... 59 K6
Arncliffe *BRAK* RG12 .... 10 C8
Arne Cl *KEMP* RG22 .... 175 K2
Arnett Av *EWKG* RG40 .... 116 D1
Arnhem Rd *NWBY* RG14 .... 13 H4
Arnside Cl *WAR/TWY* RG10 .... 46 C5
Arran Cl *DEAN* RG23 .... 173 K2
Arrowhead Rd *THLE* RG7 .... 70 E4
Arrow La *HTWY* RG27 .... 149 G3
Arrow Smith Wy *STHA* RG19 .... 86 A5
Arthur Rd *NWBY* RG14 .... 12 B6
WWKG RG41 .... 77 F7
Arthurstone Birches
BNFD RG42 .... 78 E3
Arun Cl *WWKG* RG41 .... 76 A5
Arundel Cl *FLET* GU13 .... 167 J3
Arundel Gdns *DEAN* RG23 .... 159 G4
Arundel Rd *WODY* RG5 .... 59 H7
Arwood Av *TADY* RG26 .... 109 G7
Ascension Cl *CHAM* RG24 .... 160 D2
Ascot Cl *NWBY* RG14 .... 13 J9
Ashampstead Rd
GOR/PANG RG8 .... 38 B6
THLE RG7 .... 53 F6
TLHT RG30 .... 72 C2
Ashbourne *BRAK* RG12 .... 99 G4
Ashbourne Wy *STHA* RG19 .... 85 G4
Ashburton Rd *WHIT* RG2 .... 7 M7
Ashbury Dr *CALC* RG31 .... 55 H6
Ashby Ct *WHIT* RG2 .... 73 J7
Ashcroft Cl *CAV/SC* RG4 .... 43 F7
Ashdale Pk *EWKG* RG40 .... 117 H1
Ashdown Cl *BRAK* RG12 .... 80 C7
Ashe Dr *ASC* SL5 .... 81 F6
Ashfield *CHAM* RG24 .... 145 G2
Ashford Av *CAV/SC* RG4 .... 29 F6
Ashford Hill Rd *STHA* RG19 .... 105 J6
Ash Ga *NTHA* RG18 .... 86 A3
Ash Gv *CHAM* RG24 .... 161 K5
KSCL RG20 .... 124 A7
Ash La *TADY* RG26 .... 108 B7
TADY RG26 .... 128 C4
Ashlea *HTWY* RG27 .... 164 A1
Ashlee Wk *GOR/PANG* RG8 .... 26 E3
Ashley Cl *EARL* RG6 .... 9 K8
NFNM GU10 .... 182 E5
Ashley Rd *READ* RG1 .... 6 C1
Ashman Rd *STHA* RG19 .... 86 A4
Ashmere Cl *CALC* RG31 .... 71 H2
Ashmere Ter *TLHT* RG30 .... 2 C4
Ashmoor La *CHAM* RG24 .... 162 B5
Ashmore Green Rd *NTHA* RG18 .... 65 F7
Ashmore Rd *WHIT* RG2 .... 7 L9
Ashridge Gn *BNFD* RG42 .... 10 E1
Ashridge Rd *EWKG* RG40 .... 77 J6
Ash Rd *KSCL* RG20 .... 104 C5
TLHT RG30 .... 55 K6
Ash Ter *NTHA* RG18 .... 65 G6
Ashton Cl *CALC* RG31 .... 55 H5
Ashton Rd *WWKG* RG41 .... 76 E5
Ash Tree Cl *DEAN* RG23 .... 173 K4
Ashtrees Rd *WODY* RG5 .... 59 J5
Ashurst Cl *TADY* RG26 .... 126 D1
Ashville Wy *WWKG* RG41 .... 97 F2
Ash Wy *WWKG* RG41 .... 96 C4
Ashwood *WODY* RG5 .... 75 G1
Ashwood Cl *CALC* RG31 .... 55 G7
Ashwood Dr *NWBY* RG14 .... 13 M2
Ashwood Wy *DEAN* RG23 .... 159 J4
Ashworth Dr *STHA* RG19 .... 85 H5
Askew Dr *THLE* RG7 .... 93 J4
Aspen Gdns *HTWY* RG27 .... 164 A1
Aster Cl *KEMP* RG22 .... 175 F5
Astley Cl *WWKG* RG41 .... 76 E7
Aston Av *CALC* RG31 .... 55 G5
Aston Cl *CAV/SC* RG4 .... 43 K5
Aston Ct *GOR/PANG* RG8 .... 40 C7
Aston Ferry La *HEN* RG9 .... 18 B5
Aston La *HEN* RG9 .... 18 B7
Astor Cl *WWKG* RG41 .... 76 C5
Astra Md *BNFD* RG42 .... 80 E4
Atbara Rd *FLET* GU13 .... 167 H7
Atherton Cl *TLHT* RG30 .... 56 A5
Atrebatti Rd *SHST* GU47 .... 118 D7

Attebrouche Ct *BRAK* RG12 .... 100 A5
Atte La *BNFD* RG42 .... 79 K4
Attenborough Cl *FARN* GU14 .... 151 J7
Attlee Gdns *FLET* GU13 .... 167 G7
Attwood Cl *BSTK* RG21 .... 14 A7
Auckland Rd *EARL* RG6 .... 5 C9
Auclum Cl *THLE* RG7 .... 91 C5
Auclum La *THLE* RG7 .... 91 C5
Audley Cl *NWBY* RG14 .... 84 C2
Audley St *TLHT* RG30 .... 2 B5
Audley Wy *ASC* SL5 .... 101 C1
August End *TLHT* RG30 .... 56 D5
Augustine Wk *BNFD* RG42 .... 80 B5
Augustus Dr *DEAN* RG23 .... 159 H4
Auklet Cl *KEMP* RG22 .... 174 E5
Austen Gv *KEMP* RG22 .... 175 K2
Austin Rd *WODY* RG5 .... 59 J7
Auton Pl *HEN* RG9 .... 31 G3
Autumn Cl *CAV/SC* RG4 .... 43 K5
Autumn Wk *WAR/TWY* RG10 .... 46 C2
Avalon Rd *EARL* RG6 .... 9 L5
Avebury *BRAK* RG12 .... 99 H4
Avebury Sq *READ* RG1 .... 8 B1
Avenue Rd *FLET* GU13 .... 167 G1
The Avenue *ASC* SL5 .... 81 J5
CWTH RG45 .... 118 B3
FLET GU13 .... 167 F2
THLE RG7 .... 111 C3
Averton Cl *BNFD* RG42 .... 79 J5
Avery Cl *EWKG* RG40 .... 116 E2
Avington Cl *CALC* RG31 .... 55 G5
Avondale Rd *FLET* GU13 .... 167 H1
Avon Gv *BRAK* RG12 .... 79 K5
Avon Pl *READ* RG1 .... 4 B5
Avon Rd *DEAN* RG23 .... 174 A3
Avonway *NWBY* RG14 .... 13 M1
Avon Wy *THLE* RG7 .... 89 H1
Award Rd *FLET* GU13 .... 167 G6
Axbridge *BRAK* RG12 .... 100 B3
Axbridge Rd *WHIT* RG2 .... 7 M8
Ayesgarth *FLET* GU13 .... 167 J6
Aylesford Wy *STHA* RG19 .... 86 B5
Aylesham Wy *YTLY* GU46 .... 135 G3
Aylings Cl *DEAN* RG23 .... 159 G7
Aylsham Cl *TLHT* RG30 .... 55 K5
Aylwin Cl *BSTK* RG21 .... 176 B2
Ayres La *KSCL* RG20 .... 121 J1
Ayrshire Gdns *FARN* GU14 .... 151 J6
Ayrton Senna Rd *CALC* RG31 .... 55 H6
Aysgarth *BRAK* RG12 .... 99 G4
Azalea Cl *WWKG* RG41 .... 76 A4
Azalea Gdns *FLET* GU13 .... 167 J6

B

Babbington Rd *WHIT* RG2 .... 94 A1
Bach Cl *KEMP* RG22 .... 175 J5
Back La *THLE* RG7 .... 68 C3
THLE RG7 .... 88 D1
THLE RG7 .... 93 H7
THLE RG7 .... 107 J5
THLE RG7 .... 110 B4
Backsideans *WAR/TWY* RG10 .... 46 C2
The Bader Wy *WODY* RG5 .... 75 K1
Badgemore La *HEN* RG9 .... 17 G7
Badger Dr *WAR/TWY* RG10 .... 46 C5
Badger's Bank *CHAM* RG24 .... 161 G3
Badgers Cl *FLET* GU13 .... 167 G3
Badgers Gld *THLE* RG7 .... 91 F5
Badgers Holt *YTLY* GU46 .... 135 G4
Badgers Ri *CAV/SC* RG4 .... 43 H7
Badgers Sett *CWTH* RG45 .... 118 A3
Badgers Wk *HEN* RG9 .... 45 K1
Badgers Wy *BRAK* RG12 .... 80 C6
Bagnols Wy *NWBY* RG14 .... 12 A6
Bagshot Rd *BRAK* RG12 .... 10 B5
BRAK RG12 .... 99 K4
Bagwell La *ODIM* RG29 .... 165 H4
Bailey's La *WAR/TWY* RG10 .... 61 K1
Baily Av *NTHA* RG18 .... 85 G3
Bainbridge Rd *CALC* RG31 .... 71 G2
Baird Av *KEMP* RG22 .... 175 K2
Baird Rd *WHIT* RG2 .... 95 H3

Baker St READ RG1 ...... 2 E7
Baldons Cl GOR/PANG RG8 ...... 26 E3
Balfour Crs BRAK RG12 ...... 99 J3
  NWBY RG14 ...... 103 F3
Balfour Dr CALC RG31 ...... 71 G2
Ballamoor Cl CALC RG31 ...... 71 F2
Ballard Cl KEMP RG22 ...... 175 J4
Balliol Rd CAV/SC RG4 ...... 56 E2
Balliol Wy SHST GU47 ...... 119 F7
Ball Pit Rd KSCL RG20 ...... 20 B5
Balme Cl WAR/TWY RG10 ...... 60 A2
Balmoral Wy KEMP RG22 ...... 175 F5
Balmore Dr CAV/SC RG4 ...... 57 J1
Balmore Pk CAV/SC RG4 ...... 57 H1
Bamburgh Cl WHIT RG2 ...... 7 M5
Bamford Pl CALC RG31 ...... 71 G2
Banbury Rd 100 B5
Banbury Gdns CAV/SC RG4 ...... 57 K2
Bancroft Cl CALC RG31 ...... 71 G3
Bank Side EWKG RG40 ...... 116 E2
Bankside Cl WHIT RG2 ...... 8 B7
Bannister Gdns HTWY RG27 ...... 134 D1
Bannister Pl THLE RG7 ...... 107 G2
Bannister Rd THLE RG7 ...... 90 E5
Barbara Cl FLET GU13 ...... 167 J5
Barbara's Meadow CALC RG31 ...... 55 G3
Barbel Av BSTK RG21 ...... 15 K4
Barbel Cl EARL RG6 ...... 5 H4
Barber Cl WAR/TWY RG10 ...... 60 D6
Barberry Cl FLET GU13 ...... 167 H5
Barbour Cl ODIM RG29 ...... 180 B5
Barbrook Cl CALC RG31 ...... 55 J2
Barclay Rd CALC RG31 ...... 71 J2
Barclose Av CAV/SC RG4 ...... 57 K2
Bardolph's Cl CAV/SC RG4 ...... 42 E4
Bardwell Cl KEMP RG22 ...... 159 H7
The Baredown HTWY RG27 ...... 163 G4
Barefoot Cl CALC RG31 ...... 55 G4
Barfield Rd NTHA RG18 ...... 85 F3
Barge La THLE RG7 ...... 113 H3
Barholm Cl EARL RG6 ...... 75 H4
Barkby EARL RG6 ...... 9 M8
Barker Cl WHIT RG2 ...... 115 H1
Barker Ct WAR/TWY RG10 ...... 60 E5
Barkham Ride EWKG RG40 ...... 96 B6
  EWKG RG40 ...... 116 E1
  WWKG RG41 ...... 95 K5
Barkham Rd WHIT RG2 ...... 95 H4
  WWKG RG41 ...... 95 K5
Barkham St EWKG RG40 ...... 96 B5
Barkhart Dr EWKG RG40 ...... 77 H7
Barkhart Gdns EWKG RG40 ...... 77 H7
Barkis Md SHST GU47 ...... 119 F6
Barkwith Cl EARL RG6 ...... 75 H4
Barley Md BNFD RG42 ...... 80 B5
Barley Mow Cl HTWY RG27 ...... 166 A3
Barley Wy FARN GU14 ...... 151 J3
Barlows Rd TADY RG26 ...... 126 E2
Barnard Cl CAV/SC RG4 ...... 43 K6
Barn Cl BRAK RG12 ...... 11 K3
  TLHT RG30 ...... 6 A3
Barn Crs NWBY RG14 ...... 103 G1
Barnett Ct BRAK RG12 ...... 11 H3
Barnett Gn BRAK RG12 ...... 99 J4
Barnfield YTLY GU46 ...... 135 J4
Barn La DEAN RG23 ...... 173 K4
  HEN RG9 ...... 17 F6
Barn Meadow Cl FLET GU13 ...... 183 C1
Barn Owl Wy THLE RG7 ...... 91 G4
Barnsdale Rd WHIT RG2 ...... 8 B5
Barnwood Cl TLHT RG30 ...... 2 C4
Baron Ct TLHT RG30 ...... 2 C7
Baronsmead HEN RG9 ...... 31 G1
Barracane Dr CWTH RG45 ...... 118 C4
Barracks La WWKG RG41 ...... 97 J1
Barracks Rd STHA RG19 ...... 104 E4
Barra Cl DEAN RG23 ...... 173 K2
Barrett Crs EWKG RG40 ...... 97 J1
Barrett's La WHIT RG2 ...... 95 G1
Barrington Cl EARL RG6 ...... 5 J9
Barrington Wy READ RG1 ...... 6 C1
Barron Pl READ RG24 ...... 159 G3
Barry Pl READ RG1 ...... 3 G3
Barry Sq BRAK RG12 ...... 100 A3
Barry Wy KEMP RG22 ...... 175 J5
Bartholomew Pl BNFD RG42 ...... 80 B5
Bartholomew St NWBY RG14 ...... 12 D6
Bartlemy Cl NWBY RG14 ...... 12 A9
Bartlemy Rd NWBY RG14 ...... 12 A9
Bartley Wy HTWY RG27 ...... 164 B3
Bartok Cl KEMP RG22 ...... 175 K3
Barton Rd CALC RG31 ...... 55 G7
Barton's Dr YTLY GU46 ...... 135 J3
Bartons La CHAM RG24 ...... 161 H3
Barwell Cl CWTH RG45 ...... 118 A4
Basemoors BRAK RG12 ...... 11 L3
Basil Cl EARL RG6 ...... 74 C5
Basingbourne Cl FLET GU13 ...... 167 G6
Basingbourne Rd FLET GU13 ...... 167 G6
Basing Rd CHAM RG24 ...... 15 M3
  CHAM RG24 ...... 161 G5
Basingstoke Rd HTWY RG27 ...... 131 G2
  KSCL RG20 ...... 124 B7
  TADY RG26 ...... 142 B2
  THLE RG7 ...... 88 D6
  THLE RG7 ...... 93 H2
  THLE RG7 ...... 113 J1
  WHIT RG2 ...... 7 K5
  WHIT RG2 ...... 73 J5
Basing Vw BSTK RG21 ...... 15 H3
Baskerville La HEN RG9 ...... 45 K1
Baskerville Rd CAV/SC RG4 ...... 29 F6
Baslow Rd WWKG RG41 ...... 76 A4
Basmore La HEN RG9 ...... 45 K2
Bassett Cl EARL RG6 ...... 75 F6
Batchelor Dr CHAM RG24 ...... 161 K6
Batcombe Md BRAK RG12 ...... 100 B5
Bath Rd CALC RG31 ...... 71 J1
  CAV/SC RG4 ...... 59 G4
  EARL RG6 ...... 5 M3
  NTHA RG18 ...... 84 E3
  NWBY RG14 ...... 2 D9
  READ RG1 ...... 2 D9
  THLE RG7 ...... 70 C4
  THLE RG7 ...... 87 G5
  THLE RG7 ...... 89 G2
  TLHT RG30 ...... 6 A1
  WAR/TWY RG10 ...... 47 K1
Bathurst Rd WWKG RG41 ...... 76 A4

Battens Av OVTN RG25 ...... 171 J4
Battery End NWBY RG14 ...... 103 G2
Battle Cl NWBY RG14 ...... 83 G3
Battle Rd GOR/PANG RG8 ...... 25 J4
  NWBY RG14 ...... 103 F2
Battle St READ RG1 ...... 3 H2
Batty's Barn Cl EWKG RG40 ...... 97 J2
Baughurst Rd TADY RG26 ...... 126 B4
  TADY RG26 ...... 142 B2
  THLE RG7 ...... 109 K2
The Baxendales NWBY RG14 ...... 13 J8
Bay Cl EARL RG6 ...... 8 E9
Baydon Dr READ RG1 ...... 6 D1
Bayford Dr CALC RG31 ...... 72 A2
Bayley Ct WWKG RG41 ...... 76 A5
Bayliss Rd WAR/TWY RG10 ...... 46 C3
Baynard Cl BSTK RG21 ...... 15 G1
Bay Rd BRAK RG12 ...... 11 L3
Bay Tree Ri CALC RG31 ...... 71 H1
Beach's Crs TADY RG26 ...... 127 K6
Beacon Hill Rd FLET GU13 ...... 167 J7
Beaconsfield Rd BSTK RG21 ...... 14 F7
Beaconsfield Wy EARL RG6 ...... 9 G8
Beal's La CALC RG31 ...... 55 F6
Beal's Pightle TADY RG26 ...... 142 E3
Beancroft Rd STHA RG19 ...... 85 J5
Bean Oak Rd EWKG RG40 ...... 97 K1
Bear Hl KSCL RG20 ...... 139 K1
Bear La NWBY RG14 ...... 12 E4
  WAR/TWY RG10 ...... 47 G2
Bearwood FLET GU13 ...... 167 H2
Bearwood Pth WWKG RG41 ...... 75 K4
Bearwood Rd WWKG RG41 ...... 76 A4
Beatty Dr TLHT RG30 ...... 55 K5
Beauchief Cl EARL RG6 ...... 74 C6
Beauclerk Gn HTWY RG27 ...... 165 H2
Beaufield Cl WODY RG5 ...... 59 G6
Beaufort Gdns ASC SL5 ...... 81 H6
Beaufort Rd FLET GU13 ...... 167 J4
Beaulieu Cl BRAK RG12 ...... 100 C1
Beaumont Gdns BRAK RG12 ...... 11 J9
Beaurepaire Cl TADY RG26 ...... 128 E6
Beaver Cl WWKG RG41 ...... 97 G4
Beaver La YTLY GU46 ...... 135 K4
Beavers Cl TADY RG26 ...... 108 C7
Beaver Wy WODY RG5 ...... 60 A6
Beck Ct READ RG1 ...... 3 M9
Beckett Cl DEAN RG23 ...... 159 F6
  EWKG RG40 ...... 97 K1
Beckford Av BRAK RG12 ...... 99 J4
Beckford Cl WWKG RG41 ...... 76 E5
Beckfords GOR/PANG RG8 ...... 38 D7
Beckley Cl GOR/PANG RG8 ...... 26 E3
Bec Tithe GOR/PANG RG8 ...... 40 D7
Beddington Ct CHAM RG24 ...... 161 H2
Bedford Cl NWBY RG14 ...... 103 F3
Bedford Gdns WWKG RG41 ...... 76 E6
Bedford Rd READ RG1 ...... 2 E5
Bedfordshire Down BNFD RG42 ...... 80 C4
Bedfordshire Wy WWKG RG41 ...... 96 D1
Beecham Berry KEMP RG22 ...... 175 J5
Beech Cl NTHA RG18 ...... 36 B7
  OVTN RG25 ...... 171 J2
  TADY RG26 ...... 129 H7
  TLHT RG30 ...... 91 G3
Beechcrest Vw HTWY RG27 ...... 164 A1
Beechcroft NTHA RG18 ...... 36 B7
The Beeches CALC RG31 ...... 55 J2
  GOR/PANG RG8 ...... 24 E6
  KEMP RG22 ...... 175 J6
Beech Gln BRAK RG12 ...... 10 E7
Beech Hill Rd THLE RG7 ...... 113 F2
Beech La EARL RG6 ...... 9 H7
  GOR/PANG RG8 ...... 25 J2
Beechnut Cl WWKG RG41 ...... 96 E2
Beech Ride FLET GU13 ...... 167 G4
Beech Ri CAV/SC RG4 ...... 29 F5
Beech Rd CAV/SC RG4 ...... 42 E5
  GOR/PANG RG8 ...... 41 F7
  KSCL RG20 ...... 105 F6
  WHIT RG2 ...... 8 D8
Beech Tree Cl DEAN RG23 ...... 173 K4
Beech Wk STHA RG19 ...... 85 K5
Beech Wy DEAN RG23 ...... 159 H4
Beechwood Av CALC RG31 ...... 55 J5
  WODY RG5 ...... 59 G6
Beechwood Cl ASC SL5 ...... 81 H5
  FLET GU13 ...... 167 F5
  GOR/PANG RG8 ...... 26 C5
  KEMP RG22 ...... 175 H6
Beedon Dr BRAK RG12 ...... 98 E4
Beehive La BRAK RG12 ...... 78 D7
Beehive Rd BRAK RG12 ...... 78 E7
Beeson Cl GOR/PANG RG8 ...... 26 E3
Beeston Wy EARL RG6 ...... 74 D6
Beethoven Rd KEMP RG22 ...... 175 K4
Beggars Hill Rd WODY RG5 ...... 60 A4
Beggarwood La DEAN RG23 ...... 175 F7
  KEMP RG22 ...... 175 J6
Begonia Cl KEMP RG22 ...... 175 F5
Behoes La GOR/PANG RG8 ...... 26 C2
Beighton Cl EARL RG6 ...... 74 C6
Belle Av EARL RG6 ...... 9 K7
Bellevue WHCH RG28 ...... 169 H7
Belle Vue Rd CHAM RG24 ...... 161 J5
  HEN RG9 ...... 31 G3
  READ RG1 ...... 2 E7
Bell Foundry La EWKG RG40 ...... 77 H6
Bell Holt NWBY RG14 ...... 103 F3
Bell House Gdns EWKG RG40 ...... 97 G1
Bellisle GOR/PANG RG8 ...... 41 G7
Bell La GOR/PANG RG8 ...... 23 G7
  HEN RG9 ...... 17 H7
Bell Meadow Wy HTWY RG27 ...... 164 A2
Bell Rd CHAM RG24 ...... 15 L2
Bell St HEN RG9 ...... 31 H1
  WHCH RG28 ...... 169 H7
Belmont Hts KEMP RG22 ...... 175 H7
Belmont Rd CWTH RG45 ...... 118 C2
  TLHT RG30 ...... 2 B7
Belvedere Cl FLET GU13 ...... 166 D2
Belvedere Dr NWBY RG14 ...... 12 E9
Belvedere Gdns CHAM RG24 ...... 145 H6
Belvedere Wk WWKG RG41 ...... 75 K3
Bembridge Ct CWTH RG45 ...... 117 K4

Bembridge Pl READ RG1 ...... 3 L6
Benedict Gn BNFD RG42 ...... 80 B5
Benetfeld Rd BNFD RG42 ...... 78 C4
Benett Cl NWBY RG14 ...... 83 J2
Benett Gdns NWBY RG14 ...... 83 J2
Benham Cha KSCL RG20 ...... 82 B2
Benham Hl NTHA RG18 ...... 85 F3
Benham La THLE RG7 ...... 114 A5
Bennet Cl BSTK RG21 ...... 15 H1
Bennett's Hl TLHT RG30 ...... 71 G7
Bennett Rd WHIT RG2 ...... 73 H5
Bennings Cl BNFD RG42 ...... 79 H5
Benning Wy EWKG RG40 ...... 77 H6
Bensgrove Cl GOR/PANG RG8 ...... 26 E3
Benson Cl WHIT RG2 ...... 8 B5
Bentley Cl CWTH RG45 ...... 118 A3
Benwell Cl ODIM RG29 ...... 180 B4
Beresford Rd READ RG1 ...... 2 D9
Bere Court Rd GOR/PANG RG8 ...... 53 J3
Bere Hl WHCH RG28 ...... 169 H6
Bere Rd BRAK RG12 ...... 100 B4
Beresford Rd TLHT RG30 ...... 2 C5
Berewyk Cl KEMP RG22 ...... 175 F5
Berkeley Av READ RG1 ...... 2 C9
  WHIT RG2 ...... 3 H9
Berkeley Cl FLET GU13 ...... 167 J2
Berkeley Dr KEMP RG22 ...... 176 A4
Berkeley Rd NWBY RG14 ...... 12 C5
Berkshire Circular Route
  KSCL RG20 ...... 20 A3
  KSCL RG20 ...... 21 F3
Berkshire Circular Routes
  GOR/PANG RG8 ...... 54 C3
  KSCL RG20 ...... 82 D7
  THLE RG7 ...... 51 G7
  THLE RG7 ...... 89 H1
  THLE RG7 ...... 111 G2
  WAR/TWY RG10 ...... 33 G6
Berkshire Dr CALC RG31 ...... 55 H5
  STHA RG19 ...... 86 B5
Berkshire Rd HEN RG9 ...... 31 G3
Berkshire Wy BRAK RG12 ...... 10 A3
  EWKG RG40 ...... 98 D1
Bermuda Cl CHAM RG24 ...... 160 D2
Bernadine Cl BNFD RG42 ...... 80 B5
Bernersh Cl SHST GU47 ...... 118 D7
Bernstein Rd KEMP RG22 ...... 175 H4
Berrycroft BNFD RG42 ...... 11 K1
Berrydown La OVTN RG25 ...... 171 K5
Berrylands Rd CAV/SC RG4 ...... 57 J2
  TLHT RG30 ...... 72 A5
Berrys La THLE RG7 ...... 72 C6
Berstead Cl EARL RG6 ...... 74 E5
Berwyn Cl KEMP RG22 ...... 175 F1
Bessemer Rd BSTK RG21 ...... 176 A2
Beswick Gdns BRAK RG12 ...... 80 C6
Betam Rd READ RG1 ...... 4 A6
Betchworth Av EARL RG6 ...... 9 H5
Bethesda Cl GOR/PANG RG8 ...... 38 D6
Bethesda St GOR/PANG RG8 ...... 38 D6
Betjeman Wk YTLY GU46 ...... 135 G5
Betteridge Rd STHA RG19 ...... 86 A5
Betty Grove La WWKG RG41 ...... 75 J7
Beveren Cl FARN GU14 ...... 151 J6
Beverley Cl BSTK RG21 ...... 176 C3
  NTHA RG18 ...... 85 H3
Beverley Gdns WAR/TWY RG10 ...... 46 D3
Beverley Rd CALC RG31 ...... 55 J4
The Bevers THLE RG7 ...... 111 F2
Bexley Ct TLHT RG30 ...... 2 A8
Bexmoor CHAM RG24 ...... 161 H5
Bexmoor Wy CHAM RG24 ...... 161 H5
Bibury Cl WODY RG5 ...... 75 G2
Bicester Cl WHCH RG28 ...... 169 H7
Bidden Rd ODIM RG29 ...... 179 K2
  OVTN RG25 ...... 178 E7
Bideford Cl WODY RG5 ...... 9 M2
Big Barn Gv BNFD RG42 ...... 80 A3
Bigbury Gdns WHIT RG2 ...... 7 M6
Biggs La EWKG RG40 ...... 95 J7
Billing Av EWKG RG40 ...... 116 D2
Billington Wy NTHA RG18 ...... 85 H1
Binbrook Cl EARL RG6 ...... 75 G4
Binfield Pl CHAM RG24 ...... 161 G2
Bingley Gv WODY RG5 ...... 59 J4
Birch Av FLET GU13 ...... 167 G2
  TLHT RG30 ...... 56 B5
Birch Cl CAV/SC RG4 ...... 29 G7
Birchen Cl GOR/PANG RG8 ...... 26 E3
Birches Crest KEMP RG22 ...... 175 J6
Birchetts Cl BNFD RG42 ...... 10 E1
Birch Gv BRAK RG12 ...... 11 H7
  HTWY RG27 ...... 164 A1
Birch Hill Rd BRAK RG12 ...... 99 J5
Birchland Cl THLE RG7 ...... 110 D2
Birch La ASC SL5 ...... 80 D6
  THLE RG7 ...... 110 E3
Birchmead WWKG RG41 ...... 76 C4
Birch Rd EWKG RG40 ...... 117 F1
  TADY RG26 ...... 108 B6
  THLE RG7 ...... 90 E4
Birch Side CWTH RG45 ...... 118 A2
Birch Vw WHIT RG2 ...... 8 C8
Birchview Cl YTLY GU46 ...... 135 H5
Birchwood CHAM RG24 ...... 145 G7
Birchwood Cl CAV/SC RG4 ...... 43 K6
Birchwood Rd NWBY RG14 ...... 13 M1
The Birchwoods CALC RG31 ...... 55 G5
Birdhill Av WHIT RG2 ...... 8 A7
Bird Ms EWKG RG40 ...... 97 G1
Birds La THLE RG7 ...... 87 F4
Birdwood Rd CHAM RG24 ...... 29 H7
Birkbeck Pl SHST GU47 ...... 119 F7
Birkdale BRAK RG12 ...... 99 F4
Birkhall Cl CALC RG31 ...... 71 H1
Biscuit Wy WHIT RG2 ...... 73 G6
Bishopdale BRAK RG12 ...... 10 C8
Bishops Cl FLET GU13 ...... 167 H4
  TADY RG26 ...... 108 D7
Bishops Dr EWKG RG40 ...... 77 H7
Bishop's Rd EARL RG6 ...... 5 G8
  THLE RG7 ...... 68 C3
Bishopswood La TADY RG26 ...... 108 B7

Bishopswood Rd TADY RG26 ...... 108 C7
Bittern Cl KEMP RG22 ...... 174 E4
Bitterne Av CALC RG31 ...... 55 G7
Bix Hl HEN RG9 ...... 16 B5
Blackberry Wk CHAM RG24 ...... 15 M1
  CHAM RG24 ...... 161 G4
Blackbird Cl KEMP RG22 ...... 174 E4
  THLE RG7 ...... 91 G4
Black Boy La WAR/TWY RG10 ...... 19 H7
Blackbushes Rd HTWY RG27 ...... 150 D1
Blackdown Cl ODIM RG29 ...... 175 F1
Blackdown Wy STHA RG19 ...... 85 H5
Blacklands Rd THLE RG7 ...... 86 D2
Blackley Cl EARL RG6 ...... 75 H3
Blackmeadows BRAK RG12 ...... 99 K4
Blackmoor Cl ASC SL5 ...... 81 G7
Blackmoor Wd ASC SL5 ...... 81 G7
Blackmore La CAV/SC RG4 ...... 29 H6
Blackstocks La HTWY RG27 ...... 162 E6
  EARL RG6 ...... 5 G7
Blackthorn Cl CALC RG31 ...... 55 G3
Blackthorn Dr NTHA RG18 ...... 85 J2
Blackthorn Wy DEAN RG23 ...... 159 H5
Blackwater Cl BSTK RG21 ...... 15 H5
  CAV/SC RG4 ...... 58 B1
  DEAN RG23 ...... 174 A3
  THLE RG7 ...... 93 H6
Blackwater Ri CALC RG31 ...... 71 F2
Blackwater Vw EWKG RG40 ...... 117 F6
Blaenavon CAV/SC RG4 ...... 43 G7
Blagdon Cl STHA RG19 ...... 84 C7
Blagdon Rd WHIT RG2 ...... 7 L8
Blagrave Farm La CAV/SC RG4 ...... 42 E7
Blagrave La CAV/SC RG4 ...... 56 D2
Blagrave Ri CALC RG31 ...... 55 H7
Blagrave St READ RG1 ...... 3 J5
Blagrove La WWKG RG41 ...... 96 E3
Blaire Pk YTLY GU46 ...... 135 G1
Blair Rd BSTK RG21 ...... 14 D8
Blake Cl CWTH RG45 ...... 118 D4
  EWKG RG40 ...... 77 K6
  ODIM RG29 ...... 180 B4
Blakes Cottages READ RG1 ...... 3 L6
  WAR/TWY RG10 ...... 47 G2
Blakes Ride YTLY GU46 ...... 135 G3
Blakes Rd WAR/TWY RG10 ...... 46 J1
Blamire Dr BNFD RG42 ...... 79 F4
Blanchard Cl WODY RG5 ...... 60 A5
Blandford Dr WWKG RG41 ...... 96 D3
Blandford Rd WHIT RG2 ...... 73 K6
Bland's Cl THLE RG7 ...... 90 E5
Blandy Rd HEN RG9 ...... 31 G3
Blandy's La GOR/PANG RG8 ...... 38 E6
Blane's La ASC SL5 ...... 101 F4
Blatch's Cl THLE RG7 ...... 70 C3
Bledlow Cl NWBY RG14 ...... 103 G3
Blenheim Cl WWKG RG41 ...... 96 D1
Blenheim Gdns READ RG1 ...... 4 B7
Blenheim Rd CAV/SC RG4 ...... 57 H1
  CHAM RG24 ...... 161 K6
  NWBY RG14 ...... 12 C4
  READ RG1 ...... 4 B7
Blewburton Wk BRAK RG12 ...... 11 M7
Bliss Cl KEMP RG22 ...... 175 K3
Blomfield Dl BNFD RG42 ...... 78 E7
Bloomfield Dr BRAK RG12 ...... 79 K5
Bloomfieldhatch La THLE RG7 ...... 92 C7
Blossom Av THLE RG7 ...... 70 D3
Blossom La THLE RG7 ...... 70 D3
Bloswood Dr WHCH RG28 ...... 169 G7
Bloswood La WHCH RG28 ...... 168 E4
Blount Crs BNFD RG42 ...... 79 F5
Blounts Court Rd CAV/SC RG4 ...... 29 H5
Bloxworth Cl BRAK RG12 ...... 100 C3
Bluebell Dr THLE RG7 ...... 90 E4
Bluebell Hl BRAK RG12 ...... 11 L2
Bluebell Meadow WWKG RG41 ...... 76 B3
Bluebell Wy NTHA RG18 ...... 85 J2
Bluecoats NTHA RG18 ...... 85 J3
Blue Coat Wk BRAK RG12 ...... 11 K9
Blundells Rd TLHT RG30 ...... 55 K5
Blunden Cl BSTK RG21 ...... 176 A3
Blyth Av STHA RG19 ...... 85 K5
Blythewood La ASC SL5 ...... 101 G1
Boames La KSCL RG20 ...... 102 C3
Boar's Br TADY RG26 ...... 127 K7
Bobgreen Ct WHIT RG2 ...... 93 K1
Bockmer La MLW SL7 ...... 19 G4
Bodens Ride ASC SL5 ...... 101 G4
Bodin Gdns NWBY RG14 ...... 83 K7
Bodmin Cl KEMP RG22 ...... 175 G1
  STHA RG19 ...... 85 H5
Bodmin Rd WODY RG5 ...... 9 M3
Body Rd READ RG1 ...... 3 G7
Bog La ASC SL5 ...... 100 C1
  BRAK RG12 ...... 100 C3
Boldrewood THLE RG7 ...... 90 E5
Bolingbroke Wy STHA RG19 ...... 86 A4
Bolney La HEN RG9 ...... 31 K6
Bolney Rd HEN RG9 ...... 32 A6
Bolney Trevor Dr HEN RG9 ...... 31 K7
Bolton Crs KEMP RG22 ...... 175 K1
Boltons La BNFD RG42 ...... 79 F5
Bolwell Cl WAR/TWY RG10 ...... 60 E1
Bomford Cl NTHA RG18 ...... 48 E7
Bond Cl CHAM RG24 ...... 161 F3
Bone La NWBY RG14 ...... 13 H4
Bonemill La KSCL RG20 ...... 83 G5
Bones La HEN RG9 ...... 44 D1
Boon Wy DEAN RG23 ...... 173 K2
Bosworth Gdns WODY RG5 ...... 75 H2
Botany Cl STHA RG19 ...... 86 A4
The Bothy WAR/TWY RG10 ...... 46 C2

Bottisham Cl EARL RG6 ...... 75 F6
Bottle La HTWY RG27 ...... 147 K2
Bottom La THLE RG7 ...... 70 D6
Bouldish Farm Rd ASC SL5 ...... 101 J3
Boulton Rd WHIT RG2 ...... 7 H5
Boult St READ RG1 ...... 3 L7
Boundary Cl CALC RG31 ...... 55 H7
Boundary La CAV/SC RG4 ...... 57 F2
Boundary Rd NWBY RG14 ...... 13 H5
Bounty Ri BSTK RG21 ...... 14 D7
Bounty Rd BSTK RG21 ...... 14 D7
Bourley Rd FLET GU13 ...... 167 K7
Bourn Cl EARL RG6 ...... 75 F5
Bourne Arch NTHA RG18 ...... 85 G3
Bourne Av WHIT RG2 ...... 7 K3
Bourne Cl CALC RG31 ...... 71 G2
Bourne Fld CHAM RG24 ...... 143 K6
Bourne Rd GOR/PANG RG8 ...... 40 D7
  STHA RG19 ...... 85 G3
Bourne-stevens Cl READ RG1 ...... 3 K7
The Bourne FLET GU13 ...... 167 H5
Bourton Cl TLHT RG30 ...... 56 A6
Bow Dr HTWY RG27 ...... 146 A2
Bowenhurst Gdns FLET GU13 ...... 167 H7
Bowenhurst Rd FLET GU13 ...... 167 H6
bowenhust La NFNM GU10 ...... 182 D1
Bowes Rd STHA RG19 ...... 85 J5
Bowfell Cl CALC RG31 ...... 55 H3
Bow Fld HTWY RG27 ...... 146 B2
Bow Gdns HTWY RG27 ...... 146 A2
Bow Gv HTWY RG27 ...... 146 A1
Bowland Dr BRAK RG12 ...... 100 B5
Bowling Ct HEN RG9 ...... 17 F7
Bowling Green Dr
  HTWY RG27 ...... 163 J2
Bowling Green La
  GOR/PANG RG8 ...... 41 G7
Bowling Green Rd NTHA RG18 ...... 85 F2
Bowman Rd CWTH RG45 ...... 117 K4
Bowman Rd CHAM RG24 ...... 145 G6
Bowmonts Rd TADY RG26 ...... 127 G1
Bowyer Crs EWKG RG40 ...... 77 H6
Boxford Rdg BRAK RG12 ...... 10 D7
Boyce Cl BNFD RG42 ...... 175 H4
Boyd Ct BNFD RG42 ...... 10 D2
Bracken Bank ASC SL5 ...... 81 F6
  CHAM RG24 ...... 161 G3
Bracken Cl CALC RG31 ...... 55 H4
Brackendale Wy EARL RG6 ...... 9 G1
Bracken La YTLY GU46 ...... 135 F3
The Brackens CWTH RG45 ...... 118 A2
  KEMP RG22 ...... 175 H6
Bracken Wy THLE RG7 ...... 91 F5
Brackley Av HTWY RG27 ...... 149 H4
Brackley Wy KEMP RG22 ...... 175 H3
Bracknell La HTWY RG27 ...... 149 H3
Bracknell Rd BNFD RG42 ...... 80 C2
  CWTH RG45 ...... 99 F7
  CWTH RG45 ...... 118 C2
Brackstone Cl CAV/SC RG4 ...... 3 L1
Bradbury Cl WHCH RG28 ...... 169 G7
Bradfields BRAK RG12 ...... 11 K9
Bradley-moore Sq NTHA RG18 ...... 85 K2
Bradmore Wy EARL RG6 ...... 74 D6
Bradwell Rd CALC RG31 ...... 55 H2
Braemar Dr DEAN RG23 ...... 173 K2
Braemore Cl STHA RG19 ...... 85 J6
Brahms Rd KEMP RG22 ...... 175 K4
Bramber Ms CAV/SC RG4 ...... 58 B1
Bramble Crs TLHT RG30 ...... 55 K6
Bramble Wy CHAM RG24 ...... 161 K5
Bramblegate CWTH RG45 ...... 118 A2
The Brambles CWTH RG45 ...... 117 J2
  NWBY RG14 ...... 83 H7
Bramblewood Pl FLET GU13 ...... 167 F2
Bramblings Cl KEMP RG22 ...... 174 E5
Bramblings CAV/SC RG4 ...... 43 F6
Bramblys Cl BSTK RG21 ...... 14 D6
Bramblys Dr BSTK RG21 ...... 14 C6
Bramdown Hts KEMP RG22 ...... 175 G6
Bramley Cl EARL RG6 ...... 9 H6
Bramley Crs CAV/SC RG4 ...... 29 F6
Bramley Green Rd TADY RG26 ...... 129 H7
Bramley Gv CWTH RG45 ...... 117 J3
Bramley La TADY RG26 ...... 129 G4
Bramley Rd HTWY RG27 ...... 146 A1
  TADY RG26 ...... 143 J1
  THLE RG7 ...... 110 A7
Bramling Av YTLY GU46 ...... 135 G3
Brammpton Gdns KEMP RG22 ...... 175 G7
Brampton Cha HEN RG9 ...... 31 K7
Bramshaw Rd TLHT RG30 ...... 56 B4
Bramshill Cl WHIT RG2 ...... 95 H7
Bramshot Dr FLET GU13 ...... 167 H1
Bramshott Dr HTWY RG27 ...... 164 A2
Bramwell Cl STHA RG19 ...... 86 A5
Bran Cl TLHT RG30 ...... 55 K5
Brandon Av WODY RG5 ...... 59 K4
Brandon Rd FLET GU13 ...... 167 F6
Branksomewood Rd
  FLET GU13 ...... 167 F2
Branton Cl KEMP RG22 ...... 175 H1
Brants Br BRAK RG12 ...... 11 L4
Brants Cl WHIT RG2 ...... 95 H5
Braunfels Wk KSCL RG20 ...... 12 A6
  KSCL RG20 ...... 83 G5
  NWBY RG14 ...... 12 A5
Braybrooke Dr WAR/TWY RG10 ...... 60 E3
Braybrooke Gdns
  WAR/TWY RG10 ...... 46 C3
Braybrooke Rd BNFD RG42 ...... 79 J5
  WAR/TWY RG10 ...... 46 C3
Braye Cl SHST GU47 ...... 118 D7
Brayford Rd WHIT RG2 ...... 73 K6
Bray Rd TLHT RG30 ...... 72 C2
Braziers La ASC SL5 ...... 81 G3
Breachfield KSCL RG20 ...... 121 J2
Breach La HTWY RG27 ...... 146 B2
Brean Wk EARL RG6 ...... 9 J7
Brecon Rd WODY RG5 ...... 59 J5
Bredon Rd WWKG RG41 ...... 76 E5
Brent Cl STHA RG19 ...... 85 J5
Brent Gdns WHIT RG2 ...... 7 K6
Brerewood EARL RG6 ...... 8 F8

Brewer Cl *KEMP* RG22 175 H1
Brewery Common *THLE* RG7 111 G2
Brewhouse La *HTWY* RG27 149 J4 1
Briant's Av *CAV/SC* RG4 57 K3
Briants Piece *NTHA* RG18 49 G7
Briar Cl *CAV/SC* RG4 57 H1
Briarlea Rd *THLE* RG7 110 E2
Briars Cl *GOR/PANG* RG8 40 D7
Briar Wy *TADY* RG26 127 F1
Briarwood Dr *EWKG* RG40 116 D2 1
Brickfields Cl *CHAM* RG24 161 H3 2
Brick La *FLET* GU13 167 H1
Bridge Rd *ODIM* RG29 164 B7
Bridges Cl *WWKG* RG41 76 E7
The Bridges *THLE* RG7 110 B3
Bridge St *NWBY* RG14 12 E4
OVTN RG25 171 H4
READ RG1 3 G1
READ RG1 3 H7
Bridge Wk *YTLY* GU46 135 J2
TLHT RG30 56 D4 1
Bridgewater Cl *TLHT* RG30 56 D5 2
Bridle Pth *GOR/PANG* RG8 26 D3
Bridle Rd *GOR/PANG* RG8 40 D1 1
Bridport Cl *EARL* RG6 75 G4
Brierley Pl *CALC* RG31 55 H1 1
Briff La *THLE* RG7 66 E5
THLE RG7 86 C1
Brigham Rd *READ* RG1 3 H3
Brighton Rd *EARL* RG6 5 G9
Brighton Wy *KEMP* RG22 175 J3
Brill Cl *CAV/SC* RG4 57 H1
Brimblecombe Cl *WWKG* RG41 77 F5
Brimpton Rd *THLE* RG7 87 F6
THLE RG7 107 G1
THLE RG7 107 K6
TLHT RG30 72 C2
Brinds Cl *CAV/SC* RG4 29 G6
Brinksway *FLET* GU13 167 H3
Brisbane Rd *TLHT* RG30 56 C5
Britten Rd *WHIT* RG2 7 J3
Brixham Rd *WHIT* RG2 7 K7
Broadacres *FLET* GU13 166 E3 1
Broadcommon Rd
WAR/TWY RG10 61 G7
Broadhalfpenny La *TADY* RG26 109 F7
Broad Hinton *WAR/TWY* RG10 60 D3
Broadhurst Gv *CHAM* RG24 161 G4
Broadlands Cl *CALC* RG31 71 J1
Broad La *BRAK* RG12 11 H6
NTHA RG18 66 A6
THLE RG7 86 C1
Broad Leaze *HTWY* RG27 163 K1 1
Broadmeadow End *NTHA* RG18 86 A4
Broadmoor La *CAV/SC* RG4 59 H1
Broadoak *TADY* RG26 127 G1 1
Broad Oak La *ODIM* RG29 181 F1
Broadrick Heath *BNFD* RG42 80 A5 2
Broad St *EWKG* RG40 97 H1
KSCL RG20 20 D4
READ RG1 3 H6
Broadwater La *WAR/TWY* RG10 60 D4
Broadwater Rd *WAR/TWY* RG10 60 D2
Broad Wy *THLE* RG7 112 E5
Broadway *STHA* RG19 85 J4
Brocas Dr *BSTK* RG21 15 H1
Brocas Rd *THLE* RG7 90 E6
Brockenhurst Dr *YTLY* GU46 135 J4 2
Brockenhurst Rd *BRAK* RG12 100 C1
Brock Gdns *TLHT* RG30 56 D5
Brocklands *YTLY* GU46 135 G5 1
Brockley Cl *TLHT* RG30 56 B5
Brocks La *NTHA* RG18 66 C1
Brocks Wy *HEN* RG9 45 K1
Broken Wy *KSCL* RG20 104 A6
Bromelia Cl *TADY* RG26 129 G5
Brompton Cl *EARL* RG6 75 G5 1
Brook Cl *FLET* GU13 167 H3
SHST GU47 119 F7
WWKG RG41 77 F6
Brook Dr *BRAK* RG12 11 M8
Brooke Pl *BNFD* RG42 78 E3
Brookers Cnr *CWTH* RG45 118 D3
Brooker's Hl *WHIT* RG2 94 A1
Brookers Rw *CWTH* RG45 118 D2
Brookfield Cl *CHAM* RG24 145 H7 1
Brook Gn *TADY* RG26 127 G1
Brookly Gdns *FLET* GU13 167 J1
Brooklyn Dr *CAV/SC* RG4 43 J5
The Brookmill *READ* RG1 6 D3
Brooksby Rd *CALC* RG31 55 J3
Brookside *WWKG* RG41 76 E7
Brookside Cl *EARL* RG6 75 G3
Brooks Rd *NTHA* RG18 85 K3
Brook St *WAR/TWY* RG10 60 C1
Brook St West *READ* RG1 3 G8
Brookvale Cl *BSTK* RG21 14 C5
Brookway *NWBY* RG14 84 D4
Broom Acres *FLET* GU13 167 G5
Broom Cl *CALC* RG31 71 H1 2
Broome Cl *YTLY* GU46 135 H2
Broome Ct *BRAK* RG12 10 E6
Broomfield Rd *TLHT* RG30 56 A5
Broom Gv *WWKG* RG41 96 C3
Broomhill *NFNM* GU10 183 J4
Broomrigg Rd *FLET* GU13 166 E1
Broughton Cl *TLHT* RG30 56 D4 2
Brown Cft *HTWY* RG27 163 J2
Browning Cl *CHAM* RG24 160 D3
NTHA RG18 85 H3
Browning Rd *FLET* GU13 183 F1
Brownlow Dr *BNFD* RG42 79 K5
Brownlow Rd *READ* RG1 2 D7
Brownrigg Crs *BRAK* RG12 11 M2
Browns Cl *TADY* RG26 129 F5
Brownsfield Rd *NTHA* RG18 85 H4
Brtten Rd *KEMP* RG22 175 K4
Bruan Rd *NWBY* RG14 83 J7
Bruce Rd *WODY* RG5 59 G6
Brummell Rd *NWBY* RG14 12 A1
NWBY RG14 83 H2
Brunel Dr *WODY* RG5 59 J4
Brunel Rd *BSTK* RG21 159 K5
THLE RG7 70 D4
TLHT RG30 72 B2
Brunswick *BRAK* RG12 99 H5
Brunswick Hl *READ* RG1 2 C7
Brunswick St *READ* RG1 2 D8
Bruton Wy *BRAK* RG12 100 B5
Bryanstone Cl *FLET* GU13 167 H5
Bryant Pl *GOR/PANG* RG8 41 G7 2
Brybur Cl *WHIT* RG2 74 A6
Buccaneer Cl *WODY* RG5 60 A5 1
Buchanan Dr *EWKG* RG40 116 D1
Buchanan Sq *STHA* RG19 85 K6
Buckby La *BSTK* RG21 15 K4
Buckden Cl *WODY* RG5 59 K7
Buckfast Cl *CHAM* RG24 160 B2
Buckhurst Gv *EWKG* RG40 98 A2
Buckhurst Hl *BRAK* RG12 100 C2 2
Buckhurst Wy *EARL* RG6 9 H5
Buckingham Dr *CAV/SC* RG4 43 J7
Buckingham Ga *MLW* SL7 19 J3
Buckingham Rd *NWBY* RG14 12 B7
Buckland Av *KEMP* RG22 175 J3
Buckland Rd *WHIT* RG2 7 K6
Bucklebury *BRAK* RG12 99 H5
Bucknell Av *GOR/PANG* RG8 40 D7
Bucknell Cl *CALC* RG31 72 A2
Buck Side *READ* RG1 3 G1
Buckskin La *KEMP* RG22 175 F2
Buckthorn Cl *EWKG* RG40 77 K7 1
Budd's Cl *BSTK* RG21 14 C6
Budge's Gdns *EWKG* RG40 77 J7
Budge's Rd *EWKG* RG40 77 J7
Budham Wy *BRAK* RG12 99 J4
Buffins Rd *ODIM* RG29 180 B2
Bullbrook Dr *BRAK* RG12 11 L2
Bull La *BRAK* RG12 10 F2
THLE RG7 113 J5
The Bull Meadow
GOR/PANG RG8 24 D5
Bulls Down Cl *HTWY* RG27 145 K1
Bulmershe Ct *EARL* RG6 5 K8
Bulmershe Rd *READ* RG1 4 E9
Bunce's La *GOR/PANG* RG8 41 F2
THLE RG7 91 F5
Bungler's Hl *THLE* RG7 114 E2
Bunkers Hl *NWBY* RG14 103 F3 2
Bunnian Pl *BSTK* RG21 14 F3
Bunting Cl *KEMP* RG22 174 E5
Bunting Ms *KEMP* RG22 175 F5 2
Burbage Gn *BRAK* RG12 100 C3 1
Burbidge Cl *CALC* RG31 72 A3 1
Burchell Rd *NWBY* RG14 83 H2
Burchett Coppice *EWKG* RG40 96 E7 1
Burcombe Wy *CAV/SC* RG4 57 J1
Burdens Heath *NTHA* RG18 66 B7
Burdock Cl *THLE* RG7 91 G5
Burfield *KSCL* RG20 120 B4
Burford Ct *EWKG* RG40 97 K2
Burgess Cl *ODIM* RG29 180 B2 1
WODY RG5 75 G1
Burgess Rd *BSTK* RG21 14 D2
Burghfield Rd *TLHT* RG30 72 B2 2
Burleigh La *ASC* SL5 81 H6
Burleigh Ms *CAV/SC* RG4 43 K6 2
Burleigh Rd *ASC* SL5 81 H7
Burlingham Cl *WHIT* RG2 93 K1 2
The Burlings *ASC* SL5 81 H7
Burlington Rd *TLHT* RG30 55 J6
Burlsdon Wy *BRAK* RG12 11 L2
Burnaby Cl *KEMP* RG22 175 H1
Burney Bit *TADY* RG26 127 G1
Burnham Gv *BNFD* RG42 79 K5 2
Burnham Ri *CAV/SC* RG4 43 K5
Burnham Rd *TADY* RG26 108 C6
Burniston Cl *EARL* RG6 75 H4 3
Burnley Cl *TADY* RG26 126 E2
Burn Moor Cha *BRAK* RG12 100 B5 1
Burnmoor Meadow
EWKG RG40 116 D6
Burns Av *FLET* GU13 167 J5
Burns Cl *CHAM* RG24 160 D3
WODY RG5 75 H2
Burnthouse Br *TLHT* RG30 92 B2
Burnthouse Gdns *BNFD* RG42 80 B5 2
Burnthouse La *TLHT* RG30 72 C7
Burnt Oak *EWKG* RG40 96 E7 2
Burrcroft Rd *TLHT* RG30 72 B1
Burrell Rd *KSCL* RG20 21 K7
Burrowfields *KEMP* RG22 175 G7 1
Burton Cl *WAR/TWY* RG10 60 D3
Burton's Gdns *CHAM* RG24 161 J4
Burwell Cl *EARL* RG6 75 F5
Buryfields *ODIM* RG29 180 D2
Bury Rd *DEAN* RG23 159 J5
Bury's Bank Rd *STHA* RG19 85 K7
STHA RG19 104 C1
Bushnells Dr *KSCL* RG20 123 K7 1
Bute St *TLHT* RG30 72 C1
Butler Cl *KEMP* RG22 159 H7
Butler Rd *CWTH* RG45 118 C2
Butlers Orch *CAV/SC* RG4 42 E1
Butlers Pond *GOR/PANG* RG8 40 C2
Butson Cl *NWBY* RG14 12 A4
Buttenshaw Av *WHIT* RG2 95 J7
Buttenshaw Cl *WHIT* RG2 95 K7
Buttercup Cl *EWKG* RG40 98 A1
Buttercup Pl *NTHA* RG18 85 J3
Butter Market *READ* RG1 3 J6
Buttermere Dr *KEMP* RG22 175 F3
Buttermere Gdns *BRAK* RG12 11 H5
Buttersteep Ri *ASC* SL5 101 F6
Butts Hill Rd *WODY* RG5 59 H4
Butts Meadow *HTWY* RG27 163 K2 1
The Butts *THLE* RG7 128 A1 1
The Butty *BSTK* RG21 15 K4
Buxton Av *CAV/SC* RG4 57 G1
Byefield Rd *TLHT* RG30 72 B2
Byes La *THLE* RG7 128 A2
Byeways *KSCL* RG20 120 B4
Byfields Rd *KSCL* RG20 123 K7
Byfleet Av *CHAM* RG24 161 J6
Byrd Gdns *KEMP* RG22 175 H5
Byreton Cl *EARL* RG6 9 J8
Byron Cl *CHAM* RG24 160 D2
FLET GU13 167 H3
NWBY RG14 103 J1
YTLY GU46 135 G5 2
Byron Dr *CWTH* RG45 118 C5
Byron Rd *EARL* RG6 5 H7
WAR/TWY RG10 60 D1
Bythorn Cl *EARL* RG6 75 H4
Byways *YTLY* GU46 135 G4
Bywood *BRAK* RG12 99 H5
Byworth Cl *WHIT* RG2 73 J6

C

Cabin Moss *BRAK* RG12 100 B5 2
Cadet Wy *FLET* GU13 167 J7
Cadnam Cl *DEAN* RG23 174 A2
Cadogan Cl *CAV/SC* RG4 58 B1 2
TLHT RG30 55 K6 1
Caernarvon Cl *DEAN* RG23 159 H6 1
Caesars Ga *BNFD* RG42 80 B5 3
Caesar's Wy *WHCH* RG28 169 G6
Cain Rd *BNFD* RG42 78 E7
BRAK RG12 79 F7
Cairngorm Cl *KEMP* RG22 159 G7 1
Cairngorm Rd *STHA* RG19 85 J5 1
Caistor Cl *CALC* RG31 71 G2 2
Caithness Cl *DEAN* RG23 173 K2
Calard Dr *NTHA* RG18 85 F2
Calbourne Dr *CALC* RG31 71 J2 2
Calcot Place Dr *CALC* RG31 71 K2
Calcott Pk *YTLY* GU46 135 H3
Caldbeck Dr *WODY* RG5 59 J7
Calder Cl *TLHT* RG30 56 A5
Caleta Cl *CAV/SC* RG4 58 A3 1
Calfridus Wy *BRAK* RG12 11 L6
Calleva Cl *KEMP* RG22 175 G5
Callington Rd *WHIT* RG2 7 K9
Calshot Pl *CALC* RG31 71 J2 3
Calthorpe Rd *FLET* GU13 167 F1
HTWY RG27 151 F7
Camberry Cl *BSTK* RG21 15 G9
Cambrian Wy *CALC* RG31 71 J2
EWKG RG40 97 F7
KEMP RG22 175 G1
Cambridge Rd *CWTH* RG45 118 D4
SHST GU47 119 F7
Cambridgeshire Cl *BNFD* RG42 80 C5
WWKG RG41 96 D1 2
Cambridge St *READ* RG1 2 D5
Camden Pl *CALC* RG31 71 G2 3
Camden Wk *FLET* GU13 167 K2
Camelford Cl *WHIT* RG2 7 K9
Camellia Wy *WWKG* RG41 76 C7 2
Camfield Cl *BSTK* RG21 15 G9
Campbell Cl *FLET* GU13 167 F2
Campbell Rd *TADY* RG26 129 J7
WODY RG5 75 G1
Campion Wy *EWKG* RG40 77 K7
HTWY RG27 149 J3
Camp Rd *THLE* RG7 90 B4
Campsie Cl *KEMP* RG22 159 G7
Camrose Wy *BSTK* RG21 15 G9
BSTK RG21 176 D2
Camus Cl *FLET* GU13 166 E6
Camwood Cl *BSTK* RG21 15 G9
Canal Cl *ODIM* RG29 164 B7 1
Canal View Rd *NWBY* RG14 13 M4
Canal Wy *READ* RG1 4 A6
Canberra Cl *HTWY* RG27 135 F2
Candleford Cl *BRAK* RG12 79 K5 3
Candover Cl *TADY* RG26 126 E2 2
Canhurst La *WAR/TWY* RG10 47 J1
Cannock Wy *EARL* RG6 9 M9
Cannon Hl *BRAK* RG12 99 K4
Cannon St *READ* RG1 2 D5
Canon's Ct *KSCL* RG20 123 K7
Cansfield End *NWBY* RG14 12 D3
Canterbury Cl *KEMP* RG22 175 G4 1
Canterbury Rd *WHIT* RG2 7 K5
Cantley Crs *WWKG* RG41 77 F6
Captains Gorse *GOR/PANG* RG8 38 C6
Caraway Rd *EARL* RG6 74 D5
Carbinswood La *THLE* RG7 88 A3
Carbonel Cl *DEAN* RG23 159 F6
Cardiff Rd *READ* RG1 2 F3
Cardigan Gdns *READ* RG1 8 D1
Cardigan Rd *READ* RG1 4 D9
Cardinal Cl *READ* RG1 3 J1
Carew Cl *CALC* RG31 55 G1 1
Carey Rd *EWKG* RG40 97 H2
Carey St *READ* RG1 2 F7
Carisbrooke Cl *CAV/SC* RG4 43 K6 3
DEAN RG23 159 H5
Carland Cl *EARL* RG6 74 D5
Carleton Cl *HTWY* RG27 163 J2
Carlile Gdns *WAR/TWY* RG10 46 C5
Carling Rd *CAV/SC* RG4 29 F5
Carlisle Cl *DEAN* RG23 159 H5
Carlisle Rd *CALC* RG31 55 K2
Carlton Cl *WODY* RG5 59 H7
Carlton Crs *FLET* GU13 167 J5
Carlton Rd *CAV/SC* RG4 42 E7
Carmichael Wy *KEMP* RG22 175 H4
Carnarvon Rd *READ* RG1 4 C7
Carnation Cl *EWKG* RG40 98 C7
Carnation Dr *BNFD* RG42 80 D4
Carnegie Rd *NWBY* RG14 12 F5
Carnoustie *BRAK* RG12 99 F5
Carolina Pl *EWKG* RG40 116 D1
Caroline Dr *WWKG* RG41 77 F7
Caroline St *READ* RG1 2 F5
Carpenters Cl *HTWY* RG27 146 A1
CHAM RG24 160 C1
Carpenter's Down
CHAM RG24 160 C1 1
Carrick Gdns *WODY* RG5 5 M7
WODY RG5 59 G7
Carrick La *YTLY* GU46 135 K3
Carrington Crs *TADY* RG26 126 E1
Carroll Crs *ASC* SL5 101 J2
Carron Cl *TLHT* RG30 56 B6
Carsdale Cl *READ* RG1 6 E1
Carshalton Wy *EARL* RG6 9 L9
Carston Gv *CALC* RG31 72 A2
Carter's Hl *EWKG* RG40 78 A2
Carters Ri *CALC* RG31 71 K3
Carthona Dr *FLET* GU13 167 G4
Cartmel Dr *WODY* RG5 59 G7
Cary Cl *NWBY* RG14 103 G2
Casey Ct *THLE* RG7 68 A3
Cassia Dr *EARL* RG6 74 C5 1
Castle Crs *READ* RG1 2 F8
Castle End Rd *WAR/TWY* RG10 46 E6
Castle Gv *NWBY* RG14 83 J2
Castle Hl *READ* RG1 2 F8
THLE RG7 115 F1
Castle La *NWBY* RG14 83 H1
Castle Ri *ODIM* RG29 164 B7
Castle Rd *BSTK* RG21 14 F8
Castle St *FLET* GU13 167 G4
READ RG1 3 G7
Castor Ct *FLET* GU13 167 J6 1
YTLY GU46 135 G2
Caswall Cl *BNFD* RG42 78 D4 1
Catalina Cl *WODY* RG5 60 A6
Catcliffe Wy *EARL* RG6 74 C6
Catesby Gdns *YTLY* GU46 135 F4
Catherine Rd *NWBY* RG14 12 E6
Catherine St *TLHT* RG30 2 B5
Catkin Cl *CHAM* RG24 145 G7
Caunter Rd *NWBY* RG14 83 G3 1
The Causeway *CAV/SC* RG4 4 A2
HTWY RG27 131 K2
Causmans Wy *CALC* RG31 55 H4
Cavalier Cl *CHAM* RG24 161 K5
NWBY RG14 84 B2
THLE RG7 70 C3
Cavalier Rd *CHAM* RG24 161 K5
Cavel Ct *CHAM* RG24 161 H3 3
Cavendish Ct *NWBY* RG14 84 D2
Cavendish Gdns *WWKG* RG41 75 K3
Cavendish Rd *CAV/SC* RG4 43 K6
FLET GU13 167 F6 1
Caversham Br *READ* RG1 2 F1
Caversham Park Dr *CAV/SC* RG4 43 K7
Caversham Park Rd *CAV/SC* RG4 44 A6
Caversham Rd *READ* RG1 3 G2
Cawsam Gdns *CAV/SC* RG4 57 K1
Caxton Cl *TLHT* RG30 56 D4
Cayman Cl *CHAM* RG24 160 D2
Cecil Aldin Dr *CALC* RG31 55 G1
Cedar Cl *EWKG* RG40 97 H1
TADY RG26 127 G3
Cedar Dr *BNFD* RG42 79 K5
FLET GU13 167 K2
GOR/PANG RG8 54 B1
KSCL RG20 123 K7
Cedar Gv *STHA* RG19 85 H4
Cedar Mt *NWBY* RG14 83 J7
Cedar Rd *WHIT* RG2 8 D9
The Cedars *CALC* RG31 55 J3
FLET GU13 167 J3
Cedar Tree Cl *DEAN* RG23 173 K4
Cedar Wy *DEAN* RG23 159 J4
Cedar Wood Crs *CAV/SC* RG4 57 J1
Celandine Cl *CWTH* RG45 118 D2
Celandine Ct *YTLY* GU46 135 F2
Celandine Gv *NTHA* RG18 86 A4
Cemetery Hl *ODIM* RG29 180 D2
Cemetery La *OVTN* RG25 178 E7
Cemetery Rd *FLET* GU13 167 F4
Central Wk *EWKG* RG40 97 H1 1
Centre Dr *CHAM* RG24 161 G2
Centurion Wy *KEMP* RG22 175 G6
Century Dr *THLE* RG7 93 K6
Chaffinch Cl *CALC* RG31 55 G6 1
KEMP RG22 175 F4
WWKG RG41 96 D2
Chagford Rd *WHIT* RG2 73 J5
Chain St *READ* RG1 3 H6
Chalcraft Cl *HEN* RG9 31 F3
Chalfont Cl *EARL* RG6 74 D5
Chalfont Wy *EARL* RG6 9 G9
EARL RG6 74 D6 2
Chalford Rd *NWBY* RG14 12 A5
Chalgrove Wy *CAV/SC* RG4 43 J6
Chalk Hl *HEN* RG9 31 F6
Chalkhouse Green La
CAV/SC RG4 43 H3
Chalkhousegreen La
CAV/SC RG4 43 J4
Chalkhouse Green Rd
CAV/SC RG4 42 E1
Chalk V *CHAM* RG24 161 K6
Chalky Copse *HTWY* RG27 163 K1 2
Chalky La *HTWY* RG27 182 A1
Challenor Cl *EWKG* RG40 116 E1 1
Challis Cl *KEMP* RG22 175 H2
Challis Pl *BNFD* RG42 79 F6
Challoner Cl *KEMP* RG22 175 H1
Chamberlain's Gdns
WHIT RG2 95 H5 3
Champion Rd *CAV/SC* RG4 3 L2
Champion Wy *FLET* GU13 167 H6
The Chancellor's Wy *EARL* RG6 8 C3
Chandler Rd *BSTK* RG21 176 B2
Chandlers La *YTLY* GU46 135 H2
Chandos Rd *NWBY* RG14 83 J7
Chantreys *FLET* GU13 166 E3 2
Chantry Ms *KEMP* RG22 175 G5 1
Chapel Ct *NTHA* RG18 85 K3
Chapel Hl *BSTK* RG21 14 D3
CALC RG31 55 G5
Chapel La *BNFD* RG42 78 D5
GOR/PANG RG8 37 H6
NTHA RG18 49 H5
NTHA RG18 51 F4
NTHA RG18 64 D2
STHA RG19 107 G7
TADY RG26 125 G5
THLE RG7 93 J5
THLE RG7 109 J3
Chapel Md *HTWY* RG27 134 D1 2
Chapel Pond Dr *ODIM* RG29 180 B1
Chapel Rd *KSCL* RG20 82 B1
Chapel St *NTHA* RG18 85 K4
Chaplain's Hl *CWTH* RG45 118 E4
Chapman Wk *NTHA* RG18 85 G3
Chapter Ter *HTWY* RG27 149 J4 2
Chard Cl *WODY* RG5 59 H7
Charlbury Cl *BRAK* RG12 100 C2 3
Charldon Gn *CHAM* RG24 161 H3 3
Charledown Cl *OVTN* RG25 171 H5
Charledown Rd *OVTN* RG25 171 H5
Charles Cl *HTWY* RG27 163 K2
Charles Evans Wy *CAV/SC* RG4 58 A3
Charles Richards Cl *BSTK* RG21 14 D8
Charles St *KEMP* RG22 159 J7
NWBY RG14 103 G2
READ RG1 2 E5
Charlock Cl *NTHA* RG18 85 K2
Charlotte Cl *NTHA* RG18 49 F7
Charlton Cl *EWKG* RG40 96 E7 3
Charlton Ct *SHST* GU47 118 E7
Charlton La *THLE* RG7 113 K3
Charlton Pl *NWBY* RG14 12 F2
Charlville Dr *CALC* RG31 71 G2 4
Charmwood Cl *NWBY* RG14 83 J2 1
Charndon Cl *WHIT* RG2 7 K1
Charnwood Cl *KEMP* RG22 159 G7 2
Charrington Rd *CALC* RG31 71 G2
Charterhouse Cl *BRAK* RG12 11 M9
Charter Rd *NWBY* RG14 83 J7
Charvil House Rd
WAR/TWY RG10 45 K7
Charvil La *CAV/SC* RG4 59 H1
Charvil Meadow Rd
WAR/TWY RG10 46 A7
Charwood Rd *EWKG* RG40 97 K1
Chase Gdns *BNFD* RG42 78 D3
Chaseside Av *WAR/TWY* RG10 46 C6
The Chase *CALC* RG31 71 J2
CWTH RG45 118 B2
NWBY RG14 63 J7 1
Chatham St *READ* RG1 2 F5
Chatsworth Av *WWKG* RG41 75 K4
Chatsworth Cl *CAV/SC* RG4 43 K6
Chatsworth Gn *KEMP* RG22 175 H6
Chatteris Wy *EARL* RG6 75 F5
The Chatters *THLE* RG7 115 F1
Chatton Cl *EARL* RG6 74 D6
Chaucer Cl *CAV/SC* RG4 43 H7
CHAM RG24 160 D2
EWKG RG40 98 A1 1
Chaucer Crs *NWBY* RG14 83 H2
Chaucer Rd *CWTH* RG45 118 C4
Chaucer Wy *WWKG* RG41 96 D2 1
Chaundlers Cft *NFNM* GU10 182 E7
Chavey Down Rd *BNFD* RG42 80 E4
Chazey Cl *CAV/SC* RG4 42 D4
Chazey Rd *CAV/SC* RG4 56 E1
Cheam Cl *BRAK* RG12 100 A3
Cheapside *READ* RG1 3 G5
Cheap St *KSCL* RG20 21 K6
NWBY RG14 12 E4
Cheddington Cl *TLHT* RG30 56 A7 1
Cheeseman Cl *EWKG* RG40 77 J7 1
Chelsea Cl *TLHT* RG30 56 A4
Chelwood Dr *SHST* GU47 118 A7 2
Chelwood Rd *EARL* RG6 9 K7
Cheney Cl *BNFD* RG42 78 E4
Chepstow Rd *CALC* RG31 55 H3
Chequer La *THLE* RG7 113 F6
Chequers La *HTWY* RG27 134 D2
Chequers Rd *BSTK* RG21 14 F5
Chequers Wy *WODY* RG5 5 M6
Cherberry Cl *FARN* GU14 151 J6 2
Cherbury Cl *BRAK* RG12 11 M6
Cherington Wy *ASC* SL5 81 H7 1
Cheriton Av *WAR/TWY* RG10 46 C6
Cheriton Cl *NWBY* RG14 13 G8
TADY RG26 126 E2 3
Cheriton Pl *CAV/SC* RG4 29 G6 1
Cherry Cl *CAV/SC* RG4 43 K4
HTWY RG27 164 A1
NWBY RG14 12 D1
Cherry Tree Cl *SHST* GU47 118 E7 1
Cherry Tree Dr *BRAK* RG12 11 J6
Cherry Tree Gv *WWKG* RG41 96 C3 1
Chervil Wy *THLE* RG7 91 G5
Cherwell Rd *CAV/SC* RG4 43 H6
Cheseridge Rd *KSCL* RG20 35 G2
Cheshire Pk *BNFD* RG42 80 B4
Chesilton Crs *FLET* GU13 167 H7
Chesterblade La *BRAK* RG12 100 A5
Chester Cl *NWBY* RG14 13 K9
Chesterfield Rd *BSTK* RG21 15 H8
NWBY RG14 12 E7
Chesterman St *READ* RG1 3 J9
Chesterment Wy *EARL* RG6 75 G5
Chester Pl *BSTK* RG21 14 C7
Chester St *CAV/SC* RG4 57 H3
TLHT RG30 2 A5
Chesterton Rd *NTHA* RG18 85 H2
Chestnut Av *CAV/SC* RG4 58 B1 3
WWKG RG41 76 D7
WWKG RG41 96 B1
Chestnut Cl *FARN* GU14 151 K6
HEN RG9 16 C2 1
MLW SL7 19 J3 1
THLE RG7 70 D2 1
Chestnut Crs *NWBY* RG14 12 E1
WHIT RG2 94 B3
Chestnut Dr *TLHT* RG30 91 G3
Chestnut Gv *FLET* GU13 167 J1
GOR/PANG RG8 41 J7
The Chestnuts *HEN* RG9 45 K1
Cheswell Gdns *FLET* GU13 167 F5
Chetwode Cl *EWKG* RG40 97 K1 2
Cheviot Cl *KEMP* RG22 175 G1
NWBY RG14 103 F3
Cheviot Dr *FARN* GU14 151 J6
WAR/TWY RG10 60 A1
Cheviot Rd *SHST* GU47 118 A7
Chichester Pl *KEMP* RG22 175 K2
Chichester Rd *TLHT* RG30 55 K5
Chicory Cl *EARL* RG6 8 F9
Chieveley Cl *CALC* RG31 55 H5
Chilcombe Wy *EARL* RG6 75 G4
Child Cl *EWKG* RG40 77 J6
Childrey Wy *CALC* RG31 55 G5
Chiltern Cl *FLET* GU13 167 J6
HEN RG9 30 E3
NWBY RG14 103 F3
Chiltern Ct *CAV/SC* RG4 43 J6
Chiltern Crs *EARL* RG6 5 H6
Chiltern Dr *WAR/TWY* RG10 60 A1
Chiltern Rd *CAV/SC* RG4 57 K1
HEN RG9 29 F4
SHST GU47 118 A7
Chiltern Vw *GOR/PANG* RG8 41 J7
Chiltern Wy *KEMP* RG22 175 F1
Chilton Rdg *KEMP* RG22 175 G7
Chineham La *CHAM* RG24 160 B1
CHAM RG24 160 D3
Chineham Park Ct *CHAM* RG24 160 E3
Chinnock Cl *FLET* GU13 167 G4
Chippenham Cl *EARL* RG6 74 C6 3
Chisbury Cl *BRAK* RG12 100 B4
Chittering Cl *EARL* RG6 75 F5
Chive Rd *EARL* RG6 74 D5

Chivers Cl KEMP RG22 .... 175 H5
Chivers Dr EWKG RG40 .... 116 D1 ⓵
Chives Pl BNFD RG42 .... 80 A5 ⓵
Cholmeley Pl READ RG1 .... 4 C6
Cholmeley Rd READ RG1 .... 4 C5
Cholmeley Ter READ RG1 .... 4 C6
Cholsey Cl STHA RG19 .... 86 A4
Chopin Rd READ RG1 .... 175 J4
Choseley Cl WAR/TWY RG10 .... 33 K7
Choseley Rd WAR/TWY RG10 .... 33 K7
Christchurch Cl FLET GU13 .... 167 G7 ⓵
Christchurch Dr WHIT RG2 .... 7 L2
Christchurch Rd READ RG1 .... 7 M2
Christie Hts NWBY RG14 .... 84 A7
Christie Wk YTLY GU46 .... 135 H5
Christopher Ct NWBY RG14 .... 13 H6
Christy Ct TADY RG26 .... 127 F2 ⓵
Chudleigh Gdns WHIT RG2 .... 7 L7
Church Barns Farm THLE RG7 .... 111 J3
Church Brook TADY RG26 .... 126 D3
Church Cl HEN RG9 .... 30 A2
  KSCL RG20 .... 102 B2
  WWKG RG41 .... 76 B4 ⓵
Church End La TLHT RG30 .... 56 A6
Church Ga STHA RG19 .... 85 J4
Church Gv FLET GU13 .... 167 F2
Church Hams EWKG RG40 .... 116 C2
Church Hl BNFD RG42 .... 78 D1
  KSCL RG20 .... 20 D5
  WAR/TWY RG10 .... 60 D6
Churchill Cl ODIM RG29 .... 180 B3
Churchill Cl HTWY RG27 .... 149 G4
  ODIM RG29 .... 180 C4
  TADY RG26 .... 127 G2
Churchill Crs CAV/SC RG4 .... 29 G5
Churchill Dr WWKG RG41 .... 76 A4
Churchill Rd ASC SL5 .... 81 J7
Churchill Wy BSTK RG21 .... 14 E4
Churchill Wy East BSTK RG21 .... 15 H4
Churchill Wy West BSTK RG21 .... 14 A8
  BSTK RG21 .... 159 K6
  KEMP RG22 .... 159 J6
Church Lands TADY RG26 .... 128 E6
Church La BNFD RG42 .... 78 E1
  BNFD RG42 .... 80 A1
  CHAM RG24 .... 161 J5
  DEAN RG23 .... 159 F7
  EWKG RG40 .... 96 B6
  EWKG RG40 .... 116 D4
  GOR/PANG RG8 .... 37 H6
  HEN RG9 .... 29 G3
  HEN RG9 .... 45 J3
  HTWY RG27 .... 131 K3
  HTWY RG27 .... 149 J6
  KSCL RG20 .... 82 B2
  KSCL RG20 .... 120 A1
  KSCL RG20 .... 121 K2
  NFNM GU10 .... 183 J5
  NTHA RG18 .... 51 F4
  NWBY RG14 .... 83 C3
  OVTN RG25 .... 176 B5
  READ RG1 .... 3 J8
  STHA RG19 .... 85 J4
  TADY RG26 .... 124 E7
  THLE RG7 .... 90 A3
  THLE RG7 .... 93 J3
  THLE RG7 .... 107 G2
  THLE RG7 .... 110 D7
  THLE RG7 .... 115 G2
  TLHT RG30 .... 91 K1
  WAR/TWY RG10 .... 46 E7
  WHIT RG2 .... 94 A2
  WHIT RG2 .... 95 F3
Church Ms GOR/PANG RG8 .... 41 J7 ⓵
  WODY RG5 .... 59 J5
Church Rd ASC SL5 .... 80 E6
  ASC SL5 .... 101 K2
  BRAK RG12 .... 11 C4
  EARL RG6 .... 9 J1
  FLET GU13 .... 167 F1
  FLET GU13 .... 167 G1
  KSCL RG20 .... 82 B2
  NWBY RG14 .... 13 D9
  OVTN RG25 .... 171 H4
  SHST GU47 .... 118 A7
  SHST GU47 .... 118 E7
  TADY RG26 .... 109 H7
  TADY RG26 .... 126 E3
  THLE RG7 .... 108 F1
  THLE RG7 .... 109 F1
  THLE RG7 .... 110 B3
  WDSR SL4 .... 81 F1
  WODY RG5 .... 59 J5
Church Rd East CWTH RG45 .... 118 C4
Church Rd West CWTH RG45 .... 118 C4
Church Sq BSTK RG21 .... 14 E5
Church St BSTK RG21 .... 14 E5
  CAV/SC RG4 .... 57 H1
  CWTH RG45 .... 118 C3
  HEN RG9 .... 31 G2
  NFNM GU10 .... 182 D6
  NTHA RG18 .... 36 A7
  ODIM RG29 .... 180 C2
  READ RG1 .... 3 J8
  THLE RG7 .... 70 C3
  WAR/TWY RG10 .... 46 B2
  WAR/TWY RG10 .... 60 C1
Church Vw HTWY RG27 .... 149 H5
  HTWY RG27 .... 164 A2
  THLE RG7 .... 88 D1
  YTLY GU46 .... 135 J2
Churn Cl CHAM RG24 .... 161 J4
Churn Rd KSCL RG20 .... 21 H4
Cibbons Rd CHAM RG24 .... 145 G7
Cinnamon Cl EARL RG6 .... 8 E9
Cintra Av WHIT RG2 .... 7 M2
Circle Hill Rd CWTH RG45 .... 118 D3
Circuit La TLHT RG30 .... 72 D1
City Rd CALC RG31 .... 55 G7
Clacy Gn BNFD RG42 .... 79 H5
Clanfield Crs CALC RG31 .... 55 H3
Clappers Farm Rd THLE RG7 .... 129 F1
Clapps Gate Rd TADY RG26 .... 109 H7
Clare Av EWKG RG40 .... 77 H7
Clare Ct EWKG RG40 .... 77 H1
Clarence Rd FLET GU13 .... 167 G3
  HEN RG9 .... 31 G1
Clarence Wy CALC RG31 .... 71 G2

Clarendon Cl WWKG RG41 .... 76 C4
Clarendon Gdns NWBY RG14 .... 12 F2
Clarendon Rd EARL RG6 .... 5 G9
Clares Green Rd THLE RG7 .... 93 L1
Claudius Dr DEAN RG23 .... 159 H4 ⓵
Claverdon BRAK RG12 .... 99 H5
Clay Cl CALC RG31 .... 55 G4
Clayhill Cl BRAK RG12 .... 100 C1
Clay Hill Crs NWBY RG14 .... 84 C2 ⓵
Clayhill Rd THLE RG7 .... 90 E4
Clay La EWKG RG40 .... 98 A1
  THLE RG7 .... 88 C1
Claythorpe Rd KEMP RG22 .... 175 C1
Clayton Cl HTWY RG27 .... 149 H5 ⓵
Clayton Gv BRAK RG12 .... 11 L2
Cleeve Down GOR/PANG RG8 .... 25 C4
Cleeve Rd GOR/PANG RG8 .... 24 E4
Clemence Gdns WHCH RG28 .... 169 H7 ⓵
Clements Cl THLE RG7 .... 93 H6
Clements Md CALC RG31 .... 55 G5
Clements Rd HEN RG9 .... 17 F7
Clent Rd WHIT RG2 .... 7 K3
Cleopatra Pl BNFD RG42 .... 80 B5 ⓵
Clere Gdns CHAM RG24 .... 161 G1
Clerewater Pl STHA RG19 .... 85 K4 ⓵
Clevedge Rd ODIM RG29 .... 164 B7
Clevedon Dr EARL RG6 .... 9 H8
Clevedon Rd CALC RG31 .... 55 K2
Cleveland WAR/TWY RG10 .... 60 A1 ⓵
Cleveland Cl KEMP RG22 .... 175 C1
Cleveland Gv NWBY RG14 .... 12 D3
Clevemede GOR/PANG RG8 .... 25 C3
Cleves La OVTN RG25 .... 178 E6
Cleves Gv BRAK RG12 .... 99 J3
Clifton Pk Rd CAV/SC RG4 .... 57 G2
Clifton Ri WAR/TWY RG10 .... 46 D3
Clifton Rd NWBY RG14 .... 12 A5
  WWKG RG41 .... 77 F6
Clifton St READ RG1 .... 2 E7
Clifton Ter BSTK RG21 .... 14 F3
Clintons Gn BNFD RG42 .... 10 D2
Clivedale Rd WODY RG5 .... 75 J1
Clive Gn BRAK RG12 .... 99 J3
Cloister Ms THLE RG7 .... 70 D3 ⓵
The Cloisters CAV/SC RG4 .... 57 H2
The Close ASC SL5 .... 81 G7
  BRAK RG12 .... 11 H8
  GOR/PANG RG8 .... 26 E3 ⓵
  HEN RG9 .... 31 G3
  NTHA RG18 .... 36 A7
  NTHA RG18 .... 85 G3
  TADY RG26 .... 143 G4
  THLE RG7 .... 91 F4
  WODY RG5 .... 59 J5
Clough Dr NTHA RG18 .... 48 E7 ⓵
Clove Cl EARL RG6 .... 74 C5
Clover Cl EWKG RG40 .... 77 K7
Clover Fld CHAM RG24 .... 161 G3 ⓵
Clover La YTLY GU46 .... 135 F3
Cloves Farm Wd BNFD RG42 .... 78 E7 ⓵
Club La CWTH RG45 .... 118 E3
Coach House Gdns FLET GU13 .... 151 H7
Coachman's Ct NWBY RG14 .... 84 A2 ⓵
Coach Rd ASC SL5 .... 81 H5
Coalport Wy TLHT RG30 .... 55 K4
Coates Cl KEMP RG22 .... 176 A3
Cobbett Gn KEMP RG22 .... 175 K2
Cobham Rd WODY RG5 .... 59 J6
Cochrane Cl THLE RG7 .... 91 F4
Cock-a-dobby SHST GU47 .... 118 B7 ⓵
Cock La THLE RG7 .... 68 C4
Cockney Hl TLHT RG30 .... 56 A7
Cody Cl WODY RG5 .... 60 A5
Colbeck Flet GU13 .... 167 J7
Colbred Cnr FARN GU14 .... 151 K6 ⓵
Cold Ash Hl NTHA RG18 .... 65 H6
Coldharbour Cl HEN RG9 .... 31 F3
Coldicutt St CAV/SC RG4 .... 3 L2 ⓵
Coleman Cl BSTK RG21 .... 160 D1
Colemans Moor La WODY RG5 .... 59 J7
Colemans Moor Rd WODY RG5 .... 60 A3
  WODY RG5 .... 75 J1
Coleridge Av YTLY GU46 .... 135 K4
Coleridge Cl CWTH RG45 .... 118 D4 ⓵
  WAR/TWY RG10 .... 60 E2 ⓵
Coleridge La GOR/PANG RG8 .... 53 G1
Coley Av READ RG1 .... 2 E9
Coley Hl READ RG1 .... 2 F8
Coley Park Rd READ RG1 .... 2 F8
Coley Pl READ RG1 .... 3 G8
Collaroy Rd NTHA RG18 .... 65 H7
College Piece THLE RG7 .... 110 E2 ⓵
College Rd BRAK RG12 .... 11 H7
  BSTK RG21 .... 14 B4
  EARL RG6 .... 4 E8
Colleton Dr WAR/TWY RG10 .... 60 D2
Colliers La HEN RG9 .... 29 F3
Colliers Wy TLHT RG30 .... 56 C6
Collins Cl NWBY RG14 .... 13 J1
Collins Dr NTHA RG18 .... 48 E7
Collis St WHIT RG2 .... 7 J1
Colmore La HEN RG9 .... 29 F3
Colmworth Cl EARL RG6 .... 74 D6 ⓵
Colne Valley Wy WHCH RG28 .... 170 C7 ⓵
Colne Wy BSTK RG21 .... 15 J5
Colston Cl CALC RG31 .... 71 J2 ⓵
Colthrop La STHA RG19 .... 86 C5
Coltsfoot Cl THLE RG7 .... 91 G4 ⓵
Coltsfoot Pl HTWY RG27 .... 164 B1 ⓵
Colwyn Cl YTLY GU46 .... 135 G3
Colyer Cl KEMP RG22 .... 175 H1 ⓵
  NTHA RG18 .... 49 H5
Colyton Wy GOR/PANG RG8 .... 41 H7
Combe Rd TLHT RG30 .... 56 A6
Comet Wy WODY RG5 .... 59 K6
Comfrey Cl EWKG RG40 .... 77 K6
Commercial Rd WHIT RG2 .... 7 G9
Commonfield La EWKG RG40 .... 96 A7
Common Hl THLE RG7 .... 69 J3
Common Rd STHA RG19 .... 123 K1
Commons Rd WWKG RG41 .... 76 E5
Compass Fld HTWY RG27 .... 164 A2 ⓵
Compton Av CALC RG31 .... 55 G6

Compton Cl BRAK RG12 .... 99 F4 ⓵
  EARL RG6 .... 9 M3
  FLET GU13 .... 167 J6
  HTWY RG27 .... 164 A3
  SHST GU47 .... 118 D7
Compton Rd FLET GU13 .... 167 J6
Comsaye Wk BRAK RG12 .... 99 K3 ⓵
Concorde Wy WODY RG5 .... 59 K6 ⓵
Condor Cl CALC RG31 .... 55 H2
Coney Gra BNFD RG42 .... 79 J4
Congreve Cl THLE RG7 .... 108 C1
Conifer Cl FLET GU13 .... 167 G6
  TADY RG26 .... 108 B7
Conifer Crest NWBY RG14 .... 103 F4
Conifer Dr CALC RG31 .... 55 C3
The Conifers CWTH RG45 .... 118 B1
Coningham Rd WHIT RG2 .... 93 K1
Coningsby BRAK RG12 .... 11 G7
Conisboro Av CAV/SC RG4 .... 43 F7
Conisboro Wy CAV/SC RG4 .... 43 F7
Coniston Cl STHA RG19 .... 85 F4
  WODY RG5 .... 75 H1
Coniston Dr TLHT RG30 .... 56 A3
Coniston Rd KEMP RG22 .... 175 C3
Coniston Wy FLET GU13 .... 167 F6
Connaught Cl TLHT RG30 .... 2 B7
  YTLY GU46 .... 135 G3
Connaught Rd FLET GU13 .... 167 H3 ⓵
  NWBY RG14 .... 13 G4
  TLHT RG30 .... 2 B7
Constable Cl BSTK RG21 .... 160 D4 ⓵
  WODY RG5 .... 60 A5 ⓵
Constantine Wy KEMP RG22 .... 175 F6
Constitution Rd TLHT RG30 .... 56 C5 ⓵
Consul Cl WODY RG5 .... 75 K1
Conway Dr WHIT RG2 .... 73 K7
Conway Rd CALC RG31 .... 71 H1
Conygree Cl EARL RG6 .... 74 E5
Cooke Ri BNFD RG42 .... 79 K4 ⓵
Cookham Cl SHST GU47 .... 118 D7
Cookham Rd BRAK RG12 .... 79 F7
Coombe Ct NTHA RG18 .... 85 K4
Coombe Dr FLET GU13 .... 167 K2
Coombehurst Dr BSTK RG21 .... 176 C2
Coombe Pine BRAK RG12 .... 100 A4
Coombe Rd KSCL RG20 .... 36 A2
  YTLY GU46 .... 135 G2
Coombes La WWKG RG41 .... 96 B3
Coombe Sq STHA RG19 .... 85 K4
The Coombe GOR/PANG RG8 .... 24 C5
Cooper Cl WHIT RG2 .... 73 K7
Cooper Rd HEN RG9 .... 17 F7
Coopers Ct TADY RG26 .... 129 G6
Coopers Crs NTHA RG18 .... 85 H3
Cooper's Hl HTWY RG27 .... 134 D4
Coopers La TADY RG26 .... 129 F6
Coopers Pightle CAV/SC RG4 .... 42 E1
Cope Hall La NWBY RG14 .... 102 E1
Copenhagen Cl WHIT RG2 .... 73 K7 ⓵
Copes La HTWY RG27 .... 132 D2
Copland Cl KEMP RG22 .... 175 H4
Copperdale Cl EARL RG6 .... 8 E5
Copperfield Av SHST GU47 .... 119 F6
Coppice Cl NWBY RG14 .... 13 G9
  TADY RG26 .... 126 A1
Coppice Gdns CWTH RG45 .... 118 A3
  YTLY GU46 .... 135 H4
Coppice Gn BNFD RG42 .... 79 C5
Coppice Ms DEAN RG23 .... 159 H5
Coppice Rd KSCL RG20 .... 124 B7
  WODY RG5 .... 75 H2
Copse Av CAV/SC RG4 .... 58 A2
Copse Cl CALC RG31 .... 55 J2
Copse Dr WWKG RG41 .... 77 F7
Copse Md WODY RG5 .... 59 J4
Copse Rd OVTN RG25 .... 171 J2
The Copse TADY RG26 .... 126 D1
Copse View Cl CHAM RG24 .... 145 H6 ⓵
Copse Wy EWKG RG40 .... 116 D1 ⓵
Corbett Gdns WODY RG5 .... 59 H6
Corbridge Rd WHIT RG2 .... 7 M5
Corby Cl WODY RG5 .... 59 K4
Cordale Rd BSTK RG21 .... 14 D8
Cordelia Cft BNFD RG42 .... 11 M1
Corderoy Cl STHA RG19 .... 86 A5 ⓵
Corfe Ms CAV/SC RG4 .... 58 B1
Corfield Cl EWKG RG40 .... 76 E6 ⓵
Coriander Wy EARL RG6 .... 74 C5 ⓵
Corinne Cl WHIT RG2 .... 73 J5
Corinthian Cl KEMP RG22 .... 175 H5
Corn Cft BNFD RG42 .... 80 A5 ⓵
Cornfield Rd WODY RG5 .... 59 K5
Cornfields YTLY GU46 .... 135 G3
The Cornfields KEMP RG22 .... 175 H5
Cornflower Cl WWKG RG41 .... 76 C7 ⓵
Cornish Cl KEMP RG22 .... 175 H1 ⓵
Cornwall Cl BNFD RG42 .... 80 C4
  WWKG RG41 .... 96 C1 ⓵
Cornwood Gdns WHIT RG2 .... 7 M5
Coronation Cl KSCL RG20 .... 125 J2
  ODIM RG29 .... 180 E1 ⓵
Coronation Rd ASC SL5 .... 101 K6
  BSTK RG21 .... 15 H7
  YTLY GU46 .... 135 J2
Coronation Sq EWKG RG40 .... 77 J7 ⓵
  TLHT RG30 .... 72 C2
Correlli Rd KEMP RG22 .... 176 A4
Corringway FLET GU13 .... 167 J5
Corsham Rd CALC RG31 .... 72 A3
Corsham Wy CWTH RG45 .... 118 C2
Corwen Rd TLHT RG30 .... 55 J5
Coster Cl NWBY RG14 .... 83 G2 ⓵
Cotswold Cl CALC RG31 .... 55 J4
Cotswold Rd SHST GU47 .... 118 A7 ⓵
Cotswold Wy CALC RG31 .... 55 H3
Cottage Gn HTWY RG27 .... 149 G5
Cotterell Cl BNFD RG42 .... 10 E1
Cottesmore Brook KEMP RG22 .... 99 H5
Cottesmore Rd WODY RG5 .... 59 G7
Cottington Cl KSCL RG20 .... 124 B7 ⓵
Cottle Cl BSTK RG21 .... 176 B2
Council Rd BSTK RG21 .... 14 E7
County La BNFD RG42 .... 80 B4
Courage Ct TLHT RG30 .... 72 C1 ⓵
Course Rd ASC SL5 .... 101 K1

Court Dro OVTN RG25 .... 171 G1
Courtenay Dr CAV/SC RG4 .... 43 J5
Courtlands Hl GOR/PANG RG8 .... 54 B1
Courtlands Rd NWBY RG14 .... 13 G8
Courtmoor Av FLET GU13 .... 167 G4
Courts Rd EARL RG6 .... 9 K3
The Courtyard THLE RG7 .... 70 D3
Coventry Cl KEMP RG22 .... 175 G4 ⓵
Coventry Rd READ RG1 .... 4 C6
Cove Rd FARN GU14 .... 151 J7
Covert Cl BRAK RG12 .... 11 H7
Cowdrey Cl BSTK RG21 .... 160 D4 ⓵
Cowdrey Hts CHAM RG24 .... 15 L3
Cowfold La HTWY RG27 .... 147 K4
Cow La KSCL RG20 .... 20 D4
  READ RG1 .... 2 D2
  TLHT RG30 .... 2 D4
Cowper Wy TLHT RG30 .... 6 A3
Cowslade NWBY RG14 .... 83 G2 ⓵
Cowslip Bank CHAM RG24 .... 161 G4
Cowslip Crs NTHA RG18 .... 85 J3
Coxeter Rd NWBY RG14 .... 12 A1
Coxheath Rd FLET GU13 .... 167 F5
Coxmoor Cl FLET GU13 .... 167 K6
Cox's La THLE RG7 .... 86 E4
Crabs Hl TADY RG26 .... 140 E1
Crabtree Cl NTHA RG18 .... 48 E7
Crabtree La NTHA RG18 .... 48 E7
Crabtree Wy CHAM RG24 .... 161 J7
Cradock Rd WHIT RG2 .... 7 H4
Craig Av TLHT RG30 .... 56 C5
Crail Cl WWKG RG41 .... 97 F4
Cranbourne Cl CALC RG31 .... 71 H2 ⓵
Cranbourne Gdns TLHT RG30 .... 56 A3 ⓵
Cranbourne La BSTK RG21 .... 176 A2 ⓵
Cranbrook Cl FLET GU13 .... 151 H7
Cranbury Rd TLHT RG30 .... 2 A7
Cranesfield CHAM RG24 .... 143 K6
Cranes Rd CHAM RG24 .... 143 K6
Crane Whf READ RG1 .... 3 K6
Cranford Av FLET GU13 .... 167 F6
Cranford Dr WAR/TWY RG10 .... 60 E1
Cranford Park Dr YTLY GU46 .... 135 J3
Cranmer Cl CALC RG31 .... 55 G2
Craven Dene NWBY RG14 .... 13 H2
Craven Rd NWBY RG14 .... 12 C1
  READ RG1 .... 4 A8
Crawford Cl EARL RG6 .... 9 J6
Crawford Pl NWBY RG14 .... 12 D3
Crawley Cha BNFD RG42 .... 80 E4
Crawshay Dr CAV/SC RG4 .... 43 J5
Crawts Rd OVTN RG25 .... 171 H5
Craysleaze CAV/SC RG4 .... 42 E1
Crecy Cl WWKG RG41 .... 96 D1 ⓵
Crediton Cl WODY RG5 .... 59 K7
Cremyll Rd READ RG1 .... 2 E2
Crescent Rd CALC RG31 .... 55 H4
  EWKG RG40 .... 97 H2
  READ RG1 .... 4 A6
The Crescent BRAK RG12 .... 11 H8
  EARL RG6 .... 9 L4
  FLET GU13 .... 166 D5
  HEN RG9 .... 32 A7
  THLE RG7 .... 70 D2
  THLE RG7 .... 89 F3
  THLE RG7 .... 111 F2
Cressex Cl BNFD RG42 .... 78 D4
Cressida Cha BNFD RG42 .... 80 B5 ⓵
Cressingham Rd WHIT RG2 .... 7 M7
Cresswell Rd NWBY RG14 .... 13 M1
  NWBY RG14 .... 84 D3 ⓵
Crest Ct WAR/TWY RG10 .... 46 D6
Creswell Cl WHIT RG2 .... 93 J1
Cricketers KSCL RG20 .... 82 B1
Cricketers La BNFD RG42 .... 80 D3
Cricket Field Gv CWTH RG45 .... 118 E4
Cricket Hl EWKG RG40 .... 116 E6
Cricket Hill La BLKW GU17 .... 135 J6
  YTLY GU46 .... 135 K4
Crisp Gdns BNFD RG42 .... 79 F5
Crispin Cl CAV/SC RG4 .... 42 E2
Crisp Rd HEN RG9 .... 17 F7
Crocker Cl ASC SL5 .... 81 H6
Crockford La CHAM RG24 .... 145 F6
  CHAM RG24 .... 160 E2
Crockford Pl BNFD RG42 .... 79 G5
Crockhamwell Rd WODY RG5 .... 59 H7
Crocus Md NTHA RG18 .... 85 K3
Crocus Wy WWKG RG41 .... 76 C7 ⓵
Croft Cl WWKG RG41 .... 97 F5
Crofters Meadow
  CHAM RG24 .... 161 G3 ⓵
Croft La NFNM GU10 .... 182 D7
  NWBY RG14 .... 12 B2
  YTLY GU46 .... 135 H2
Crofton Cl BRAK RG12 .... 100 B3
Croft Rd DEAN RG23 .... 173 K2
  EWKG RG40 .... 97 F6
  GOR/PANG RG8 .... 25 F5
  NWBY RG14 .... 12 D9
  THLE RG7 .... 93 K3
  THLE RG7 .... 110 E2
The Crofts KEMP RG22 .... 175 H6
The Croft BNFD RG42 .... 79 J5 ⓵
Croft Wy GOR/PANG RG8 .... 26 E3
Cromer Cl CALC RG31 .... 55 H4 ⓵
Cromwell Cl CHAM RG24 .... 161 J5
  HEN RG9 .... 31 G3 ⓵
Cromwell Rd BSTK RG21 .... 14 D2
  CAV/SC RG4 .... 57 J3
  HEN RG9 .... 31 H3
  NWBY RG14 .... 84 B2
Crondall End YTLY GU46 .... 135 H2
Crondall Rd NFNM GU10 .... 182 D1
Crookham Cl TADY RG26 .... 126 E3 ⓵
Crookham Reach FLET GU13 .... 167 F6
Crookham Rd FLET GU13 .... 167 G6
Cropmark Wy KEMP RG22 .... 175 G5
Cropper Cl STHA RG19 .... 86 B4
Crosby Gdns YTLY GU46 .... 135 F2
Crosfields Cl WHIT RG2 .... 94 B2
Crossborough Hl BSTK RG21 .... 15 H7
Cross Fell BRAK RG12 .... 10 C8
Cross Gates Cl BRAK RG12 .... 100 C3
Crossland Rd READ RG1 .... 3 J7
Cross La THLE RG7 .... 92 B7
  THLE RG7 .... 112 E1
Cross St BSTK RG21 .... 14 E6

  EWKG RG40 .... 97 H1 ⓵
  READ RG1 .... 3 J6
Crowfield Dr STHA RG19 .... 85 G4
Crown Acre Cl STHA RG19 .... 85 H4 ⓵
Crownfields ODIM RG29 .... 180 C2
Crown Gdns READ RG1 .... 167 J3
Crown La CHAM RG24 .... 161 H5
  HTWY RG27 .... 162 E4
  THLE RG7 .... 70 D3 ⓵
Crown Pl READ RG1 .... 3 L8
  SHST GU47 .... 119 F7 ⓵
Crown Rw BRAK RG12 .... 100 A4
Crown St READ RG1 .... 3 J8
Crowsley Rd HEN RG9 .... 31 K7
Crowsley Wy CAV/SC RG4 .... 29 F6
Crowthorne Rd BRAK RG12 .... 10 C9
  BRAK RG12 .... 99 G6
Crowthorne Rd North
  BRAK RG12 .... 10 F6
Crutchley Rd EWKG RG40 .... 77 H7
Cuddesdon Cl GOR/PANG RG8 .... 26 E3 ⓵
Cufaude La TADY RG26 .... 145 G4
Cuffelle Cl CHAM RG24 .... 145 H7
Culford Cl EARL RG6 .... 75 G4
Cullen Cl YTLY GU46 .... 135 H4
Culloden Wy WWKG RG41 .... 96 D1
Culver Cft BNFD RG42 .... 79 F5
Culver La EARL RG6 .... 5 H7
Culver Rd BSTK RG21 .... 14 C9
  NWBY RG14 .... 83 J7 ⓵
  READ RG1 .... 4 E8
  SHST GU47 .... 118 E7
Cumberland Av KEMP RG22 .... 175 K3 ⓵
Cumberland Dr BRAK RG12 .... 11 K2
Cumberland Rd READ RG1 .... 4 B6
Cumberland Wy WWKG RG41 .... 96 C1 ⓵
Cumnor Wy BRAK RG12 .... 11 M7
Curlew Cl KEMP RG22 .... 175 F3
  STHA RG19 .... 85 H4 ⓵
Curlew Dr CALC RG31 .... 55 H7
Curleys Wy THLE RG7 .... 114 A2 ⓵
Curling Wy NWBY RG14 .... 13 K1
Curl Wy WWKG RG41 .... 97 F2
Curridge Gn NTHA RG18 .... 64 D2
Curridge Rd NWBY RG14 .... 64 B3
Curtis Rd CALC RG31 .... 71 G1
Curzon Dr FLET GU13 .... 167 H6
Curzon St TLHT RG30 .... 2 B5
Cutbush Cl EARL RG6 .... 74 E6
Cutbush La EARL RG6 .... 9 M9
  EARL RG6 .... 74 D6
  WHIT RG2 .... 94 B1
The Cuttings NTHA RG18 .... 36 A7
Cwmcarn CAV/SC RG4 .... 43 G6
Cygnet Cl STHA RG19 .... 85 G4
Cypress Cl EWKG RG40 .... 97 F7
Cypress Dr FLET GU13 .... 167 K2
Cypress Wy WODY RG5 .... 59 K7
Cyprus Rd KEMP RG22 .... 175 H7
Cyril Vokins Rd NWBY RG14 .... 84 D5

D

Dacre Av CAV/SC RG4 .... 58 B1
Daffodil Cl KEMP RG22 .... 175 F4
Dahlia Cl KEMP RG22 .... 175 F4 ⓵
Dairy La HEN RG9 .... 18 A1
Dalby Cl WAR/TWY RG10 .... 60 E5
Dalby Crs NWBY RG14 .... 13 H9
Dalcross BRAK RG12 .... 100 B4
Dale Rd WHIT RG2 .... 7 J1
Dalewood KEMP RG22 .... 175 G4
Dalton Cl TLHT RG30 .... 55 K5 ⓵
Damar Gdns HEN RG9 .... 31 H3
Damsel Pth BSTK RG21 .... 15 K5
Dancers Meadow CHAM RG24 .... 144 A7
Dances La WHCH RG28 .... 169 H6
Danebury Rd KEMP RG22 .... 175 G6
Daneshill Dr CHAM RG24 .... 161 G3
Dankworth Rd KEMP RG22 .... 175 H4
Danvers Cl STHA RG19 .... 85 J5 ⓵
Danvers Dr FLET GU13 .... 166 E7
Danywern Dr WWKG RG41 .... 76 B4
Daphne Dr FLET GU13 .... 183 F1
Darby La GOR/PANG RG8 .... 38 E7
Darby V BNFD RG42 .... 79 J4
Darell Rd CAV/SC RG4 .... 57 G2
Dare's La NFNM GU10 .... 183 F3
Dark La CALC RG31 .... 55 G3
  CHAM RG24 .... 143 K7
  THLE RG7 .... 53 F6
  WAR/TWY RG10 .... 46 C2
Darleydale Cl SHST GU47 .... 118 E6 ⓵
Darlington Rd BSTK RG21 .... 14 D1
Darset Av FLET GU13 .... 167 H1
Dart Cl EWKG RG40 .... 116 E1
  NTHA RG18 .... 85 G2
Dartington Av WODY RG5 .... 75 G2
Dartmouth Cl BRAK RG12 .... 11 M5
Darwall Dr ASC SL5 .... 81 G7
Darwin Cl WHIT RG2 .... 7 H9
Dashwood Cl BRAK RG12 .... 11 J2
Dauntless Rd THLE RG7 .... 91 G4
Davenport Rd BRAK RG12 .... 11 L2
Daventry Ct BRAK RG12 .... 10 E1
Davis St WAR/TWY RG10 .... 76 C2
Davis Wy WAR/TWY RG10 .... 76 C2
Davy Cl EWKG RG40 .... 97 H2
  KEMP RG22 .... 159 K6
Dawlish Rd WHIT RG2 .... 7 L7
Dawnay Cl ASC SL5 .... 81 J6
Deacon Cl EWKG RG40 .... 77 H6
Deacons La NTHA RG18 .... 49 H6
Deacon Wy TLHT RG30 .... 56 B3
Deadman's La GOR/PANG RG8 .... 27 H6
  GOR/PANG RG8 .... 41 G1
  STHA RG19 .... 104 A2
  THLE RG7 .... 70 B2
Deadmoor La KSCL RG20 .... 103 H6
Deane's Cl BSTK RG21 .... 15 G2
Deanfield Av HEN RG9 .... 31 G2
Deanfield Rd HEN RG9 .... 31 F2
Dean Gv EWKG RG40 .... 77 H7
Deans Farm CAV/SC RG4 .... 4 A2
Deansgate BRAK RG12 .... 99 H5
Deansgate Rd READ RG1 .... 3 J8

Deanswood Rd *TADY* RG26 .... 126 D1
De Beauvoir Rd *READ* RG1 .... 4 C7
De Bohun Rd *READ* RG1 .... 3 J4
Decouttere Cl *FLET* GU13 .... 167 H6
Deepdale *BRAK* RG12 .... 10 C7
Deepdene Cl *READ* RG1 .... 2 D7
Deepfield Rd *BRAK* RG12 .... 11 J3
Deep La *BSTK* RG21 .... 14 A5
Dee Rd *TLHT* RG30 .... 56 B6
Deerhurst Av *WWKG* RG41 .... 76 B4
Deer Rd *TLHT* RG30 .... 56 B6
Deer Rock Hl *BRAK* RG12 .... 99 K4
Deer's La *COR/PANG* RG8 .... 27 H1
Delafield Dr *CALC* RG31 .... 71 G2
Delamere Rd *EARL* RG6 .... 5 J5
Delane Dr *WWKG* RG41 .... 76 A4
Delaney Cl *TLHT* RG30 .... 56 A5
Delft Cl *TLHT* RG30 .... 56 A5 ⬚
Delibes Rd *KEMP* RG22 .... 176 A4
Delius Cl *KEMP* RG22 .... 175 K3
Dellands *OVTN* RG25 .... 171 H5
Dellands La *OVTN* RG25 .... 171 G4
Deller St *BNFD* RG42 .... 79 G5
Dellfield *DEAN* RG23 .... 174 A1
Dell Rd *CALC* RG31 .... 55 H3
       EWKG RG40 .... 117 F5
The Dell *KSCL* RG20 .... 124 A7
       READ RG1 .... 3 L8
       YTLY GU46 .... 135 H4
The Delph *EARL* RG6 .... 75 G4
De Montfort Rd *NWBY* RG14 ...... 83 G2
       READ RG1 .... 3 H3
Denbeigh Pl *READ* RG1 .... 2 F2
Denbury Gdns *WHIT* RG2 .... 73 K6 ⬚
Denby Wy *TLHT* RG30 .... 56 A4
Dene Cl *BRAK* RG12 .... 11 H1
       BRAK RG12 .... 79 K5 ⬚
       EARL RG6 .... 9 H6
Dene Wy *NWBY* RG14 .... 83 J2
Denham Dr *KEMP* RG22 .... 175 H2
       YTLY GU46 .... 135 K4 ⬚
Denham Gv *BRAK* RG12 .... 99 K3
Denman Cl *FLET* GU13 .... 167 K2
Denmark Av *WODY* RG5 .... 59 K4
Denmark Rd *NWBY* RG14 .... 13 G4
       READ RG1 .... 4 A7
Denmark St *EWKG* RG40 .... 97 G2
Denmead Ct *BRAK* RG12 .... 100 B4
Denmead *TADY* RG26 .... 126 E1
Denning Cl *FLET* GU13 .... 167 H4
Dennisford Rd *KSCL* RG20 .... 20 E6
Dennose Cl *EARL* RG6 .... 9 H9
Denton Cl *STHA* RG19 .... 85 H5
Denton Rd *EWKG* RG40 .... 97 H2
Deptford La *ODIM* RG29 .... 179 K1
Derby Flds *ODIM* RG29 .... 164 B5
Derby Rd *CAV/SC* RG4 .... 57 J2
       NWBY RG14 .... 12 D7
Derbyshire Gn *BNFD* RG42 .... 80 C5
Derby St *READ* RG1 .... 2 E5
Derrick Cl *CALC* RG31 .... 71 H2 ⬚
Derwent Cl *WWKG* RG41 .... 96 D1 ⬚
Derwent Rd *KEMP* RG22 .... 175 F3
       STHA RG19 .... 85 F4
Deveron Dr *TLHT* RG30 .... 56 B5
Dever Wy *DEAN* RG23 .... 174 A3
The Devil's Hwy *CWTH* RG45 .... 117 K3
Devil's Hl *HEN* RG9 .... 30 A5
De-vitre Gn *EWKG* RG40 .... 78 A7
Devitt Cl *EARL* RG6 .... 8 D9
Devon Cha *BNFD* RG42 .... 80 B4 ⬚
       BNFD RG42 .... 80 C4 ⬚
Devon Cl *FARN* GU14 .... 151 J4
       WWKG RG41 .... 96 D1
Devon Dr *CAV/SC* RG4 .... 58 B1
Devonshire Gdns *CALC* RG31 ...... 55 G1
Devonshire Pk *WHIT* RG2 .... 8 D7
Devonshire Pl *BSTK* RG21 .... 14 C7
Dewe La *TLHT* RG30 .... 71 K4
Dewpond Wk *CHAM* RG24 .... 161 G3
Dexter Wy *FARN* GU14 .... 151 J6 ⬚
Diamond Wy *WWKG* RG41 .... 76 D7 ⬚
Diana Cl *KEMP* RG22 .... 175 K1
       THLE RG7 .... 93 H6
Dianthus Pl *BNFD* RG42 .... 80 E4
Dibley Cl *KEMP* RG22 .... 175 H1
Dickens Cl *CAV/SC* RG4 .... 4 A1
Dickens La *CHAM* RG24 .... 161 H7
       OVTN RG25 .... 177 G2
Dickens Wy *YTLY* GU46 .... 135 H4
Dieppe Cl *WWKG* RG41 .... 96 D1 ⬚
Digby Rd *NWBY* RG14 .... 12 B1
       NWBY RG14 .... 83 H2
Dilly La *HTWY* RG27 .... 149 H6
Dines Wy *NTHA* RG18 .... 49 C6
Dinorben Av *FLET* GU13 .... 167 H4
Dinorben Beeches *FLET* GU13 .... 167 H4
Dinorben Cl *FLET* GU13 .... 167 G4
Dippenhall St *NFNM* GU10 .... 182 E6
Ditchfield La *EWKG* RG40 .... 96 D7
Ditchling *BRAK* RG12 .... 99 H5
The Dittons *EWKG* RG40 .... 116 E2 ⬚
Dixon Rd *HTWY* RG27 .... 145 J2
Dobsons La *HEN* RG9 .... 17 F1
Doctors La *NTHA* RG18 .... 49 F7
Doddington Cl *EARL* RG6 .... 75 F5
Dodsells Well *EWKG* RG40 .... 96 E7 ⬚
Dog La *COR/PANG* RG8 .... 37 H6
       HEN RG9 .... 29 H3
Doles Hl *WWKG* RG41 .... 96 C4
Doles La *WWKG* RG41 .... 96 D4
Dollis Gn *TADY* RG26 .... 129 C6
Dolman Rd *NWBY* RG14 .... 12 E1
       NWBY RG14 .... 83 K2 ⬚
Dolphin Cl *WWKG* RG41 .... 76 B5
Dominica Cl *CHAM* RG24 .... 160 D1
Domomyclose *STHA* RG19 .... 85 K4
Donaldson Wy *WODY* RG5 .... 59 K5
Doncaster Rd *BRAK* RG12 .... 10 A6
       BRAK RG12 .... 99 F1
Don Cl *THLE* RG7 .... 93 J6
Donegal Cl *CAV/SC* RG4 .... 57 K2
Donkin Hl *CAV/SC* RG4 .... 57 K2
Donnington Cl *THLE* RG7 .... 67 K6
Donnington Gdns *READ* RG1 .... 4 B8
Donnington Pk *NWBY* RG14 .... 83 J1
Donnington Pl *WWKG* RG41 .... 76 C4 ⬚
Donnington Rd *READ* RG1 .... 4 B7
Donnington Sq *NWBY* RG14 .... 83 J2

Donnybrook *BRAK* RG12 .... 99 H5
Dora's Green La *NFNM* GU10 ..... 183 H6
Dorchester Cl *DEAN* RG23 .... 159 G6
Dorchester Ct *TLHT* RG30 .... 56 D7
Dorchester Rd *HTWY* RG27 .... 163 K2
Dorchester Wy *ODIM* RG29 .... 163 J7
Dorking Wy *CALC* RG31 .... 71 F2
Dormer Cl *READ* RG45 .... 118 B3
       NWBY RG14 .... 103 H2
Dorothy St *READ* RG1 .... 3 J8
Dorrel Cl *KEMP* RG22 .... 175 G6
Dorset St *TLHT* RG30 .... 56 D5
Dorset V *BNFD* RG42 .... 80 B4
Dorset Wy *WWKG* RG41 .... 96 D2
Doswell Wy *BSTK* RG21 .... 15 G2
Doublet Cl *STHA* RG19 .... 85 F4
Douglas Gra *WAR/TWY* RG10 ...... 76 C2
Douglas Ride *KSCL* RG20 .... 120 B1
Dove Cl *EARL* RG6 .... 74 C6 ⬚
       KEMP RG22 .... 174 E3
Dovecote Rd *WHIT* RG2 .... 73 J7
Dovedale Cl *CAV/SC* RG4 .... 57 G2
       SHST GU47 .... 118 C6
Dove La *HEN* RG9 .... 28 E3
Dover Cl *DEAN* RG23 .... 159 J5
Dover St *READ* RG1 .... 3 G8
Doveton Wy *NWBY* RG14 .... 13 H1
Dowding Rd *WODY* RG5 .... 59 K6 ⬚
Dowding Ct *CWTH* RG45 .... 118 D2 ⬚
Downend La *KSCL* RG20 .... 48 A2
Downing Rd *CALC* RG31 .... 55 H5
Down La *OVTN* RG25 .... 178 D2
Downmill Rd *BRAK* RG12 .... 10 B4
Downshire Sq *READ* RG1 .... 2 D8
Downshire Wy *BNFD* RG42 .... 10 D2
       BRAK RG12 .... 10 D4
Downsland Rd *BSTK* RG21 .... 14 B6
Downs Rd *KSCL* RG20 .... 22 B7
Downs Wy *CALC* RG31 .... 55 H3
Doyle Cl *EWKG* RG40 .... 135 H4 ⬚
Dragonfly Dr *CHAM* RG24 .... 161 G3 ⬚
Drake Cl *EWKG* RG40 .... 116 D1
Draper Cl *STHA* RG19 .... 85 J5
Draycott *BRAK* RG12 .... 100 B3
Drayton Cl *BRAK* RG12 .... 11 J4
Drayton Rd *TLHT* RG30 .... 56 C5
Dresden Wy *TLHT* RG30 .... 56 A4 ⬚
Drewett Cl *WHIT* RG2 .... 93 K1
Driftway Cl *EARL* RG6 .... 75 F5
Driftway Rd *HTWY* RG27 .... 164 B2 ⬚
The Drive *DEAN* RG23 .... 174 A3
       EARL RG6 .... 5 G6
       NWBY RG14 .... 12 B9
Droitwich Cl *BRAK* RG12 .... 11 K6
Drome Pth *WWKG* RG41 .... 75 K3
Drove La *NTHA* RG18 .... 65 G4
Drovers End *FARN* GU14 .... 151 K6
Drovers Wy *BRAK* RG12 .... 100 C1
       WODY RG5 .... 75 H1
Droxford Crs *TADY* RG26 .... 126 D2
Druce Wy *STHA* RG19 .... 85 J4
Drummond Cl *BRAK* RG12 .... 80 C6 ⬚
Drury La *THLE* RG7 .... 111 G4
Dryden *BRAK* RG12 .... 99 H5
Dryden Cl *CHAM* RG24 .... 160 D3
       NTHA RG18 .... 85 H7
Duchess Cl *CWTH* RG45 .... 118 C1 ⬚
Duddon Wy *BSTK* RG21 .... 15 K5
Dudley Cl *CALC* RG31 .... 55 K4
       DEAN RG23 .... 159 G6
Dudley Ms *CALC* RG31 .... 55 K4 ⬚
Duffield Rd *BNFD* RG42 .... 10 E1
Dukeshill Rd *BNFD* RG42 .... 10 C7
Dukes Md *FLET* GU13 .... 166 D3
Duke's Ride *CWTH* RG45 .... 118 A4
       THLE RG7 .... 128 A1
Duke St *HEN* RG9 .... 31 H1
       READ RG1 .... 3 J6
Dukes Wd *CWTH* RG45 .... 118 C3
Dulnan Cl *TLHT* RG30 .... 56 B5
Dulverton Gdns *WHIT* RG2 .... 7 M8
Dumas Cl *YTLY* GU46 .... 135 H4 ⬚
Du Maurier Cl *FLET* GU13 .... 183 F1 ⬚
Dumbarton Av *CAV/SC* RG4 .... 44 B7
Dunaways Cl *EARL* RG6 .... 75 G3
Dunbar Dr *WODY* RG5 .... 59 K7
Duncan Dr *EWKG* RG40 .... 97 J2
Duncan Gdns *GOR/PANG* RG8 ..... 55 H7 ⬚
Duncan Rd *WODY* RG5 .... 59 H7
Dundas Cl *BRAK* RG12 .... 10 E7
Dundela Cl *WODY* RG5 .... 59 H7
Dunford Pl *BNFD* RG42 .... 79 F5
Dungells Farm Cl *YTLY* GU46 .... 135 J5 ⬚
Dungells La *YTLY* GU46 .... 135 H4
Dunholme Cl *EARL* RG6 .... 9 G9
Dunkirk Cl *WWKG* RG41 .... 96 D1 ⬚
Dunley's Hl *ODIM* RG29 .... 180 B1
Dunluce Gdns *GOR/PANG* RG8 ... 40 D7 ⬚
Dunmow Hl *FLET* GU13 .... 167 H1
Dunnock Wy *WAR/TWY* RG10 .... 46 D1 ⬚
Dunoon Cl *CALC* RG31 .... 71 K2 ⬚
Dunsfold Rd *TLHT* RG30 .... 56 A6
Dunsford Crs *DEAN* RG23 .... 159 H4
Dunsmore Gdns *YTLY* GU46 ..... 135 F4
Dunstall Cl *CALC* RG31 .... 55 J5 ⬚
Dunstan Rd *NTHA* RG18 .... 85 K3
Dunstans Dr *WWKG* RG41 .... 76 A4
Dunster Cl *CAV/SC* RG4 .... 43 K6
Dunt Av *WAR/TWY* RG10 .... 76 D2
Dunt La *WAR/TWY* RG10 .... 76 D1
Durand Rd *EARL* RG6 .... 9 G9
Durant Wy *CALC* RG31 .... 55 J2
Durbidges *STHA* RG19 .... 123 K1
Durham Cl *WHIT* RG2 .... 73 K6
Durham Rd *SHST* GU47 .... 119 F6
Durham Wy *KEMP* RG22 .... 175 G4 ⬚
Durley Md *BRAK* RG12 .... 100 C3
Durnsford Av *FLET* GU13 .... 167 H4
Dwyer Rd *TLHT* RG30 .... 72 A2 ⬚
Dyer Rd *EWKG* RG40 .... 77 K7
Dysons Cl *WHIT* RG2 .... 12 B4
Dysonswood La *CAV/SC* RG4 ...... 43 H7

E

Eagle Cl *CWTH* RG45 .... 118 B1
       KEMP RG22 .... 174 E4 ⬚
       WWKG RG41 .... 96 E2 ⬚
Eagle Rd *KSCL* RG20 .... 105 G6
Eagles Nest *SHST* GU47 .... 118 B7 ⬚
Earle Cft *BNFD* RG42 .... 79 K5 ⬚
Earley Hill Rd *EARL* RG6 .... 9 C2
Earley Pl *READ* RG1 .... 3 J6
Earlsbourne *FLET* GU13 .... 167 J7
Earlsfield Cl *CAV/SC* RG4 .... 58 B1
Earlswood *BRAK* RG12 .... 99 J5
Easby Wy *EARL* RG6 .... 75 G5
Easington Dr *EARL* RG6 .... 75 H4
Eastbury Av *CALC* RG31 .... 55 G5
Eastcourt Av *EARL* RG6 .... 5 H8
Eastern Av *READ* RG1 .... 4 D9
Eastern La *CWTH* RG45 .... 119 G4
Eastern Rd *BRAK* RG12 .... 11 K4
Eastfield Av *BSTK* RG21 .... 15 G5
Eastfield La *GOR/PANG* RG8 .... 26 D5
       GOR/PANG RG8 .... 26 C5
Easthampstead Rd *BRAK* RG12 ... 10 C3
       EWKG RG40 .... 97 J1
Eastheath Av *WWKG* RG41 .... 97 F3
Eastheath Gdns *WWKG* RG41 ... 97 G4 ⬚
East La *KSCL* RG20 .... 48 A3
Eastlyn Rd *TADY* RG26 .... 109 H7
East Park Farm Dr
       WAR/TWY RG10 .... 60 A1
Eastrop La *BSTK* RG21 .... 15 G5
Eastrop Rbt *BSTK* RG21 .... 15 G4
East Stratton Cl *BRAK* RG12 ..... 100 C3 ⬚
East St *READ* RG1 .... 3 K7
East View La *WAR/TWY* RG10 .... 46 D3
Eastwood Rd *WODY* RG5 .... 75 H2
Eaton Pl *READ* RG1 .... 2 F6
Ebborn Sq *EARL* RG6 .... 75 F6 ⬚
Eccinswell Rd *KSCL* RG20 .... 123 J7
Eccles Cl *CAV/SC* RG4 .... 57 K3 ⬚
Eddington Rd *BRAK* RG12 .... 99 F4
Edenhall Cl *CALC* RG31 .... 55 J2
Edenham Cl *EARL* RG6 .... 75 H4
Edenham Crs *READ* RG1 .... 6 C1
Eden Wy *WWKG* RG41 .... 76 A5
Edgar Milward Cl *TLHT* RG30 ...... 56 A4
Edgbarrow Ri *SHST* GU47 .... 118 B6
Edgbarrowhill Star *CWTH* RG45 . 118 B5
Edgcombe La *NWBY* RG14 .... 84 B2
Edgcumbe Park Dr *CWTH* RG45 118 B3
Edgedale Cl *CWTH* RG45 .... 118 C4 ⬚
Edgehill Cl *READ* RG1 .... 175 G1
Edgehill St *READ* RG1 .... 7 J1
Edgehill St *READ* RG45 .... 118 B1 ⬚
Edinburgh Rd *TLHT* RG30 .... 2 C6
Edmonds Ct *BRAK* RG12 .... 11 H1
Edney Cl *FLET* GU13 .... 167 J5
Edward Rd *WAR/TWY* RG10 .... 46 A7
Edwin Cl *STHA* RG19 .... 86 A4
Eeklo Pl *NWBY* RG14 .... 12 F8
Egerton Rd *WHIT* RG2 .... 7 M6
Eggleton Cl *FLET* GU13 .... 167 F6 ⬚
Egremont Dr *EARL* RG6 .... 9 M6
       EARL RG6 .... 75 G4 ⬚
Elan Cl *TLHT* RG30 .... 56 A6
Elbow Cnr *BSTK* RG21 .... 14 E5
Eldart Cl *TLHT* RG30 .... 56 C6
Elderberry Bank *CHAM* RG24 ... 161 G3
Elderberry Wy *EARL* RG6 .... 75 G5 ⬚
Elder Cl *CALC* RG31 .... 55 H4
Eldon Pl *READ* RG1 .... 3 M7
Eldon Rd *READ* RG1 .... 3 M7
Eldon Sq *READ* RG1 .... 3 M7
Eldon St *READ* RG1 .... 4 A7
Eldon Ter *READ* RG1 .... 3 M7
Elford Cl *EARL* RG6 .... 9 M9
Elgar Av *CWTH* RG45 .... 118 C2
Elgar Cl *KEMP* RG22 .... 175 K4
Elgar Rd *WHIT* RG2 .... 7 H1
Elgar Rd South *WHIT* RG2 .... 7 J5
Elgarth Dr *EWKG* RG40 .... 96 E7 ⬚
Elgin Rd *BLKW* GU17 .... 151 K1
Eliot Cl *CAV/SC* RG4 .... 57 H1
       NTHA RG18 .... 85 H2
Elizabeth Av *NWBY* RG14 .... 103 G1
Elizabeth Cl *BRAK* RG12 .... 11 H8
       HEN RG9 .... 30 D2
Elizabeth Dr *FLET* GU13 .... 167 H6
Elizabeth Rd *EWKG* RG40 .... 97 J1
       HEN RG9 .... 30 E3
       KEMP RG22 .... 159 K7
Elizabeth Rout Cl *THLE* RG7 .... 93 K5
Ellenborough Cl *BRAK* RG12 ...... 11 J2
Ellen Dr *FARN* GU14 .... 151 K6
Ellen Gdns *TADY* RG26 .... 129 F6
Ellerton Cl *THLE* RG7 .... 70 D2 ⬚
Ellesfield Dr *BRAK* RG12 .... 99 F2
Ellesmere Cl *CAV/SC* RG4 .... 57 J2
Ellington Dr *KEMP* RG22 .... 175 H5
Elliot Ri *ASC* SL5 .... 81 G7
Elliots Wy *READ* RG1 .... 3 J1
Ellison Wy *EWKG* RG40 .... 97 G1
Ellis Rd *CWTH* RG45 .... 118 C2
Ellis's Hl *WHIT* RG2 .... 95 J3
Elm Bank *YTLY* GU46 .... 135 H2 ⬚
Elm Ct *CAV/SC* RG4 .... 29 G7
Elmcroft *GOR/PANG* RG8 .... 25 F6 ⬚
Elm Dr *TLHT* RG30 .... 91 G2
Elm Farm Gv *KSCL* RG20 .... 124 A7 ⬚
       NTHA RG18 .... 85 G2
Elmhurst Rd *GOR/PANG* RG8 ..... 25 F4
       NTHA RG18 .... 85 F2
       READ RG1 .... 8 B2
Elm La *EARL* RG6 .... 8 B1
Elmleigh Ct *CAV/SC* RG4 .... 57 K3 ⬚
Elmley Cl *WWKG* RG41 .... 76 E5
Elm Lodge Av *TLHT* RG30 .... 2 A5
Elm Park Rd *TLHT* RG30 .... 2 B7
Elm Rd *CAV/SC* RG4 .... 42 E5

       CHAM RG24 .... 159 J1
       EARL RG6 .... 8 E8
       OVTN RG25 .... 171 J2
Elms Av *WHIT* RG2 .... 85 K4
Elms Rd *EWKG* RG40 .... 97 G2
       FLET GU13 .... 167 K2
       HTWY RG27 .... 163 K1 ⬚
Elmstone Dr *CALC* RG31 .... 55 H4
Elmwood Wy *DEAN* RG23 .... 159 H4
Elsley Rd *CALC* RG31 .... 55 J2
Elstow Av *CAV/SC* RG4 .... 43 K6
Elstree Cl *CAV/SC* RG4 .... 55 J3
Eltham Av *CAV/SC* RG4 .... 44 B7
Elvaston Wy *TLHT* RG30 .... 56 A6
Elveden Cl *EARL* RG6 .... 75 H4
Elvendon La *GOR/PANG* RG8 ...... 41 G7 ⬚
Elvendon Rd *GOR/PANG* RG8 ..... 25 G4
Elvetham Cl *FLET* GU13 .... 151 G7
Elvetham La *HTWY* RG27 .... 150 A2
Elvetham Pl *HTWY* RG27 .... 151 F7
Elvetham Rd *FLET* GU13 .... 166 E1
Elyham *GOR/PANG* RG8 .... 41 G7 ⬚
Emblen Crs *WHIT* RG2 .... 95 H5
Embrook Wy *CALC* RG31 .... 71 F2 ⬚
Emerald Cl *WWKG* RG41 .... 76 D7 ⬚
Emery Acres *GOR/PANG* RG8 ..... 38 D6
Emery Down Cl *BRAK* RG12 ..... 100 D1 ⬚
Emma La *WAR/TWY* RG10 .... 46 D2
Emm Cl *WWKG* RG41 .... 76 E6
Emmbrook Rd *WWKG* RG41 ...... 76 E6
Emmbrook V *WWKG* RG41 .... 77 F5
Emm Cl *WWKG* RG41 .... 76 E6
Emmens La *GOR/PANG* RG8 .... 27 K1
Emmer Green Ct *CAV/SC* RG4 ..... 43 K7
Emmets Nest *BNFD* RG42 .... 78 D4
Emmets Pk *BNFD* RG42 .... 78 D4 ⬚
Emmview Cl *WWKG* RG41 .... 76 E7 ⬚
Empress Rd *CALC* RG31 .... 71 H1
Enborne Cl *CALC* RG31 .... 55 H5 ⬚
Enborne Gdns *BRAK* RG12 .... 80 A5
Enborne Gv *NWBY* RG14 .... 12 B6
Enborne Pl *NWBY* RG14 .... 12 B6
Enborne Rd *KSCL* RG20 .... 83 F6
       NWBY RG14 .... 12 B6
Enborne St *KSCL* RG20 .... 102 D4
Enborne Wy *THLE* RG7 .... 107 G2
Englefield Rd *THLE* RG7 .... 70 C2
Englemere Pk *ASC* SL5 .... 101 G2
Englemere Rd *BNFD* RG42 .... 79 G5
Ennerdale *BRAK* RG12 .... 10 C7
Ennerdale Cl *KEMP* RG22 .... 175 G2
Ennerdale Rd *WHIT* RG2 .... 8 B5
Ennerdale Wy *STHA* RG19 ...... 85 F4 ⬚
Enstone Rd *WODY* RG5 .... 59 K5
Enterprise Ct *CHAM* RG24 .... 160 E4
Enterprise Dr *STHA* RG19 .... 86 B5
Epping Cl *READ* RG1 .... 2 F7
Epping Wy *BRAK* RG12 .... 100 C2
Epsom Ct *READ* RG1 .... 2 E9
Epsom Crs *NWBY* RG14 .... 13 H8
Equine Wy *NWBY* RG14 .... 104 A1
Equinne Wy *NWBY* RG14 .... 104 A1
Erica Dr *EWKG* RG40 .... 97 J2
Eric Av *CAV/SC* RG4 .... 43 H6
Eriswell Cl *EARL* RG6 .... 75 H4
Erleigh Court Dr *EARL* RG6 .... 5 G6
Erleigh Court Gdns *EARL* RG6 ...... 5 G6
Erleigh Dene *NWBY* RG14 .... 12 C8
Erleigh Rd *READ* RG1 .... 4 A8
Erskine Rd *TADY* RG26 .... 109 J7
Esher Cl *KEMP* RG22 .... 175 J3
Eskdale Rd *WWKG* RG41 .... 75 K2
Essame Cl *EWKG* RG40 .... 97 J1
Essenden Ri *BNFD* RG42 .... 80 C5
Essex Ri *BSTK* RG21 .... 14 D5
Essex St *NWBY* RG14 .... 103 G1
       WHIT RG2 .... 7 K2
Essex Wy *CAV/SC* RG4 .... 43 H1
Ester Carling La *HEN* RG9 .... 28 E3
Eton Cl *KEMP* RG22 .... 175 F6
Europa Cl *FLET* GU13 .... 129 G6
Eustace Crs *EWKG* RG40 .... 77 K7
Evedon *BRAK* RG12 .... 99 J5
Evelyn Ct *WODY* RG5 .... 75 J1
Evendon's Cl *WWKG* RG41 .... 97 F4
Evendon's La *WWKG* RG41 .... 96 C4
Everest Rd *CWTH* RG45 .... 118 C2
Evergreen Dr *CALC* RG31 .... 72 A2 ⬚
Evergreen Wy *WWKG* RG41 ..... 96 E3 ⬚
Everington La *NTHA* RG18 .... 90 B4
Eversley Rd *WHIT* RG2 .... 95 H5
Eversley St *WHIT* RG27 .... 115 K7
Evesham Rd *CAV/SC* RG4 .... 43 J7
Evesham Wk *SHST* GU47 .... 118 D7
Evingar Gdns *WHCH* RG28 .... 169 H6
Evingar Rd *WHCH* RG28 .... 169 H6
Evreux Cr *STHA* RG19 .... 86 A5 ⬚
Ewhurst Rd *TADY* RG26 .... 142 B3
Ewshot La *FLET* GU13 .... 183 G1
Exbourne Rd *WHIT* RG2 .... 73 K6
Exeter Cl *KEMP* RG22 .... 175 G5
Exeter Gdns *YTLY* GU46 .... 135 G2
Exmoor Cl *KEMP* RG22 .... 175 G1
Exmoor Rd *STHA* RG19 .... 85 H4
Express Wy *NWBY* RG14 .... 84 D5
Eynsford Cl *CAV/SC* RG4 .... 44 B7 ⬚
Eynsham Cl *WODY* RG5 .... 59 H5

F

Fairacre *KSCL* RG20 .... 120 C1
Faircross *BRAK* RG12 .... 10 E7
Faircross Quarters *NTHA* RG18 ... 48 E7
Faircross Rd *TLHT* RG30 .... 72 D1 ⬚
Fairfax *BNFD* RG42 .... 10 D2
Fairfax Cl *CAV/SC* RG4 .... 57 J3
Fairfax Pl *NWBY* RG14 .... 84 D1 ⬚
Fairfield *KSCL* RG20 .... 21 J7
       WHCH RG28 .... 169 H1
Fairfields Rd *BSTK* RG21 .... 14 E8
Fairford Rd *CALC* RG31 .... 55 H3
Fairland Cl *FLET* GU13 .... 167 J3
Fair Lawn Gn *EARL* RG6 .... 8 E9
Fairlawn Rd *TADY* RG26 .... 127 G2

Fairlop Cl *CALC* RG31 .... 71 J2 ⬚
Fairmead Rd *WHIT* RG2 .... 94 B3
Fairmile *FLET* GU13 .... 167 H5
Fair Mile *HEN* RG9 .... 16 E5
Fair Oak La *THLE* RG7 .... 129 K2
Fairoak Wy *TADY* RG26 .... 108 A7
Fairsted Cl *TLHT* RG30 .... 56 B5 ⬚
Fairthorne Ri *CHAM* RG24 .... 161 K6 ⬚
Fairview Av *EARL* RG6 .... 5 J9
Fairview Meadow *DEAN* RG23 .. 174 A4
Fairview Rd *EWKG* RG40 .... 97 H2
Fairwater Dr *WODY* RG5 .... 5 M9
Fairway Av *TLHT* RG30 .... 71 H4
Fairway Dr *WAR/TWY* RG10 ..... 45 K7 ⬚
Faithfull Cl *BNFD* RG42 .... 79 J4
Fakenham Cl *EARL* RG6 .... 74 D6 ⬚
Fakenham Wy *SHST* GU47 .... 118 C7
Falcon Av *WHIT* RG2 .... 74 C5
Falcon Cl *KEMP* RG22 .... 174 E3
Falcon Coppice *KSCL* RG20 ..... 120 C1 ⬚
Falcon Flds *TADY* RG26 .... 108 E6
Falcon House Gdns *KSCL* RG20 . 120 B1
Falcon Wy *WWKG* RG41 .... 96 E1 ⬚
       YTLY GU46 .... 135 G3 ⬚
Falkland Dr *NWBY* RG14 .... 12 C9
Falkland Garth *NWBY* RG14 ..... 103 C1
Falkland Rd *CHAM* RG24 .... 160 D1 ⬚
       NWBY RG14 .... 103 C2
Falkners Cl *FARN* GU14 .... 151 K6
Fallowfield *FARN* GU14 .... 151 K6 ⬚
       YTLY GU46 .... 135 G2
Fallowfield Cl *CAV/SC* RG4 .... 57 J1
Falmouth Rd *WHIT* RG2 .... 73 K7
Falmouth Wy *STHA* RG19 .... 86 A4
Falstaff Av *EARL* RG6 .... 8 E7
Fanes Cl *BNFD* RG42 .... 10 B2
Fannys La *THLE* RG7 .... 66 C5
Faraday Cl *WHIT* RG2 .... 115 H1 ⬚
Faraday Rd *CHAM* RG24 .... 160 E3
       NWBY RG14 .... 13 C3
Faraday Wy *EWKG* RG40 .... 95 K7
Fareham Dr *YTLY* GU46 .... 135 G2 ⬚
Faringdon Cl *SHST* GU47 .... 118 D7
Faringdon Dr *BRAK* RG12 .... 11 J9
Farleigh Ms *CAV/SC* RG4 .... 44 B7
Farleigh Ri *BSTK* RG21 .... 176 D2
Farleigh Rd *OVTN* RG25 .... 176 C3
Farley Copse *BNFD* RG42 .... 79 F6
Farman Cl *WODY* RG5 .... 60 A5
Farm Cl *BNFD* RG42 .... 10 A1
       CWTH RG45 .... 118 D1
       GOR/PANG RG8 .... 41 H7
       YTLY GU46 .... 135 J4
Farm Dr *CALC* RG31 .... 55 G7
       FARN GU14 .... 151 J6
Farmers Cl *WHIT* RG2 .... 93 K1 ⬚
Farmers End *WAR/TWY* RG10 ..... 60 A1
Farm Ground Cl *HTWY* RG27 ..... 164 B2 ⬚
Farmhouse Wy *FLET* GU13 ...... 167 F6
Farm La *NFNM* GU10 .... 182 D7
Farm Rd *GOR/PANG* RG8 .... 25 F5
Farm Vw *YTLY* GU46 .... 135 H4
Farm View Dr *CHAM* RG24 .... 145 H7
Farnham Cl *BRAK* RG12 .... 11 J4
Farnham Dr *CAV/SC* RG4 .... 58 B1
Farnham Rd *ODIM* RG29 .... 180 E1
Farningham *BRAK* RG12 .... 100 B4
Farnsfield Cl *EARL* RG6 .... 74 D6 ⬚
Faroe Cl *CHAM* RG24 .... 160 E2
Farriers Cl *TADY* RG26 .... 129 G6
       WODY RG5 .... 59 H6
Farriers La *KSCL* RG20 .... 20 D4
Farringdon Wy *TADY* RG26 ...... 126 E2
Far Rd *HEN* RG9 .... 31 J3
Farrowdene Rd *WHIT* RG2 .... 73 K6
Fatherson Rd *READ* RG1 .... 4 B7
Faversham Rd *SHST* GU47 .... 118 E7 ⬚
Fawcett Crs *WODY* RG5 .... 59 G7
Fawconer Rd *KSCL* RG20 .... 124 A7
Fawler Md *BRAK* RG12 .... 100 C2 ⬚
Fawley Bottom La *HEN* RG9 .... 16 D5
Fawley Rd *TLHT* RG30 .... 72 D1
Faygate Wy *EARL* RG6 .... 74 E5
Fayrewood Cha *KEMP* RG22 .... 175 G5 ⬚
Feathers La *BSTK* RG21 .... 14 F6
Feld Wy *CHAM* RG24 .... 161 H4
Felixstowe Cl *EARL* RG6 .... 75 G4
The Fells *CALC* RG31 .... 55 F7 ⬚
Felstead Cl *EARL* RG6 .... 8 E7
Felthorpe Cl *EARL* RG6 .... 74 D6 ⬚
Felton Wy *CALC* RG31 .... 55 H5
Fencote *BRAK* RG12 .... 100 A5
Fennel Cl *CHAM* RG24 .... 145 H1
       EARL RG6 .... 74 C5 ⬚
       NWBY RG14 .... 84 C2
Ferbies *FLET* GU13 .... 167 H5
Ferguson Cl *BSTK* RG21 .... 176 B2
Fernbank *EWKG* RG40 .... 116 C1 ⬚
Fernbank Crs *ASC* SL5 .... 81 G6
Fernbank Pl *ASC* SL5 .... 81 F6
Fernbank Rd *ASC* SL5 .... 81 G7
Fernbrook Rd *CAV/SC* RG4 .... 42 E7
Fern Cl *CALC* RG31 .... 71 H1
       CWTH RG45 .... 118 C1
Ferndale Av *TLHT* RG30 .... 72 A2
Ferndale Cl *CALC* RG31 .... 55 K2 ⬚
Ferndale Ct *STHA* RG19 .... 85 J4
Ferndale Gdns *HTWY* RG27 ..... 163 K1 ⬚
Ferndale Rd *FLET* GU13 .... 167 G6
Fern Dr *FLET* GU13 .... 167 G6
Ferne *GOR/PANG* RG8 .... 25 F4 ⬚
Fern Gln *CALC* RG31 .... 55 H4 ⬚
Fernhill Cl *BNFD* RG42 .... 79 G5
Fernhurst Rd *CALC* RG31 .... 71 H2 ⬚
Ferrard Cl *ASC* SL5 .... 81 G6
Ferrell Fld *HTWY* RG27 .... 163 J2
Ferry La *HEN* RG9 .... 18 C4
       MLW SL7 .... 19 G5
       WAR/TWY RG10 .... 46 B2
Fidler's La *KSCL* RG20 .... 20 D4
Fidlers Wk *WAR/TWY* RG10 .... 46 B2
Field Cl *THLE* RG7 .... 91 G5
Fielden Pl *BRAK* RG12 .... 11 H3
The Fielders *HTWY* RG27 .... 134 D3
Fieldfare Av *YTLY* GU46 .... 135 F3
Field Gate Dr *KSCL* RG20 .... 123 K7
Field House Cl *ASC* SL5 .... 101 K6
Fielding Gdns *CWTH* RG45 .... 118 B4

Field Pk BRAK RG12 ...... 11 K1
Fieldridge NWBY RG14 ...... 84 B2
Field Rd READ RG1 ...... 2 F8
Field Vw CAV/SC RG4 ...... 57 J2
Fieldway FLET GU13 ...... 166 E3
WWKG RG41 ...... 76 C4
Fifth Rd NWBY RG14 ...... 12 A8
NWBY RG14 ...... 83 G6
Fifth St STHA RG19 ...... 104 E3
Filbert Cl CALC RG31 ...... 55 H5
Filey Rd READ RG1 ...... 4 D6
Finbeck Wy EARL RG6 ...... 74 C1
Fincham End Dr CWTH RG45 ...... 118 A4
Finchampstead Rd EWKG RG40 ...... 97 F6
EWKG RG40 ...... 116 E1
EWKG RG40 ...... 117 F1
Finch Cl TADY RG26 ...... 127 F2
Finch Rd EARL RG6 ...... 9 M4
Finch Wy THLE RG7 ...... 91 G4
Finmere BRAK RG12 ...... 99 K4
Finstock Cl EARL RG6 ...... 75 G5
Finstock Gn BRAK RG12 ...... 100 C2
Fir Cl FLET GU13 ...... 167 G3
Fir Cottage Rd EWKG RG40 ...... 96 D7
Fircroft Cl CALC RG31 ...... 55 H4
Firecrest Rd KEMP RG22 ...... 174 E6
Fire Thorn Cl FLET GU13 ...... 167 G5
Firglen Dr YTLY GU46 ...... 135 J2
Firgrove Rd HTWY RG27 ...... 134 D3
YTLY GU46 ...... 135 G3
Firlands BRAK RG12 ...... 11 H9
Fir's End THLE RG7 ...... 91 F5
Firs La ODIM RG29 ...... 180 B2
TLHT RG30 ...... 6 B2
Firs Rd CALC RG31 ...... 55 H7
First Av THLE RG7 ...... 109 F6
The Firs NTHA RG18 ...... 85 G3
First St STHA RG19 ...... 105 F3
Firs Wy DEAN RG23 ...... 159 G4
WHCH RG28 ...... 169 H7
Firth Cl THLE RG7 ...... 128 A1
Fir Tree Cl ASC SL5 ...... 101 K5
Fir Tree La NWBY RG14 ...... 84 D3
Firtree Wy FLET GU13 ...... 167 G3
Fisher Gn BNFD RG42 ...... 78 C4
Fisherman's La THLE RG7 ...... 108 D1
Fishers Ct CAV/SC RG4 ...... 43 K6
Fisher's La NTHA RG18 ...... 65 F5
Fishponds Cl WWKG RG41 ...... 97 F3
Fishponds Rd WWKG RG41 ...... 97 F3
Fiske Cl KEMP RG22 ...... 159 H7
Fitzroy Crs WODY RG5 ...... 59 K7
Fitzroy Rd FLET GU13 ...... 166 E2
Five Acre CALC RG31 ...... 55 G4
Flag Staff Sq STHA RG19 ...... 85 K6
Flambards CAV/SC RG4 ...... 57 K3
Flamborough Cl EARL RG6 ...... 75 H4
Flamingo Cl WWKG RG41 ...... 96 D2
Flaxfield Ct BSTK RG21 ...... 14 D5
Flaxfield Rd BSTK RG21 ...... 14 D5
Flaxman Cl EARL RG6 ...... 8 E8
Flecker Cl NTHA RG18 ...... 85 H2
Fleet Cl WWKG RG41 ...... 96 D1
Fleetham Gdns EARL RG6 ...... 9 L9
Fleet Hl EWKG RG40 ...... 116 B6
Fleet La EWKG RG40 ...... 116 A6
Fleet Rd FLET GU13 ...... 167 G2
HTWY RG27 ...... 150 B5
Fleetwood Cl NWBY RG14 ...... 84 C2
Fleming Cl WHIT RG2 ...... 115 H1
Fleming Rd NWBY RG14 ...... 13 G3
Fletcher Cl BSTK RG21 ...... 14 B7
Fletcher Gdns BNFD RG42 ...... 78 E6
Flexford Cl KSCL RG20 ...... 120 C4
Flexford Gn BRAK RG12 ...... 99 F4
Flintgrove BRAK RG12 ...... 11 J1
Flodden Dr CALC RG31 ...... 71 J2
Floral Wy NTHA RG18 ...... 85 J2
NTHA RG18 ...... 86 A3
Floreat Gdns NWBY RG14 ...... 12 A7
Florence Cl YTLY GU46 ...... 135 H3
Florence Portal Cl WHCH RG28 ...... 170 C7
Florence Rd FLET GU13 ...... 167 J5
Florence Wk READ RG1 ...... 4 B6
Florence Wy CHAM RG24 ...... 159 H3
Florian Gdns TLHT RG30 ...... 72 C1
Flower's Hl CAV/SC RG4 ...... 54 B1
Flowers Piece GOR/PANG RG8 ...... 37 J6
Fobney St READ RG1 ...... 3 H7
Fokerham Rd STHA RG19 ...... 86 A5
Folder's La BNFD RG42 ...... 79 K5
Folly Cl FLET GU13 ...... 167 H4
Folly Gn GOR/PANG RG8 ...... 26 D3
Folly La TADY RG26 ...... 129 J4
THLE RG7 ...... 90 E2
Folly Orchard Rd
GOR/PANG RG8 ...... 26 D3
The Folly NWBY RG14 ...... 13 G8
Fontwell Cl TLHT RG30 ...... 72 A1
Fontwell Rd NWBY RG14 ...... 13 G8
The Forbury READ RG1 ...... 3 J5
Forbury Rd READ RG1 ...... 3 J5
Fordham Wy EARL RG6 ...... 75 F5
Ford La ODIM RG29 ...... 179 J4
THLE RG7 ...... 114 D4
Fordwells Dr BRAK RG12 ...... 100 C2
The Forehead THLE RG7 ...... 112 A4
Forest Cl ASC SL5 ...... 101 F1
TADY RG26 ...... 108 B7
Forest Dean FARN GU14 ...... 151 K6
WHIT RG2 ...... 73 K7
Forest Dr CHAM RG24 ...... 145 G4
Forest End FLET GU13 ...... 167 G5
Forest End Rd SHST GU47 ...... 118 A7
Foresters Sq BRAK RG12 ...... 11 M6
Foresters Wy CWTH RG45 ...... 99 F7
CWTH RG45 ...... 119 G1
Forest Hl TLHT RG30 ...... 56 A3
Forest La TADY RG26 ...... 129 G1
Forest Rd ASC SL5 ...... 81 G4
BNFD RG42 ...... 78 C4
BNFD RG42 ...... 79 K3
BNFD RG42 ...... 80 C3
CWTH RG45 ...... 118 D3
EWKG RG40 ...... 77 F4
WWKG RG41 ...... 76 E5

Forge Cl CAV/SC RG4 ...... 3 M2
TADY RG26 ...... 129 H7
Forge Hl NTHA RG18 ...... 36 B7
Formby Cl EARL RG6 ...... 75 H3
Forndon Cl EARL RG6 ...... 75 H4
Fosseway WCTH RG45 ...... 118 A3
Fosters La WODY RG5 ...... 59 H7
Fountains Cl WHIT RG2 ...... 160 B2
Fountains Garth BRAK RG12 ...... 10 C6
Four Acre Coppice
HTWY RG27 ...... 164 B1
HTWY RG27 ...... 164 B2
Four Lanes Cl CHAM RG24 ...... 145 H1
Four Oaks KSCL RG20 ...... 120 C3
Fowler Cl EARL RG6 ...... 9 G6
Fowlers La BNFD RG42 ...... 10 E2
Foxborough THLE RG7 ...... 114 A2
Fox Cl THLE RG7 ...... 91 F4
Foxcombe Dr CALC RG31 ...... 55 H6
Foxcote EWKG RG40 ...... 117 F1
Fox Cft FLET GU13 ...... 167 H6
Foxdown OVTN RG25 ...... 171 H2
Fox Dr YTLY GU46 ...... 135 J2
Foxes Wk WAR/TWY RG10 ...... 59 K2
Foxglove Cl BNFD RG42 ...... 80 D4
KEMP RG22 ...... 175 F5
WWKG RG41 ...... 76 C7
Foxglove Gdns READ RG1 ...... 2 D5
Foxglove Wy NTHA RG18 ...... 85 K2
Foxhays Rd WHIT RG2 ...... 74 A6
Foxhill Cl CAV/SC RG4 ...... 44 D7
Foxhill La CAV/SC RG4 ...... 44 A5
Foxhill Rd READ RG1 ...... 4 C9
Foxhunter Wy STHA RG19 ...... 84 E4
Foxhunt Gv CALC RG31 ...... 72 A2
Fox La DEAN RG23 ...... 174 B1
HTWY RG27 ...... 134 E1
Foxley La BRAK RG12 ...... 78 C4
Foxmoor Cl DEAN RG23 ...... 174 A1
Fox Rd BRAK RG12 ...... 11 H8
Fox's Furlong CHAM RG24 ...... 145 J6
Fox's La KSCL RG20 ...... 139 K1
Fox Wy NFNM GU10 ...... 183 J4
Foxwood FARN GU14 ...... 151 K2
Foye La FLET GU13 ...... 167 J6
Foyle Pk BSTK RG21 ...... 176 C2
Framlingham Dr CAV/SC RG4 ...... 44 B7
Frampton Cl WODY RG5 ...... 59 H4
Frances Rd BSTK RG21 ...... 14 D7
The Frances NTHA RG18 ...... 85 J3
Francis Gdns BNFD RG42 ...... 80 A4
Francis St READ RG1 ...... 3 J9
Franklin Av HTWY RG27 ...... 149 G3
TADY RG26 ...... 108 D7
Franklin St READ RG1 ...... 2 E7
Fraser Av CAV/SC RG4 ...... 43 K6
Fraser Cl CHAM RG24 ...... 161 K5
Fraser Rd BNFD RG42 ...... 10 E1
Frederick Pl WWKG RG41 ...... 97 F1
Freeborn Wy BRAK RG12 ...... 11 M3
Freelands Dr FLET GU13 ...... 167 F6
Freemantle Cl BSTK RG21 ...... 160 E4
Freemantle La BSTK RG21 ...... 160 E4
Frensham BRAK RG12 ...... 100 A4
Frensham Av FLET GU13 ...... 167 K2
Frensham Cl YTLY GU46 ...... 135 G3
Frensham Gn WHIT RG2 ...... 74 C5
Frensham Rd CWTH RG45 ...... 118 C1
Frere Av FLET GU13 ...... 167 F4
Frescade Crs BSTK RG21 ...... 14 C8
Freshfield Cl EARL RG6 ...... 75 H3
Freshwater Rd READ RG1 ...... 4 C5
Freshwood Dr YTLY GU46 ...... 135 H5
Friars Keep BRAK RG12 ...... 10 F7
Friars Rd NWBY RG14 ...... 12 E9
Friar St READ RG1 ...... 3 J5
Friday St HEN RG9 ...... 31 H2
Friendship Wy BRAK RG12 ...... 10 F6
Friesian Cl FARN GU14 ...... 151 J6
Frieth Cl EARL RG6 ...... 9 G8
Frilsham Rd TLHT RG30 ...... 72 C2
Frimley Cl WODY RG5 ...... 59 G5
Fringford Cl EARL RG6 ...... 75 F5
Frithmead Cl BSTK RG21 ...... 176 B2
Frobisher BRAK RG12 ...... 99 K5
Frodsham Wy SHST GU47 ...... 119 F6
Froud Cl HTWY RG27 ...... 163 J3
Frouds La THLE RG7 ...... 88 C5
Froxfield Av READ RG1 ...... 6 D1
Froxfield Down BRAK RG12 ...... 100 C3
Fry's La YTLY GU46 ...... 135 K2
Fuchsia Cl CALC RG31 ...... 71 H1
Fugelmere Rd FLET GU13 ...... 167 K1
Fulbrook Dr ODIM RG29 ...... 180 C4
Fullbrook Cl WWKG RG41 ...... 77 F5
Fullbrook Crs CALC RG31 ...... 55 J2
Fuller Cl STHA RG19 ...... 86 A5
Fuller's La THLE RG7 ...... 92 C3
Fullerton Wy TADY RG26 ...... 127 F2
Fulmar Cl KEMP RG22 ...... 174 E6
Fulmead Rd TLHT RG30 ...... 56 D5
Fulmer Cl EARL RG6 ...... 75 F5
Further Vell-mead FLET GU13 ...... 167 F7
Furze Hill Crs CWTH RG45 ...... 118 D4
Furze Rd TADY RG26 ...... 108 C6
Fuzzy Dro KEMP RG22 ...... 174 D6
Fyfield Rd STHA RG19 ...... 85 J5
Fylingdales STHA RG19 ...... 85 H5
Fylingdales Cl KEMP RG22 ...... 175 F1

G

Gables Rd FLET GU13 ...... 167 G7
Gables Wy STHA RG19 ...... 86 C5
The Gabriels NWBY RG14 ...... 103 G2

Gage Cl CHAM RG24 ...... 161 G4
Gainsborough Cl WODY RG5 ...... 59 K7
Gainsborough Crs HEN RG9 ...... 31 F3
Gainsborough Dr ASC SL5 ...... 101 G1
Gainsborough Hl HEN RG9 ...... 31 G3
Gainsborough Rd BSTK RG21 ...... 176 D2
HEN RG9 ...... 31 F3
TLHT RG30 ...... 72 C1
Gairn Cl TLHT RG30 ...... 56 B6
Galley La STHA RG19 ...... 105 J7
The Gallops KSCL RG20 ...... 20 D5
The Gallop YTLY GU46 ...... 135 J2
Galloway Cl FARN GU14 ...... 151 K6
KEMP RG22 ...... 175 G1
Gally Hill Rd FLET GU13 ...... 167 G7
Galsworthy Dr CAV/SC RG4 ...... 44 A7
Gander Dr CHAM RG24 ...... 159 H3
Gannet Cl KEMP RG22 ...... 174 E5
Gap Wy GOR/PANG RG8 ...... 26 E3
Garden Cl HTWY RG27 ...... 163 J2
KSCL RG20 ...... 124 A7
Garden Close La NWBY RG14 ...... 103 G4
Gardeners La GOR/PANG RG8 ...... 53 F1
Garde Rd CAV/SC RG4 ...... 59 H2
Gardners Rd BNFD RG42 ...... 80 A4
Garford Crs NWBY RG14 ...... 83 G7
Garlands Cl THLE RG7 ...... 91 F5
Garnet Fld YTLY GU46 ...... 135 F4
Garnet Hl READ RG1 ...... 2 F8
Garnet St READ RG1 ...... 3 F8
Garrard St READ RG1 ...... 3 H5
Garrett Cl KSCL RG20 ...... 123 K6
Garrett Rd EWKG RG40 ...... 96 D7
Garston Cl TLHT RG30 ...... 72 B2
Garston Crs CALC RG31 ...... 71 G1
Garston Gv EWKG RG40 ...... 96 E6
Garswood BRAK RG12 ...... 100 A4
Garth Cl WWKG RG41 ...... 76 B4
Garth La THLE RG7 ...... 88 D5
Garth Rd THLE RG7 ...... 111 F3
Garth Sq BNFD RG42 ...... 79 J5
Gaskells End CAV/SC RG4 ...... 42 E4
Gas La WAR/TWY RG10 ...... 60 C1
Gaston La ODIM RG29 ...... 179 J6
Gas Works Rd READ RG1 ...... 3 M6
Gatcombe Cl CALC RG31 ...... 71 J2
Gatehampton Rd
GOR/PANG RG8 ...... 25 G7
The Gates FARN GU14 ...... 151 K6
Gayhurst Cl CAV/SC RG4 ...... 44 A6
Gaywood Dr NWBY RG14 ...... 13 L1
Gazelle Cl WWKG RG41 ...... 75 K3
Geffers Ride ASC SL5 ...... 101 H1
Gelder Cl EARL RG6 ...... 75 G5
Geoffreyson Rd CAV/SC RG4 ...... 42 E7
Georgeham Rd SHST GU47 ...... 118 E6
George Rd FLET GU13 ...... 167 J2
George St BSTK RG21 ...... 14 B5
KSCL RG20 ...... 123 K7
READ RG1 ...... 2 E5
READ RG1 ...... 3 K3
Georgia Gdns TADY RG26 ...... 127 H1
Geranium Cl CWTH RG45 ...... 98 C7
German Rd READ RG1 ...... 3 H1
Gershwin Rd KEMP RG22 ...... 175 H4
Gibbins La BNFD RG42 ...... 80 A3
Gibbs Cl EWKG RG40 ...... 116 D2
Gibbs Wy YTLY GU46 ...... 135 G5
Gifford Cl CAV/SC RG4 ...... 44 B7
Gilbard Ct CHAM RG24 ...... 145 H7
Gilbert Wy EWKG RG40 ...... 96 D7
Giles Rd TADY RG26 ...... 127 F1
Gillette Wy WHIT RG2 ...... 7 J6
Gillies Dr CHAM RG24 ...... 159 H3
Gillotts Cl HEN RG9 ...... 30 E4
Gillott's La HEN RG9 ...... 30 E4
Gill Ri BNFD RG42 ...... 79 K4
Gilroy Cl NWBY RG14 ...... 103 H2
Gingells Farm Rd
WAR/TWY RG10 ...... 46 A7
Gipsy La BRAK RG12 ...... 11 J4
EARL RG6 ...... 75 G5
EWKG RG40 ...... 97 H2
TLHT RG30 ...... 55 K4
WWKG RG41 ...... 75 J7
Girton Cl SHST GU47 ...... 119 F7
Glade Cl CHAM RG24 ...... 161 G1
The Glade CALC RG31 ...... 55 H1
NWBY RG14 ...... 83 J7
Gladridge Cl EARL RG6 ...... 9 K3
Gladstone La NTHA RG18 ...... 65 H6
Glaisdale STHA RG19 ...... 85 H5
Glamis Cl DEAN RG23 ...... 173 K2
Glamis Wy CALC RG31 ...... 71 G2
Glastonbury Cl CHAM RG24 ...... 160 B3
Glaston Hill Rd HTWY RG27 ...... 134 A1
Glebe Cl TADY RG26 ...... 127 F2
Glebe Ct FLET GU13 ...... 167 G2
Glebefields NWBY RG14 ...... 84 A2
Glebe Gdns CAV/SC RG4 ...... 59 H2
Glebelands STHA RG19 ...... 85 H4
Glebelands Rd EWKG RG40 ...... 77 G7
Glebe La CAV/SC RG4 ...... 59 H2
DEAN RG23 ...... 159 F7
HTWY RG27 ...... 149 J5
KSCL RG20 ...... 82 B2
Glebe Meadow OVTN RG25 ...... 171 H4
Glebe Ride GOR/PANG RG8 ...... 24 E5
Glebe Rd GOR/PANG RG8 ...... 41 G7
NFNM GU10 ...... 182 E6
WHIT RG2 ...... 7 L2
The Glebe GOR/PANG RG8 ...... 37 G1
Glebewood BRAK RG12 ...... 11 G9
Glenavon Gdns YTLY GU46 ...... 135 J5
Glenbeigh Ter READ RG1 ...... 2 C8
Glendale Av NWBY RG14 ...... 103 F3
Glendale Pk FLET GU13 ...... 166 D1
Glendale Rd TADY RG26 ...... 108 D7
Glendevon Rd WODY RG5 ...... 59 J5
Glenfield Cl STHA RG19 ...... 85 J5
Glennon Cl TLHT RG30 ...... 72 D2
Glenrhondda CAV/SC RG4 ...... 43 G7
Glen Rd FLET GU13 ...... 167 G3
Glenrosa Rd TLHT RG30 ...... 56 A5
The Glen TADY RG26 ...... 109 H7
Glenwood BRAK RG12 ...... 11 K8
Glenwood Dr CALC RG31 ...... 55 H6

Gloucester Dr KEMP RG22 ...... 175 G5
Gloucester Pl BNFD RG42 ...... 80 C5
Gloucester Rd NWBY RG14 ...... 12 B5
TLHT RG30 ...... 2 A7
Glyncastle CAV/SC RG4 ...... 43 G7
Goaters Rd ASC SL5 ...... 81 F7
Goat La BSTK RG21 ...... 15 G5
Goddard Cl WHIT RG2 ...... 94 B2
Goddard Ct WWKG RG41 ...... 76 A5
Goddard Dr THLE RG7 ...... 87 G4
Goddards Cl HTWY RG27 ...... 146 A2
Goddards Firs DEAN RG23 ...... 174 B4
Godstow Cl WODY RG5 ...... 59 H5
Goldcrest Cl CALC RG31 ...... 55 G7
Goldcrest Wy CALC RG31 ...... 55 G7
Gold Cup La ASC SL5 ...... 81 G6
Golden Orb Wd BNFD RG42 ...... 78 E6
Golding Cl STHA RG19 ...... 86 A4
Goldsmid Rd READ RG1 ...... 2 E7
Goldsmith Cl EWKG RG40 ...... 96 D6
NTHA RG18 ...... 85 H2
Goldsmith Wy CWTH RG45 ...... 118 C4
Goldthorpe Gdns EARL RG6 ...... 74 C6
Goldwell Dr NWBY RG14 ...... 12 C2
Gondreville Gdns FLET GU13 ...... 167 F7
Gooch Cl WAR/TWY RG10 ...... 60 E2
Goodboy's La THLE RG7 ...... 92 B6
Goodchild Rd EWKG RG40 ...... 97 J1
Goodings Gn EWKG RG40 ...... 97 K1
Goodliffe Gdns CALC RG31 ...... 55 H1
Goodman Cl BSTK RG21 ...... 14 A7
Goodrich Cl CAV/SC RG4 ...... 44 B7
Goodways Dr BRAK RG12 ...... 11 H4
Goodwin Cl CALC RG31 ...... 71 K2
Goodwood Cl THLE RG7 ...... 90 E5
Goodwood Wy NWBY RG14 ...... 13 K8
Goose Gn HTWY RG27 ...... 163 J1
Goose Green Wy STHA RG19 ...... 85 K4
Goose La HTWY RG27 ...... 163 K1
Gordon Av FLET GU13 ...... 167 J5
Gordon Cl BSTK RG21 ...... 15 H2
Gordon Crs KSCL RG20 ...... 21 J7
Gordon Pl CWTH RG45 ...... 118 E5
NTHA RG18 ...... 85 F2
NWBY RG14 ...... 13 G5
Gordon Wk YTLY GU46 ...... 135 K4
Goring La THLE RG7 ...... 90 E6
Goring Rd GOR/PANG RG8 ...... 26 C4
Gorrick Sq WWKG RG41 ...... 97 G4
Gorse Cottage Dr NTHA RG18 ...... 59 K5
Gorse Dr WODY RG5 ...... 59 K5
Gorselands CAV/SC RG4 ...... 43 H6
NWBY RG14 ...... 103 G3
TADY RG26 ...... 127 F1
YTLY GU46 ...... 135 H5
Gorse Ride North EWKG RG40 ...... 116 D1
Gorse Ride South EWKG RG40 ...... 116 D1
Gorseway FLET GU13 ...... 167 H4
Gosbrook Rd CAV/SC RG4 ...... 3 M1
READ RG1 ...... 3 J1
Gosforth Cl EARL RG6 ...... 75 G4
Gough Rd FLET GU13 ...... 167 F1
Gough's La BRAK RG12 ...... 80 A5
Gower Crs HTWY RG27 ...... 164 A2
Gower St READ RG1 ...... 2 D6
Gracemere Crs KEMP RG22 ...... 174 E5
Graces La KSCL RG20 ...... 48 A5
Graffham Ct EARL RG6 ...... 74 C6
Grafton Rd TLHT RG30 ...... 55 J6
Grafton Wy KEMP RG22 ...... 159 J7
Graham Cl CALC RG31 ...... 71 K2
Grahame Av GOR/PANG RG8 ...... 40 C7
Grainger Cl KEMP RG22 ...... 175 K3
Grampian Rd SHST GU47 ...... 118 A6
Grampian Wy KEMP RG22 ...... 175 G1
Granby Ct READ RG1 ...... 4 C7
Granby End THLE RG7 ...... 91 G4
Granby Gdns EARL RG6 ...... 4 C7
Grange Av CWTH RG45 ...... 118 C2
EARL RG6 ...... 4 F8
HEN RG9 ...... 29 H3
Grange Cl GOR/PANG RG8 ...... 24 E6
Grange La HTWY RG27 ...... 149 G5
Grangely Cl CALC RG31 ...... 71 J2
Grange Rd BRAK RG12 ...... 11 H2
FLET GU13 ...... 167 G6
HEN RG9 ...... 31 H2
The Grange NWBY RG14 ...... 103 F3
Grantham Cl SHST GU47 ...... 119 F7
Grantham Rd CALC RG31 ...... 72 A2
Grantley Dr FLET GU13 ...... 167 G4
Grant Rd CWTH RG45 ...... 118 D4
Granville Rd TLHT RG30 ...... 72 C1
Grasmere Av TLHT RG30 ...... 56 A3
Grasmere Cl WWKG RG41 ...... 76 A5
Grass Hl CAV/SC RG4 ...... 57 F2
Grassington Pl STHA RG19 ...... 85 J4
Grassmead STHA RG19 ...... 86 A5
Gratton Rd WHIT RG2 ...... 73 K6
Gratwicke Rd TLHT RG30 ...... 55 K5
Gravel Hl CAV/SC RG4 ...... 43 F6
HEN RG9 ...... 29 G5
KSCL RG20 ...... 82 B2
Gravel Hill Crs HEN RG9 ...... 29 G5
Gravelly Cl TADY RG26 ...... 127 F3
Gravel Rd CAV/SC RG4 ...... 44 C3
FLET GU13 ...... 167 J5
Graveney Dr CAV/SC RG4 ...... 57 F2
Gravett Cl HEN RG9 ...... 31 F3
Grays Crs WODY RG5 ...... 5 M5
Grazeley Rd THLE RG7 ...... 93 H3
Great Binfields Crs CHAM RG24 ...... 161 G3
Great Binfields Rd CHAM RG24 ...... 161 G4
Great Hollands Rd BRAK RG12 ...... 99 G4
Great Hollands Sq BRAK RG12 ...... 99 G4
Great Knollys St READ RG1 ...... 2 E5
Great La WHCH RG28 ...... 169 H7
Great Lea Ter THLE RG7 ...... 93 H2
Great Oaks Cha CHAM RG24 ...... 161 G4
Great Sheldons Coppice
HTWY RG27 ...... 163 J1
Grebe Cl KEMP RG22 ...... 174 E6
Greenacre KSCL RG20 ...... 124 A7
Green Acre Mt TLHT RG30 ...... 55 J5
Greenacres KSCL RG20 ...... 120 B1
Greenacres Av WWKG RG41 ...... 75 K4

Greenacres La WWKG RG41 ...... 75 K3
Greenbirch Cl KEMP RG22 ...... 174 E5
Greenbury Cl DEAN RG23 ...... 159 H6
Green Cft EWKG RG40 ...... 77 K6
Green Dean Hl CAV/SC RG4 ...... 42 C2
Green Dr EWKG RG40 ...... 97 J3
Green End Cl THLE RG7 ...... 93 J5
Green End YTLY GU46 ...... 135 J2
Greenfields Rd WHIT RG2 ...... 73 J6
Greenfield Wy CWTH RG45 ...... 118 B1
Greenfinch Cl CALC RG31 ...... 55 G7
Green Finch Cl CWTH RG45 ...... 118 A2
Green Glades FLET GU13 ...... 167 G6
Greenham Cl WODY RG5 ...... 59 K7
Greenham Rd NWBY RG14 ...... 12 F6
Greenham Wd BRAK RG12 ...... 99 K5
Greenhaven YTLY GU46 ...... 135 G4
Greenhow BRAK RG12 ...... 10 C6
Greenidge Cl READ RG1 ...... 6 C2
Greenlands KSCL RG20 ...... 102 B7
Greenlands Rd KSCL RG20 ...... 124 A7
NWBY RG14 ...... 13 G9
Green La CAV/SC RG4 ...... 29 G6
CAV/SC RG4 ...... 44 D3
EWKG RG40 ...... 78 B4
GOR/PANG RG8 ...... 26 E4
GOR/PANG RG8 ...... 40 B7
HEN RG9 ...... 31 G3
HTWY RG27 ...... 149 H5
KSCL RG20 ...... 48 A6
NWBY RG14 ...... 12 B5
STHA RG19 ...... 85 H4
TADY RG26 ...... 127 H5
THLE RG7 ...... 68 C3
THLE RG7 ...... 90 B5
THLE RG7 ...... 130 A1
WAR/TWY RG10 ...... 76 D3
WWKG RG41 ...... 76 C5
YTLY GU46 ...... 135 G2
Greenleas Av CAV/SC RG4 ...... 43 J5
Greenleas Cl YTLY GU46 ...... 135 H2
Green Leys FLET GU13 ...... 167 G7
Greenmoor GOR/PANG RG8 ...... 26 E3
Green Rd EARL RG6 ...... 8 F1
Greenside CWTH RG45 ...... 118 A3
Green Springs NFNM GU10 ...... 182 E5
Greensward La WHIT RG2 ...... 95 H4
The Green BRAK RG12 ...... 10 F8
OVTN RG25 ...... 171 J4
TADY RG26 ...... 127 F3
THLE RG7 ...... 70 B4
WHCH RG28 ...... 169 H6
WWKG RG41 ...... 76 D7
Greenway HTWY RG27 ...... 146 A2
Greenways FLET GU13 ...... 167 G5
KSCL RG20 ...... 102 B7
SHST GU47 ...... 118 C7
Green Wd ASC SL5 ...... 81 F6
Greenwood Dr CHAM RG24 ...... 145 G6
Greenwood Gv WWKG RG41 ...... 76 C3
Greenwood Rd CWTH RG45 ...... 118 D5
TLHT RG30 ...... 72 A1
Greenwoods WHCH RG28 ...... 169 H6
Gregory Cl BSTK RG21 ...... 160 D4
EARL RG6 ...... 75 F6
Greig Rd KEMP RG22 ...... 175 J3
Grensell Cl HTWY RG27 ...... 134 D1
Grenville Dr FLET GU13 ...... 167 F4
Gresham Wy TLHT RG30 ...... 56 B3
Gresley Rd BSTK RG21 ...... 15 J1
CHAM RG24 ...... 15 K1
Greyberry Copse Rd STHA RG19 ...... 84 C7
Greyfriars Rd READ RG1 ...... 3 H5
Greyhound La OVTN RG25 ...... 171 H5
Greys Ct READ RG1 ...... 3 L7
Greys Hl HEN RG9 ...... 31 G2
Greys Rd HEN RG9 ...... 30 D3
Greystoke Ct CWTH RG45 ...... 118 B4
Greystoke Rd CAV/SC RG4 ...... 57 K1
Greywell Cl TADY RG26 ...... 126 D1
Greywell Rd CHAM RG24 ...... 162 A6
HTWY RG27 ...... 163 F7
Griffin Wy North HTWY RG27 ...... 148 A7
Griffin Wy South HTWY RG27 ...... 148 A7
HTWY RG27 ...... 164 B2
Griffiths Cl STHA RG19 ...... 86 A5
Grimmer Wy GOR/PANG RG8 ...... 26 E3
Grindle Cl NTHA RG18 ...... 85 H2
Grosvenor Cl KEMP RG22 ...... 175 G7
Grosvenor Rd CAV/SC RG4 ...... 57 K2
Grove Cl BSTK RG21 ...... 15 H9
EWKG RG40 ...... 117 K1
Grove Hl CAV/SC RG4 ...... 57 H1
Groveland Pl TLHT RG30 ...... 56 C5
Groveland Rd NWBY RG14 ...... 83 G2
Grovelands Av WWKG RG41 ...... 76 C4
Grovelands Cl WWKG RG41 ...... 76 C3
Grovelands Rd THLE RG7 ...... 93 K5
TLHT RG30 ...... 56 C5
Groves Lea THLE RG7 ...... 110 E2
The Grove ASC SL5 ...... 81 F6
NTHA RG18 ...... 85 J3
READ RG1 ...... 3 L7
WAR/TWY RG10 ...... 46 C7
Guerdon Pl BRAK RG12 ...... 100 A5
Guernsey Cl CHAM RG24 ...... 160 D5
Guernsey Dr FARN GU14 ...... 151 J6
Guildford Rd FLET GU13 ...... 167 K2
Guinea Ct CHAM RG24 ...... 145 H7
Gun St READ RG1 ...... 3 H6
Gurney Cl CAV/SC RG4 ...... 42 E7
Gurney Dr CAV/SC RG4 ...... 56 E1
Guttridge La TADY RG26 ...... 126 D1
Gwyn Cl NWBY RG14 ...... 83 J7
Gwynne Cl CALC RG31 ...... 55 J2

H

Hackwood La OVTN RG25 176 C6
Hackwood Rd BSTK RG21 14 F7
BSTK RG21 176 D2
Hackwood Road Rbt BSTK RG21 15 G8
Haddon Dr WODY RG5 59 H5
Hadleigh Pl BSTK RG21 14 D5
Hadleigh Ri CAV/SC RG4 44 B7
Hadrians Wy DEAN RG23 159 H4 2
Hafod CAV/SC RG4 43 G6
Hagbourne Cl GOR/PANG RG8 26 E3 9
Hagley Rd FLET GU13 167 F1
WHIT RG2 7 K3
Haig La FLET GU13 167 J6
Hailsham Cl SHST GU47 118 E7 3
Hailstone Rd BSTK RG21 160 C3
Halcyon Ter TLHT RG30 55 K5 2
Haldane Rd CAV/SC RG4 43 F7
Hale End BRAK RG12 100 C2
Halewood BRAK RG12 99 G4
Halfacre Cl THLE RG7 93 J4
Halifax Pl NTHA RG18 85 H3 1
Hallbrook Gdns BNFD RG42 79 F5
Halley Dr ASC SL5 81 G7
Hall Farm Crs YTLY GU46 135 H4
Halliday Cl BSTK RG21 176 B2
Hall La YTLY GU46 135 H4
Halls La WHIT RG2 74 B5
Halls Rd TLHT RG30 55 H7
Halpin Cl CALC RG31 71 H2
Halstead Cl WODY RG5 59 H6
The Halters NWBY RG14 104 A1 1
Hamble Cl DEAN RG23 174 A3 2
Hamble Ct BSTK RG21 15 K5
Hambledon Cl EARL RG6 75 H5
Hamble Dr TADY RG26 127 G1
Hamborne Ga NWBY RG14 83 G6
Ham Br STHA RG19 84 D4
NWBY RG14 13 M4
Hambridge La NWBY RG14 84 D5
Hambridge Rd NWBY RG14 13 J5
NWBY RG14 84 D4
Hamdens NWBY RG14 103 F2
Hamelyn Rd BSTK RG21 14 C7
Hamilton Av HEN RG9 31 H2
Hamilton Cl NWBY RG14 12 F9
Hamilton Rd FLET GU13 167 J5 1
READ RG1 4 D8
WAR/TWY RG10 46 D2
Ham La TADY RG26 125 J3
Hamlet St BNFD RG42 11 L1
The Hamlet CAV/SC RG4 28 C6
Hammond Cl STHA RG19 85 K5
Hammond Rd BSTK RG21 14 D8
Hammonds Heath THLE RG7 111 G2
Hampden Rd CAV/SC RG4 57 J3
Hampshire Cl KEMP RG22 175 F1
Hampshire Ri BNFD RG42 80 C4 2
Hampshire Wy WWKG RG41 96 C1
Hampstead Norreys Rd
NTHA RG18 49 G6
Hampton Cl FLET GU13 167 H7
Hampton Rd NWBY RG14 12 D7
Hanbury Dr CALC RG31 71 J2 7
Hancombe Rd SHST GU47 118 B6
Handcroft Cl NFNM GU10 182 E4
Handel Cl KEMP RG22 175 K3
Handford La YTLY GU46 135 J4
Hangerfield Cl YTLY GU46 135 H4
Hanger Rd TADY RG26 108 C7
Hanmore Rd CHAM RG24 161 F1
Hannam's Farm NFNM GU10 182 D6 1
Hanningtons Wy THLE RG7 91 H4
Hanover Dr FARN GU14 151 K6
Hanover Gdns BRAK RG12 99 G5 1
BSTK RG21 176 B2
Hanwood Cl WODY RG5 5 M4
Hanworth Cl BRAK RG12 99 K4 4
Hanworth Rd BRAK RG12 99 H5
Harcourt Cl HEN RG9 31 F2
Harcourt Dr EARL RG6 8 E7
Harcourt Rd BRAK RG12 99 J4
Harding Rd WODY RG5 5 M5
Hardings La HTWY RG27 149 J4 3
Hardwell Wy BRAK RG12 11 M7
Hardwick Rd GOR/PANG RG8 40 C5
TLHT RG30 56 A6
Hardy Av YTLY GU46 135 H5
Hardy Cl CAV/SC RG4 3 L1
CAV/SC RG4 57 K3
NTHA RG18 85 H2 2
Hardy Gn CWTH RG45 118 C4
Hardy La BSTK RG21 14 B7
Hardys Fld KSCL RG20 123 K6
Harebell Cl HTWY RG27 149 J3 1
Harebell Dr NTHA RG18 85 K3
Harebell Gdns HTWY RG27 149 J3
Harefield Cl WWKG RG41 76 B4 2
Hare's La HTWY RG27 149 K2
Harewood Dr NTHA RG18 65 H6
Harfield Cl HTWY RG27 163 K2 2
Harlech Av CAV/SC RG4 44 B7
Harlech Cl DEAN RG23 159 H6
Harley Rd READ RG1 3 J1
Harlington Wy FLET GU13 167 F3
Harlton Cl EARL RG6 75 F6 5
Harman Ct WWKG RG41 76 A4
Harmans Water Rd BRAK RG12 11 J9
BRAK RG12 100 A3
Harmar Cl EWKG RG40 97 K1
Harmsworth Rd TADY RG26 126 E1 1
Harness Cl WHIT RG2 93 J1 1
Harpdon Pde YTLY GU46 135 J2 2
Harpsden Rd HEN RG9 31 H3
Harpsden Wy HEN RG9 31 H4
Harpton Cl YTLY GU46 135 J2
Harrier Cl WODY RG5 59 K7
Harrington Cl EARL RG6 9 M7
NWBY RG14 84 C2
Harris Cl WODY RG5 60 A5
Harris Hl KEMP RG22 175 G5
Harrison Cl WAR/TWY RG10 60 E2
Harrogate Rd CAV/SC RG4 57 F1
Harroway WHCH RG28 169 G3
Harrow Ct READ RG1 2 E8
Harrow Wy OVTN RG25 172 E1
The Harrow Wy KEMP RG22 175 K3
Hart Cl BNFD RG42 79 H5
Hart Dyke Cl WWKG RG41 97 G5
Hartford Bridge Flats
HTWY RG27 150 B1
Hartford Ct HTWY RG27 149 H4 1
Hartford Rd HTWY RG27 149 H4
Hartigan Pl WODY RG5 59 K5 2
Hartland Rd WHIT RG2 73 J5
Hartley Court Rd THLE RG7 93 G1
Hartley Gdns TADY RG26 126 E2
Hartley La HTWY RG27 130 C7
Hartley Meadow
WHCH RG28 169 G7 2
Hartleys THLE RG7 127 K1
Hartmead Rd STHA RG19 85 K4
Hartsbourne Rd EARL RG6 9 G6
Harts Cl WHIT RG2 95 H5 4
Harts Hill Rd NTHA RG18 85 K3
Hartshill Rd TADY RG26 126 C1
Harts La KSCL RG20 121 H3
THLE RG7 90 A2
Hartsleaf Cl FLET GU13 167 G3 1
Harts Leap Cl SHST GU47 118 B7
Hartslock Ct GOR/PANG RG8 40 A6
Hartslock Vw GOR/PANG RG8 39 H2
Hartslock Wy CALC RG31 55 H3
Hart St READ RG1 2 D5
Hartswood CHAM RG24 161 F1
Harvard Cl WODY RG5 60 A5
Harvard Rd SHST GU47 119 G7
Harvest Cl CALC RG31 55 G7 2
YTLY GU46 135 G5
Harvest Crs FARN GU14 151 J5
Harvest Gn NWBY RG14 12 B8
Harvest Ride BNFD RG42 79 H4
BNFD RG42 80 A4
BNFD RG42 80 B5
Harvest Wy CHAM RG24 161 G3
Harveys Fld OVTN RG25 171 H4
Harwich Cl EARL RG6 75 G5 3
Harwood Ri KSCL RG20 102 C7
Hastings Cl DEAN RG23 159 G6
TLHT RG30 72 B2 4
Hatch Cl THLE RG7 67 K7
Hatchet La ASC SL5 81 K3
WDSR SL4 81 K2
Hatchets La NTHA RG18 50 D6
Hatchgate Cl NTHA RG18 85 H1
Hatchgate Copse BRAK RG12 99 F4
Hatch Gate La WAR/TWY RG10 32 E4
WAR/TWY RG10 33 F5
Hatchgate Md HTWY RG27 163 K1 5
Hatch La CHAM RG24 161 J6
THLE RG7 87 K1
TLHT RG30 91 J1
Hatch Ride CWTH RG45 118 C1
EWKG RG40 98 A7
Hatchwarren Gdns
KEMP RG22 175 K5 1
Hatchwarren La KEMP RG22 175 H5
Hatch Warren La KEMP RG22 175 K5
KEMP RG22 176 A3
Hatfield Ct CALC RG31 71 G2 6
Hatford Rd TLHT RG30 72 C2
Hathaway Gdns CHAM RG24 160 D3
Hatherley Rd READ RG1 4 C8
Hatton Hl GOR/PANG RG8 37 J5
Haughurst Hl STHA RG19 125 J1
Havelock Rd WWKG RG41 97 F1 1
Havelock St WWKG RG41 97 F1 2
Haversham Dr BRAK RG12 99 J4
Hawkchurch Rd WHIT RG2 74 A6
Hawk Cl KEMP RG22 174 E4 2
Hawkedon Wy EARL RG6 75 G4
Hawker Wy WODY RG5 59 K7
Hawkesbury Dr CALC RG31 71 K3
Hawkes Cl HTWY RG27 149 H3
WWKG RG41 77 F7
Hawkfield La BSTK RG21 14 D7
Hawkins Cl BRAK RG12 80 D7
Hawkins Gv FLET GU13 166 E5
Hawkins Wy EWKG RG40 97 K1
FLET GU13 167 K3 1
Hawk La BRAK RG12 11 J8
Hawkley Dr TADY RG26 127 F2
Hawksworth Rd THLE RG7 91 G4
Hawkwell FLET GU13 167 J7
Haw La GOR/PANG RG8 37 F5
Hawley Cl CALC RG31 71 H2 5
Hawthorn Cl BNFD RG42 10 C1
Hawthorne Rd CAV/SC RG4 58 B2
Hawthornes CALC RG31 55 G3 1
Hawthorn Gdns WHIT RG2 8 C7
Hawthorn Ri HTWY RG27 164 A1 3
Hawthorn Rd NWBY RG14 12 E1
The Hawthorns TADY RG26 126 B1 1
WAR/TWY RG10 59 K2
Hawthorn Wy CAV/SC RG4 59 H3
DEAN RG23 159 H5
Haydn Rd KEMP RG22 175 J4
Haydon La KSCL RG20 20 D4
Hayes La WWKG RG41 96 B3
Hayfield Cl CALC RG31 55 H5
Hayley Gn BNFD RG42 80 C3
Hayley La ODIM RG29 180 A7
Hay Rd READ RG1 6 F2
Haywarden Pl HTWY RG27 149 J3
Haywards Cl HEN RG9 31 F2
The Haywards NTHA RG18 85 J3
Haywood BRAK RG12 99 K5
Haywood Ct EARL RG6 4 E6
Haywood Dr FLET GU13 167 H4
Haywood Wy TLHT RG30 72 A1
Hazelbank EWKG RG40 116 C2
Hazel Cl DEAN RG23 174 A3
TLHT RG30 91 G2
WWKG RG41 96 E2 4
Hazel Coppice HTWY RG27 164 A1 4
Hazel Crs WHIT RG2 8 C7
Hazeldene CHAM RG24 161 G1 1
KSCL RG20 48 A4 1
Hazel Dr WODY RG5 9 M2
Hazeley Cl HTWY RG27 149 H3
Hazel Gdns CAV/SC RG4 29 G5
Hazel Gn TADY RG26 108 A7 1
Hazel Gv NTHA RG18 85 J2
Hazell Hl BRAK RG12 11 G6
Hazelmoor La CAV/SC RG4 28 D7
Hazel Rd CALC RG31 55 H1
Hazelwood Cl CALC RG31 55 H4 4
DEAN RG23 159 J4
Hazelwood Dr DEAN RG23 159 J4
Hazelwood La BNFD RG42 79 H2
Hazely Cl HTWY RG27 149 H3
Heacham Cl EARL RG6 74 D6 7
Headington Cl EWKG RG40 77 J6 1
KEMP RG22 175 J4 1
Headington Dr EWKG RG40 77 J6
Headley Cl WODY RG5 59 K5 3
Headley Rd WODY RG5 59 H6
Headley Rd East WODY RG5 59 J6
Heardman Cl STHA RG19 86 A5
Hearmon Cl YTLY GU46 135 J3
Hearn Rd WODY RG5 75 H1
Hearns La CAV/SC RG4 28 D6
Hearn Wk BRAK RG12 11 L2
Heath Cl WWKG RG41 97 G3
Heath Dr CAV/SC RG4 44 D3
Heath End Rd TADY RG26 108 B7
Heather Cl CAV/SC RG4 29 G6
EWKG RG40 116 D1 4
Heatherden Cl WHIT RG2 73 K7
Heatherdene Av CWTH RG45 117 K4
Heather Dr FLET GU13 167 G6
NTHA RG18 85 J2
TADY RG26 108 C6
Heather Gv HTWY RG27 149 H3
Heather La HTWY RG27 163 F6
Heathermount Dr CWTH RG45 118 A2
Heather Row La HTWY RG27 163 G6
Heatherway CWTH RG45 118 B3
Heather Wy KEMP RG22 175 F5
Heathfield Av HEN RG9 44 E2
TLHT RG30 55 J6
Heathfield Cl HEN RG9 44 E2
Heathfield Ct FLET GU13 167 F4
Heathfield Rd KEMP RG22 175 J5
Heath Hill Rd North
CWTH RG45 118 C3
Heath Hill Rd South
CWTH RG45 118 C3
Heathlands KSCL RG20 120 D1
TADY RG26 108 B7 1
Heathlands Rd EWKG RG40 98 A4
Heath La NFNM GU10 182 E6
NTHA RG18 85 H2
Heathmoors BRAK RG12 99 K3 2
Heath Ride CWTH RG45 117 J4
EWKG RG40 117 F2
Heath Rd EARL RG6 9 H2
TADY RG26 109 H7
THLE RG7 68 D4
Heathrow Copse TADY RG26 126 A1
Heathview HTWY RG27 164 B1 3
Heathway ASC SL5 81 H6
CALC RG31 55 H5 2
Heathwood Cl YTLY GU46 135 J2 3
Hebbecastle Down BNFD RG42 79 J4
Hebden Cl STHA RG19 85 H6
The Hedgerows CHAM RG24 161 H3
Hedgeway NWBY RG14 13 K1
Heelas Rd WWKG RG41 97 F1
Hele Cl BSTK RG21 176 B2
Helksham Cl SHST GU47 118 E7 4
Helmsdale BRAK RG12 100 B3
Helmsdale Cl TLHT RG30 56 C5
Helston Gdns WHIT RG2 7 K9
Hemdean Hl CAV/SC RG4 57 H2
Hemdean Ri CAV/SC RG4 57 H2
Hemdean Rd CAV/SC RG4 57 H1
Hemmyng Cnr BNFD RG42 79 K4 2
Hengrave Cl EARL RG6 75 H4 7
Henley Gdns YTLY GU46 135 J4
Henley Rd CAV/SC RG4 44 D7
CAV/SC RG4 57 J2
HEN RG9 45 F4
WAR/TWY RG10 33 G1
Henley Wood Rd EARL RG6 75 G2
The Henrys NTHA RG18 85 J3
Henry St READ RG1 3 J8
Henshaw Crs NWBY RG14 83 G7
Henwick Cl NTHA RG18 85 F1
Henwick La NTHA RG18 85 F2
Henwood Copse GOR/PANG RG8 38 D6
Hepplewhite Cl TADY RG26 108 B7
Hepplewhite Dr KEMP RG22 175 F5
Herald Wy WODY RG5 59 K7
Herbert Cl BRAK RG12 99 J3
Herbert Rd FLET GU13 167 F2
Hereford Cl ODIM RG29 180 B2 2
Hereford Md FARN GU14 151 J6 4
Hereford Rd DEAN RG23 159 H6
Herewood Cl NWBY RG14 12 C1
Heritage Pk DEAN RG23 175 G7
Hermes Cl FLET GU13 167 K2
Hermitage Dr ASC SL5 81 H7
WAR/TWY RG10 46 C7
Hermitage Rd NTHA RG18 65 G4
Hermits Cl THLE RG7 91 G4
Heroes Wk WHIT RG2 73 J7
Heron Cl ASC SL5 81 G6
FLET GU13 167 K6
Herondale BRAK RG12 99 K5
Heron Dr WAR/TWY RG10 46 D6
Heron Island CAV/SC RG4 3 L2
Heron Pk CHAM RG24 161 G2
Heron Rd WWKG RG41 96 D1
Heron Shaw GOR/PANG RG8 25 F4 3
Heron's Wy EWKG RG40 77 J7
Heron Wy KEMP RG22 174 E4
READ RG1 6 C3
STHA RG19 85 G4
THLE RG7 88 E4
Herriard Wy TADY RG26 126 E2 4
Herriot Ct YTLY GU46 135 H5
Hertford Cl CAV/SC RG4 44 A6
WWKG RG41 96 D2
Hewett Av CAV/SC RG4 56 E1
Hewett Cl CAV/SC RG4 56 E1
Hexham Cl SHST GU47 118 E6
Hexham Rd WHIT RG2 7 M5
Highams Cl KSCL RG20 124 A7
High Beech BRAK RG12 100 C2 6
Highbridge Cl CAV/SC RG4 44 B7
Highbridge Whf READ RG1 3 K6
Highbury Rd CALC RG31 55 F6
Highcliffe Cl WODY RG5 59 J4
Highdown FLET GU13 167 H1
Highdown Av CAV/SC RG4 43 H6
Highdown Hill Rd CAV/SC RG4 43 H5
Highdowns KEMP RG22 175 H6
High Dr KEMP RG22 175 H2
Higher Alham BRAK RG12 100 B5 3
BRAK RG12 100 B5 3
BRAK RG12 100 B5 3
Higher Md CHAM RG24 161 G3
Highfield BRAK RG12 99 G4
EARL RG6 9 J7
Highfield Av NWBY RG14 12 E5
Highfield Cha BSTK RG21 14 B5
Highfield Cl EWKG RG40 97 G1
Highfield Pk WAR/TWY RG10 46 E2
Highfield Rd CALC RG31 55 G1
NWBY RG14 12 D9
Highgate Rd WODY RG5 75 G1
Highgrove St READ RG1 7 L1
Highgrove Ter READ RG1 3 K9
Highland Dr DEAN RG23 173 K2
FARN GU14 151 J7
Highlands Av WWKG RG41 96 B2
Highlands La HEN RG9 30 D4
Highlands Rd KEMP RG22 175 F1
Highmead Cl WHIT RG2 8 C7
High Meadow CAV/SC RG4 56 E2
Highmoor Rd CAV/SC RG4 57 G2
Highmoors CHAM RG24 145 F7
High St ASC SL5 101 J1
BRAK RG12 10 F3
CAV/SC RG4 59 G2
CWTH RG45 118 D4
GOR/PANG RG8 24 D5
GOR/PANG RG8 40 C5
HTWY RG27 149 J4
KSCL RG20 20 D5
KSCL RG20 21 J7
KSCL RG20 48 A4
ODIM RG29 180 C2
OVTN RG25 171 H4
SHST GU47 118 A7
STHA RG19 85 J4
THLE RG7 70 D3
WAR/TWY RG10 46 C3
WAR/TWY RG10 46 C7
High Tree Dr EARL RG6 5 J9
Highview CALC RG31 71 G1
Highway CWTH RG45 118 B3
Highwood Cl NWBY RG14 84 A1
YTLY GU46 135 H5
Highwood Rdg KEMP RG22 175 G6
Highworth Wy CALC RG31 55 G3
Hilary Cl WHIT RG2 73 K7
Hilary Dr CWTH RG45 118 C2
Hilborn Wy EWKG RG40 95 K6
Hilbury Rd EARL RG6 9 H6
Hilcot Rd TLHT RG30 2 A5
Hildens Dr CALC RG31 55 H6
Hillary Rd BSTK RG21 14 B1
Hillberry BRAK RG12 99 K5
Hill Bottom Cl GOR/PANG RG8 40 D1
Hillbrow WHIT RG2 8 C9
Hill Cl NWBY RG14 103 G1
Hill Copse Vw BRAK RG12 11 L2
Hillcrest FLET GU13 151 H7 1
Hillcrest Ct DEAN RG23 159 G5 1
Hillcrest La HEN RG9 29 G4
Hill Gdns GOR/PANG RG8 24 D5
Hillhouse La STHA RG19 106 B7
STHA RG19 124 B1
Hill Lands WAR/TWY RG10 46 C2
Hill Meadow OVTN RG25 171 H2
Hill Rd DEAN RG23 173 K3
NWBY RG14 12 A2
WHIT RG2 95 J6
Hillside GOR/PANG RG8 40 C4
TADY RG26 126 A5
THLE RG7 91 H4
Hillside Cl FLET GU13 166 D5
Hillside Dr BNFD RG42 78 D4
Hillside Pk WHIT RG2 8 E9
Hillside Rd EARL RG6 75 G3
ODIM RG29 180 E3
Hill St READ RG1 3 J9
Hilltop Rd CAV/SC RG4 42 E7
EARL RG6 5 K5
OVTN RG25 171 J2
WAR/TWY RG10 46 D5
Hilltop Vw YTLY GU46 135 G4
Hillview Cl CALC RG31 55 G3
Hill View Rd KEMP RG22 175 K1
Hilmanton EARL RG6 74 C6
Hindhead Rd EARL RG6 9 G6
Hinton Cl CWTH RG45 118 C1
TADY RG26 126 E2
Hinton Dr CWTH RG45 118 C1
Hinton Rd WAR/TWY RG10 60 E5
Hirstwood TLHT RG30 55 K4 3
Hirtes Av WHIT RG2 94 B2 1
Hitches La FLET GU13 166 D4
Hitherhooks Hl BNFD RG42 79 F5 1
Hocketts Cl GOR/PANG RG8 40 D1
Hockford La THLE RG7 107 H5
Hockham Rd KSCL RG20 21 J6
Hodgedale La WAR/TWY RG10 33 J5
Hodge La ASC SL5 81 K3
Hodsoll Rd READ RG1 2 E4
Hogarth Av TLHT RG30 72 A1
Hogarth Cl BSTK RG21 15 L7
Hogmoor La WAR/TWY RG10 60 E4
Hogwood La EWKG RG40 115 K2
Holbeche Cl YTLY GU46 135 F4
Holbeck BRAK RG12 99 G4
Holbein Cl BSTK RG21 15 J9
Holberton Rd WHIT RG2 74 A6
Holborne Cl NWBY RG14 103 F3
Holford Cl CALC RG31 55 H5 3
Holkam Cl TLHT RG30 56 A4 2
Holland Gdns FLET GU13 167 H3
Holland Pines BRAK RG12 99 G5
Holland Rd TLHT RG30 55 J6
The Hollands STHA RG19 85 K4
Hollicombe Cl TLHT RG30 55 K6 2
The Hollies NWBY RG14 103 G3
Hollow La WHIT RG2 94 B2
Hollowshot La KSCL RG20 139 K1
TADY RG26 140 D2
Hollybush La HTWY RG27 134 D1
TADY RG26 126 C7
THLE RG7 90 E5
Hollybush Ride EWKG RG40 117 H3
Holly Cl TADY RG26 129 H7
Hollydale Cl WHIT RG2 74 A5
Holly Dr CHAM RG24 161 K5
Hollyhock Cl KEMP RG22 175 F4
Holly La GOR/PANG RG8 37 J6
NTHA RG18 66 C3
THLE RG7 128 A1
Hollym Cl EARL RG6 75 H4
Holly Orch WWKG RG41 96 E2 5
Holly Rd WODY RG5 59 K7
Holly Spring La BRAK RG12 11 J1
Hollytrees FLET GU13 167 F5
Holmbury Av CWTH RG45 118 B1
Holmdene THLE RG7 91 G4 3
Holme Cl CWTH RG45 118 B1
Holmemoor Dr CAV/SC RG4 59 G3
Holme Park Farm La CAV/SC RG4 5 M2
Holmes Cl KEMP RG22 175 H6 2
WWKG RG41 97 F3
Holmes Crs WWKG RG41 97 F3
Holmes Rd EARL RG6 9 G2
Holmewood Cl WWKG RG41 97 F5
Holmlea Rd GOR/PANG RG8 25 F6
Holmwood Av TLHT RG30 72 A1
Holst Cl KEMP RG22 175 K5
Holsworthy Cl EARL RG6 75 H3 3
Holt Cottages STHA RG19 125 G1
Holt La HTWY RG27 164 B4
TADY RG26 125 G5
WWKG RG41 77 F7
Holton Heath BRAK RG12 100 C2 7
Holt Wy HTWY RG27 164 B1
Holy Barn Cl KEMP RG22 175 F3
Holybrook Crs TLHT RG30 72 B2 5
Holybrook Rd READ RG1 6 E1
Holyhook Cl CWTH RG45 118 B2
Holyrood Cl CAV/SC RG4 44 A6
Holywell Ct STHA RG19 85 J4 1
Hombrook Dr BNFD RG42 79 F6
Home Cft CALC RG31 55 G4
Home Farm Cl WHIT RG2 7 K4
Home Farm Rd HTWY RG27 150 C3
Homelands Wy HEN RG9 31 G2 1
Home Mead Cl NWBY RG14 83 H7
Home Park Rd YTLY GU46 135 H3
Homesteads Rd KEMP RG22 175 F3
Honeybottom Rd TADY RG26 108 E7
Honey End La TLHT RG30 56 B7
Honey Hl EWKG RG40 98 A5
Honeyhill Rd BNFD RG42 10 C2
Honey La MDHD SL6 33 K1
Honey Meadow Cl CAV/SC RG4 4 C1
Honeysuckle Cl CWTH RG45 118 B1
KEMP RG22 175 F4 2
YTLY GU46 135 F3 1
Honister Gdns FLET GU13 167 K1
Honiton Rd WHIT RG2 7 L7
Hook Common HTWY RG27 163 J4
Hookend La GOR/PANG RG8 27 J2
Hook End La GOR/PANG RG8 38 D5
Hook La TADY RG26 125 J3
TADY RG26 157 K3
Hook Rd HTWY RG27 147 K5
HTWY RG27 163 K4
KSCL RG20 124 B7
ODIM RG29 163 J7
ODIM RG29 164 B6
Hoopersmead OVTN RG25 176 B5
Hoopers Wy DEAN RG23 174 A3
Hoops Wy WHIT RG2 73 G6
Hope Av BRAK RG12 100 B5
Hopfield Rd HTWY RG27 149 H5
Hop Gdn FLET GU13 167 F7
Hop Garden Rd HTWY RG27 163 J2
Hop Gdns HEN RG9 31 G1
Hopton Garth CHAM RG24 161 H2
Hopwood Cl NWBY RG14 13 L1
Horatio Av BNFD RG42 11 M1
Horewood Rd BRAK RG12 99 J4
Hormer Cl SHST GU47 118 E7 5
Hornbeam Cl GOR/PANG RG8 41 H7 1
SHST GU47 118 E7 6
WWKG RG41 96 C4
Hornbeam Dr EARL RG6 75 G5
Hornbeam Pl HTWY RG27 164 A1 5
Hornbeams THLE RG7 113 K1
Hornby Av BRAK RG12 100 A5
Horncastle Dr TLHT RG30 72 A1 2
Horndean Rd BRAK RG12 100 C4 1
Horne Rd STHA RG19 85 J5
Hornsea Cl TLHT RG30 55 K4 4
Horn St KSCL RG20 21 K6
The Horse Cl CAV/SC RG4 57 K1
Horse Gate Ride ASC SL5 101 K4
Horsepond Rd CAV/SC RG4 28 C6
Horseshoe Crs THLE RG7 91 F4
Horseshoe End NWBY RG14 104 A1 2
Horseshoe Pk GOR/PANG RG8 40 C7
Horseshoe Rd GOR/PANG RG8 40 C7
Horsham Rd SHST GU47 118 E7
Horsnape Gdns BNFD RG42 78 C4 2
Horsneile La BNFD RG42 10 E1
Horwood Gdns BSTK RG21 176 A2
Hose Hl THLE RG7 71 F7
Hosier St READ RG1 3 H6
Hound Green Cl HTWY RG27 132 A6
Houndmills Rd BSTK RG21 159 K5
Howard Cl FLET GU13 167 K2
Howard Rd BSTK RG21 15 G9
EWKG RG40 97 H2
NWBY RG14 12 E7
Howard St READ RG1 2 F6
Howell Cl BNFD RG42 79 K4
Howes Gdns FLET GU13 167 F5
Howth Dr WODY RG5 59 G6
Hubbard Cl WAR/TWY RG10 60 E2
Hubbard Rd BSTK RG21 14 A1
Hubberholme BRAK RG12 10 D5
Huckleberry Cl
GOR/PANG RG8 55 H1 4
Huddington Gld HTWY RG27 135 F4

Hudson Rd WODY RG5 75 J1
Hudsons Meadow HTWY RG27 132 A6
Hughes Rd EWKG RG40 77 J7
Hugh Fraser Dr CALC RG31 55 H7
Huish La OVTN RG25 177 J2
Hulbert Wy KEMP RG22 175 H2
Hulfords La HTWY RG27 149 K1
Humber Cl NTHA RG18 85 G2
WWKG RG41 76 D7
Hungerford Dr READ RG1 6 D1
Hungerford La THLE RG7 68 B4
WAR/TWY RG10 61 H3
Hunnels Cl FLET GU13 183 F1
Hunters Cha CAV/SC RG4 43 G7
Hunters Cl DEAN RG23 174 A1
Hunter's Hl THLE RG7 90 E4
Hunters Wy THLE RG7 93 H6
Huntingdon Cl EARL RG6 75 H4
Hunts Cl HTWY RG27 164 B2 5
Huntsmans Meadow ASC SL5 81 J6
Huntsmoor Rd TADY RG26 108 D7
TADY RG26 126 C1
Hurricane Wy WODY RG5 59 K6
Hursley Cl TLHT RG30 55 K6 5
Hurst Park Rd WAR/TWY RG10 60 D3
Hurst Rd WAR/TWY RG10 60 D2
The Hurst HTWY RG27 166 A2
Hurst Wy WHIT RG2 73 G6
Hurstwood ASC SL5 101 K4
Huscarle Wy CALC RG31 55 H1 5
Huson Rd BNFD RG42 79 K5
Hutsons Cl EWKG RG40 77 J6
Hutton Cl EARL RG6 9 G8
NWBY RG14 13 G1
Hyacinth Cl KEMP RG22 175 F4 5
Hyde End La STHA RG19 106 E3
THLE RG7 93 K3
Hyde End Rd THLE RG7 93 K5
Hyde La KSCL RG20 123 F3
NFNM GU10 182 C5
Hydes Platt THLE RG7 128 A1
The Hydes CALC RG31 55 H1 6
Hyperion Wy WHIT RG2 7 J5
Hythe Cl BRAK RG12 11 M9

I

Ibstock Cl TLHT RG30 56 C6
Ibstone Av CAV/SC RG4 44 B7
Ibworth La TADY RG26 140 E7
Icknield Pl GOR/PANG RG8 25 G3
Icknield Rd GOR/PANG RG8 25 G3
Ilbury Cl WHIT RG2 94 B2
Ilchester Ms CAV/SC RG4 44 B6 1
Ilex Cl CAV/SC RG4 29 G7
TADY RG26 109 H7
YTLY GU46 135 G3
Ilfracombe Wy EARL RG6 75 H3
Ilkley Rd CAV/SC RG4 57 F2
Ilkley Wy STHA RG19 85 H5
Illingworth Av CAV/SC RG4 44 B7
Illingworth Gv BRAK RG12 80 C6
Ilsley Cl CAV/SC RG4 29 G6 2
Ilsley Rd KSCL RG20 21 H7
Imperial Wy WHIT RG2 73 H7
Impstone Rd TADY RG26 109 J7
Inchwood BRAK RG12 99 K6
Ingle Gln EWKG RG40 117 F1 2
Ingleton BRAK RG12 10 D6
Inglewood Cl CAV/SC RG4 29 G6
Inglewood Ct TLHT RG30 56 D7 2
Inglewood Dr KEMP RG22 175 G6
Inhams Wy THLE RG7 127 K1
Inhurst La STHA RG19 107 K7
Inhurst Wy TADY RG26 108 C7
Inkpen Cl TLHT RG30 72 B2 6
Inkpen Gdns CHAM RG24 161 H3
Innings La BNFD RG42 11 K1
Instow Rd EARL RG6 9 K7
Invergordon Cl CALC RG31 71 K2 1
Iris Cl KEMP RG22 175 F5
Irvine Wy EARL RG6 75 F6 5
Irwell Cl BSTK RG21 15 J5
Isaac Newton Rd WHIT RG2 95 J7
Isis Cl WWKG RG41 76 A5
Island Farm Rd THLE RG7 90 D6
Island Rd WHIT RG2 6 E6
Islandstone La WAR/TWY RG10 61 F7
Itchel La NFNM GU10 182 C5
Itchen Cl DEAN RG23 174 A3
Ivanhoe Rd EWKG RG40 115 K2
Ivar Gdns CHAM RG24 161 H3
Ives Cl YTLY GU46 135 G2
Ivybank CALC RG31 55 H4
Ivydene Rd TLHT RG30 56 D4
Ivy Down La DEAN RG23 173 H1
Ivyhole Hl HTWY RG27 150 C2

J

Jackdaw Cl KEMP RG22 174 E4
Jackson Cl BRAK RG12 99 J3 1
Jacksons La CAV/SC RG4 42 B7
Jacob Cl BNFD RG42 78 E7 3
James Cl BSTK RG21 160 D4
James's La TLHT RG30 91 J3
James St READ RG1 2 E6
Jameston BRAK RG12 99 K6
James Watt Rd EWKG RG40 95 K7
Janson Ct READ RG1 2 E8
Japonica Cl WWKG RG41 96 C3 2
Jaques's La THLE RG7 90 E1
Jarvis Cl HTWY RG27 134 D1
Jarvis Dr WAR/TWY RG10 46 C6
Jasmine Cl WWKG RG41 76 C7 6
Jasmine Rd KEMP RG22 175 G4
Jay Cl EARL RG6 9 K9
EARL RG6 74 E5
Jays Cl KEMP RG22 176 B3
Jedburgh Cl STHA RG19 86 A4
Jefferson Cl CAV/SC RG4 43 K5
Jefferson Rd BSTK RG21 160 C4
Jenkins Cl TLHT RG30 56 D7 3
Jenner Wk CALC RG31 55 F6 1
Jennetts Cl THLE RG7 68 B3
Jenny's Wk YTLY GU46 135 K3
Jerome Cnr CWTH RG45 118 D5
Jerome Rd WODY RG5 59 G7
Jerrymoor Hl EWKG RG40 96 E7 6
Jersey Cl CHAM RG24 160 D1
FARN GU14 151 J6 5
Jesmond Dene NWBY RG14 12 C2
Jesse Ter READ RG1 2 F7
Jessett Dr FLET GU13 167 F7
Jevington BRAK RG12 99 K5
Jibbs Meadow TADY RG26 129 G6 1
Jig's La North BNFD RG42 80 B4 2
Jig's La South BNFD RG42 11 L1
BNFD RG42 80 B5 11
Jobson Cl WHCH RG28 169 H7 2
Jock's La BNFD RG42 79 F6
Joel Cl EARL RG6 9 G6
John Hunt Cl STHA RG19 86 A5 5
John Morgan Cl HTWY RG27 148 A7 1
HTWY RG27 163 K1 6
John Nike Wy BRAK RG12 78 D7
Johnson Dr EWKG RG40 117 G1
Johnson Wy FLET GU13 167 G5
Jonathan Hl KSCL RG20 104 A5
Jones Cnr ASC SL5 81 H6
Jordan Cl CAV/SC RG4 44 B7
THLE RG7 94 A6
Jordan's La THLE RG7 90 E5
Joseph Ct BNFD RG42 80 B4 3
Josephine Ct TLHT RG30 2 B8
Josey Cl CAV/SC RG4 29 G5 1
Jouldings La HTWY RG27 115 G4
Joule Rd BSTK RG21 14 B1
Jubilee Av ASC SL5 81 H6
WWKG RG41 77 F7
Jubilee Cl ASC SL5 81 H6
TADY RG26 109 H7
Jubilee Rd BSTK RG21 14 E7
EARL RG6 5 G9
EWKG RG40 116 E5
NWBY RG14 13 G6
Jubilee Sq READ RG1 3 K8
Juliet Gdns BNFD RG42 80 C5 1
Julius Cl CHAM RG24 159 H3
Julius Hl BNFD RG42 80 C5 2
Julkes La WHIT RG2 75 H7
Junction Rd READ RG1 4 C8
Junction Ter NWBY RG14 13 J5
June Dr DEAN RG23 159 G6
Juniper BRAK RG12 99 K6
Juniper Cl CHAM RG24 145 H6
The Junipers WWKG RG41 96 C3
Juniper Wy CALC RG31 55 J3
Jupiter Wy WWKG RG41 96 E1
Justice Cl STHA RG19 86 A5
Jutland Cl WWKG RG41 96 D1 10

K

Katesgrove La READ RG1 3 H8
Kathleen Cl BSTK RG21 176 B2 2
Kathleen Sanders Ct
THLE RG7 70 D2 3
Kaynes Pk ASC SL5 81 H6
Keane Cl WODY RG5 59 H5
Kearsley Rd TLHT RG30 56 D7
Keates Gn BNFD RG42 10 F1
Keats Cl CHAM RG24 160 D2
WODY RG5 75 H1
Keats Rd WODY RG5 75 H2
Keats Wy CWTH RG45 118 C1
YTLY GU46 135 G5
Keble Wy SHST GU47 119 F6
Keepers Combe BRAK RG12 100 A4
Keephatch Rd EWKG RG40 77 K6
Keeps Md KSCL RG20 123 K6
Keighley Cl STHA RG19 85 H5
Kelburne Cl WWKG RG41 76 B3
Keldholme BRAK RG12 10 D6
Kelmscott Cl CAV/SC RG4 57 F2
Kelsey Av EWKG RG40 116 D2
Kelsey Gv YTLY GU46 135 K4
Kelton Cl EARL RG6 75 H4
Kelvedon Wy CAV/SC RG4 43 F7
Kelvin Cl WHIT RG2 115 H1 2
Kelvin Hl KEMP RG22 175 K2
Kelvin Rd NWBY RG14 13 G2
Kemble Ct CALC RG31 71 J2 3
Kemerton Cl CALC RG31 71 J2 2
Kempshott Gdns KEMP RG22 175 F4 4
Kempshott Gv KEMP RG22 159 F7 1
Kempshott La KEMP RG22 175 F3
Kempton Cl NWBY RG14 13 K8
Kenavon Dr READ RG1 3 L5
Kendal Av CAV/SC RG4 44 A7
WHIT RG2 94 B1 1
Kendal Cl NTHA RG18 85 H3
Kendal Gdns KEMP RG22 175 G3
Kendrick Cl EWKG RG40 97 G2
Kendrick Rd NWBY RG14 103 G3
READ RG1 3 L8
Kenilworth Av BRAK RG12 11 H1
TLHT RG30 6 A2
Kenilworth Crs FLET GU13 167 K1
Kenilworth Rd DEAN RG23 159 G5 2
FLET GU13 167 J6
Kenmore Cl FLET GU13 167 J2
Kennedy Cl NWBY RG14 103 G2
Kennedy Dr GOR/PANG RG8 40 C7
Kennedy Gdns EARL RG6 9 J5
Kennel Av ASC SL5 81 J6
Kennel Cl ASC SL5 81 J6
Kennel Gn ASC SL5 81 H6
Kennel La BNFD RG42 79 J5
Kennel Ride ASC SL5 81 J5
Kennel Wd ASC SL5 81 J6
Kennet Cl BSTK RG21 15 J5
STHA RG19 85 K4
Kennet Ct WWKG RG41 96 E1 3
Kennet Pl THLE RG7 91 G4
Kennet Rd NWBY RG14 12 D5
Kennet Side NWBY RG14 13 J4
READ RG1 3 L6
Kennet St READ RG1 3 L6
Kennet Wy DEAN RG23 174 A3
Kennylands Rd CAV/SC RG4 29 G7
Kensington Cl EARL RG6 74 E5
Kensington Rd TLHT RG30 2 A6
Kent Cl WWKG RG41 96 C2
Kent Folly BNFD RG42 80 C4
Kentigern Dr CWTH RG45 119 F3
Kenton Cl BRAK RG12 11 J4
Kenton Rd EARL RG6 9 M4
Kenton's La WAR/TWY RG10 32 C3
Kent Rd FLET GU13 167 J2
TLHT RG30 2 A7
Kentwood Cl TLHT RG30 55 K4
Kentwood Hl CALC RG31 55 K3
TLHT RG30 55 K4
Kenwith Av FLET GU13 167 K2 1
Kerchers Fld OVTN RG25 171 H5
Kerfield Wy HTWY RG27 164 A2 3
Kernham Dr CALC RG31 55 G3 2
Kerris Wy EARL RG6 74 D5
Kerry Cl FARN GU14 151 J5 1
Kersey Crs NWBY RG14 83 H2
Kersley Crs ODIM RG29 180 B4
Kesteven Wy WWKG RG41 96 D1 11
Keston Cl CAV/SC RG4 57 K2
Kestrel Cl NFNM GU10 183 J5
STHA RG19 85 G4 1
Kestrel Rd KEMP RG22 174 E3
Kestrel Wy THLE RG7 91 G3
TLHT RG30 72 B2
WWKG RG41 96 D1
Keswick Cl TLHT RG30 55 J6
Keswick Gdns WODY RG5 75 H1
Ketcher Gn BNFD RG42 78 D2
Ketelbey Ri KEMP RG22 176 A5
Kettering Cl CALC RG31 71 K2
Kevin Cl KSCL RG20 124 C7
Kevins Dr YTLY GU46 135 K2
Kevins Gv FLET GU13 167 J7
Keynes Cl FLET GU13 167 J7
Keynsham Wy SHST GU47 118 E6
Kibble Gn BRAK RG12 99 K4
Kibblewhite Crs
WAR/TWY RG10 46 C6 1
Kidmore End Rd CAV/SC RG4 43 H4
Kidmore La CAV/SC RG4 29 F7
CAV/SC RG4 42 E1
Kidmore Rd CAV/SC RG4 43 F6
Kilburn Cl CALC RG31 71 J2 10
Kildare Gdns CAV/SC RG4 57 K2
Kilmington Cl BRAK RG12 100 B5 4
Kiln Cl NTHA RG18 49 G6
Kiln Dr NTHA RG18 64 D1
Kiln Gdns HTWY RG27 149 H4
Kiln Hl THLE RG7 114 E1
Kiln La BRAK RG12 10 C4
CALC RG31 55 F5
HEN RG9 45 F2
TADY RG26 143 F5
THLE RG7 111 H3
Kiln Ride EWKG RG40 97 F7
EWKG RG40 117 F1
GOR/PANG RG8 38 C7
Kiln Ride Extension
EWKG RG40 117 F2
Kiln Rd CAV/SC RG4 43 K5
CHAM RG24 143 K7
NWBY RG14 84 B2
Kilnsea Dr EARL RG6 75 G4
Kiln View Rd WHIT RG2 8 A7
Kilowna Cl WAR/TWY RG10 59 K1
Kimbell Rd KEMP RG22 176 A2
Kimber Cl CHAM RG24 161 G1
Kimberley BRAK RG12 99 K6
FLET GU13 167 J7
Kimberley Cl READ RG1 6 C1
Kimberley Rd KEMP RG22 175 K1
Kimbers Dr NWBY RG14 83 F2
Kimbers La TADY RG26 127 G4
Kimmeridge BRAK RG12 100 B4 1
Kimpton Cl WHIT RG2 74 B6
King Edwards Cl ASC SL5 81 H6 1
King Edwards Ri ASC SL5 81 H6
King Edwards Rd ASC SL5 81 H6
Kingfisher Cl FLET GU13 167 H6
KEMP RG22 174 E3
THLE RG7 89 F4 1
Kingfisher Ct WAR/TWY RG10 60 D2 1
Kingfisher Dr WODY RG5 5 M9
YTLY GU46 135 G3
Kingfisher Pl READ RG1 3 K3
King James Wy HEN RG9 31 F3
King John Rd KSCL RG20 124 A7
King Johns Rd ODIM RG29 164 B7
Kingsbridge Hl THLE RG7 113 H2
Kingsbridge Rd NWBY RG14 12 A7
WHIT RG2 7 K7
Kingsclere Rd BSTK RG21 14 B1
DEAN RG23 158 D1
OVTN RG25 171 H2
Kingscroft FLET GU13 167 H3
Kingsdown Cl EARL RG6 9 J8
Kings Farm La HEN RG9 30 A5
Kingsford Cl WODY RG5 75 K1
Kings Furlong Dr BSTK RG21 14 B8
Kingsgate St READ RG1 4 B7
Kings Keep FLET GU13 167 H5
Kingsland Gra NWBY RG14 83 H7
Kingsley Cl CWTH RG45 118 C5
NWBY RG14 84 A1
WAR/TWY RG10 45 K7
WHIT RG2 73 J7
Kingsley Pk WHCH RG28 169 H6
Kingsley Rd HTWY RG27 134 B1
King's Meadow OVTN RG25 171 H4
King's Meadow Rd READ RG1 3 K4
Kingsmere Rd BNFD RG42 10 A1
Kingsmill Rd BSTK RG21 176 B2
Kings Orch DEAN RG23 174 A4
Kings Pightle CHAM RG24 145 G7
King's Ride ASC SL5 101 F2
King's Rd CAV/SC RG4 3 K1
CWTH RG45 118 C4
FLET GU13 167 J2
HEN RG9 31 G1
HEN RG9 31 G1
KEMP RG22 175 K1
NWBY RG14 12 F5
READ RG1 3 K6
THLE RG7 109 K7
Kings Rd West NWBY RG14 12 F5
Kingston Gdns WHIT RG2 7 L7
Kingston La THLE RG7 90 B1
King St ODIM RG29 180 D1
READ RG1 3 J6
THLE RG7 111 F2
King Street La WWKG RG41 76 A5
Kings Wk WHCH RG28 169 H7
Kingsway CAV/SC RG4 44 B6
Kings Wd MLW SL7 19 J3 2
Kinross Av ASC SL5 101 J3
Kinross Ct ASC SL5 101 J3
Kinson Rd TLHT RG30 56 B4
Kintyre Cl DEAN RG23 173 K2
Kipling Cl NTHA RG18 85 H2
YTLY GU46 135 H5 1
Kipling Wk KEMP RG22 175 K1
Kirkfell Cl CALC RG31 55 H3
Kirkham Cl CAV/SC RG4 44 B6
SHST GU47 118 E6 3
Kirkstall Ct CALC RG31 71 J2 11
Kirkwood Crs THLE RG7 90 E4 2
Kirton Cl TLHT RG30 56 C6
Kirtons Farm Rd TLHT RG30 72 D5
Kittiwake Cl WODY RG5 60 A6
Kitwood Dr EARL RG6 75 H5
Knappe Cl HEN RG9 31 F3
Knapp La TADY RG26 127 G3
The Knapp EARL RG6 9 J3
Knight Cl FLET GU13 166 D5
Knighton Cl CAV/SC RG4 57 H2
Knightsbridge Dr STHA RG19 105 G5
Knight St BSTK RG21 14 A7
Knights Wy CAV/SC RG4 43 J7
Knightswood BRAK RG12 99 J6
Knoll Cl FLET GU13 167 H1
Knoll Rd FLET GU13 167 H1
The Knoll CALC RG31 55 G3 3
Knollys Rd THLE RG7 109 J7
Knossington Cl EARL RG6 9 M8
Knott La THLE RG7 88 E3
Knowle Cl CAV/SC RG4 56 E1
Knowle Crs KSCL RG20 124 A7
Knowle Rd WODY RG5 75 H2
Knowles Av CWTH RG45 118 A3
Knowsley Rd CALC RG31 55 G2
Knox Cl FLET GU13 166 E6
Knox Gn BNFD RG42 78 D3
Kybes La THLE RG7 92 E3
Kyle Cl BRAK RG12 10 E6

L

Laburnum Gdns WHIT RG2 8 C9
Laburnum Gv NWBY RG14 12 E1
Laburnum Rd WWKG RG41 76 B5
Laburnum Wy DEAN RG23 159 J5
Lackmore Gdns GOR/PANG RG8 26 E3
Ladbroke Cl WODY RG5 59 J7
Ladwell Cl NWBY RG14 103 G3
Ladybank BRAK RG12 99 J6
Lady Jane Ct CAV/SC RG4 57 J2
Ladymask Cl CALC RG31 72 A2 2
Laffans Rd ODIM RG29 180 C4
The Laffords THLE RG7 68 D4
Lake End Wy CWTH RG45 118 B4
Lakelands TADY RG26 108 A7 2
Lakeside BNFD RG42 79 K5
EARL RG6 9 J6
Lakeside Ct FARN GU14 151 J7
Lakeside Dr HTWY RG27 133 G5
Lalande Cl WWKG RG41 96 D1 12
Lamb Cl NTHA RG18 85 H2
Lambdens Hl THLE RG7 69 G5
Lambdens Wk TADY RG26 126 E1 2
Lambeth Ct TLHT RG30 56 A6 1
Lambfields THLE RG7 70 C3 2
Lamborne Cl SHST GU47 118 B7
Lambourne Cl CALC RG31 55 J5 4
Lambourne Rd CAV/SC RG4 29 F6
Lambourn Rd KSCL RG20 83 F1
Lambourn Valley Wy KSCL RG20 62 E6
NWBY RG14 12 B4
Lambridge La HEN RG9 16 E7
Lambridge Wood Rd HEN RG9 16 E6
Lambs La THLE RG7 93 H7
Lambs Rw CHAM RG24 161 G4
Lamden Wy THLE RG7 91 G4
Lamerton Rd WHIT RG2 73 J5
Lammas Md BNFD RG42 79 F5
Lamorna Crs CALC RG31 55 H4
Lamp Acres NWBY RG14 84 A2
Lampards Cl HTWY RG27 147 J4
Lanark Cl WODY RG5 59 K7
Lancashire Hl BNFD RG42 80 C4 3
Lancaster Cl NTHA RG18 85 H3
READ RG1 7 M1
Lancaster Gdns EARL RG6 9 J5
Lancaster Rd BSTK RG21 14 C2
Lancing Cl TLHT RG30 2 B7
Landen Ct EWKG RG40 97 G3
Landrake Crs WHIT RG2 7 L9
Landseer Cl BSTK RG21 15 J9
Landsend La WODY RG5 60 A3
Lane End TADY RG26 129 G7
Lane End Cl WHIT RG2 94 B1 2
Laneswood THLE RG7 110 D3
The Lane TADY RG26 126 E1
Langborough Rd EWKG RG40 97 H2
Langdale Dr ASC SL5 81 H7
Langdale Gdns EARL RG6 8 E8
Langford Cl CAV/SC RG4 43 K7
Langhams Wy WAR/TWY RG10 46 C2
Langley Cl FLET GU13 167 G7
Langley Common Rd
EWKG RG40 95 J6
Langley Hl CALC RG31 71 H1
Langley Hill Cl TLHT RG30 55 H7
Laniver Cl EARL RG6 9 J9
Lansdowne Gdns THLE RG7 93 K6
Lansdowne Rd TLHT RG30 55 J6
Lansley Rd BSTK RG21 160 C3 1
Lapin La KEMP RG22 175 G7
Lapwing Cl CALC RG31 55 G7
Lapwing Ri WHCH RG28 169 G6
Larch Av WWKG RG41 77 F7
Larch Cl NWBY RG14 83 G2
TLHT RG30 91 G3
Larch Dr KSCL RG20 124 A7
WODY RG5 75 G1
Larchfield Rd FLET GU13 167 H4
Larchside Cl THLE RG7 93 J5
Larchwood CHAM RG24 145 G7 2
Larges Bridge Dr BRAK RG12 11 H5
Larges La BRAK RG12 11 H4
Larissa Cl CALC RG31 55 K4 3
Lark Cl KEMP RG22 174 E4
Larkes-meade EARL RG6 9 G9
Larkfield CHAM RG24 145 G7
Larks Barrow Hl WHCH RG28 169 H2
Larkspur Cl WWKG RG41 76 C7
Larkspur Gdns NTHA RG18 86 A3
Larkswood Cl CALC RG31 55 J2 3
SHST GU47 118 B7 3
Larkswood Dr CWTH RG45 118 C3
Larmer Cl FLET GU13 166 E4
Lashbrook Rd HEN RG9 32 A7
Latimer BRAK RG12 99 J6
Latimer Dr CALC RG31 71 H2 6
Latimer Rd WWKG RG41 97 G2
Laud Cl NWBY RG14 84 C2
WHIT RG2 7 H1
Laud's Cl HEN RG9 31 F2
Laud Wy EWKG RG40 97 K1
Launceston Av CAV/SC RG4 44 B6 2
Launcestone Cl EARL RG6 9 J7
Laundry La HTWY RG27 132 A4
Lauradale BRAK RG12 10 D7
Laurel Cl ODIM RG29 180 B1
WWKG RG41 96 E2
Laurel Dr CALC RG31 55 G5
The Laurels BSTK RG21 15 H2
FLET GU13 167 H2
GOR/PANG RG8 40 C7 1
Lavell's La THLE RG7 129 H1
Lavender Rd KEMP RG22 175 F5
Lavenham Dr WODY RG5 59 J5
Laverstoke La WHCH RG28 170 D7
Lawford Crs YTLY GU46 135 J3
Lawrence Cl CHAM RG24 160 D2
EWKG RG40 97 J1
Lawrencedale Ct BSTK RG21 14 B6
Lawrence Gv BNFD RG42 78 E6
Lawrence Rd FLET GU13 167 G3
TLHT RG30 56 B5
Lawrences La NTHA RG18 85 J1
Lawson Dr CAV/SC RG4 43 F7
Lay Fld HTWY RG27 163 J2
Layleys Gn NTHA RG18 64 E2 1
Laytom Ri CALC RG31 55 H2
Lea Cl BSTK RG21 15 K4
TLHT RG30 72 B3
Lea Cft CWTH RG45 118 C2
Leafield Copse BRAK RG12 100 C2
Lea Rd CAV/SC RG4 29 G7
Lea Springs FLET GU13 166 E4
The Lea EWKG RG40 96 E7
FLET GU13 166 E4
Leaver Rd HEN RG9 31 F2
Leaves Gn BRAK RG12 100 A4
Leawood Rd FLET GU13 166 E4 1
Le Borowe FLET GU13 167 F7
Ledbury Cl TLHT RG30 56 D5 3
Ledbury Dr CALC RG31 71 J2 12
Ledran Cl EARL RG6 75 F6 7
Lefroy Av BSTK RG21 15 G1
Lefroy's Fld NFNM GU10 182 E4
Leger Cl FLET GU13 167 F6
Lehar Cl KEMP RG22 175 J4
Leicester BRAK RG12 100 A5
Leicester Cl HEN RG9 17 G7
Leigh Fld THLE RG7 110 E2
Leipzig Barracks FLET GU13 183 J2
Leipzig Rd FLET GU13 183 J1
Leiston Cl EARL RG6 75 G5 4
Leith Cl CWTH RG45 118 B1
Lemart Cl TLHT RG30 55 K5 3
Lemington Gv BRAK RG12 99 J4 1
Leney Cl EWKG RG40 77 J6
Lenham Cl WWKG RG41 76 C5
Lennel Gdns FLET GU13 167 K5
Lennon Wy KEMP RG22 175 H5
Lennox Cl CALC RG31 71 G2 7
Lennox Rd EARL RG6 9 H1
Leopold Wk READ RG1 4 A6 1
Leppington BRAK RG12 99 J6
Lesford Rd READ RG1 6 C3
Leslie Southern Ct NWBY RG14 13 G2
Lestock Wy FLET GU13 167 K2
Letcombe Sq BRAK RG12 100 C2
Letcombe St READ RG1 3 J7
Leverkusen Rd BRAK RG12 10 F6
Levignen Cl FLET GU13 166 E6
Lewis Cl BSTK RG21 15 H1
Lewisham Wy SHST GU47 118 E7
Lexington Gv WHIT RG2 93 K1 4
Leyburn Cl WODY RG5 59 K5
Leyland Gdns WHIT RG2 94 B2
Leys Gdns NWBY RG14 12 D2
Leyside CWTH RG45 118 B3
Lichfield Cl EARL RG6 9 M9
Lichfields BRAK RG12 11 M3
Liddell Cl EWKG RG40 116 D5
Liddell Wy ASC SL5 101 J3
Lidstone Cl EARL RG6 75 G5
Liebenrood Rd TLHT RG30 56 D7 4
Lightfoot Gv BSTK RG21 176 C2
Lightsfield DEAN RG23 174 A2
Lightwood BRAK RG12 100 A4
Lilac Cl GOR/PANG RG8 41 J7 2
The Lilacs WWKG RG41 96 B4
Lilac Wy DEAN RG23 159 J5
Lily Cl KEMP RG22 175 F5
Lily Hill Dr BRAK RG12 11 M4
Lily Hill Rd BRAK RG12 11 M3
BRAK RG12 80 C7
Lima Ct READ RG1 2 E8
Limbrey Hl OVTN RG25 178 E7
Lime Cl NWBY RG14 13 M2
WWKG RG41 96 E2
Limecroft YTLY GU46 135 H4
Lime Dr FARN GU14 151 J6 5

Limefield Cl *EARL* RG6 .... 75 H3
Limerick Cl *BNFD* RG42 .... 10 C1
Limes Av *KSCL* RG20 .... 121 K2
The Limes *TADY* RG26 .... 129 J7
Limetree Av *KSCL* RG20 .... 120 E7
Limetree Rd *GOR/PANG* RG8 .... 24 E5
Lime Tree Wy *CHAM* RG24 .... 145 F7
Lime Wk *BRAK* RG12 .... 11 H7
Limmer Cl *WWKG* RG41 .... 96 B3
Limmerhill Rd *WWKG* RG41 .... 96 D2
Lincoln Cl *KEMP* RG22 .... 175 C5
  WWKG RG41 .... 75 K4
Lincoln Gdns *WAR/TWY* RG10 .... 46 C7
Lincoln Rd *WHIT* RG2 .... 7 L4
Lincolnshire Gdns *BNFD* RG42 .... 80 B5
Lindberg Wy *WODY* RG5 .... 60 A4
Lind Cl *EARL* RG6 .... 9 K7
Linden Av *CHAM* RG24 .... 161 J6
  ODIM RG29 .... 164 E7
Linden Cl *NWBY* RG14 .... 12 C1
  WWKG RG41 .... 96 E3
Linden Hill La *WAR/TWY* RG10 .... 47 H2
Lindenhill Rd *BNFD* RG42 .... 10 A2
Linden Rd *WHIT* RG2 .... 8 C8
  WODY RG5 .... 75 C2
Lindsey Cl *WWKG* RG41 .... 96 D1
Lines Rd *WAR/TWY* RG10 .... 60 D7
  WAR/TWY RG10 .... 76 E2
  WAR/TWY RG10 .... 77 F2
The Lines *KSCL* RG20 .... 124 A6
Lingfield Cl *CHAM* RG24 .... 161 K6
Lingfield Rd *NWBY* RG14 .... 13 J9
Lingholm Cl *TLHT* RG30 .... 72 A1
Lingmala Gv *FLET* GU13 .... 167 G3
Lingwood *BRAK* RG12 .... 99 K4
Link Rd *KSCL* RG20 .... 124 B7
  NWBY RG14 .... 12 E6
Links Dr *TLHT* RG30 .... 56 B5
The Links *ASC* SL5 .... 81 H7
The Link *YTLY* GU46 .... 135 H2
Link Wy *NTHA* RG18 .... 85 G3
  DEAN RG23 .... 174 A3
  WHIT RG2 .... 95 H5
Linkway *CWTH* RG45 .... 118 A3
  FLET GU13 .... 167 G5
Linnet Cl *CALC* RG31 .... 55 C7
  KEMP RG22 .... 175 F2
Linton Cl *TADY* RG26 .... 127 F2
Lion Cl *OVTN* RG25 .... 171 H5
Lion Wy *FLET* GU13 .... 167 J6
Lipscomb Cl *EARL* RG18 .... 49 C7
Lipscombe Cl *NWBY* RG14 .... 12 A5
Liscombe *BRAK* RG12 .... 99 J5
Lisle Cl *NWBY* RG14 .... 83 J2
Lismore Cl *WODY* RG5 .... 59 K5
Lismoyne Cl *FLET* GU13 .... 167 G1
Lister Cl *GOR/PANG* RG8 .... 41 H7
Lister Rd *KEMP* RG22 .... 175 K2
Littington Cl *EARL* RG6 .... 75 F6
Little Aldershot La *STHA* RG19 .... 107 K6
Little Basing *CHAM* RG24 .... 161 C4
Little Bowden La
  GOR/PANG RG8 .... 39 J7
  YTLY GU46 .... 135 C4
Little Copse *FLET* GU13 .... 167 C4
Littlecote Dr *READ* RG1 .... 2 D9
Little Croft Rd *GOR/PANG* RG8 .... 25 F6
Littledale Cl *BRAK* RG12 .... 11 L5
Little Dean La *OVTN* RG25 .... 179 H7
Little Fallow *CHAM* RG24 .... 161 C4
Little Frith *EWKG* RG40 .... 117 H2
Little Glebe *CAV/SC* RG4 .... 59 H7
Little Heath Rd *CALC* RG31 .... 55 F6
Little Hill Rd *WAR/TWY* RG10 .... 76 C2
Little Hoddington Cl
  OVTN RG25 .... 179 F7
Littlejohn's La *TLHT* RG30 .... 2 A3
Little John's La *TLHT* RG30 .... 56 D5
Little Knowle Hl *KSCL* RG20 .... 124 C5
  STHA RG19 .... 124 E3
Little La *THLE* RG7 .... 86 D1
Little London Rd *THLE* RG7 .... 127 K3
Little Moor *SHST* GU47 .... 118 D7
Little Oak Dr *CALC* RG31 .... 55 H5
Little Ringdale *BRAK* RG12 .... 11 M8
Littlestead Cl *CAV/SC* RG4 .... 44 B6
Little St *READ* RG1 .... 2 D5
Little Vigo *YTLY* GU46 .... 135 C5
Litton Gdns *DEAN* RG23 .... 174 A3
Litton Rd *WHIT* RG2 .... 8 A4
Liverpool Rd *READ* RG1 .... 4 C5
Livery Cl *READ* RG1 .... 3 K7
Livingstone Gdns *WODY* RG5 .... 75 H1
Livingstone Rd *NWBY* RG14 .... 13 G5
Llangar Gv *CWTH* RG45 .... 118 B3
Llanvair Cl *ASC* SL5 .... 101 K4
Llanvair Dr *ASC* SL5 .... 101 J5
Llewellyn Pk *WAR/TWY* RG10 .... 46 B6
Lloyd's La *TADY* RG26 .... 141 K5
Lochinver *BRAK* RG12 .... 99 J5
Lock Pl *READ* RG1 .... 4 A6
Lockram La *THLE* RG7 .... 91 H6
Locksbridge La *TADY* RG26 .... 128 C7
Lockside Ct *THLE* RG7 .... 89 F4
Locks Ride *ASC* SL5 .... 81 F5
Lockstile Md *GOR/PANG* RG8 .... 25 F4
Lockstile Wy *GOR/PANG* RG8 .... 25 F5
Lockton Cha *ASC* SL5 .... 101 C1
Loddon Br *EARL* RG6 .... 75 J3
Loddon Bridge Rd *EARL* RG6 .... 75 J2
  WODY RG5 .... 75 J1
Loddon Dr *BSTK* RG21 .... 15 J5
  WAR/TWY RG10 .... 46 A3
Loddon Hall Rd *WAR/TWY* RG10 .... 46 C7
Lodge Rd *WAR/TWY* RG10 .... 60 D5
Logan Cl *TLHT* RG30 .... 56 A6
Loggon Rd *BSTK* RG21 .... 176 B3
Lomond Av *CAV/SC* RG4 .... 44 B7
Lomond Cl *DEAN* RG23 .... 173 K3
Londlandes *FLET* GU13 .... 167 F7
London Rd *ASC* SL5 .... 100 D1
  BNFD RG42 .... 78 D7
  BNFD RG42 .... 98 C1
  BRAK RG12 .... 11 J3
  BSTK RG21 .... 14 F6
  CHAM RG24 .... 161 J7
  EARL RG6 .... 5 J4

  EWKG RG40 .... 97 K1
  HTWY RG27 .... 148 D7
  HTWY RG27 .... 149 H5
  HTWY RG27 .... 162 D4
  NWBY RG14 .... 12 E2
  ODIM RG29 .... 164 F7
  ODIM RG29 .... 180 D1
  OVTN RG25 .... 171 C5
  READ RG1 .... 3 L8
  STHA RG19 .... 85 K4
  WAR/TWY RG10 .... 46 D6
  WHCH RG28 .... 169 K7
London St *READ* RG1 .... 3 K6
  WHCH RG28 .... 169 H7
Longacre *NWBY* RG14 .... 83 C7
Longacre Ri *CHAM* RG24 .... 161 F1
Long Barn La *WHIT* RG2 .... 7 K5
Longbridge Cl *HTWY* RG27 .... 146 B1
Longbridge Rd *TADY* RG26 .... 129 C6
Long Copse Cha *CHAM* RG24 .... 161 F1
Longcroft Rd *KSCL* RG20 .... 123 K6
  STHA RG19 .... 85 K5
Long Cross La *KEMP* RG22 .... 175 F6
Longdon Rd *WWKG* RG41 .... 76 B5
Longdown Rd *FLET* GU13 .... 167 G5
Longfield Rd *WAR/TWY* RG10 .... 46 C6
Long Gv *TADY* RG26 .... 108 A6
  THLE RG7 .... 86 C2
Long Hill Rd *ASC* SL5 .... 80 E6
  BRAK RG12 .... 80 D7
Longhurst Cl *CAV/SC* RG4 .... 57 K2
Long La *CALC* RG31 .... 55 G1
  CHAM RG24 .... 161 H1
  NTHA RG18 .... 64 E4
  NWBY RG14 .... 64 B7
  ODIM RG29 .... 180 E4
Longleat Dr *CALC* RG31 .... 55 G2
Longmead *FLET* GU13 .... 167 H5
  KSCL RG20 .... 102 C7
Long Mickle *SHST* GU47 .... 118 B7
Longmoor La *THLE* RG7 .... 111 F1
Longmoor Rd *BSTK* RG21 .... 14 C7
Longmoors *BNFD* RG42 .... 79 F6
Longmore Rd *WHIT* RG2 .... 94 A1
Longridge Cl *TLHT* RG30 .... 56 C6
Longroden La *OVTN* RG25 .... 177 J5
Longs Ct *WHCH* RG28 .... 169 H7
Longshot La *BRAK* RG12 .... 79 F7
Longstock Cl *CHAM* RG24 .... 145 J6
Long's Wy *EWKG* RG40 .... 77 K7
Long Toll *GOR/PANG* RG8 .... 27 F6
Longwater La *EWKG* RG40 .... 116 D6
Longwater Rd *BRAK* RG12 .... 99 K4
  EWKG RG40 .... 116 C6
  HTWY RG27 .... 134 E1
Longworth Av *CALC* RG31 .... 55 C6
Lordsfield Gdns *OVTN* RG25 .... 171 C4
Lordswood *THLE* RG7 .... 127 K1
Lorne Pl *READ* RG1 .... 2 D6
Lorne St *READ* RG1 .... 2 D6
Loughborough *BRAK* RG12 .... 100 B4
Loundyes Cl *NTHA* RG18 .... 85 G3
Lovatt Cl *CALC* RG31 .... 55 G6
Lovedean Ct *BRAK* RG12 .... 100 B4
Lovegroves *CHAM* RG24 .... 145 H7
Lovelace Rd *BRAK* RG12 .... 99 F2
Love La *KSCL* RG20 .... 124 A7
  NWBY RG14 .... 83 J1
  ODIM RG29 .... 180 C3
Lovell Cl *HEN* RG9 .... 31 F3
Lovel Rd *ASC* SL5 .... 81 J2
Loveridge Cl *BSTK* RG21 .... 176 B2
Loverock Rd *TLHT* RG30 .... 2 A3
  TLHT RG30 .... 56 D4
Loves Cl *THLE* RG7 .... 90 E4
Loves Wd *THLE* RG7 .... 110 E3
Lowbury *BRAK* RG12 .... 11 M7
Lower Armour Rd *CALC* RG31 .... 55 J4
Lower Broadmoor Rd
  CWTH RG45 .... 118 E4
Lower Brook St *BSTK* RG21 .... 14 A5
  READ RG1 .... 3 H8
Lower Canes *YTLY* GU46 .... 135 F3
Lower Chestnut Dr *BSTK* RG21 .... 14 A9
Lower Church Rd *SHST* GU47 .... 117 K7
Lower Common *HTWY* RG27 .... 115 H7
Lower Earley Wy *EARL* RG6 .... 75 H5
Lower Earley Way (North)
  EARL RG6 .... 75 J4
Lower Earley Way (West)
  WHIT RG2 .... 74 B7
Lower Elmstone Dr *CALC* RG31 .... 55 H4
Lower Evingar Rd *WHCH* RG28 .... 169 H7
Lower Farm Ct *STHA* RG19 .... 84 B3
Lower Field Rd *READ* RG1 .... 3 K3
Lower Henley Rd *CAV/SC* RG4 .... 57 K3
Lower Meadow Rd *WHIT* RG2 .... 8 A7
Lower Moor *YTLY* GU46 .... 135 J4
Lower Mt *READ* RG1 .... 8 A1
Lower Pool Rd *HTWY* RG27 .... 133 G5
Lower Sandhurst Rd
  EWKG RG40 .... 117 F6
Lower Wy *STHA* RG19 .... 84 E4
Lower Wokingham Rd
  EWKG RG40 .... 117 J2
Lower Wote St *BSTK* RG21 .... 14 F4
Lowes Cl *HEN* RG9 .... 32 A7
Lowfield Cl *CAV/SC* RG4 .... 58 B1
Lowfield Rd *CAV/SC* RG4 .... 44 A7
  CAV/SC RG4 .... 58 A1
Lowlands Rd *KEMP* RG22 .... 175 F1
Lowther Cl *WWKG* RG41 .... 76 E6
Lowther Rd *WWKG* RG41 .... 76 D5
Loxwood *EARL* RG6 .... 9 L8
Loxwood Av *FLET* GU13 .... 167 F4
Loyalty La *CHAM* RG24 .... 161 J5
Lucas Cl *YTLY* GU46 .... 135 J4
Lucey Cl *CALC* RG31 .... 55 G3
Luckley Pth *EWKG* RG40 .... 97 H1
Luckley Rd *WWKG* RG41 .... 97 G4
Luckley Wd *WWKG* RG41 .... 97 G4
Ludlow *BRAK* RG12 .... 99 J5
Ludlow Cl *DEAN* RG23 .... 159 J6
Ludlow Gdns *DEAN* RG23 .... 159 J6
Luker Av *HEN* RG9 .... 17 F7

Lulworth Rd *WHIT* RG2 .... 73 K6
Lunds Farm Rd *WODY* RG5 .... 59 K5
Lundy Cl *CHAM* RG24 .... 160 E2
Lundy La *TLHT* RG30 .... 56 D6
Lune Cl *BSTK* RG21 .... 15 J5
Lupin Cl *READ* RG2 .... 175 F4
Luscombe Cl *CAV/SC* RG4 .... 58 A3
Lutman's Hvn *WAR/TWY* RG10 .... 33 K6
Lutterworth Cl *BNFD* RG42 .... 79 K5
Lutyens Cl *CHAM* RG24 .... 161 C3
Lycroft Cl *GOR/PANG* RG8 .... 25 F4
Lydbury *BRAK* RG12 .... 100 C1
Lyde Cl *DEAN* RG23 .... 174 A3
Lydford Rd *READ* RG1 .... 8 C1
Lydney *BRAK* RG12 .... 99 J5
Lyefield Ct *CAV/SC* RG4 .... 43 J6
Lyford Rd *BSTK* RG21 .... 14 F2
Lyme Gv *CALC* RG31 .... 55 J4
Lymington Av *YTLY* GU46 .... 135 H4
Lymington Cl *KEMP* RG22 .... 175 G6
Lymington Ga *CAV/SC* RG4 .... 43 F7
Lynch Hl *WHCH* RG28 .... 169 H7
Lynch Hill Pk *WHCH* RG28 .... 169 J7
The Lynch *OVTN* RG25 .... 171 F4
  WHCH RG28 .... 169 J7
Lyndford Ter *FLET* GU13 .... 167 G4
Lyndhurst Cl *BRAK* RG12 .... 100 D1
Lyndhurst Dr *READ* RG2 .... 175 H6
Lyndhurst Rd *ASC* SL5 .... 101 K2
Lyneham Rd *CWTH* RG45 .... 118 C3
Lynmouth Rd *READ* RG1 .... 3 H3
Lynton Cl *WODY* RG5 .... 9 M2
Lynwood Cha *BRAK* RG12 .... 79 K5
Lynwood Gdns *HTWY* RG27 .... 163 K2
Lyon Cl *STHA* RG19 .... 86 A5
Lyon Oaks *BNFD* RG42 .... 79 J4
Lyon Rd *CWTH* RG45 .... 118 D2
Lyon Sq *TLHT* RG30 .... 56 B6
Lysander Cl *WODY* RG5 .... 59 K5
Lytchet Minster Cl
  BRAK RG12 .... 100 C3
Lytham *BRAK* RG12 .... 99 F4
Lytham Cl *TLHT* RG30 .... 72 D2
Lytham End *CALC* RG31 .... 55 G2
Lytham Rd *WODY* RG5 .... 59 H6
Lytton Rd *BSTK* RG21 .... 15 H5

M

Mabbs La *HTWY* RG27 .... 149 H6
Macbeth Ct *BNFD* RG42 .... 11 L1
Mace Cl *EARL* RG6 .... 74 D5
Mackay Cl *CALC* RG31 .... 71 K3
Macphail Cl *EWKG* RG40 .... 77 K6
Macrae Rd *YTLY* GU46 .... 135 H5
Madeira Cl *CHAM* RG24 .... 160 E2
Madeley Rd *FLET* GU13 .... 167 J5
Madingley *BRAK* RG12 .... 99 J6
Magdalene Rd *SHST* GU47 .... 119 C6
Magill Cl *THLE* RG7 .... 93 J5
Magnolia Cl *SHST* GU47 .... 118 E7
Magnolia Wy *FLET* GU13 .... 167 H4
  WWKG RG41 .... 96 E2
Magnus Dr *KEMP* RG22 .... 175 G5
Magpie Cl *KEMP* RG22 .... 174 E4
  NFNM GU10 .... 183 J4
  STHA RG19 .... 85 G4
Magpie Wy *CALC* RG31 .... 55 C7
Mahler Cl *KEMP* RG22 .... 176 A4
Maiden Erlegh Dr *EARL* RG6 .... 9 J3
Maidenhead Rd *BNFD* RG42 .... 79 J1
  EWKG RG40 .... 77 K3
Maiden Pl *EARL* RG6 .... 75 G4
Main Dr *READ* RG2 .... 80 E5
Mainprize Rd *BRAK* RG12 .... 11 L2
Main Rd *TADY* RG26 .... 127 G3
Main St *STHA* RG19 .... 105 F3
Maitland Rd *READ* RG1 .... 2 D7
Maiwand Gdns *TLHT* RG30 .... 55 J6
Maize La *BNFD* RG42 .... 80 A4
Majendie Cl *NWBY* RG14 .... 83 G3
Majestic Rd *KEMP* RG22 .... 175 F7
Makepeace Rd *BNFD* RG42 .... 79 J5
Maker Cl *TLHT* RG30 .... 72 C1
Makins Rd *HEN* RG9 .... 31 F5
Maldive Rd *CHAM* RG24 .... 160 E2
Maldon Cl *TLHT* RG30 .... 2 A8
Malham Fell *BRAK* RG12 .... 10 D7
Malham Gdns *KEMP* RG22 .... 175 G7
Malham Rd *STHA* RG19 .... 85 H4
Mallard Cl *EARL* RG6 .... 9 G6
  KEMP RG22 .... 174 E5
  WAR/TWY RG10 .... 60 D2
Mallard Ct *NWBY* RG14 .... 12 C4
Mallard Rw *READ* RG1 .... 3 H8
Mallard Wy *THLE* RG7 .... 88 E4
  YTLY GU46 .... 135 G3
Mallory Av *CAV/SC* RG4 .... 43 K6
Mallowdale Rd *BRAK* RG12 .... 100 B5
Malone Rd *WODY* RG5 .... 59 G7
Malshanger La *DEAN* RG23 .... 173 K1
Malta Cl *CHAM* RG24 .... 160 D2
Maltby Wy *EARL* RG6 .... 74 C6
Malt Hl *BNFD* RG42 .... 80 B1
Malthouse Cl *FLET* GU13 .... 167 H6
Malthouse La *READ* RG1 .... 2 F5
  TADY RG26 .... 127 G3
Maltings Pl *READ* RG1 .... 3 H7
The Maltings *TADY* RG26 .... 129 G7
Malvern Cl *KEMP* RG22 .... 175 F1
  WODY RG5 .... 59 J7
Malvern Ct *NWBY* RG14 .... 12 D7
  READ RG1 .... 4 B9
Malvern Wy *WAR/TWY* RG10 .... 46 C5
Managua Cl *CAV/SC* RG4 .... 58 A3
Manchester Rd *READ* RG1 .... 4 D5
Mandeville La *TLHT* RG30 .... 72 A1
Manea Cl *EARL* RG6 .... 75 F6
Manley James Cl *ODIM* RG29 .... 180 D7
Manners Rd *WODY* RG5 .... 59 G6
Mannock Wy *WODY* RG5 .... 60 A5
Manor Cl *BNFD* RG42 .... 79 H5
  KEMP RG22 .... 175 F6

Manor Ct *FLET* GU13 .... 167 H7
Manor Crs *KSCL* RG20 .... 21 J7
Manor Farm La *GOR/PANG* RG8 .... 54 B3
Manor Farm Rd *WHIT* RG2 .... 7 J8
Manor House Dr *ASC* SL5 .... 81 K5
Manor La *CHAM* RG24 .... 161 J5
  NTHA RG18 .... 49 C4
  NTHA RG18 .... 84 D3
  STHA RG19 .... 106 E1
Manor Park Cl *TLHT* RG30 .... 55 H7
Manor Park Dr *EWKG* RG40 .... 116 C2
  EWKG RG40 .... 116 D2
  YTLY GU46 .... 135 J4
Manor Pl *NWBY* RG14 .... 83 G2
Manor Rd *CHAM* RG24 .... 143 K7
  GOR/PANG RG8 .... 24 E5
  GOR/PANG RG8 .... 40 B5
  HEN RG9 .... 31 G3
  WHIT RG2 .... 97 F5
Manor Wood Ga *HEN* RG9 .... 31 K7
Manse La *TADY* RG26 .... 127 G3
Mansell Ct *WHIT* RG2 .... 8 D7
Mansell Dr *NWBY* RG14 .... 109 K1
Mansion Dr *HTWY* RG27 .... 133 G5
Manston Dr *BRAK* RG12 .... 99 J4
Maple Cl *CAV/SC* RG4 .... 29 H7
  SHST GU47 .... 118 A7
  WWKG RG41 .... 76 C3
Maple Ct *GOR/PANG* RG8 .... 24 E5
Maple Crs *BSTK* RG21 .... 160 C4
Maple Gdns *WHIT* RG2 .... 8 C7
  YTLY GU46 .... 135 J4
Maple Gv *TADY* RG26 .... 126 E1
Maplehurst Cha *KEMP* RG22 .... 175 G6
Maple La *GOR/PANG* RG8 .... 38 E7
Marathon Cl *WODY* RG5 .... 60 A5
Marbull Wy *BNFD* RG42 .... 79 J4
Marchant Cl *STHA* RG19 .... 104 C1
Marcheria Cl *BRAK* RG12 .... 99 J4
Marchwood Av *CAV/SC* RG4 .... 43 K4
Marconi Rd *NWBY* RG14 .... 13 G2
Marefield *EARL* RG6 .... 9 L7
Mareshall Av *BNFD* RG42 .... 79 J4
Marfleet Cl *EARL* RG6 .... 75 H4
Margaret Cl *WHIT* RG2 .... 73 K7
Margaret Rd *EWKG* RG40 .... 159 J7
Marigold Cl *CWTH* RG45 .... 118 A1
  KEMP RG22 .... 175 F4
Mariners Cl *TADY* RG26 .... 127 G3
Mariners La *THLE* RG7 .... 68 D3
Marino Wy *EWKG* RG40 .... 115 K2
Markby Wy *EARL* RG6 .... 75 H4
Market Pl *BSTK* RG21 .... 14 F6
  HEN RG9 .... 31 G1
  READ RG1 .... 3 J6
Market St *BRAK* RG12 .... 10 F3
  NWBY RG14 .... 12 E5
Marks Rd *WWKG* RG41 .... 77 F6
Marlborough Av *READ* RG1 .... 8 B2
Marlborough Ct *READ* RG1 .... 2 E9
Marlborough Gdns
  DEAN RG23 .... 174 A2
Marlborough Wy *CALC* RG31 .... 71 G2
Marling Cl *CALC* RG31 .... 55 H3
The Marlowes *NWBY* RG14 .... 83 J7
Marlow Rd *HEN* RG9 .... 17 H7
Marl's La *CHAM* RG24 .... 144 C6
Marlston Rd *NTHA* RG18 .... 65 H1
Marmion Rd *HEN* RG9 .... 31 H3
Marsack St *CAV/SC* RG4 .... 57 K3
Marsden Ct *WHCH* RG28 .... 170 D6
Marshall Cl *GOR/PANG* RG8 .... 55 J1
Marshall Gdns *BSTK* RG21 .... 14 F1
Marshalls Ct *NWBY* RG14 .... 83 G3
Marshcourt *CHAM* RG24 .... 161 G3
Marshland Sq *CAV/SC* RG4 .... 43 J7
Marsh La *HTWY* RG27 .... 134 E2
  NTHA RG18 .... 64 C2
  NWBY RG14 .... 12 E3
Marsh Rd *NTHA* RG18 .... 85 K3
Marston Dr *NWBY* RG14 .... 84 C2
Marston Wy *ASC* SL5 .... 81 H7
Marten Pl *CALC* RG31 .... 55 G2
Martin Cl *BSTK* RG21 .... 160 D4
  WODY RG5 .... 59 H7
Martineau La *WAR/TWY* RG10 .... 60 D6
Martins Cl *WWKG* RG41 .... 77 G6
Martins La *BRAK* RG12 .... 11 L5
Martins St *EARL* RG6 .... 9 M9
The Martins *STHA* RG19 .... 86 A5
Martins Wd *CHAM* RG24 .... 145 G7
Maryland *EWKG* RG40 .... 116 C1
Mary Md *BNFD* RG42 .... 80 A4
Masefield Rd *NTHA* RG18 .... 85 H3
Mason Cl *YTLY* GU46 .... 135 K4
Mason St *READ* RG1 .... 2 C5
Master Cl *WODY* RG5 .... 60 A5
Mathias Wk *KEMP* RG22 .... 175 J6
Matilda Dr *KEMP* RG22 .... 175 G5
Matlock Rd *CAV/SC* RG4 .... 57 J7
Matthews Cha *BNFD* RG42 .... 79 G5
Matthews Cl *STHA* RG19 .... 85 G4
Matthewsgreen Rd *WWKG* RG41 .... 77 F6
Mattock Wy *CHAM* RG24 .... 145 G7
Mawbray Cl *EARL* RG6 .... 9 M6
Maw Cl *KEMP* RG22 .... 176 A4
Maxine Cl *SHST* GU47 .... 118 C7
Maxwell Cl *WODY* RG5 .... 59 H5
Maybrick Cl *SHST* GU47 .... 118 A7
Maybrook *CHAM* RG24 .... 145 G6
May Cl *CHAM* RG24 .... 161 K5
Mayfair *TLHT* RG30 .... 55 H1
Mayfair Dr *NWBY* RG14 .... 12 A7

Mayfield Av *CALC* RG31 .... 71 G2
Mayfield Cl *HTWY* RG27 .... 134 C1
Mayfield Dr *CAV/SC* RG4 .... 57 K2
Mayfield Rdg *DEAN* RG23 .... 175 G7
May Flds *WWKG* RG41 .... 75 K5
Mayflower Cl *CHAM* RG24 .... 161 F1
Mayflower Dr *YTLY* GU46 .... 135 F2
The Maying *WHIT* RG2 .... 93 J1
Maynard Cl *NTHA* RG18 .... 85 H2
Maynard's Wd *CHAM* RG24 .... 161 F1
Mayors La *NWBY* RG14 .... 12 E5
Mayow Cl *STHA* RG19 .... 86 A5
May Pk *CALC* RG31 .... 71 K2
Mays Cl *EARL* RG6 .... 9 J1
Mays La *EARL* RG6 .... 9 K3
Mays Rd *EWKG* RG40 .... 97 K1
Mc Carthy Wy *EWKG* RG40 .... 96 E7
Mccartney Wk *KEMP* RG22 .... 175 K5
Mccrae's Wk *WAR/TWY* RG10 .... 46 C2
Mcnair Cl *EARL* RG6 .... 9 G9
  EARL RG6 .... 74 D5
Mead Cl *CALC* RG31 .... 55 G7
Meadham La *OVTN* RG25 .... 139 J7
Mead La *GOR/PANG* RG8 .... 39 F6
Meadow Cl *GOR/PANG* RG8 .... 25 F5
  STHA RG19 .... 85 H4
Meadow Crs *KSCL* RG20 .... 21 K6
Meadowcroft Rd *WHIT* RG2 .... 73 J6
Meadowland *CHAM* RG24 .... 145 F7
Meadow La *HTWY* RG27 .... 149 H4
Meadow Pound *WHCH* RG28 .... 169 J7
Meadowridge *KEMP* RG22 .... 175 H7
Meadow Rd *BSTK* RG21 .... 176 B3
  EARL RG6 .... 75 G3
  HEN RG9 .... 31 H2
  NWBY RG14 .... 12 D9
  READ RG1 .... 4 A4
  WWKG RG41 .... 97 F2
Meadowside *CALC* RG31 .... 55 G4
Meadowside Rd *GOR/PANG* RG8 .... 40 C7
The Meadows *HTWY* RG27 .... 146 A1
Meadowsweet Cl *NTHA* RG18 .... 85 K3
Meadow Vw *FLET* GU13 .... 167 F6
  WHCH RG28 .... 169 G7
  WWKG RG41 .... 76 C3
Meadow Wk *WWKG* RG41 .... 97 F1
Meadow Wy *BNFD* RG42 .... 79 H5
  THLE RG7 .... 70 C3
  WWKG RG41 .... 97 F2
The Mead *CHAM* RG24 .... 161 J5
The Meadway *TLHT* RG30 .... 55 K6
The Mearings *TLHT* RG30 .... 55 K6
Measham Wy *EARL* RG6 .... 9 L9
Meavy Gdns *WHIT* RG2 .... 7 K8
Mede Cl *OVTN* RG25 .... 171 J5
Medill Cl *GOR/PANG* RG8 .... 26 D5
Medina Cl *WWKG* RG41 .... 96 D1
Medina Gdns *DEAN* RG23 .... 174 A3
Medonte Cl *FLET* GU13 .... 167 J3
Medway Av *DEAN* RG23 .... 174 A2
Medway Cl *NTHA* RG18 .... 85 G2
  WWKG RG41 .... 76 E7
Meitner Cl *TADY* RG26 .... 129 G5
Melbourne Av *WODY* RG41 .... 76 B5
Meldreth Wy *EARL* RG6 .... 75 F5
Meldrum Cl *NWBY* RG14 .... 103 F2
Melford Gdns *KEMP* RG22 .... 175 F2
Melford Gn *CAV/SC* RG4 .... 44 B6
Melksham Cl *EARL* RG6 .... 74 B6
Melling Cl *EARL* RG6 .... 75 H3
Melody Cl *WWKG* RG41 .... 76 B3
Melrose *BRAK* RG12 .... 99 J6
Melrose Av *EARL* RG6 .... 9 G2
Melrose Gdns *WHIT* RG2 .... 95 H5
Membury Wk *BRAK* RG12 .... 11 M8
  BRAK RG12 .... 100 C2
Memorial Av *HEN* RG9 .... 45 H2
Memorial Rd *HTWY* RG27 .... 163 K3
Mendip Cl *KEMP* RG22 .... 175 F1
  WAR/TWY RG10 .... 60 A1
Mendip Dr *CALC* RG31 .... 55 F7
Mendip Rd *BRAK* RG12 .... 11 M9
  READ RG1 .... 100 B3
Menpes Rd *CALC* RG31 .... 55 H1
Meon Cl *TADY* RG26 .... 108 D7
Meon Rd *DEAN* RG23 .... 174 A3
Mercer Cl *KEMP* RG22 .... 175 K6
Merchants Pl *READ* RG1 .... 3 H5
Mercury Av *WWKG* RG41 .... 96 D1
Mereoak La *THLE* RG7 .... 93 H2
Merivale *FLET* GU13 .... 166 E3
Merlewood *BRAK* RG12 .... 11 J9
Merlin Clove *BNFD* RG42 .... 80 E4
Merlin Md *KEMP* RG22 .... 174 E6
Mermaid Cl *WWKG* RG41 .... 76 A4
Merriatt Cl *BSTK* RG21 .... 176 C2
Merrileas Gdns *KEMP* RG22 .... 175 F4
Merrivale Gdns *WHIT* RG2 .... 7 K9
Merron Cl *YTLY* GU46 .... 135 H4
Merrydown La *CHAM* RG24 .... 161 H1
Merryfield *CHAM* RG24 .... 145 F7
Merryhill Green La
  WWKG RG41 .... 76 C3
Merryman Dr *CWTH* RG45 .... 118 A2
Merryweather Cl *EWKG* RG40 .... 96 E6
Mersey Wy *NTHA* RG18 .... 85 G2
Merthyr V *CAV/SC* RG4 .... 43 H6
Merton Cl *SHST* GU47 .... 119 C6
Merton Rd *BSTK* RG21 .... 14 B2
Merton Rd North *WHIT* RG2 .... 7 K9
Merton Rd South *WHIT* RG2 .... 73 J5
Meteor Cl *WODY* RG5 .... 59 K6
The Mews *READ* RG1 .... 4 D8
  TADY RG26 .... 129 J7
Meyrick Dr *NWBY* RG14 .... 103 F3
Michaelmas Cl *YTLY* GU46 .... 135 J5
Michael Way *CALC* RG31 .... 100 C4
Micklands Rd *CAV/SC* RG4 .... 58 A1
Mickle Hl *SHST* GU47 .... 118 B7
Middle Cl *NWBY* RG14 .... 103 C1
Middlefields *WAR/TWY* RG10 .... 46 D6
Middle Md *HTWY* RG27 .... 163 K2
Middleton Ct *NWBY* RG14 .... 84 D2
Middleton Gdns *BSTK* RG21 .... 14 F1
Midiane Cl *BSTK* RG21 .... 176 B2

Midsummer Meadow
CAV/SC RG4 .... 43 G6 🔲
Midwinter Cl TLHT RG30 .... 55 K5 🔲
Milbanke Ct BRAK RG12 .... 10 B3
Milbanke Wy BRAK RG12 .... 10 B3
Mildmay Ct ODIM RG29 .... 180 D2
Milestone Av WAR/TWY RG10 .... 45 J6
  WAR/TWY RG10 .... 59 K1
Milestone Crs WAR/TWY RG10 ...... 59 K1
Miles Wy WODY RG5 .... 59 K6
Milkhouse Rd KSCL RG20 .... 82 A1
Milkingpen La CHAM RG24 .... 161 J4
Millard Cl BSTK RG21 .... 160 A4
Millbank Crs WODY RG5 .... 59 J7
Millbridge Rd YTLY GU46 .... 135 G1
Mill Cl HEN RG9 .... 16 C2
  WWKG RG41 .... 76 E7
Mill Cnr FARN GU14 .... 151 K5 🔲
Milldown Av GOR/PANG RG8 .... 25 F4
Milldown Rd GOR/PANG RG8 .... 25 F4
Millers Cl GOR/PANG RG8 .... 24 E4
Millers Gv CALC RG31 .... 71 K2
Millers Rd TADY RG26 .... 126 E1
Milley La WAR/TWY RG10 .... 47 G4
Millford Rd READ RG1 .... 2 F3
Mill Gn BNFD RG42 .... 79 F5
  CAV/SC RG4 .... 3 L2
Millgreen La STHA RG19 .... 106 A6
Millins Cl SHST GU47 .... 118 E7
Mill La BRAK RG12 .... 99 H3
  CALC RG31 .... 71 K2
  CAV/SC RG4 .... 42 D3
  EARL RG6 .... 75 H4
  HEN RG9 .... 31 J3
  HEN RG9 .... 45 K2
  HTWY RG27 .... 146 E3
  KSCL RG20 .... 123 F5
  NWBY RG14 .... 12 F4
  ODIM RG29 .... 164 A7
  READ RG1 .... 3 J7
  TADY RG26 .... 129 K6
  THLE RG7 .... 89 F4
  THLE RG7 .... 129 K4
  WWKG RG41 .... 75 J5
  YTLY GU46 .... 135 J1
Millmead WWKG RG41 .... 77 F7
Millmere YTLY GU46 .... 135 J2
Mill Reef Cl STHA RG19 .... 84 E4
Mill Ride ASC SL5 .... 81 G6 🔲
Mill Rd CAV/SC RG4 .... 3 L2
  CHAM RG24 .... 159 H3
  GOR/PANG RG8 .... 25 F4
  HEN RG9 .... 46 A1
  TLHT RG30 .... 71 K4
Millworth La WHIT RG2 .... 94 B3
Milman Cl BRAK RG12 .... 80 D7 🔲
Milman Rd WHIT RG2 .... 7 K2
Milsom Cl WHIT RG2 .... 94 B2 🔲
Milton Cl BRAK RG12 .... 99 J4
  CHAM RG24 .... 160 D3
  HEN RG9 .... 31 G1
Milton Ct EWKG RG40 .... 77 G7
Milton Dr EWKG RG40 .... 77 G7
Milton Gdns EWKG RG40 .... 77 G7
Milton Rd EARL RG6 .... 5 G7
  EWKG RG40 .... 97 G1
  WWKG RG41 .... 77 G7
Milton Wy WAR/TWY RG10 .... 46 E7 🔲
Milward Gdns BRAK RG12 .... 78 D7
Minchens La TADY RG26 .... 129 C4
Minchin Gn BNFD RG42 .... 78 D3 🔲
Minden Cl CHAM RG24 .... 161 F1 🔲
  WWKG RG41 .... 96 D1 🔲🔲
Ministry Rd STHA RG19 .... 105 F3
Minley Gv FARN GU14 .... 151 J7 🔲
Minley Rd FARN GU14 .... 151 J4
Minstead Cl BRAK RG12 .... 100 C1
  TADY RG26 .... 126 E3
Minstead Dr YTLY GU46 .... 135 H4
Minster St READ RG1 .... 3 H6
Mint Cl EARL RG6 .... 5 J7
Minton Cl TLHT RG30 .... 56 A5 🔲
Mire La WAR/TWY RG10 .... 61 J1
Mistletoe Rd YTLY GU46 .... 135 J5
Mitcham Cl WHIT RG2 .... 7 K2
Mitchell Av HTWY RG27 .... 149 H5
Mitchell Gdns KEMP RG22 .... 175 H5 🔲
Mitchell Wy WODY RG5 .... 59 K6
Mitford Cl WHIT RG2 .... 74 A6
Moat Cl TADY RG26 .... 129 F5
Modbury Gdns WHIT RG2 .... 7 M7
Mohawk Wy WODY RG5 .... 60 A6
Mole Rd WHIT RG2 .... 95 J2
  WWKG RG41 .... 75 K6
Moles Cl EWKG RG40 .... 97 J2
Mollison Cl WODY RG5 .... 60 A5
Molly Millar Br WWKG RG41 .... 97 G3
Molly Millar's La WWKG RG41 .... 97 F2
Monachus La HTWY RG27 .... 149 J3
Monarch Cl KEMP RG22 .... 175 F6
Mongers Piece CHAM RG24 .... 145 H6
Monksbarn WHIT RG2 .... 8 B7
Monk Sherborne Rd
  TADY RG26 .... 142 C3
Monkshood Cl EWKG RG40 .... 77 K7
Monks La NWBY RG14 .... 103 H1
Monks Ri FLET GU13 .... 166 E2 🔲
Monks Wy TLHT RG30 .... 6 A2
Monkswood Cl HEN RG9 .... 103 G1 🔲
Monks Wood Crs TADY RG26 .... 126 E2 🔲
Monktons La THLE RG7 .... 108 E7 🔲
Mons Cl WWKG RG41 .... 96 D1 🔲🔲
Montacute Dr STHA RG19 .... 86 A5 🔲
Montague Cl EWKG RG40 .... 77 K7
Montague Pl BSTK RG21 .... 14 F8
Montague St CAV/SC RG4 .... 3 L1
  READ RG1 .... 3 G4
Montague Ter NWBY RG14 .... 12 E9
Monteagle La YTLY GU46 .... 135 G4
Montgomery Dr THLE RG7 .... 93 J3
Montgomery Rd NWBY RG14 .... 12 A9
Montpelier Dr CAV/SC RG4 .... 44 B7 🔲
Montrose Cl FLET GU13 .... 167 J3
Montserrat Cl WHIT RG2 .... 160 D1 🔲
Montserrat Rd CHAM RG24 .... 160 D1
Monument Cl NWBY RG14 .... 103 G1 🔲
Moor Cl EWKG RG40 .... 116 D1
  SHST GU47 .... 119 F7

Moor Copse Cl EARL RG6 .... 9 K5
Moordale Av BNFD RG42 .... 10 B1
  BNFD RG42 .... 79 F6
Moore Rd FLET GU13 .... 167 H6
Moore Rd FLET GU13 .... 167 H6
Moores Gn BNFD RG42 .... 77 K6
Moorfoot Gdns KEMP RG22 .... 175 G1
Moorings Av KEMP RG22 .... 175 F6
Moorhen Dr EARL RG6 .... 74 E5
The Moorings BSTK RG21 .... 15 K4
Moorlands Cl FLET GU13 .... 167 J3 🔲
The Moors GOR/PANG RG8 .... 40 C7
  STHA RG19 .... 85 J5
Moor Vw CHAM RG24 .... 161 J4
Morden Cl BRAK RG12 .... 100 C2 🔲
Morecambe Av CAV/SC RG4 .... 43 F7
Moreleigh Cl WHIT RG2 .... 73 K6 🔲
Moreton Cl FLET GU13 .... 167 G7
Morgan Rd READ RG1 .... 7 L1
Morgaston Rd TADY RG26 .... 144 A3
Moriston Cl TLHT RG30 .... 56 C5
Morlais CAV/SC RG4 .... 43 G7
Morlands Av TLHT RG30 .... 72 B1 🔲
Morley Cl YTLY GU46 .... 135 G4
Morley Rd BSTK RG21 .... 176 B3
Mornington Av EWKG RG40 .... 96 E7
Mornington Cl TADY RG26 .... 108 A7
Morpeth Cl WHIT RG2 .... 7 M5
Morris St HTWY RG27 .... 163 H3
Morse Rd KEMP RG22 .... 175 K4
Mortimer Cl HTWY RG27 .... 149 G6 🔲
  WHIT RG2 .... 73 K7
Mortimer Gdns TADY RG26 .... 127 F2
Mortimer La BSTK RG21 .... 14 D5
  THLE RG7 .... 111 J1
  THLE RG7 .... 129 J1
Moss Cl CAV/SC RG4 .... 57 K2
Moulsham Copse La YTLY GU46 . 135 G2
Moulsham La YTLY GU46 .... 135 G2
Moulshay La HTWY RG27 .... 145 K5
Mountbatten Cl NWBY RG14 .... 84 B2 🔲
Mountbatten Ri SHST GU47 .... 118 A7
Mountbatten Sq KSCL RG20 .... 120 C3
  NWBY RG14 .... 12 E8
Mountfield GOR/PANG RG8 .... 25 F4 🔲
Mount La BRAK RG12 .... 11 G5
Mount Pleasant BRAK RG12 .... 11 H5
  HTWY RG27 .... 149 J4
  READ RG1 .... 3 K9 🔲
  SHST GU47 .... 118 B7 🔲
  TADY RG26 .... 126 D1
  WWKG RG41 .... 97 F1
Mount Pleasant Gv READ RG1 .... 3 K9
Mount Rd KSCL RG20 .... 120 C2
  NTHA RG18 .... 85 J3
Mount St WHIT RG2 .... 7 J1
The Mount CAV/SC RG4 .... 57 G2
  FLET GU13 .... 167 H1
  WHIT RG2 .... 7 M1
Mount Vw HEN RG9 .... 17 G7
Mourne Cl KEMP RG22 .... 159 G7
Mowbray Dr TLHT RG30 .... 56 B5
Mower Cl EWKG RG40 .... 78 A7 🔲
Mowforth Cl GOR/PANG RG8 .... 26 D2 🔲
Mozart Cl KEMP RG22 .... 175 K4
Mud La HTWY RG27 .... 115 J7
Muirfield Cl READ RG1 .... 4 A7
Mulberry Cl CWTH RG45 .... 118 C4
  WODY RG5 .... 59 H7
Mulberry Wy WHAM RG24 .... 145 G7
  THLE RG7 .... 70 D4
Mulfords Hl TADY RG26 .... 108 E7
  TADY RG26 .... 127 F1
Mull Cl DEAN RG23 .... 173 K2
Mullins Cl BSTK RG21 .... 160 C3
Mumbery Hl WAR/TWY RG10 ...... 46 D3
Munday Ct BNFD RG42 .... 79 F5 🔲
Mundesley St READ RG1 .... 3 J8
Munkle Marsh STHA RG19 .... 86 B4 🔲
Munnings Ct BSTK RG21 .... 15 J9
Munro Av WODY RG5 .... 75 J2
Murdoch Rd EWKG RG40 .... 97 H2
Murray Rd WWKG RG41 .... 97 F1
Murrell Green Rd HTWY RG27 ... 148 D5
Murrellhill La BNFD RG42 .... 78 D6
Musgrave Cl KEMP RG22 .... 175 J4 🔲
Mushroom Castle BNFD RG42 ...... 80 E4
Musket Copse CHAM RG24 .... 161 H5
Mustard La CAV/SC RG4 .... 59 H4
Mutton Cl THLE RG7 .... 70 D3 🔲
Mutton Oaks BNFD RG42 .... 78 E6
Myland Cl BSTK RG21 .... 160 D3 🔲
Mylne Sq EWKG RG40 .... 97 J1 🔲
Mylum Cl WHIT RG2 .... 93 K1 🔲
Myrtle Cl CALC RG31 .... 55 H7 🔲
  THLE RG7 .... 91 G4
Myton Wk THLE RG7 .... 70 D3

N

Nabbs Hill CALC RG31 .... 71 H1 🔲
Napier Cl CWTH RG45 .... 118 D4
Napier Rd CWTH RG45 .... 118 D4
  READ RG1 .... 3 M4
Napoleon Dr DEAN RG23 .... 159 H4
Napper Cl ASC SL5 .... 81 F7
Narromine Dr CALC RG31 .... 72 A2
Naseby BRAK RG12 .... 99 J6
Naseby Ri NWBY RG14 .... 84 C2
Nash Cl BSTK RG21 .... 15 G1
  EARL RG6 .... 9 G5
Nash Gdns ASC SL5 .... 81 G7
Nash Grove La EWKG RG40 .... 96 D5
Nash Pk BNFD RG42 .... 78 C4
Nately Rd OVTN RG25 .... 179 G1
The Naylors THLE RG7 .... 114 A2
Neals La CAV/SC RG4 .... 28 C1
Neath Gdns TLHT RG30 .... 56 A6 🔲
Neath La BSTK RG21 .... 15 J4
Nelson Cl CALC RG31 .... 11 M3
Nelson Rd CAV/SC RG4 .... 3 L1
  EARL RG6 .... 9 J8
Nelson's La WAR/TWY RG10 .... 72 E7
Neptune Cl WWKG RG41 .... 96 D1 🔲🔲
Netherhouse Moor
  FLET GU13 .... 166 E4 🔲
Netherton BRAK RG12 .... 10 D7

Netley Cl CAV/SC RG4 .... 44 B6
Nettlecombe BRAK RG12 .... 100 A3
Nevelle Cl BNFD RG42 .... 78 E6
Neville Cl BSTK RG21 .... 176 C2
Neville Dr STHA RG19 .... 85 K4
Nevis Rd CALC RG31 .... 55 J2 🔲
Newalls Ri WAR/TWY RG10 .... 46 D2
Newark Rd BLKW GU17 .... 151 K1
Newark St READ RG1 .... 3 K8
New Barn Cl FLET GU13 .... 166 E4 🔲
New Bath Rd WAR/TWY RG10 ...... 46 A7
  WAR/TWY RG10 .... 59 K1
Newbery Cl CALC RG31 .... 55 J4 🔲
Newbold Rd NWBY RG14 .... 83 G2 🔲
Newbolt Cl NTHA RG18 .... 85 H2
New Bright St READ RG1 .... 3 H8
Newbury Cl WAR/TWY RG10 .... 60 A1
Newbury Hl NTHA RG18 .... 36 A7
Newbury La KSCL RG20 .... 21 J7
Newbury Rd KSCL RG20 .... 123 K6
  NTHA RG18 .... 49 F7
  WHCH RG28 .... 169 J3
Newbury St WHCH RG28 .... 169 H7
Newcastle Rd WHIT RG2 .... 7 M4
Newchurch Rd TADY RG26 .... 108 D7
Newell Gn BNFD RG42 .... 79 K3
Newell's La CAV/SC RG4 .... 42 C5
Newfield Rd CAV/SC RG4 .... 29 G5
New Forest Ride BRAK RG12 ...... 100 B5
New Hl GOR/PANG RG8 .... 41 H7
Newhurst Gdns BNFD RG42 .... 80 A3
Newlands FLET GU13 .... 167 H5
Newlands Av CAV/SC RG4 .... 57 J2
Newlands Cl YTLY GU46 .... 135 J4
New Lane Hl TLHT RG30 .... 55 K7
  TLHT RG30 .... 72 A1
Newlyn Gdns WHIT RG2 .... 7 K9
Newmarket Cl EARL RG6 .... 75 G4
New Meadow ASC SL5 .... 81 G6
New Mill La HTWY RG27 .... 115 H6
New Mill Rd HTWY RG27 .... 115 H6
Newnham La CHAM RG24 .... 162 A3
  HTWY RG27 .... 163 F2
Newnham Pk HTWY RG27 .... 163 J3 🔲
Newnham Rd HTWY RG27 .... 163 G3
Newport Cl NWBY RG14 .... 13 H2
Newport Rd NWBY RG14 .... 13 H1
  READ RG1 .... 3 G2
New Rd ASC SL5 .... 81 J5
  BRAK RG12 .... 11 K3
  BSTK RG21 .... 14 F6
  CWTH RG45 .... 118 D3
  FLET GU13 .... 167 J5
  HEN RG9 .... 45 K1
  HTWY RG27 .... 134 D2
  HTWY RG27 .... 149 H4
  HTWY RG27 .... 163 K2
  NWBY RG14 .... 13 G7
  ODIM RG29 .... 164 B7
  READ RG1 .... 8 B2
  STHA RG19 .... 104 C1
  TADY RG26 .... 126 E2
  TADY RG26 .... 127 H6
  THLE RG7 .... 91 J7
  WAR/TWY RG10 .... 46 C5
  WAR/TWY RG10 .... 46 E6
  WWKG RG41 .... 75 K6
New Road Hl HTWY RG27 .... 87 J4
New St BSTK RG21 .... 14 E6
  HEN RG9 .... 31 H1
  THLE RG7 .... 130 B1
Newton Av CAV/SC RG4 .... 44 A7
Newtown TADY RG26 .... 108 D7
  TADY RG26 .... 126 D1
Newtown Gdns HEN RG9 .... 31 H3
Newtown Rd HEN RG9 .... 31 J3
  NWBY RG14 .... 12 E8
  NWBY RG14 .... 103 K2
New Wy THLE RG7 .... 68 D4
New Wokingham Rd
  CWTH RG45 .... 118 B1
Niagara Rd HEN RG9 .... 31 H3
Nicholas Rd HEN RG9 .... 30 E3
Nideggan Cl STHA RG19 .... 85 J4
Nightingale Cl BRAK RG12 .... 11 H9
Nightingale Gdns CHAM RG24 .. 159 H3
  HTWY RG27 .... 163 K2
Nightingale La THLE RG7 .... 111 J2
Nightingale Ri OVTN RG25 .... 171 J5
Nightingale Rd WODY RG5 .... 75 G2
The Nightingales NWBY RG14 ..... 12 F9
Nightjar Cl NFNM GU10 .... 183 J4
Nimrod Cl WODY RG5 .... 59 K6
Nimrod Wy WHIT RG2 .... 7 J2
Nine Mile Ride CWTH RG45 .... 99 H6
  EWKG RG40 .... 116 C2
Nire Rd CAV/SC RG4 .... 58 B2
Noakes Hl GOR/PANG RG8 .... 37 J5
Norcot Rd TLHT RG30 .... 55 K5
Norden Cl BSTK RG21 .... 14 F2
Nores Rd WHIT RG2 .... 74 A7
Norfolk Cha BNFD RG42 .... 80 C5
Norfolk Cl WWKG RG41 .... 96 D1
Norfolk Rd TLHT RG30 .... 56 D6
Norlands NTHA RG18 .... 85 H2
Norman Av HEN RG9 .... 31 H2
Norman Keep BNFD RG42 .... 80 C6
Norman Pl READ RG1 .... 3 J3
Norman Rd CAV/SC RG4 .... 57 K1
Normanstead Rd CALC RG31 .... 55 H5
  BSTK RG21 .... 160 C3 🔲
Normanton Rd BSTK RG21 .... 160 C4 🔲
Normay Ri NWBY RG14 .... 103 F3
Normoor Rd THLE RG7 .... 90 E6
Norn Hl BSTK RG21 .... 15 H2
Norn Hill Cl BSTK RG21 .... 15 H2
Norreys Av EWKG RG40 .... 77 J7
Norris Rd EARL RG6 .... 4 F8
Northam Cl EARL RG6 .... 75 H3
Northampton Cl BRAK RG12 .... 11 K6
Northbourne Cl EARL RG6 .... 9 J8
Northbrook Copse
  BRAK RG12 .... 100 C4 🔲
Northbrook Rd CAV/SC RG4 .... 44 A7
Northbrook St NWBY RG14 .... 12 E3
Northbury Av WAR/TWY RG10 .... 46 D7
Northbury La WAR/TWY RG10 .... 46 D6

Northcott BRAK RG12 .... 99 H6
Northcourt Av WHIT RG2 .... 8 A3
Northcroft La NWBY RG14 .... 12 B3
North Dr THLE RG7 .... 70 C7
Northern Av NWBY RG14 .... 83 K1
Northfield Av HEN RG9 .... 31 K7
Northfield Cl FLET GU13 .... 167 J5 🔲
Northfield End HEN RG9 .... 17 G7
Northfield Rd FLET GU13 .... 167 J5
  HEN RG9 .... 32 A7
  HTWY RG27 .... 146 A1
  NTHA RG18 .... 85 G3
  READ RG1 .... 3 G3
Newbery Cl CALC RG31 .... 55 J4 🔲
North Gn BRAK RG12 .... 11 K2
Northington Cl BRAK RG12 .... 100 C4 🔲
North Lodge Dr ASC SL5 .... 81 F7
North Rd ASC SL5 .... 80 E6
North St CAV/SC RG4 .... 57 J3
  KSCL RG20 .... 124 A7
  READ RG1 .... 2 F5
  WDSR SL4 .... 81 J1
Northumberland Av WHIT RG2 ...... 7 L4
  WHIT RG2 .... 73 K6
Northumberland Cl
  BNFD RG42 .... 80 C5 🔲
North View Rd TADY RG26 .... 127 G2
North Wk THLE RG7 .... 70 D2 🔲
North Warnborough St
  ODIM RG29 .... 180 A1
  NWBY RG14 .... 13 G6
  WWKG RG41 .... 76 D7
Northwood Dr NWBY RG14 .... 13 J1
Norton Cl NWBY RG14 .... 103 F3
Norton Ride CHAM RG24 .... 161 G4
  READ RG1 .... 4 D6
  THLE RG7 .... 113 K6
  WODY RG5 .... 75 J1
Norwich Dr WODY RG5 .... 5 M5
Norwood Rd READ RG1 .... 4 B6
Notton Wy EARL RG6 .... 74 C6
Novello Cl KEMP RG22 .... 175 J5
Nuffield Dr SHST GU47 .... 119 G7
Nuffield Rd WHIT RG2 .... 115 J1
Nugee Ct CWTH RG45 .... 118 C4
Nuneaton BRAK RG12 .... 100 B4
Nunhide La GOR/PANG RG8 .... 54 E4
Nun's Acre GOR/PANG RG8 .... 24 E4
Nursery Cl CHAM RG24 .... 145 H7 🔲
  HEN RG9 .... 31 K7
  HTWY RG27 .... 163 K1 🔲
  WAR/TWY RG10 .... 60 D5
Nursery Gdns GOR/PANG RG8 ..... 41 G7
Nutbean La THLE RG7 .... 114 C3
Nuthatch Cl NFNM GU10 .... 183 J5
Nuthatch Dr EARL RG6 .... 9 K3
Nuthurst BRAK RG12 .... 11 L9
  BRAK RG12 .... 100 B3
Nut La WAR/TWY RG10 .... 47 K6
Nutley BRAK RG12 .... 99 H6
Nutley Cl YTLY GU46 .... 135 J4
Nutmeg Cl EARL RG6 .... 8 F9
Nutter's La WHIT RG2 .... 94 D6

O

Oak Av SHST GU47 .... 118 E7
Oak Cl DEAN RG23 .... 174 A3
  OVTN RG25 .... 171 H5
Oakdale BRAK RG12 .... 100 A4
Oakdale Cl CALC RG31 .... 55 H5
Oakdene GOR/PANG RG8 .... 26 E4 🔲
  THLE RG7 .... 91 F6
Oakdown Cl GOR/PANG RG8 .... 40 D1
Oak Dr NWBY RG14 .... 12 C6
  THLE RG7 .... 90 E5
  WODY RG5 .... 59 K7
Oaken Copse FLET GU13 .... 167 H5
Oak End Wy THLE RG7 .... 89 F3
Oakengates BRAK RG12 .... 99 H5
Oaken Gv NWBY RG14 .... 83 G7
Oakfield Rd TADY RG26 .... 109 H7
Oakfields Cl KSCL RG20 .... 122 E5
Oakham Cl CALC RG31 .... 55 J3 🔲
Oak Hanger Cl HTWY RG27 .... 164 A2 🔲
Oakland Rd WHCH RG28 .... 169 H7
Oaklands NTHA RG18 .... 64 B3
  YTLY GU46 .... 135 J3
Oaklands Cl ASC SL5 .... 81 J5
Oaklands Dr ASC SL5 .... 81 K5
  WWKG RG41 .... 97 F3
Oaklands La CWTH RG45 .... 118 B2
Oaklands Pk WWKG RG41 .... 97 F3
Oaklands Wy DEAN RG23 .... 159 H5
Oaklea Dr HTWY RG27 .... 115 G7
Oaklea Gdns TADY RG26 .... 129 J7
Oakley Dr FLET GU13 .... 167 H3
Oakley La DEAN RG23 .... 173 K3
Oakley Rd CAV/SC RG4 .... 57 G1
  NWBY RG14 .... 13 L1
  TADY RG26 .... 140 C7
Oakmead TADY RG26 .... 129 F5
Oakridge Rd BSTK RG21 .... 160 B4
Oakside Wy WHIT RG2 .... 74 B6
Oaks Rd HEN RG9 .... 31 K7
The Oaks BRAK RG12 .... 11 J3
  FLET GU13 .... 166 E2
  TADY RG26 .... 126 D4
  YTLY GU46 .... 135 H3
Oak Tree Cl TADY RG26 .... 108 E7 🔲
Oak Tree Copse CALC RG31 .... 55 K2 🔲
Oak Tree Dr HTWY RG27 .... 164 A1
Oak Tree Rd CALC RG31 .... 55 J3
  STHA RG19 .... 85 K3
Oak Tree Wk GOR/PANG RG8 .... 41 J7
Oaktree Av SHST GU47 .... 118 D7
Oak Vw CALC RG31 .... 55 H5
Oak Wy WODY RG5 .... 75 G2
Oakwood CHAM RG24 .... 145 G4
  FLET GU13 .... 167 H7
Oakwood Rd BRAK RG12 .... 11 M3
Oareborough BRAK RG12 .... 11 M9
Oareborough La NTHA RG18 .... 49 F3
Oasthouse Dr FARN GU14 .... 151 K6

Oatlands Rd WHIT RG2 .... 94 C2
Oban Cl DEAN RG23 .... 173 K2 🔲
Oban Gdns WODY RG5 .... 75 H2
O'bee Gdns TADY RG26 .... 108 B7
Ochil Cl KEMP RG22 .... 175 G1
Octavia BRAK RG12 .... 99 H6
Octavian Cl KEMP RG22 .... 175 G5
Oddfellows Rd NWBY RG14 .... 12 D5
Odell Cl EARL RG6 .... 74 E6
Odette Gdns TADY RG26 .... 108 E7
Odiham Av CAV/SC RG4 .... 44 B7
Odiham Rd HTWY RG27 .... 114 A7
  HTWY RG27 .... 165 F4
  NFNM GU10 .... 183 G4
  THLE RG7 .... 113 K5
Officers Rw TADY RG26 .... 129 J7
Ogmore Cl TLHT RG30 .... 55 K6 🔲
Okingham Cl SHST GU47 .... 118 E7 🔲
Old Acre La WAR/TWY RG10 .... 46 A7
Old Barn Cl CAV/SC RG4 .... 43 H6
Old Bath Rd CAV/SC RG4 .... 5 M3
  CAV/SC RG4 .... 59 H3
  NWBY RG14 .... 12 C2
  WAR/TWY RG10 .... 59 K1
Oldberg Gdns KEMP RG22 .... 176 A4 🔲
Old Bracknell Cl BRAK RG12 .... 10 E5
Old Bracknell La East
  BRAK RG12 .... 10 E5
Old Bracknell La West
  BRAK RG12 .... 10 D5
Oldbury BRAK RG12 .... 10 B5
Old Common Rd BRAK RG12 .... 15 J7
Old Copse Gdns HEN RG9 .... 29 G5
Oldcorne Hollow HTWY RG27 ... 135 F4
Old Cove Rd FARN GU14 .... 151 J7
Old Down Cl KEMP RG22 .... 175 F3
Old Elm Dr TLHT RG30 .... 55 J5 🔲
Old Farm Crs CALC RG31 .... 55 H3 🔲
Old Farm Dr BRAK RG12 .... 79 K5
Oldfield Cl EARL RG6 .... 9 K2
Oldfield Vw HTWY RG27 .... 149 H5 🔲
Old Forest Rd WWKG RG41 .... 77 F4 🔲
Old Kempshott La KEMP RG22 ... 175 F1
Old Lands Hl BRAK RG12 .... 11 J1
Old La STHA RG19 .... 107 F7
The Old La READ RG1 .... 6 E2
Old Mill Ct WAR/TWY RG10 .... 60 E6
Old Newtown Rd NWBY RG14 ... 12 D7 🔲
The Old Orch CALC RG31 .... 71 K2
Old Pharmacy Ct
  CWTH RG45 .... 118 D4 🔲
Old Potbridge Rd HTWY RG27 ... 165 F2 🔲
Old Priory La BNFD RG42 .... 80 A4
Old Pumphouse Cl FLET GU13 ... 167 J1
Old Reading Rd BSTK RG21 .... 15 G4
Old Sawmill La CWTH RG45 ...... 118 D2
Old School Cl FLET GU13 .... 167 H2 🔲
  HTWY RG27 .... 149 J4 🔲
Old School La YTLY GU46 .... 135 H3
Old School Rd HTWY RG27 .... 163 H5
Oldstead BRAK RG12 .... 100 A3
Old St KSCL RG20 .... 34 B7
  NTHA RG18 .... 48 C4
  NTHA RG18 .... 48 E5
Old Vyne La TADY RG26 .... 142 C1
Old Welmore YTLY GU46 .... 135 K4
Old Whitley Wood La WHIT RG2 ... 93 K1
Old Wokingham Rd
  CWTH RG45 .... 118 D1
  EWKG RG40 .... 98 C5
Old Wooseehill La WWKG RG41 ... 76 E7
Old Worting Rd KEMP RG22 .... 159 H7
Oleander Cl CWTH RG45 .... 118 A1
Oliver Dr CALC RG31 .... 71 G1
Oliver Rd ASC SL5 .... 101 K2
Olivers Cl TADY RG26 .... 129 H7
Oliver's La TADY RG26 .... 129 K5
Oliver's Wk CHAM RG24 .... 161 G4
Ollerton BRAK RG12 .... 99 H6
Omer's Ri THLE RG7 .... 90 E4
Onslow Cl CHAM RG24 .... 161 F2
Onslow Dr ASC SL5 .... 81 K5
Onslow Gdns CAV/SC RG4 .... 57 K2
Opal Wy WWKG RG41 .... 76 D7 🔲
Opladen Wy BRAK RG12 .... 99 K3
Oracle Pkwy EARL RG6 .... 4 F4
Orbit Cl EWKG RG40 .... 116 C2
Orchard Av CAV/SC RG4 .... 29 F6
Orchard Cha WAR/TWY RG10 ...... 60 E6
Orchard Cl CALC RG31 .... 55 G1
  EWKG RG40 .... 97 J1
  HEN RG9 .... 31 K7
  HEN RG9 .... 45 H2
  NTHA RG18 .... 84 B2
  NWBY RG14 .... 84 B2
  THLE RG7 .... 93 J5
  THLE RG7 .... 93 J5
Orchard Coombe
  GOR/PANG RG8 .... 40 C1
Orchard Ct BRAK RG12 .... 11 G4
Orchardene NWBY RG14 .... 13 H2
Orchard Est WAR/TWY RG10 .... 46 D7
Orchard Fld CAV/SC RG4 .... 28 D6 🔲
Orchard Gv CAV/SC RG4 .... 58 B1
Orchard Pl EWKG RG40 .... 97 H1
Orchard Rd KEMP RG22 .... 159 H7
  THLE RG7 .... 111 G3
  WAR/TWY RG10 .... 60 E6
Orchard Rd BSTK RG21 .... 3 H8
The Orchard OVTN RG25 .... 171 H4
  TADY RG26 .... 127 G1
  THLE RG7 .... 70 D2 🔲
Oregon Av CALC RG31 .... 55 H2
Oregon Wk EWKG RG40 .... 116 C1 🔲
Orion BRAK RG12 .... 99 H6
Orkney Cl CALC RG31 .... 71 K2
  CHAM RG24 .... 160 C2
Ormathwaites Cnr
  BNFD RG42 .... 80 B5 🔲🔲
Ormonde Rd WWKG RG41 .... 97 F2
Ormsby St READ RG1 .... 2 D6
Orrin Cl TLHT RG30 .... 56 B5
Orts Rd READ RG1 .... 3 M6
Orville Cl WODY RG5 .... 59 K6
Orwell Cl CAV/SC RG4 .... 57 G1
Osborne Cl BSTK RG21 .... 14 C1
  BSTK RG21 .... 160 B4
Osborne Dr FLET GU13 .... 167 J4

Osborne La *BNFD* RG42 .... **79** K3
Osborne Rd *EWKG* RG40 .... **97** H1
TLHT RG30 .... **56** C5
Osborn Wy *HTWY* RG27 .... **164** A3
Osler Cl *TADY* RG26 .... **129** G6
Osman's Cl *BNFD* RG42 .... **80** E5
Osprey Cl *KEMP* RG22 .... **174** E3
Osprey Rd *KEMP* RG22 .... **174** E3
Osterley Cl *EWKG* RG40 .... **98** A2
Osterley Dr *CAV/SC* RG4 .... **44** B6
Oswald Cl *BNFD* RG42 .... **80** A4
Otterbourne Crs *TADY* RG26 ... **126** E3
Otter Cl *CWTH* RG45 .... **118** B1
Overbridge Sq *NWBY* RG14 .... **13** M4
NWBY RG14 .... **84** D5
Overbury Av *WWKG* RG41 ...... **76** E5
Overdown Rd *CALC* RG31 ...... **55** J2
Overlanders End *CALC* RG31 ... **55** K2
Owen Rd *NWBY* RG14 .... **84** A1
Owl Cl *WWKG* RG41 .... **96** D2
Owston *EARL* RG6 .... **9** L7
Oxenhope *BRAK* RG12 .... **10** C8
Oxford Rd *CALC* RG31 .... **41** H7
CALC RG31 .... **55** J1
KSCL RG20 .... **48** B4
NWBY RG14 .... **12** D1
NWBY RG14 .... **83** J2
READ RG1 .... **2** F6
SHST GU47 .... **119** F6
TLHT RG30 .... **2** B5
TLHT RG30 .... **56** C5
WWKG RG41 .... **97** F1
Oxford St *CAV/SC* RG4 .... **57** H3
NWBY RG14 .... **12** D2
Oyster Cl *KEMP* RG22 .... **175** F5

P

Pack And Prime La *HEN* RG9 .... **31** F1
Packenham Rd *BSTK* RG21 ...... **14** B7
Pack La *DEAN* RG23 .... **174** A1
KEMP RG22 .... **175** F2
Packman Dr *WAR/TWY* RG10 ... **46** C6
Paddick Cl *CAV/SC* RG4 .... **59** H2
Paddick Dr *EARL* RG6 .... **9** J7
Paddock Cl *HTWY* RG27 .... **149** H5
Paddockfields *CHAM* RG24 ..... **161** J4
Paddock Hts *WAR/TWY* RG10 ... **60** D1
Paddock Rd *CAV/SC* RG4 .... **4** A2
KEMP RG22 .... **175** J1
NWBY RG14 .... **12** D8
The Paddock *BRAK* RG12 .... **11** H6
CWTH RG45 .... **118** B2
HTWY RG27 .... **149** J5
KSCL RG20 .... **123** K7
WAR/TWY RG10 .... **13** K5
Padstow Gdns *WHIT* RG2 .... **7** K9
Padwick Cl *BSTK* RG21 .... **14** C7
Padworth La *THLE* RG7 .... **89** H4
Padworth Rd *THLE* RG7 .... **90** D7
Page's Cft *EWKG* RG40 .... **97** J3
Pages Orch *CAV/SC* RG4 .... **29** F6
Paice Gn *EWKG* RG40 .... **77** J7
Paices Hl *THLE* RG7 .... **108** D4
Painters Pightle *HTWY* RG27 ... **163** J2
Pakenham Rd *BRAK* RG12 ...... **100** A3
Palace Ga *ODIM* RG29 .... **180** C1
Pale La *HTWY* RG27 .... **150** C6
HTWY RG27 .... **166** B1
Palmera Av *CALC* RG31 .... **71** H2
Palmer Cl *BSTK* RG21 .... **160** D3
EWKG RG40 .... **98** B7
Palmer Park Av *EARL* RG6 .... **4** E7
Palmer School Rd *EWKG* RG40 . **97** H1
Palmer's La *THLE* RG7 .... **91** F5
THLE RG7 .... **92** B4
Palmerstone Rd *EARL* RG6 ...... **5** H7
Pamber Heath Rd *TADY* RG26 ... **127** G1
Pamber Rd *THLE* RG7 .... **109** K7
Pangbourne Hl *GOR/PANG* RG8 . **40** B7
Pangbourne Rd *GOR/PANG* RG8 . **39** H7
GOR/PANG RG8 .... **53** F1
Pangbourne St *TLHT* RG30 ...... **56** C5
Pankhurst Dr *BRAK* RG12 ...... **100** A3
Pankridge St *NFNM* GU10 ...... **182** E5
Pantile Dr *HTWY* RG27 .... **164** B2
Pantings La *KSCL* RG20 .... **120** C3
Papermakers *OVTN* RG25 .... **171** J5
Paprika Cl *EARL* RG6 .... **8** F9
The Parade *TADY* RG26 .... **108** E7
WODY RG5 .... **59** J5
Paradise Rd *HEN* RG9 .... **31** F2
Paradise Wy *THLE* RG7 .... **67** K2
Pardown *DEAN* RG23 .... **174** A5
Park Av *CHAM* RG24 .... **161** J6
NTHA RG18 .... **85** J3
Park Cl *CAV/SC* RG4 .... **29** H5
DEAN RG23 .... **173** K2
Parkcorner La *WHIT* RG2 .... **95** J1
Park Crs *TLHT* RG30 .... **56** B7
Park End *NWBY* RG14 .... **12** F2
Parkfields *YTLY* GU46 .... **135** J4
Park Gdns *BSTK* RG21 .... **15** H8
Park Hl *FLET* GU13 .... **167** G2
Parkhill Dr *CALC* RG31 .... **55** J3
Parkhouse La *TLHT* RG30 .... **2** A8
Parkland Dr *BRAK* RG12 .... **11** M2
Park La *BNFD* RG42 .... **79** F5
CALC RG31 .... **55** H6
CHAM RG24 .... **161** J6
EWKG RG40 .... **115** K5
GOR/PANG RG8 .... **27** K5
NTHA RG18 .... **85** J3
THLE RG7 .... **111** H6
THLE RG7 .... **112** C6
WAR/TWY RG10 .... **60** A2
Park La *FLET* GU13 .... **167** G6
Park Rd *BRAK* RG12 .... **11** J2
EWKG RG40 .... **97** G1
HEN RG9 .... **31** F1
Parkside *HEN* RG9 .... **31** F1
Parkside Rd *BSTK* RG21 .... **15** C8
NTHA RG18 .... **85** J2
TLHT RG30 .... **2** A8
Park St *NWBY* RG14 .... **12** C4

Park View Dr North
WAR/TWY RG10 .... **45** K6
Park View Dr South
WAR/TWY RG10 .... **45** K7
Park Wk *GOR/PANG* RG8 .... **41** J7
Park Wall La *GOR/PANG* RG8.... **38** E4
Park Wy *NWBY* RG14 .... **12** E2
Parkway *CWTH* RG45 .... **118** B3
Parkway Dr *CAV/SC* RG4 .... **59** G2
Parkwood Cl *CHAM* RG24 ...... **145** G6
Parsley Cl *EARL* RG6 .... **8** F9
Parsons Cl *FLET* GU13 .... **167** G6
NWBY RG14 .... **12** A5
WHIT RG2 .... **115** K1
Parthia Cl *READ* RG1 .... **3** H8
Part La *THLE* RG7 .... **113** K5
Partridge Av *YTLY* GU46 .... **135** G3
Partridge Dr *CALC* RG31 .... **55** G7
Pasture Cl *EARL* RG6 .... **74** E6
Paterson Cl *KEMP* RG22 .... **175** H5
Patrick Gdns *BNFD* RG42 .... **80** B5
Patrick Rd *READ* RG1 .... **3** J1
Patriot Pl *READ* RG1 .... **3** M6
Patten Ash Dr *EWKG* RG40 ..... **77** K7
Patten Av *YTLY* GU46 .... **135** H4
Pattinson Rd *WHIT* RG2 .... **94** A1
Paulet Pl *CHAM* RG24 .... **161** J5
Paul's Fld *HTWY* RG27 .... **134** D1
Pavenham Cl *EARL* RG6 .... **74** D6
Pavy Cl *STHA* RG19 .... **86** A5
Pawmers Md *FLET* GU13 .... **183** F1
Paxton Cl *KEMP* RG22 .... **175** G5
Payley Dr *EWKG* RG40 .... **77** K6
Paynes Cl *STHA* RG19 .... **123** K1
Paynesdown Rd *STHA* RG19 ... **85** G4
Peachey Dr *STHA* RG19 .... **86** A5
Peach St *EWKG* RG40 .... **97** H1
Peacock La *BRAK* RG12 .... **98** E2
Pearce's Orch *HEN* RG9 .... **17** G7
Pearson Rd *CAV/SC* RG4 .... **59** G2
Pearson Wy *WODY* RG5 .... **75** H1
Pear Tree Av *FLET* GU13 .... **167** G3
Pear Tree La *NWBY* RG14 ...... **84** B2
Pease Hl *THLE* RG7 .... **67** G6
Peatmoor Cl *FLET* GU13 .... **167** F1
Peat Moor Cl *FLET* GU13 .... **167** F1
Peddlars Gv *YTLY* GU46 .... **135** K3
Peel Cl *CAV/SC* RG4 .... **58** A3
Peel Ct *HTWY* RG27 .... **149** H4
Peel Gdns *KSCL* RG20 .... **123** K6
Pegasus Cl *STHA* RG19 .... **85** F3
Pegasus Ct *CALC* RG31 .... **55** H6
Peggotts Pl *SHST* GU47 .... **119** F6
Peg's Gn *TLHT* RG30 .... **56** C6
Peg's Green Cl *TLHT* RG30 ..... **56** C7
Pelham Cl *CHAM* RG24 .... **161** J6
Pelican La *NWBY* RG14 .... **12** E2
Pelican Rd *TADY* RG26 .... **109** H6
Pell St *READ* RG1 .... **3** J9
Pelton Rd *BSTK* RG21 .... **14** B3
Pemberton Gdns *CALC* RG31 ... **71** J2
Pembroke *BRAK* RG12 .... **99** G5
Pembroke Cl *THLE* RG7 .... **91** H4
Pembroke Pl *CAV/SC* RG4 ...... **57** K2
Pembroke Rd *DEAN* RG23 ..... **159** G6
NWBY RG14 .... **12** D3
Pemerton Rd *BSTK* RG21 ...... **15** H1
Pendals Cl *NTHA* RG18 .... **36** A7
Pendennis Av *CAV/SC* RG4 .... **44** B6
Pendennis Cl *DEAN* RG23 ..... **159** G5
Pendine Pl *BRAK* RG12 .... **99** J3
Pendlebury *BRAK* RG12 .... **99** H5
Pendred Rd *WHIT* RG2 .... **93** K1
Penn Cl *CAV/SC* RG4 .... **43** H6
Pennfields *WAR/TWY* RG10 .... **46** D6
Pennine Cl *CALC* RG31 .... **55** C7
Pennine Wy *KEMP* RG22 .... **175** G1
WAR/TWY RG10 .... **60** A1
Penn Rd *NWBY* RG14 .... **83** G2
Pennypiece *GOR/PANG* RG8 .... **25** F4
Pennyroyal Ct *READ* RG1 .... **3** G9
Penny's Hatch *KSCL* RG20 ..... **124** B7
Penrith Rd *BSTK* RG21 .... **14** C6
Penroath Av *TLHT* RG30 .... **56** D7
Penrose Av *WODY* RG5 .... **59** H7
Penrose Cl *NWBY* RG14 .... **83** J2
Pensford Cl *CWTH* RG45 .... **118** C1
Pentland Cl *KEMP* RG22 .... **175** G1
TLHT RG30 .... **72** A1
Penwood Gdns *EWKG* RG40 ... **98** E4
Penwood Hts *KSCL* RG20 ...... **120** D1
Penwood Rd *KSCL* RG20 .... **103** F5
Peppard Hl *HEN* RG9 .... **29** G3
Peppard Rd *CAV/SC* RG4 .... **29** H6
CAV/SC RG4 .... **43** K5
CAV/SC RG4 .... **57** K1
Pepper La *EARL* RG6 .... **8** C4
Peregrine Cl *BRAK* RG12 .... **10** F9
BRAK RG12 .... **99** J3
WWKG RG41 .... **96** E2
Periam Cl *HEN* RG9 .... **31** F3
Perkins Wy *WWKG* RG41 ...... **97** F2
Perry Dr *FLET* GU13 .... **166** E2
Perryhill Dr *SHST* GU47 .... **118** A7
Perry Oaks *BRAK* RG12 .... **11** M4
Perry Wy *BRAK* RG12 .... **11** M3
Perseverance Hl *HEN* RG9 ..... **30** D6
Pershore Rd *CHAM* RG24 ...... **160** C2
Perth Cl *WODY* RG5 .... **59** K4
Peterhouse Cl *SHST* GU47 ..... **119** G6
Petersfield Cl *CHAM* RG24 .... **145** J6
Petrel Cl *WWKG* RG41 .... **96** D2
Petrel Cft *KEMP* RG22 .... **175** F4
Petty's Brook Rd *CHAM* RG24 . **145** G6
Petunia Cl *KEMP* RG22 .... **175** F4
Petworth Av *CALC* RG31 ...... **72** A3
Petworth Cl *KEMP* RG22 ...... **175** G6
Pevensey Av *CAV/SC* RG4 ..... **44** B7
Pewsey V *BRAK* RG12 .... **100** C3
Pheaben's Fld *TADY* RG26 ..... **129** F6
Pheasant Cl *KEMP* RG22 .... **174** E4
Pheby Rd *KEMP* RG22 .... **175** J2
Phillimore Rd *CAV/SC* RG4 .... **43** K4
Phillips Cl *WODY* RG5 .... **60** A4

Phoebe Ct *READ* RG1 .... **3** H9
Phoenix Cl *WWKG* RG41 .... **96** D1
Phoenix Ct *HTWY* RG27 .... **149** G6
KSCL RG20 .... **124** A7
Phoenix Park Ter *BSTK* RG21 .. **14** E3
Phoenix Ter *HTWY* RG27 ...... **149** G6
Phyllis Court Dr *HEN* RG9 ..... **17** H7
Pickering Rd *CAV/SC* RG4 ..... **44** A5
Picket Post Cl *BRAK* RG12 .... **100** D1
Picketts La *GOR/PANG* RG8 ... **53** H1
Pickwell Cl *EARL* RG6 .... **9** M8
Picton Wy *CAV/SC* RG4 .... **57** J1
Piercefield *CALC* RG31 .... **71** G2
Pierce's Hl *CALC* RG31 .... **55** H4
Pigeon Cl *BNFD* RG42 .... **129** H7
Pigeonhouse La *WDSR* SL4 .... **81** H1
Pigeons Farm Rd *STHA* RG19 . **104** C1
Piggott's Rd *CAV/SC* RG4 ...... **3** M2
Pigott Rd *EWKG* RG40 .... **77** J7
Pikeshaw Wy *CALC* RG31 ..... **55** H3
Pike St *NWBY* RG14 .... **13** H1
Pilcot Rd *HTWY* RG27 .... **166** C5
Pimento Dr *EARL* RG6 .... **8** F9
Pimpernel Pl *NTHA* RG18 ..... **86** A3
Pimpernel Wy *CHAM* RG24 ... **161** G4
Pincents La *CALC* RG31 .... **71** F2
THLE RG7 .... **71** F1
Pinchcut *THLE* RG7 .... **71** H7
Pinchington La *NWBY* RG14 ... **103** K1
Pindar Pl *NWBY* RG14 .... **84** D2
Pine Croft Rd *WWKG* RG41 .... **97** F5
Pine Dr *EWKG* RG40 .... **117** F1
THLE RG7 .... **110** E2
Pinefields Cl *CWTH* RG45 ..... **118** C3
Pine Gv *FLET* GU13 .... **167** J6
WAR/TWY RG10 .... **46** C7
Pinehill Rd *CWTH* RG45 .... **118** C4
Pinehurst *TADY* RG26 .... **126** E2
Pine Rdg *NWBY* RG14 .... **84** B2
Pine Ridge Rd *THLE* RG7 ...... **91** F5
Pines *FLET* GU13 .... **167** G1
The Pines *WAR/TWY* RG10 .... **46** D5
Pinetree Ct *CAV/SC* RG4 .... **43** H7
Pinewood Av *CWTH* RG45 .... **118** D2
Pinewood Cl *TADY* RG26 ...... **108** A7
Pinewood Dr *KSCL* RG20 ...... **103** K6
Pinewood Hl *FLET* GU13 ...... **167** K1
Pingewood Cl *TLHT* RG30 ..... **72** B5
Pingewood Rd North *TLHT* RG30.. **72** B4
Pingewood Rd South
TLHT RG30 .... **72** C7
Pinkerton Rd *KEMP* RG22 ..... **175** H1
Pinks La *TADY* RG26 .... **108** B7
Pinnell Cl *KEMP* RG22 .... **175** H6
Pintail Cl *KEMP* RG22 .... **174** E5
Pipers Cft *FLET* GU13 .... **167** H7
Pipers La *STHA* RG19 .... **86** A6
Pipers Wy *STHA* RG19 .... **86** B5
Pipit Cl *STHA* RG19 .... **85** G4
Pipsons Cl *YTLY* GU46 .... **135** J3
Pitcairn Cl *CHAM* RG24 .... **160** D1
Pitch Pl *BNFD* RG42 .... **78** E3
Pitcroft Av *EARL* RG6 .... **5** G9
Pitfield La *THLE* RG7 .... **111** H4
Pitford Rd *WODY* RG5 .... **59** J5
Pither Rd *ODIM* RG29 .... **180** B4
Pitman Cl *KEMP* RG22 .... **175** G2
Pittard Rd *BSTK* RG21 .... **14** B8
Pitts Cl *BNFD* RG42 .... **78** D4
Pitt's La *EARL* RG6 .... **5** K6
Plantagenet Pk *BNFD* RG42 ... **80** C6
Plantation Cl *NTHA* RG18 ..... **64** E1
Plantation Rd *TADY* RG26 ..... **108** B6
Players Gn *WODY* RG5 .... **75** H1
Playhatch Rd *CAV/SC* RG4 .... **44** D7
Play Platt *THLE* RG7 .... **70** C2
Pleasant Hl *TADY* RG26 .... **126** E1
Ploughlands *BNFD* RG42 ...... **10** A1
Plough La *EWKG* RG40 .... **78** A7
HEN RG9 .... **45** H3
HTWY RG27 .... **132** E6
Plough Rd *YTLY* GU46 .... **135** K2
Plover Cl *KEMP* RG22 .... **175** F3
WWKG RG41 .... **96** E2
Plowden Wy *HEN* RG9 .... **45** H3
Plumpton Rd *NWBY* RG14 .... **13** J8
Plumtrees *EARL* RG6 .... **9** K8
Plymouth Av *WODY* RG5 ...... **9** M1
Plympton Cl *EARL* RG6 .... **75** H3
Pocket Cl *BRAK* RG12 .... **78** E7
Poffley Pl *STHA* RG19 .... **86** B4
Pointers Cl *KSCL* RG20 .... **48** A3
Poland La *ODIM* RG29 .... **164** D5
Polehampton Cl *WAR/TWY* RG10.. **60** C1
Polkerris Wy *FLET* GU13 ...... **167** J7
Pollardrow Av *BNFD* RG42 .... **10** A2
Pollards Wy *CALC* RG31 .... **71** H2
Polmear Cl *FLET* GU13 .... **167** J7
Polsted Rd *CALC* RG31 .... **55** J4
Polyanthus Wy *CWTH* RG45 .. **98** C7
Pond Cl *NWBY* RG14 .... **103** G1
OVTN RG25 .... **171** H6
Pond Cft *YTLY* GU46 .... **135** K3
Pond End Rd *CAV/SC* RG4 .... **29** H5
Pond Head La *WODY* RG5 ..... **75** G2
Pond La *CAV/SC* RG4 .... **42** A6
NTHA RG18 .... **49** H6
Pond Moor Rd *BRAK* RG12 ... **10** E9
Pond Rd *STHA* RG19 .... **129** H7
Pondtail Cl *FLET* GU13 .... **167** K3
Pondtail Gdns *FLET* GU13 .... **167** K3
Pondtail Rd *FLET* GU13 .... **167** K3
Pondview Cl *FLET* GU13 ...... **167** K1
Poole Cl *TLHT* RG30 .... **56** A6
Pool Rd *WHIT* RG2 .... **149** H3
Poors Farm Rd *CHAM* RG24 .. **162** B3
Popes Hl *KSCL* RG20 .... **123** K7
Popeswood Rd *BNFD* RG42 ... **78** E6
Popham Cl *BRAK* RG12 .... **100** C3
Poplar Av *TLHT* RG30 .... **72** A1
Poplar La *WAR/TWY* RG10 .... **60** L4
WWKG RG41 .... **76** C5
Poplar Pl *NWBY* RG14 .... **83** K2
The Poplars *ASC* SL5 .... **101** K3
Popley Wy *CHAM* RG24 ...... **160** D2

Poppy Dr *NTHA* RG18 .... **86** A3
Poppy Flds *CHAM* RG24 ...... **161** H3
Poppy Pl *EWKG* RG40 .... **97** G1
Poppy Rd *NWBY* RG14 .... **71** H1
Porchester *ASC* SL5 .... **101** K2
Porchester Rd *NWBY* RG14 ... **12** E8
Porchfield *EARL* RG6 .... **9** H9
Porlock Cl *STHA* RG19 .... **85** J5
Porlock Pl *CALC* RG31 .... **71** H2
Portacre Ri *BSTK* RG21 .... **14** A8
Porter End *NWBY* RG14 ...... **13** H9
Porter Rd *KEMP* RG22 .... **176** A3
Portia Gv *BNFD* RG42 .... **11** M1
Portiswood Cl *TADY* RG26 .... **127** C1
Portland Dr *FLET* GU13 .... **167** G7
Portland Gdns *TLHT* RG30 ... **55** H6
Portman Cl *BNFD* RG42 .... **10** C2
Portman Rd *TLHT* RG30 ...... **56** C4
Portmeirion Gdns *TLHT* RG30 . **56** A4
Portrush Cl *WODY* RG5 .... **59** C7
Portway *TADY* RG26 .... **108** A7
THLE RG7 .... **113** K6
Portway Cl *READ* RG1 .... **2** D9
Portway Pl *DEAN* RG23 ...... **159** G6
Post Horn La *HTWY* RG27 .... **147** H5
Post Horn Pl *CALC* RG31 ..... **72** A2
Posting House Ms *NWBY* RG14 . **12** B1
Post Office La *THLE* RG7 ...... **91** H2
Potbridge Rd *ODIM* RG29 .... **164** E3
Potkiln La *GOR/PANG* RG8 .... **26** D5
Pot La *CHAM* RG24 .... **162** C3
Potters La *HTWY* RG27 .... **130** C6
Pottery Rd *TLHT* RG30 .... **55** K4
Poultons Cl *OVTN* RG25 ...... **171** H6
Poultons Rd *OVTN* RG25 ..... **171** H5
Pound Cl *TADY* RG26 .... **129** F6
Poundfield Wy *WAR/TWY* RG10 . **60** C2
Pound La *CAV/SC* RG4 .... **59** G2
KSCL RG20 .... **121** H3
NWBY RG14 .... **83** J3
STHA RG19 .... **85** F4
WAR/TWY RG10 .... **77** G1
Pound Meadow *HTWY* RG27 . **146** B2
Pound Rd *OVTN* RG25 .... **171** J5
Pound St *NWBY* RG14 .... **12** D6
Poveys Md *KSCL* RG20 .... **124** B7
Poyle Gdns *BRAK* RG12 ...... **11** J1
Poynings Crs *BSTK* RG21 ..... **176** D2
Poyntz Rd *OVTN* RG25 .... **171** H4
Prescott *BRAK* RG12 .... **99** G5
Preston Pl *NWBY* RG14 ...... **84** C2
Preston Rd *WHIT* RG2 .... **7** J2
Price Gdns *BNFD* RG42 ...... **79** J4
Prides Crossing *ASC* SL5 ..... **81** K5
Priest Av *EWKG* RG40 .... **98** A2
Priest Hl *CAV/SC* RG4 .... **57** H2
Priestley Rd *CHAM* RG24 .... **159** K4
Priestwood Av *BNFD* RG42 ... **10** A1
Priestwood Court Rd
BNFD RG42 .... **10** A1
Primrose Cl *GOR/PANG* RG8 .. **41** H7
Primrose Dr *HTWY* RG27 ..... **149** H3
Primrose Gdns *KEMP* RG22 ... **175** G7
Primrose La *WWKG* RG41 .... **76** B3
Primrose Wk *BRAK* RG12 ..... **99** K3
Primrose Wy *SHST* GU47 ..... **118** C7
Prince Albert Dr *ASC* SL5 ..... **101** G2
Prince Andrew Wy *ASC* SL5 ... **81** C7
Prince Consort Dr *ASC* SL5 ... **101** G2
Prince Dr *SHST* GU47 .... **118** B7
Prince Hold Rd *STHA* RG19 ... **85** F4
Prince of Wales Av *TLHT* RG30 . **2** A6
Princes' Crs *KEMP* RG22 ...... **175** K1
Princess Marina Dr *EWKG* RG40.. **95** K6
WHIT RG2 .... **95** J7
WHIT RG2 .... **115** J1
Prince's St *READ* RG1 .... **3** M7
Prince William Dr *CALC* RG31 . **55** H4
Priors Cl *KSCL* RG20 .... **124** A7
Prior's Ct *READ* RG1 .... **3** B1
Priors Court Rd *NWBY* RG18 .. **48** B5
Priors Keep *FLET* GU13 ...... **167** K3
Priors Wd *CWTH* RG45 .... **117** J4
Priory Av *CAV/SC* RG4 .... **57** H3
Priory Cl *FLET* GU13 .... **166** E3
Priory Ct *WWKG* RG41 .... **76** B3
Priory Gdns *CHAM* RG24 .... **161** J4
Priory La *BRAK* RG12 .... **79** K5
WHCH RG28 .... **170** B5
Priory Rd *NWBY* RG14 .... **104** A2
Priory Rd *ASC* SL5 .... **80** E6
NWBY RG14 .... **13** G6
The Priory *WWKG* RG41 ..... **76** B3
Priory Wk *BRAK* RG12 .... **100** C2
Pritchard Cl *STHA* RG19 ..... **104** C1
Privet Cl *EARL* RG6 .... **74** E5
Privett Cl *CHAM* RG24 .... **161** H3
Proctors Rd *EWKG* RG40 .... **98** A1
Promenade Rd *READ* RG1 .... **3** G1
Prospect Pl *NWBY* RG14 ..... **12** E7
Prospect St *CAV/SC* RG4 ..... **57** H3
READ RG1 .... **2** E7
Provident Wy *BSTK* RG21 .... **14** E4
Pudding Hl *WAR/TWY* RG10 .. **33** J5
Puffers Wy *NWBY* RG14 ..... **12** A5
Puffin Cl *KEMP* RG22 .... **174** E6
Pump La *THLE* RG7 .... **92** D5
Purbrook Cl *BRAK* RG12 ..... **100** B4
Purbrook Rd *TADY* RG26 .... **126** D1
Purcell Cl *KEMP* RG22 .... **176** A3
Purcell Rd *CWTH* RG45 ...... **118** C1
Purfield Dr *WAR/TWY* RG10 .. **46** D2
Purley La *GOR/PANG* RG8 .... **41** H7
Purley Ri *GOR/PANG* RG8 .... **40** E7
Purley Village *GOR/PANG* RG8 . **41** H7
Purley Wy *GOR/PANG* RG8 ... **40** D7
Pursers Farm *THLE* RG7 ..... **93** J4
Purslane *EWKG* RG40 .... **97** J2
Puttenham Rd *CHAM* RG24 .. **145** H7
Pyegrove Cha *BRAK* RG12 ... **100** D5
Pyotts Copse *CHAM* RG24 ... **161** H2
Pyotts Ct *CHAM* RG24 .... **161** H2
Pyotts Hl *CHAM* RG24 .... **161** H2

Q

Quadrant Ct *BRAK* RG12 ...... **11** L5
Qualitas *BRAK* RG12 .... **99** G6
Quantock Av *CAV/SC* RG4 .... **44** A7
Quantock Cl *WAR/TWY* RG10 . **60** A1
The Quantocks *STHA* RG19 ... **85** J5
Quarrington Cl *STHA* RG19 ... **85** K5
Quarry La *HEN* RG9 .... **31** K7
YTLY GU46 .... **135** K4
Quartz Cl *WWKG* RG41 ...... **76** C7
Queen Annes Ga *CAV/SC* RG4 . **57** K1
Queen Cl *HEN* RG9 .... **31** H2
Queen Mary Av *BSTK* RG21 .. **14** F2
Queen Mary Cl *FLET* GU13 ... **167** G1
Queensborough Dr *CAV/SC* RG4 .. **43** F7
Queen's Cottages *READ* RG1 .. **3** K5
The Queen's Dr *EARL* RG6 .... **8** B3
Queens Pine *BRAK* RG12 ..... **100** B4
Queen's Pl *ASC* SL5 .... **101** K1
Queens Ride *CWTH* RG45 .... **118** D1
Queen's Rd *BSTK* RG21 ...... **14** B4
CAV/SC RG4 .... **3** K2
FLET GU13 .... **167** H4
KSCL RG20 .... **124** B7
NWBY RG14 .... **13** G6
ODIM RG29 .... **180** B1
READ RG1 .... **3** K6
Queen St *CAV/SC* RG4 .... **57** H2
HEN RG9 .... **31** H2
Queensway *CAV/SC* RG4 ..... **44** A6
Queen Victoria St *READ* RG1 . **3** J4
Quelm La *BNFD* RG42 .... **79** J4
Quentin Rd *WODY* RG5 ...... **59** G7
Quilter Rd *KEMP* RG22 ...... **175** J3
Quince Tree Wy *HTWY* RG27 . **164** A2
Quintilis *BRAK* RG12 .... **99** G6

R

Rachaels Lake Vw
BNFD RG42 .... **80** B5
Rackstraw Rd *SHST* GU47 .... **118** E7
Radbourne Rd *CALC* RG31 ... **71** J2
Radcliffe Wy *BNFD* RG42 ..... **79** F6
Radcot Cl *WODY* RG5 .... **59** H4
Radford Gdns *BSTK* RG21 .... **176** A2
Radical Ride *EWKG* RG40 .... **116** E1
Radnor Cl *HEN* RG9 .... **31** H1
Radnor Rd *BRAK* RG12 ...... **100** C1
EARL RG6 .... **9** L5
Radstock La *EARL* RG6 ...... **9** J7
Radstock Rd *READ* RG1 ...... **4** D6
Ragdale *THLE* RG7 .... **91** F4
Raggleswood Cl *EARL* RG6 ... **9** L5
Raghill *THLE* RG7 .... **109** G2
Raglan Gdns *CAV/SC* RG4 .... **57** K1
Ragley Ms *CAV/SC* RG4 ...... **44** A3
Railside *THLE* RG7 .... **88** C5
Railton Cl *WHIT* RG2 .... **74** A7
Railway Wy *NWBY* RG14 ..... **13** C5
Rainbow Cl *CHAM* RG24 ..... **161** K6
Rainbow Pk *WWKG* RG41 .... **76** A5
Rainham Cl *KEMP* RG22 ..... **174** E5
Rainworth Cl *EARL* RG6 ..... **74** D6
Raleigh Cl *WODY* RG5 .... **75** H1
Ralphs Ride *BRAK* RG12 ..... **11** L5
Ram Aly *STHA* RG19 .... **124** D1
Ramptons La *THLE* RG7 ..... **110** A2
Rampton's Meadow
TADY RG26 .... **127** G2
Ramsbury Cl *BRAK* RG12 .... **99** F4
Ramsbury Dr *EARL* RG6 ..... **9** H4
Ramsdell Cl *TADY* RG26 ..... **126** E3
Ramsdell Rd *TADY* RG26 .... **141** F1
TADY RG26 .... **143** G1
Ramsey Cl *EARL* RG6 .... **75** H4
Ramslade Rd *BRAK* RG12 .... **11** J8
Rances La *EWKG* RG40 ...... **97** K1
Randall Md *BNFD* RG42 ..... **78** C4
Randolph Rd *READ* RG1 ..... **3** G2
Ranelagh Crs *ASC* SL5 .... **81** F6
Ranelagh Dr *BRAK* RG12 .... **11** H5
Range Rd *EWKG* RG40 ...... **117** G1
Rangewood Av *CALC* RG31 .. **72** A3
Raphael Cl *BSTK* RG21 ...... **15** K8
Rapley Gn *BRAK* RG12 ...... **99** K4
Ratby Cl *EARL* RG6 .... **9** L8
Ravel Cl *KEMP* RG22 .... **175** J3
Ravelin Cl *NFNM* GU10 ..... **182** E7
Raven Cl *YTLY* GU46 .... **135** G3
Ravenglass Cl *EARL* RG6 .... **9** M7
Raven Rd *HTWY* RG27 ...... **163** K2
Ravensbourne Dr *WODY* RG5 . **59** H5
Ravens Cft *HTWY* RG27 ..... **164** B2
Ravenscroft Rd *HEN* RG9 .... **31** G1
Ravensdale Rd *ASC* SL5 ..... **101** K3
Ravenswood Av *CWTH* RG45 . **117** K3
Ravensworth Rd *THLE* RG7 .. **110** D2
Rawlings Rd *HTWY* RG27 .... **164** A3
Rayleigh Rd *BSTK* RG21 ..... **15** K8
Reade's La *CAV/SC* RG4 ..... **28** A7
Reading Rd *CAV/SC* RG4 .... **28** A7
CHAM RG24 .... **145** F4
EARL RG6 .... **160** E3
EWKG RG40 .... **115** J4
GOR/PANG RG8 .... **24** D5
GOR/PANG RG8 .... **37** G2
GOR/PANG RG8 .... **40** C7
HEN RG9 .... **31** H3
HTWY RG27 .... **134** C1
HTWY RG27 .... **146** A2
HTWY RG27 .... **163** K1
HTWY RG27 .... **164** A1
HTWY RG27 .... **90** E7
THLE RG7 .... **109** J3
TLHT RG30 .... **91** H3
WHIT RG2 .... **95** F3
WODY RG5 .... **59** G5
WWKG RG41 .... **76** A4
YTLY GU46 .... **135** F2
Reading Rd North *FLET* GU13 . **166** E1

Reading Rd South FLET GU13...... 167 H4
Rebecca Cl FLET GU13 .... 183 F1
Recreation La THLE RG7 .... 93 J5
Recreation Rd ODIM RG29 .... 180 B2
  THLE RG7 .... 91 F5
  TLHT RG30 .... 55 K5
  WAR/TWY RG10 .... 46 D2
Rectory Cl BRAK RG12 .... 11 G7
  EWKG RG40 .... 97 H1
  NWBY RG14 .... 12 C7
  TADY RG26 .... 127 F3
Rectory La BRAK RG12 .... 10 E9
  TADY RG26 .... 140 D2
Rectory Rd CAV/SC RG4 .... 57 H5
  DEAN RG23 .... 173 H3
  EWKG RG40 .... 97 H1
  GOR/PANG RG8 .... 23 K4
  HTWY RG27 .... 163 K5
  THLE RG7 .... 109 J1
Redberry Cl CAV/SC RG4 .... 44 A7
Redbridge La THLE RG7 .... 15 M5
Red Cottage Dr CALC RG31 .... 71 H2
Red Cross Rd GOR/PANG RG8 .... 25 F5
Redditch BRAK RG12 .... 100 A5
Redfield Ct NWBY RG14 .... 13 M2
Redfields La NWFNM GU10....... 183 F3
Redgauntlet EWKG RG40 .... 116 D2
Redhatch Dr EARL RG6 .... 8 F7
Red HI HEN RG9 .... 30 C6
  HTWY RG27 .... 148 D1
Red House Cl EARL RG6 .... 74 E6
Red House Dr CAV/SC RG4 .... 29 C6
Redlake La EWKG RG40 .... 98 A4
Redlands La NFNM GU10....... 182 E5
Redlands Pl WWKG RG41 .... 96 E5
Redlands Rd READ RG1 .... 8 A2
Red La GOR/PANG RG8....... 26 D2
  THLE RG7 .... 109 G3
Red Lion La BSTK RG21 .... 14 F6
  OVTN RG25 .... 171 H4
Red Rose BNFD RG42 .... 78 D3
Redruth Gdns WHIT RG2 .... 7 K9
Red Shute HI NTHA RG18....... 65 F2
Redvers Rd BRAK RG12 .... 99 J3
Redwing Cl KEMP RG22 .... 174 E5
Redwood Av WODY RG5 .... 75 K1
Redwoods Wy FLET GU13 .... 167 J7
Redwood Wy CALC RG31....... 55 J2
Reeds Av EARL RG6 .... 8 F6
Reed's HI BRAK RG12 .... 99 J3
Reeves Wy WWKG RG41 .... 97 F3
Regent Cl EARL RG6 .... 75 F5
  FLET GU13 .... 167 H3
Regent Ct READ RG1 .... 3 G4
Regent St FLET GU13 .... 167 H3
  READ RG1 .... 4 D6
Regis Cl WHIT RG2 .... 74 A7
Regnum Dr NWBY RG14 .... 84 A2
Rembrandt Cl BSTK RG21........... 15 K8
  WWKG RG41 .... 96 C1
Rembrandt Wy READ RG1........... 6 D1
Remembrance Gdns
  CHAM RG24 .... 161 G1
Remembrance Rd NWBY RG14 .... 12 A6
Remenham Church La HEN RG9 .. 17 K6
Remenham La HEN RG9 .... 31 J1
Renault Rd WODY RG5........... 59 K7
Renoir Cl BSTK RG21........... 15 K9
Renown Wy CHAM RG24 .... 145 G6
Repton Rd EARL RG6........... 9 M4
Restormel Cl DEAN RG23....... 159 G5
Restwood Cl TLHT RG30 .... 72 D2
Retford Cl WODY RG5 .... 59 J4
Reuben's Crs TADY RG26 .... 126 E2
Reynards Cl TADY RG26 .... 126 E1
  WWKG RG41 .... 76 B4
Reynolds Cl BSTK RG21 .... 15 K7
Reyntiens Vw ODIM RG29 .... 180 D3
Rhigos CAV/SC RG4........... 43 G6
Rhine Cl CAV/SC RG4........... 58 A3
Rhodes Cl EARL RG6........... 75 H3
Rhododendron Cl ASC SL5 .... 81 H5
Rhododendron Wk ASC SL5 .... 81 H5
Ribbleton Cl EARL RG6 .... 75 H3
Ribble Wy BSTK RG21 .... 15 J5
Richard Cl FLET GU13 .... 167 H4
Richborough Cl EARL RG6....... 9 J8
Richfield Av READ RG1........... 2 E2
Richfield Pl READ RG1 .... 2 E2
Richmond Cl FLET GU13 .... 167 H3
Richmond Ri WWKG RG41 .... 76 D7
Richmond Rd BSTK RG21 .... 14 D2
  CAV/SC RG4........... 57 F1
  TLHT RG30 .... 56 D5
Rickman Cl BRAK RG12 .... 99 K4
  WHIT RG2 .... 95 H6
  WODY RG5 .... 75 C1
Riddings La STHA RG19 .... 106 D6
Rider's La THLE RG7 .... 92 B3
Ridge Cl KEMP RG22 .... 175 H1
Ridge Hall Cl CAV/SC RG4 .... 57 F2
Ridge La HTWY RG27 .... 163 H1
Ridgemount Cl CALC RG31 .... 55 C3
The Ridge GOR/PANG RG8....... 39 J4
  NTHA RG18 .... 65 H5
Ridge Wy WAR/TWY RG10 .... 46 C3
Ridgeway DID OX11 .... 21 F1
  DID OX11 .... 22 B3
  GOR/PANG RG8 .... 25 F3
Ridgeway La NTHA RG18....... 49 G6
The Ridgeway BRAK RG12 .... 11 G6
  CAV/SC RG4........... 57 H2
  WODY RG5 .... 75 J1
The Ridings CAV/SC RG4........... 43 K4
Riding Wy WWKG RG41 .... 96 C1
Ridley Cl FLET GU13 .... 167 G4
Ridlington Cl EARL RG6 .... 75 H4
Righton Cl WAR/TWY RG10 .... 60 A2
Riley La CHAM RG24 .... 161 J4
Riley Rd TLHT RG30 .... 56 A5
Rimes's La TADY RG26 .... 126 C3
Ringmead BRAK RG12 .... 99 F5
Ringshall Gdns TADY RG26 .... 129 F6
The Ring BRAK RG12 .... 10 F4
Ringway North CHAM RG24 .... 159 K4
Ringway South BSTK RG21 .... 14 D9
  BSTK RG21 .... 176 B2
Ringway West DEAN RG23 .... 159 K4

KEMP RG22 .... 159 K7
Ringwood Cl BRAK RG12 .... 99 G5
Ringwood Rd TLHT RG30 .... 56 A4
Ripley Rd TLHT RG30 .... 56 B4
Ripplesmere BRAK RG12 .... 11 K9
The Rise CAV/SC RG4........... 57 J1
  CWTH RG45 .... 118 A3
  WODY RG5 .... 115 K6
  NTHA RG18 .... 65 H6
  WWKG RG41 .... 77 F7
Rissington Cl CALC RG31....... 55 K2
Rivacres GOR/PANG RG8 .... 40 D1
Riverdene Dr WWKG RG41 .... 75 J3
River Gdns GOR/PANG RG8 .... 41 J7
Rivermead Rd WODY RG5 .... 75 J1
River Pk NWBY RG14 .... 13 H3
River Rd CAV/SC RG4........... 56 E2
  READ RG1 .... 3 H9
  YTLY GU46 .... 135 G2
Riversdale Ct READ RG1........... 4 C5
Riverside Cl CHAM RG24 .... 161 J4
  OVTN RG25 .... 171 J4
Riverview Rd GOR/PANG RG8....... 40 B6
Robert Mays Rd ODIM RG29 .... 180 B2
Robertsfield STHA RG19 .... 84 E4
Roberts Gv WWKG RG41 .... 96 A5
Robertson Cl NWBY RG14 .... 84 A7
Robin Cl KEMP RG22 .... 175 H4
  THLE RG7 .... 91 G4
Robindale Av EARL RG6 .... 75 C3
Robinhood La WWKG RG41 .... 76 B4
Robin Hood Wy WWKG RG41 .... 76 B3
Robins Cl NWBY RG14 .... 103 J1
Robins Grove Crs YTLY GU46 .... 135 C3
Robinson Ct EARL RG6 .... 9 C9
Roby Dr BRAK RG12 .... 100 A5
Rochester Av WODY RG5........... 59 K6
Rochester Cl KEMP RG22 .... 175 G4
Rochester Gv FLET GU13 .... 167 G3
Rochford Rd BSTK RG21 .... 14 C5
Rockbourne Gdns TLHT RG30 ... 56 B4
Rockingham Rd NWBY RG14 .... 12 C5
Roding Cl BSTK RG21 .... 15 J5
Roebuck Est BNFD RG42 .... 78 D5
Roebuck Ri CALC RG31........... 55 J2
Roebuts Cl NWBY RG14 .... 83 J7
Roentgen Rd CHAM RG24 .... 15 M1
  CHAM RG24 .... 161 G5
Rokeby Cl BRAK RG12 .... 11 J3
  NWBY RG14 .... 103 K1
Rokeby Dr CAV/SC RG4........... 42 E4
Roke La ODIM RG29 .... 181 F3
Rokes Pl YTLY GU46 .... 135 F3
Roman Ride CWTH RG45 .... 117 J3
Roman Rd DEAN RG23 .... 159 G6
Romans Fld THLE RG7 .... 110 A7
  THLE RG7 .... 128 A1
Romans Ga THLE RG7 .... 109 J7
Roman Wy BNFD RG42 .... 80 C6
  DEAN RG23 .... 159 F6
  EARL RG6 .... 75 C3
  NTHA RG18 .... 85 F3
Romany Cl TLHT RG30 .... 56 B4
Romany La TLHT RG30 .... 56 B4
Romeo HI BNFD RG42 .... 80 C6
Romsey Cl CHAM RG24 .... 160 B2
Romsey Rd TLHT RG30 .... 56 B4
Rona Ct TLHT RG30 .... 56 C5
Rook Cl WWKG RG41 .... 96 D2
The Rookery WHCH RG28 .... 169 H7
Rooksdown Av CHAM RG24 .... 159 H3
Rooksdown La CHAM RG24 .... 159 H2
Rooksfield KSCL RG20 .... 105 F6
Rookswood BNFD RG42 .... 79 J5
  KSCL RG20 .... 82 C1
Rookswood Cl HTWY RG27 .... 164 A2
Rookswood Av SHST GU47 .... 119 F7
Rope Wk STHA RG19 .... 85 H4
Ropley Cl TADY RG26 .... 126 C1
Rosary Gdns YTLY GU46 .... 135 J3
Rosebay WWKG RG40 .... 77 K6
Rose Bay Gdns HTWY RG27 .... 164 B1
Roseberry Cl KEMP RG22 .... 175 G2
Rosebery Rd CAV/SC RG4........... 42 E5
Rose Cl KEMP RG22 .... 175 C4
  WODY RG5 .... 60 A6
Rosecroft Wy WHIT RG2 .... 94 B2
Rosedale EARL RG6 .... 74 D3
Rosedale Crs EARL RG6 .... 5 H4
Rosedale Gdns BRAK RG12 .... 10 D9
  STHA RG19 .... 85 H5
Rosedene Gdns FLET GU13 .... 167 G1
Rose HI BNFD RG42 .... 78 D3
Rosehill Pk CAV/SC RG4........... 43 K5
Rosehip Wy CHAM RG24 .... 161 G4
Rose Hodson Pl DEAN RG23 .... 159 H4
Rose Kiln La WHIT RG2 .... 7 G1
Rose La WAR/TWY RG10 .... 33 F3
Rosemary Av EARL RG6 .... 74 C5
Rosemary Dr TADY RG26 .... 126 E3
Rosemead Av CALC RG31 .... 55 C2
Rose St EWKG RG40 .... 97 H1
Rose Wk FLET GU13 .... 167 G1
  READ RG1 .... 3 H7
Rosewood WODY RG5........... 75 G2
Rosier Cl STHA RG19 .... 86 A5
Roslyn Rd WODY RG5........... 59 K7
Ross Cl BSTK RG21 .... 176 B2
Rossendale Rd CAV/SC RG4 .... 58 A2
Rosset Cl BRAK RG12 .... 10 E8
Rossington Pl WHIT RG2 .... 73 K6
Rossini Cl KEMP RG22 .... 175 K4
Ross Rd READ RG1 .... 2 F3
Rothay Ct BSTK RG21 .... 15 J5
Rotherfield Av WWKG RG41 .... 77 F7
Rotherfield Cl THLE RG7 .... 70 E2
Rotherfield Rd HEN RG9 .... 31 G4
Rotherwick La HTWY RG27 .... 146 E2
Rotherwick Rd TADY RG26 .... 126 C1
Rothwell Gdns WODY RG5 .... 59 J4
Rotten HI OVTN RG25 .... 170 E6
Rotten Row HI THLE RG7 .... 88 C3
Roughgrove Copse BNFD RG42 .... 78 C4
Roundabouts La WWKG RG41 .... 76 C4

Round End NWBY RG14 .... 103 G3
Roundfield THLE RG7 .... 86 C1
Roundhead Rd THLE RG7 .... 70 C3
Roundmead Rd BSTK RG21 .... 14 C6
Roundshead Dr BNFD RG42 .... 80 A5
Rounton Rd FLET GU13 .... 167 H6
Routh La TLHT RG30 .... 55 K7
Rowallan Cl CAV/SC RG4........... 44 A4
Rowan Cl CAV/SC RG4........... 29 G7
  FLET GU13 .... 167 K2
  WWKG RG41 .... 96 E2
Rowan Dl FLET GU13 .... 167 G6
Rowan Dr CWTH RG45 .... 118 D1
  NWBY RG14 .... 83 K2
  WAR/TWY RG10 .... 46 D7
Rowan Rd TADY RG26 .... 127 F2
Rowanmead TLHT RG30 .... 91 G3
Rowcroft Rd WHIT RG2 .... 115 J1
Rowdell Dr WHIT RG2 .... 74 A5
Rowe Ct TLHT RG30 .... 56 C5
Rowland's Cl THLE RG7 .... 110 B3
Rowland Wy EARL RG6 .... 8 E7
Row La CAV/SC RG4........... 44 B4
Rowley Cl BRAK RG12 .... 11 M5
Rowley Rd WHIT RG2 .... 7 K3
Royal Av CALC RG31 .... 71 G2
Royal Cl DEAN RG23 .... 175 F7
Royal Oak Dr CWTH RG45 .... 98 C7
Royal Wy WHIT RG2 .... 73 G6
Roy Cl NTHA RG18 .... 48 E7
Roycroft La EWKG RG40 .... 96 D7
Royston Cl TLHT RG30 .... 56 A6
Rubens Cl BSTK RG21 .... 176 E2
Ruby Cl WWKG RG41 .... 76 D7
Rudland Cl STHA RG19 .... 85 J5
Rufford Cl FLET GU13 .... 167 H5
Rufus Isaacs Rd CAV/SC RG4 .... 57 J3
Rugby Cl SHST GU47 .... 119 F7
Rupert Cl HEN RG9 .... 17 H7
Rupert Rd NWBY RG14 .... 83 J7
Rupert St READ RG1........... 4 B7
Ruscombe La WAR/TWY RG10 .... 46 D7
Ruscombe Pk WAR/TWY RG10 .... 46 D7
Rushall Cl EARL RG6 .... 74 B7
Rushbrook Rd WODY RG5........... 5 M7
  WODY RG5 .... 59 G6
Rushden Dr WHIT RG2 .... 74 B5
The Rushes BSTK RG21 .... 15 K5
Rushey Wy EARL RG6........... 9 K9
  EARL RG6 .... 74 D5
Rushmoor Cl FLET GU13 .... 167 H4
Rushmoor Gdns CALC RG31 .... 71 G2
Ruskin Cl BSTK RG21 .... 15 L8
Ruskin Ct CWTH RG45 .... 118 A4
Ruskin Wy WWKG RG41 .... 96 C1
Russell Cl BRAK RG12 .... 100 A6
Russell Rd BSTK RG21 .... 14 F8
  CAV/SC RG4........... 42 E5
  NWBY RG14 .... 12 B5
Russell St READ RG1........... 2 F7
Russell Wy WWKG RG41 .... 76 A5
Russet Cl CAV/SC RG4........... 29 F6
Russet Gld CAV/SC RG4........... 43 K5
  THLE RG7 .... 91 G5
Russetts Dr FLET GU13 .... 167 H3
Russley Gn EWKG RG40 .... 97 F6
Rustic Gln FLET GU13 .... 167 G6
Rustington Cl EARL RG6 .... 74 E5
Ruston Wy ASC SL5 .... 81 H7
Rutherford Rd CHAM RG24 .... 160 E3
Rutland Rd TLHT RG30 .... 2 A7
Rydal Av TLHT RG30 .... 56 A3
Rydal Dr FLET GU13 .... 167 F6
  STHA RG19 .... 85 F4
Ryebeck Rd FLET GU13 .... 167 H6
Rye Cl BRAK RG12 .... 80 A5
  FARN GU14 .... 151 K5
Rye Cft FLET GU13 .... 167 F7
Ryecroft Cl WAR/TWY RG10 .... 46 D2
  WODY RG5 .... 59 H4
Ryehurst La BNFD RG42 .... 79 G1
Ryeish La FARN GU14 .... 151 K5
Ryeland Cl FLET GU13 .... 167 H6
Ryelaw Rd FLET GU13 .... 167 H6
Ryemead La WDSR SL4 .... 81 F1
Ryhill Wy EARL RG6 .... 74 B6
Rylstone Rd TLHT RG30 .... 2 A4
Ryves Av YTLY GU46 .... 135 F4

S

Sackville St READ RG1 .... 3 G5
Saddleback Wy FARN GU14 .... 151 J6
Sadler's Cl WWKG RG41 .... 76 C5
Sadlers End WWKG RG41 .... 76 A7
Sadler's La WWKG RG41 .... 76 C6
The Sadlers CALC RG31 .... 55 G4
Saffron Cl CHAM RG24 .... 145 G6
  EARL RG6 .... 9 M4
  NWBY RG14 .... 12 D3
Saffron Rd BRAK RG12 .... 10 E8
Sage Cl EARL RG6 .... 74 D5
Sagecroft Rd NTHA RG18 .... 85 H2
Sage Rd CALC RG31........... 55 H2
Sage Wk BNFD RG42 .... 80 A5
Sainfoin La DEAN RG23 .... 174 A4
St Andrews BRAK RG12 .... 99 F4
St Andrews Cl CWTH RG45 .... 118 A4
St Andrew's Rd CAV/SC RG4 .... 57 G1
  HEN RG9 .... 31 G3
  KEMP RG22 .... 175 J1
St Anne's Cl HEN RG9 .... 31 G2
St Anne's Rd CAV/SC RG4 .... 57 H3
St Anthonys Cl BNFD RG42 .... 10 D1
St Barbara's Rd TADY RG26 .... 129 J7
St Barnabas Rd CAV/SC RG4........... 43 H6
  WHIT RG2 .... 8 E9
St Bartholomews Rd EARL RG6 .... 4 E6
St Birinus Rd CALC RG31 .... 71 H1
St Catherine's Cl WWKG RG41....... 75 K5
St Catherine's HI THLE RG7 .... 110 D3
St Christophers Cl
  CHAM RG24 .... 175 H1
St Christophers Gdns ASC SL5 .... 81 G6
St Cross Rd NFNM GU10 .... 182 E1
St David's Cl CAV/SC RG4........... 43 G7

ODIM RG29 .... 180 B2
St David's Rd KEMP RG22 .... 175 K1
  KEMP RG22 .... 12 D5
St Donats Pl NWBY RG14 .... 12 F6
St Edward's Rd EARL RG6 .... 5 G8
St Elizabeth Cl WHIT RG2 .... 73 J7
St Gabriels Lea CHAM RG24 .... 145 H7
St George's Av NWBY RG14 .... 12 B6
St George's Rd TLHT RG30 .... 56 C5
St Giles Cl READ RG1 .... 3 J8
St Giles Ct READ RG1 .... 3 J8
St Helier Cl WWKG RG41 .... 97 G4
St Ives Cl THLE RG7 .... 70 C3
St James Cl GOR/PANG RG8........... 40 B6
  WAR/TWY RG10 .... 46 D7
St James Rd EWKG RG40 .... 96 D7
  FLET GU13 .... 167 G3
St John Cl TADY RG26 .... 129 H7
St Johns Cl HTWY RG27 .... 164 A2
  WODY RG5 .... 59 J5
St John's HI READ RG1 .... 3 M6
St John's Piece DEAN RG23 .... 174 A4
St John's Rd ASC SL5 .... 81 J5
  CAV/SC RG4........... 3 L1
  CAV/SC RG4........... 57 K3
  DEAN RG23 .... 174 A2
  HTWY RG27 .... 149 J5
  NWBY RG14 .... 12 E7
  READ RG1 .... 3 M7
  STHA RG19 .... 85 H4
  THLE RG7 .... 111 F3
St John's St READ RG1 .... 3 M6
St Joseph's Crs CHAM RG24 .... 161 G1
St Katherine's Rd HEN RG9 .... 31 G4
St Leonard's Av CHAM RG24 .... 145 H7
St Lukes Wy CAV/SC RG4........... 57 J1
St Marks Cl STHA RG19 .... 85 H4
St Mark's Rd BNFD RG42 .... 78 D6
  HEN RG9 .... 31 G3
St Mary's Av GOR/PANG RG8........... 41 H7
  TADY RG26 .... 129 J7
St Mary's Butts READ RG1........... 3 H6
St Mary's Cl HEN RG9 .... 30 D3
St Mary's Ct BSTK RG21 .... 15 G5
St Marys La WDSR SL4 .... 81 G1
St Mary's Rd HTWY RG27 .... 149 H5
  KSCL RG20 .... 124 A7
  NWBY RG14 .... 12 F2
  THLE RG7 .... 111 F3
  WWKG RG41 .... 76 A5
St Mary's Wy THLE RG7 .... 91 H4
St Michaels Cl FLET GU13 .... 167 K3
St Michaels Rd WAR/TWY RG10....... 46 D6
St Michaels La THLE RG7 .... 90 C2
St Michael's Rd KEMP RG22 .... 175 H1
  NWBY RG14 .... 12 C6
  TLHT RG30 .... 55 K6
St Neot's Rd HTWY RG27 .... 133 J2
St Nicholas Cl FLET GU13 .... 167 G2
St Nicholas Cl KEMP RG22 .... 159 J7
St Nicholas' Rd NWBY RG14 .... 12 D5
St Patrick's Av WAR/TWY RG10....... 45 K7
St Patrick's Cl KEMP RG22 .... 175 K1
St Paul's Ct READ RG1 .... 3 G9
St Paul's Ga WWKG RG41 .... 97 F1
St Paul's Rd KEMP RG22 .... 175 K1
St Peter's Av CAV/SC RG4........... 57 F1
St Peter's Gdns YTLY GU46 .... 135 J3
St Peter's HI CAV/SC RG4........... 57 G2
St Peter's Rd EARL RG6 .... 5 G9
  KEMP RG22 .... 175 H1
St Richards Rd NWBY RG14 .... 84 A2
St Ronans Rd TLHT RG30 .... 56 C5
St Saviour's Rd READ RG1 .... 6 E2
St Sebastian's Cl EWKG RG40 .... 97 K7
St Stephens Cl READ RG1 .... 3 H1
St Thomas' Cl BSTK RG21 .... 14 C6
Salamanca CWTH RG45 .... 117 K3
Salcombe Dr EARL RG6 .... 9 K3
Salcombe Rd NWBY RG14 .... 12 A7
  WHIT RG2 .... 8 A6
Saleby Cl EARL RG6 .... 74 H4
Salford Cl WHIT RG2 .... 94 B2
Salisbury Cl ODIM RG29 .... 180 B2
  WWKG RG41 .... 97 F5
Salisbury Gdns KEMP RG22 .... 159 H7
Salisbury Rd TLHT RG30 .... 2 C4
Salmon Cl THLE RG7 .... 93 J5
Salmond Rd WHIT RG2 .... 93 K1
Salmons Rd ODIM RG29 .... 180 B2
Saltersgate Cl EARL RG6 .... 75 G4
Salters Heath Rd TADY RG26 .... 143 G4
Salwey Cl BRAK RG12 .... 99 J4
Samian Pl BNFD RG42 .... 79 F5
Sampage Cl WHIT RG2 .... 93 K1
Sampson Pk BNFD RG42 .... 78 E6
Sanctuary Cl TLHT RG30 .... 55 K5
Sandbanks Dr KEMP RG22 .... 175 G5
Sandcroft Rd CAV/SC RG4........... 43 F6
Sandford Cl GOR/PANG RG8 .... 26 E3
  KSCL RG20 .... 124 C7
Sandford Down BRAK RG12 .... 100 C3
Sandford Dr WODY RG5........... 59 J4
Sandford La WODY RG5 .... 60 A6
Sandford Rd TADY RG26 .... 126 C5
Sandgate Av TLHT RG30 .... 56 A3
Sandhills Wy WHIT RG2 .... 47 J1
Sandhurst Rd CWTH RG45 .... 118 C5
  EWKG RG40 .... 97 G7
  YTLY GU46 .... 135 K5
Sandleford Cl WHIT RG2 .... 93 K1
Sandown Av CALC RG31 .... 71 G2
Sandown Wy NWBY RG14 .... 13 J8
Sandpiper Wy KEMP RG22 .... 174 E5
Sandpit HI KSCL RG20 .... 103 F5
Sandpit La CAV/SC RG4........... 44 B3
  THLE RG7 .... 114 E3
Sandringham Wy CALC RG31 .... 71 G2
Sandstone Cl WWKG RG41 .... 76 B5
Sandy Cl NTHA RG18........... 64 E2
Sandy La ASC SL5 .... 81 F6
  BRAK RG12 .... 11 G1
  FLET GU13 .... 167 H7
  HTWY RG27 .... 149 J5
  NTHA RG18 .... 64 E2
  SHST GU47 .... 118 A7
  TADY RG26 .... 127 G1

WWKG RG41 .... 96 B3
Sandys Cl KEMP RG22 .... 175 K1
Sandys Rd KEMP RG22 .... 159 K7
Sapley La OVTN RG25 .... 171 H5
Sapphire Cl WWKG RG41 .... 76 C7
Sargood Cl STHA RG19 .... 85 K5
Sarisbury Cl TADY RG26 .... 126 D1
Sarum BRAK RG12 .... 99 F6
Sarum Crs EWKG RG40 .... 77 J7
Sarum HI BSTK RG21 .... 14 D6
Sarum Rd TADY RG26 .... 108 D7
Saturn Cl WWKG RG41 .... 96 D1
Saturn Cft BNFD RG42 .... 80 E4
Savernake Cl TLHT RG30 .... 56 A6
Savernake Wy BRAK RG12 .... 100 C4
Savory Wk BNFD RG42 .... 78 D4
Sawmill Rd NTHA RG18 .... 65 F2
Sawpit Rd WAR/TWY RG10 .... 60 D6
Sawtry Cl EARL RG6 .... 75 H4
Sawyers Ley THLE RG7 .... 91 J7
Saxby Cl THLE RG7 .... 91 J7
Saxon Ct STHA RG19 .... 85 F4
Saxon Dr BNFD RG42 .... 80 C6
Saxon Wy CHAM RG24 .... 161 G4
Sayers Cl NWBY RG14 .... 84 A7
Scafell Cl CALC RG31 .... 55 G3
Scania Wk BNFD RG42 .... 80 E4
Scarlatti Rd KEMP RG22 .... 176 A4
Scarletts La WAR/TWY RG10 .... 47 A4
Scholars Cl CAV/SC RG4........... 57 G2
School HI CWTH RG45 .... 118 E4
  SHST GU47 .... 118 B7
  WAR/TWY RG10 .... 46 C3
School La CAV/SC RG4........... 43 J7
  KSCL RG20 .... 62 A2
  MLW SL7 .... 19 G4
  READ RG1 .... 3 H1
  THLE RG7 .... 90 E5
  THLE RG7 .... 110 A7
  THLE RG7 .... 114 B4
  WAR/TWY RG10 .... 46 C2
  YTLY GU46 .... 135 G3
School Rd CALC RG31........... 97 J1
  EWKG RG40 .... 97 J1
  KSCL RG20 .... 21 K7
  THLE RG7 .... 89 J6
  THLE RG7 .... 114 B4
  TLHT RG30 .... 91 H1
  WAR/TWY RG10 .... 60 E6
  WHIT RG2 .... 95 J5
School Ter READ RG1 .... 4 B5
Schroeder Cl BSTK RG21 .... 176 B2
Schubert Rd KEMP RG22 .... 175 K4
Scotney Rd BSTK RG21 .... 160 C4
Scots Dr WWKG RG41 .... 76 D7
Scottalls La NTHA RG18 .... 36 A7
Scott Cl CAV/SC RG4........... 43 H7
  WODY RG5 .... 59 K6
Scott Ter BNFD RG42 .... 11 M1
Scours La TLHT RG30 .... 56 C4
Scratchface La NTHA RG18 .... 52 A6
Scrivens Md STHA RG19 .... 86 A4
Scures Rd HTWY RG27 .... 163 J2
Seaford Gdns WODY RG5 .... 59 H7
Seaford Rd EWKG RG40 .... 97 J1
Seagull Cl KEMP RG22 .... 174 E4
Seal Rd BSTK RG21 .... 14 F5
Searing Wy TADY RG26 .... 108 D7
Searles Farm La TLHT RG30 .... 72 C5
Searl's La HTWY RG27 .... 148 A6
Seaton Gdns WHIT RG2 .... 7 M7
Second Av THLE RG7 .... 109 F6
Second St STHA RG19 .... 104 E4
Seddon HI BNFD RG42 .... 79 J4
Sedgefield Cl CAV/SC RG4........... 29 G5
Sedgefield Rd NWBY RG14 .... 13 J9
Sedge Gv NTHA RG18 .... 85 K3
Sedgewell Rd CAV/SC RG4........... 29 G6
Segsbury Gv BRAK RG12 .... 11 M7
Selborne Cl HTWY RG27 .... 164 A2
Selborne Gdns TLHT RG30 .... 56 B4
Selcourt Cl WODY RG5 .... 59 G5
Sellafield Wy EARL RG6 .... 9 M7
Selsdon Av WODY RG5 .... 59 J5
Selsey Wy EARL RG6 .... 74 E6
Selva Ct READ RG1 .... 3 L9
Selwyn Dr YTLY GU46 .... 135 G3
Sen Cl BNFD RG42 .... 79 K4
Send Rd CAV/SC RG4........... 3 M2
Setley Wy BRAK RG12 .... 100 C1
Seton Dr CALC RG31 .... 72 A1
  HTWY RG27 .... 163 J3
The Sett YTLY GU46 .... 135 G4
Sevenoaks Dr THLE RG7 .... 93 H4
Sevenoaks Rd EARL RG6 .... 9 K5
Seventh St STHA RG19 .... 104 E3
The Severals CHAM RG24 .... 143 K7
Severn Cl NTHA RG18 .... 85 G2
Severn Gdns DEAN RG23 .... 174 A3
Severn Wy BSTK RG21 .... 15 K5
  TLHT RG30 .... 56 A7
Sewell Av WWKG RG41 .... 77 F6
Sewell Cl NTHA RG18 .... 65 H5
Seymour Av WHIT RG2 .... 94 B2
Seymour Rd KEMP RG22 .... 175 H2
Shackleton Wy WODY RG5 .... 59 K6
Shaftesbury Cl BRAK RG12 .... 11 J9
Shaftesbury Rd TLHT RG30 .... 56 C5
Shakespeare Cl CAV/SC RG4........... 44 A7
Shakespeare Rd CHAM RG24 .... 160 D3
  NTHA RG18 .... 85 H3
Shakespeare Wy BNFD RG42 .... 11 M1
  BNFD RG42 .... 80 D5
  BNFD RG42 .... 80 C5
Shaldon Wy FLET GU13 .... 166 E3
Sharnwood Dr CALC RG31........... 72 A1
Sharpethorpe Cl EARL RG6 .... 74 E5
Shaw Farm Rd NWBY RG14 .... 84 A2
Shaw HI NWBY RG14 .... 84 A2
Shaw La TADY RG26 .... 126 C5
Shaw Pk CWTH RG45 .... 118 C5
Shaw Pightle HTWY RG27 .... 163 J2
Shaw Rd NWBY RG14 .... 13 G1
  READ RG1 .... 2 F9
Sheep Wk CAV/SC RG4........... 57 J1
Sheepwash La KSCL RG20 .... 103 K6
  TADY RG26 .... 142 C4
Sheepways La CAV/SC RG4........... 42 C4

Sheerlands Rd *EWKG* RG40 .... 115 H2
Shefford Crs *EWKG* RG40 .... 77 J6
Sheldon's La *HTWY* RG27 .... 163 K2
Sheldon's Rd *HTWY* RG27 .... 163 K2
Shelley Av *BRAK* RG12 .... 11 M3
Shelley Cl *CHAM* RG24 .... 160 D3
  FLET GU13 .... 167 H3
  MLW SL7 .... 19 J3
  WODY RG5 .... 75 H2
Shelley Rd *NTHA* RG18 .... 85 H3
Shelley Wk *YTLY* GU46 .... 135 G4
Shenstone Cl *EWKG* RG40 .... 97 F7
Shenstone Rd *WHIT* RG2 .... 7 K4
Shepherds Av *EARL* RG6 .... 5 K4
Shepherds Hl *BRAK* RG12 .... 11 H1
  EARL RG6 .... 5 L4
  KSCL RG20 .... 35 K1
Shepherd's House La *EARL* RG6 .... 5 G4
Shepherds La *BNFD* RG42 .... 79 H5
  CAV/SC RG4 .... 42 E6
  MDHD SL6 .... 19 J6
Shepherds Mt *KSCL* RG20 .... 35 K1
Shepherds Hl *KSCL* RG20 .... 21 K7
Shepherds Wk *EARL* RG6 .... 5 M4
Shepherds Wy *CWTH* RG45 .... 117 K4
Shepley Dr *TLHT* RG30 .... 72 D2
Sheppard Rd *BSTK* RG21 .... 176 B2
Sheraton Av *KEMP* RG22 .... 175 G5
Sheraton Dr *CALC* RG31 .... 55 G4
Sherborne Rd *BSTK* RG21 .... 14 C1
  CHAM RG24 .... 160 A1
Sherbourne La *WODY* RG5 .... 59 J5
Sherfield Cl *WHIT* RG2 .... 8 A4
Sherfield Dr *WHIT* RG2 .... 8 A4
Sherfield Rd *TADY* RG26 .... 129 G6
Sheridan Av *CAV/SC* RG4 .... 57 G1
Sheridan Wy *WWKG* RG41 .... 96 D2
Sherlock Lea *HTWY* RG27 .... 134 C2
Sherman Rd *READ* RG1 .... 3 J8
Sherrardmead *NWBY* RG14 .... 84 A2
Sherring Cl *BNFD* RG42 .... 79 K5
Sherwood Cl *BRAK* RG12 .... 80 D7
  KEMP RG22 .... 175 H6
Sherwood Gdns *HEN* RG9 .... 31 F3
Sherwood Ri *GOR/PANG* RG8 .... 55 G1
Sherwood Rd *WWKG* RG41 .... 76 B4
Sherwood St *TLHT* RG30 .... 56 D5
Shetland Rd *CHAM* RG24 .... 160 D2
Shetland Wy *FARN* GU14 .... 151 J6
Shilling Cl *TLHT* RG30 .... 56 C7
Shinfield Ri *WHIT* RG2 .... 8 D9
Shinfield Rd *WHIT* RG2 .... 8 D9
  WHIT RG2 .... 74 B5
  WHIT RG2 .... 94 B1
Shiplake Bottom *HEN* RG9 .... 29 F4
Shipley Cl *WODY* RG5 .... 59 K4
Shipton Cl *CALC* RG31 .... 55 H3
Shipton Wy *KEMP* RG22 .... 175 H2
Shire Av *FARN* GU14 .... 151 K7
The Shires *WWKG* RG41 .... 96 D3
Shires Wy *YTLY* GU46 .... 135 J1
Shirley Av *WHIT* RG2 .... 73 K7
Shirvell's Hl *GOR/PANG* RG8 .... 26 C4
Shooter's Hl *GOR/PANG* RG8 .... 39 J4
Shooters Wy *BSTK* RG21 .... 15 C1
  WHIT RG2 .... 73 G6
Shop La *NWBY* RG14 .... 83 G7
Shorland Oaks *BNFD* RG42 .... 79 K4
Shortheath La *THLE* RG7 .... 90 C4
Short St *CAV/SC* RG4 .... 57 J3
  GOR/PANG RG8 .... 40 C7
  READ RG1 .... 3 K9
The Short *GOR/PANG* RG8 .... 41 J7
Shropshire Gdns *BNFD* RG42 .... 80 C5
Shrubland Dr *TLHT* RG30 .... 72 B2
Shute End *EWKG* RG40 .... 97 C1
Shyshack La *TADY* RG26 .... 108 B7
Sian Cl *FLET* GU13 .... 167 J6
Sibelius Cl *KEMP* RG22 .... 175 K5
Sibley Park Rd *EARL* RG6 .... 9 G8
Sibson *EARL* RG6 .... 9 L7
Sidestrand Rd *NWBY* RG14 .... 83 G7
Sidlaw Cl *KEMP* RG22 .... 175 F1
Sidmouth Grange Cl *EARL* RG6 .... 5 J6
Sidmouth Grange Rd *EARL* RG6 .... 5 J6
Sidmouth St *READ* RG1 .... 3 L7
Silbury Cl *CALC* RG31 .... 71 G2
Silchester Rd *TADY* RG26 .... 108 E7
  TADY RG26 .... 127 K4
  TLHT RG30 .... 72 D2
Silk Mill La *OVTN* RG25 .... 171 G4
Silver Birch Cl *FLET* GU13 .... 167 G6
Silver Birches *WWKG* RG41 .... 96 B4
Silverdale *FLET* GU13 .... 167 H5
Silverdale Rd *EARL* RG6 .... 9 K5
  TADY RG26 .... 108 D7
  WAR/TWY RG10 .... 46 C3
Silver Fox Crs *WODY* RG5 .... 59 G7
Silverglades *YTLY* GU46 .... 135 H5
Silver La *THLE* RG7 .... 89 K7
Silver Park Cl *FLET* GU13 .... 167 J5
Silver St *READ* RG1 .... 3 K8
Silverthorne Dr *CAV/SC* RG4 .... 42 E6
Silvester Cl *BSTK* RG21 .... 15 H1
Silvester Wy *FLET* GU13 .... 167 K7
Silwood *BRAK* RG12 .... 99 F6
Simkins Cl *BNFD* RG42 .... 80 E4
Simmonds Rd *BNFD* RG42 .... 79 F6
Simmonds St *READ* RG1 .... 3 H7
Simmons Fld *NTHA* RG18 .... 86 A3
Simmons Flds *WAR/TWY* RG10 .... 60 A2
Simms Farm La *THLE* RG7 .... 110 E4
Simons Cl *CALC* RG31 .... 55 H7
Simon's La *WWKG* RG41 .... 76 C6
Simons Rd *CHAM* RG24 .... 161 G1
Sims Cl *TADY* RG26 .... 129 J7
Sindle Cl *WWKG* RG41 .... 76 A4
Sindlesham Rd *WHIT* RG2 .... 95 H4
Singers Hl *HEN* RG9 .... 31 H3
Sirius Cl *WWKG* RG41 .... 96 E1
Sixth St *STHA* RG19 .... 104 E3
Skarries Vw *CAV/SC* RG4 .... 42 E4
Skates La *TADY* RG26 .... 127 G4
Skeffling Cl *EARL* RG6 .... 75 H4
Skelmerdale Wy *EARL* RG6 .... 75 H3

Skelton Flds *BNFD* RG42 .... 79 K5
Skerritt Wy *GOR/PANG* RG8 .... 55 J1
Skilman Dr *STHA* RG19 .... 86 A4
Skilton Rd *CALC* RG31 .... 55 H1
Skimpedhill La *BRAK* RG12 .... 10 E3
Skinner's Green La *KSCL* RG20 .... 102 C2
Skippetts La East *BSTK* RG21 .... 176 D2
Skippetts La West *BSTK* RG21 .... 176 C2
Skippons Cl *NWBY* RG14 .... 103 F2
Skye Cl *CALC* RG31 .... 71 K2
Skylark Ri *WHCH* RG28 .... 169 G6
Skyllings *NWBY* RG14 .... 13 J2
Slaidburn Gn *BRAK* RG12 .... 100 B5
Slanting Hl *NTHA* RG18 .... 65 G1
The Slopes *CAV/SC* RG4 .... 58 A3
Smallfield Dr *HTWY* RG27 .... 164 B2
Smallmead Rd *WHIT* RG2 .... 6 F9
  WHIT RG2 .... 72 E5
Smallridge *KSCL* RG20 .... 103 F4
Smith Cl *CAV/SC* RG4 .... 29 G6
Smith Sq *BRAK* RG12 .... 11 J3
The Smithy *TADY* RG26 .... 129 G6
Snake La *KSCL* RG20 .... 82 D1
Snowberry Cl *WWKG* RG41 .... 96 E2
Snowden Dr *CALC* RG31 .... 55 F7
Snowdon Cl *STHA* RG19 .... 85 J5
Snowdrop Cl *KEMP* RG22 .... 175 F4
Snowdrop Copse *NTHA* RG18 .... 86 A3
Snowdrop Gv *WWKG* RG41 .... 76 B3
Soane End *CAV/SC* RG4 .... 43 H6
Soham Cl *EARL* RG6 .... 75 F6
Soke Rd *THLE* RG7 .... 109 H4
Solby's Rd *BSTK* RG21 .... 14 C5
Soldiers Ri *EWKG* RG40 .... 117 J1
Solent Dr *KEMP* RG22 .... 175 G5
Somerset Cl *WWKG* RG41 .... 96 C1
Somerset Gv *BNFD* RG42 .... 80 C5
Somerstown Ct *READ* RG1 .... 2 E7
Somerton Gdns *EARL* RG6 .... 9 H7
Somerton Gv *STHA* RG19 .... 85 H5
Somerville Cl *WWKG* RG41 .... 96 C3
Somerville Crs *YTLY* GU46 .... 135 K3
Sonning Cl *KEMP* RG22 .... 174 E5
Sonning La *CAV/SC* RG4 .... 5 M2
  CAV/SC RG4 .... 59 G3
Sonning Mdw *CAV/SC* RG4 .... 5 L2
Soper Gv *BSTK* RG21 .... 14 E2
Sopwith Cl *WODY* RG5 .... 59 K6
Sorrel Cl *EWKG* RG40 .... 77 K6
  NWBY RG14 .... 84 C2
  THLE RG7 .... 91 G4
Sorrell's Cl *CHAM* RG24 .... 145 G7
Southampton St *READ* RG1 .... 3 J8
Southbury La *WAR/TWY* RG10 .... 46 E7
  WAR/TWY RG10 .... 61 F1
Southby Dr *FLET* GU13 .... 167 J2
South Cl *EWKG* RG40 .... 97 H2
  MLW SL7 .... 19 J3
Southcote Farm La *TLHT* RG30 .... 6 A2
Southcote La *TLHT* RG30 .... 72 B2
Southcote Rd *TLHT* RG30 .... 2 B9
Southdown Rd *CAV/SC* RG4 .... 43 J7
  STHA RG19 .... 84 E3
  TADY RG26 .... 108 D7
South Dr *CAV/SC* RG4 .... 5 M3
  EARL RG6 .... 8 E8
  EWKG RG40 .... 97 H2
  THLE RG7 .... 70 C7
  WHIT RG2 .... 8 D8
Southend *NTHA* RG18 .... 85 H1
Southend Rd *BSTK* RG21 .... 14 C5
South End Rd *THLE* RG7 .... 68 B4
Southerndene Cl *CALC* RG31 .... 55 J3
Southern Haye *HTWY* RG27 .... 149 H5
Southern Hl *READ* RG1 .... 8 A2
Southern Rd *BSTK* RG21 .... 14 E7
Southglade *WHIT* RG2 .... 74 A6
South Gv *FARN* GU14 .... 151 K6
South Ham Rd *KEMP* RG22 .... 159 K7
South Hill Rd *BRAK* RG12 .... 99 J4
Southington Cl *OVTN* RG25 .... 171 F4
Southington La *OVTN* RG25 .... 171 G4
South Lake Crs *WODY* RG5 .... 75 H1
Southlands *CHAM* RG24 .... 145 F7
Southlands Cl *EWKG* RG40 .... 97 J2
Southlands Rd *EWKG* RG40 .... 97 J3
South Lynn Crs *BRAK* RG12 .... 99 J3
South Meadow *CWTH* RG45 .... 118 C5
South Rdg *ODIM* RG29 .... 180 D2
South Rd *CWTH* RG45 .... 119 F5
  EWKG RG40 .... 99 F6
  HEN RG9 .... 28 C2
  KSCL RG20 .... 124 B7
South St *READ* RG1 .... 3 K7
  READ RG1 .... 57 J3
South View Av *CAV/SC* RG4 .... 57 J3
Southview Cl *WAR/TWY* RG10 .... 46 D6
South View Cottages
  WHCH RG28 .... 170 B5
South View Pk *CAV/SC* RG4 .... 57 K3
Southwark Cl *YTLY* GU46 .... 135 H3
Southwick Ct *BRAK* RG12 .... 100 B4
Southwold *BRAK* RG12 .... 99 F6
Southwold Cl *EARL* RG6 .... 75 G4
Southwood *EWKG* RG40 .... 97 J3
Southwood Gdns *THLE* RG7 .... 91 F4
Southwood Rd *FARN* GU14 .... 151 K1
Sovereign Wy *CALC* RG31 .... 71 H1
Spackman Cl *STHA* RG19 .... 85 J5
Span Hl *HEN* RG9 .... 44 E5
Sparrow Cl *WWKG* RG41 .... 96 D2
Sparrowhawk Cl *NFNM* GU10 .... 183 J4
Sparvells *HTWY* RG27 .... 134 D1
Speckled Wood Rd *CHAM* RG24 .... 160 C2
Speedwell Wy *NTHA* RG18 .... 86 A3
Speen Hill Cl *NWBY* RG14 .... 12 A2
Speen La *NWBY* RG14 .... 12 B2
Speen Lodge Ct *NWBY* RG14 .... 12 A1
Speen Pl *NWBY* RG14 .... 12 A1
Spencer Cl *FLET* GU13 .... 167 H2
  TADY RG26 .... 109 H7
  WWKG RG41 .... 96 C1
Spencer Rd *BNFD* RG42 .... 10 B2
  NWBY RG14 .... 103 G2
  WHIT RG2 .... 73 J7
Sperrin Cl *KEMP* RG22 .... 175 G1
Spey Rd *TLHT* RG30 .... 56 B5

Spiers Cl *TADY* RG26 .... 127 G1
Spinis *BRAK* RG12 .... 99 F6
Spinner Gn *BRAK* RG12 .... 10 D9
Spinney Cl *CAV/SC* RG4 .... 43 J5
The Spinney *EWKG* RG40 .... 96 E7
  FLET GU13 .... 166 E3
  HTWY RG27 .... 163 K1
  YTLY GU46 .... 135 H2
Spitfire Wy *WODY* RG5 .... 59 K6
The Splash *BNFD* RG42 .... 79 J4
Spode Cl *TLHT* RG30 .... 55 K5
Sprat's Hatch La *HTWY* RG27 .... 165 K4
  ODIM RG29 .... 165 J6
Spriggs Cl *STHA* RG19 .... 85 J5
Spring Cl *CHAM* RG24 .... 143 K6
  GOR/PANG RG8 .... 39 G7
Springdale *EARL* RG6 .... 9 J7
  EWKG RG40 .... 96 D7
Springfield *GOR/PANG* RG8 .... 25 F3
Springfield End *GOR/PANG* RG8 .... 25 F3
  NWBY RG14 .... 83 K7
Springfield La *FLET* GU13 .... 167 F2
Springfield Pk *WAR/TWY* RG10 .... 60 D1
Springfield Rd *BRAK* RG12 .... 78 D7
  TADY RG26 .... 109 H7
Spring Gdns *THLE* RG7 .... 93 J6
Spring Gv *READ* RG1 .... 3 K9
Springhill Rd *GOR/PANG* RG8 .... 25 F3
Spring La *CAV/SC* RG4 .... 44 E6
  KSCL RG20 .... 121 J3
  NTHA RG18 .... 65 H1
  THLE RG7 .... 109 F2
  THLE RG7 .... 111 F1
  THLE RG7 .... 113 J3
Spring Meadow *BRAK* RG12 .... 11 K1
The Springs *THLE* RG7 .... 129 J1
Spring Wk *WAR/TWY* RG10 .... 46 C5
Springwell La *HTWY* RG27 .... 149 J2
Springwood La *HEN* RG9 .... 29 G3
Spring Wood La *THLE* RG7 .... 91 F5
Spring Woods *FLET* GU13 .... 167 G4
  SHST GU47 .... 118 D7
Spruce Rd *WODY* RG5 .... 59 K7
Spurcroft Rd *STHA* RG19 .... 85 J5
The Spur *WAR/TWY* RG10 .... 46 D1
Squarefield Gdns *HTWY* RG27 .... 164 B1
The Square *THLE* RG7 .... 93 J5
Squirrels Drey *CWTH* RG45 .... 118 A3
Squirrels Wy *EARL* RG6 .... 9 K8
Stable Cl *HTWY* RG27 .... 163 J2
  THLE RG7 .... 91 F4
Stable Vw *NWBY* RG14 .... 84 A2
Stable Vw *YTLY* GU46 .... 135 J2
Staddlestone Cl *CALC* RG31 .... 55 H3
Stadium Wy *TLHT* RG30 .... 56 C4
Stafford Cl *WODY* RG5 .... 59 J6
Staffordshire Cl *TLHT* RG30 .... 56 A4
Staffordshire Cft *BNFD* RG42 .... 80 C4
Stag Hl *KEMP* RG22 .... 175 J2
Stanbrook Cl *THLE* RG7 .... 68 D5
Stanfield Rd *WHIT* RG2 .... 126 E1
Stanford Rd *KEMP* RG22 .... 175 J5
Stanham Rd *TLHT* RG30 .... 56 A5
Stanhope Rd *WHIT* RG2 .... 7 M5
Stanlake La *WAR/TWY* RG10 .... 60 E1
Stanley Gv *READ* RG1 .... 2 D5
Stanley Rd *EWKG* RG40 .... 97 K1
  NWBY RG14 .... 13 G6
Stanley St *READ* RG1 .... 3 G6
Stanmore Cl *ASC* SL5 .... 101 K2
Stanmore Gdns *THLE* RG7 .... 110 E3
Stanmore Rd *KSCL* RG20 .... 20 D4
  KSCL RG20 .... 34 A2
Stanshawe Rd *READ* RG1 .... 3 G4
Stanton Cl *EARL* RG6 .... 9 L3
Stanton Rd *FLET* GU13 .... 167 F3
Stapleford Rd *TLHT* RG30 .... 72 D2
Staplehurst *BRAK* RG12 .... 99 F5
Stapleton Cl *NWBY* RG14 .... 103 F2
Star Hl *HTWY* RG27 .... 150 A1
Star La *KSCL* RG20 .... 120 C3
  WAR/TWY RG10 .... 33 H5
Starling Cl *KEMP* RG22 .... 174 E4
  WWKG RG41 .... 96 E2
Starlings Dr *CALC* RG31 .... 55 G7
Starmead Dr *EWKG* RG40 .... 97 J2
Starting Gates *NWBY* RG14 .... 13 J8
Statham St *BNFD* RG42 .... 79 F6
Station Ap *READ* RG1 .... 3 H4
Station Hl *ASC* SL5 .... 101 K1
  OVTN RG25 .... 171 J2
  READ RG1 .... 3 H4
Station Rd *BRAK* RG12 .... 10 F4
  DEAN RG23 .... 173 J2
  EARL RG6 .... 9 M3
  EWKG RG40 .... 97 G1
  GOR/PANG RG8 .... 25 C4
  HEN RG9 .... 31 H2
  HEN RG9 .... 31 K7
  HTWY RG27 .... 163 K2
  KSCL RG20 .... 102 D5
  NWBY RG14 .... 12 E6
  NWBY RG14 .... 83 G2
  OVTN RG25 .... 171 J4
  OVTN RG25 .... 176 C5
  READ RG1 .... 3 H5
  STHA RG19 .... 85 K4
  THLE RG7 .... 70 D3
  THLE RG7 .... 87 K5
  THLE RG7 .... 111 K3
  WAR/TWY RG10 .... 46 B3
  WAR/TWY RG10 .... 60 C1
  WHCH RG28 .... 169 H6
Staverton Cl *EWKG* RG40 .... 98 A1
Staverton Rd *WHIT* RG2 .... 7 M7
Steeple Wk *EARL* RG6 .... 9 J7
Steerforth Copse *SHST* GU47 .... 119 F6
Steggles Ct *WODY* RG5 .... 59 G5
Stephanie Chase Ct
  EWKG RG40 .... 77 J7
  WWKG RG41 .... 96 C1
Stephen Cl *WAR/TWY* RG10 .... 60 E2
Stephen's Cl *THLE* RG7 .... 110 E2
Stephens Firs *THLE* RG7 .... 110 D2
Stephenson Cl *NTHA* RG18 .... 85 H3
Stephenson Rd *WHIT* RG2 .... 115 K1

Stephens Rd *TADY* RG26 .... 127 F1
  THLE RG7 .... 110 E2
Sterling Wy *TLHT* RG30 .... 56 B4
Stevens La *HEN* RG9 .... 28 E3
Stevens Rd *WWKG* RG41 .... 135 K4
Stevenson Dr *BNFD* RG42 .... 78 D3
Stilton Cl *EARL* RG6 .... 75 H4
Stilwell Cl *YTLY* GU46 .... 135 K3
Stirling Cl *CAV/SC* RG4 .... 44 A6
Stirling Wy *NTHA* RG18 .... 85 H3
Stirrup Pightle *NWBY* RG14 .... 104 A1
Stockbridge Cl *CHAM* RG24 .... 145 J6
Stockbridge Wy *YTLY* GU46 .... 135 J5
Stockbury Cl *EARL* RG6 .... 9 J9
Stocker Cl *BSTK* RG21 .... 176 B2
Stockton Av *CAV/SC* RG4 .... 167 C1
Stockton Pk *FLET* GU13 .... 167 G1
Stockton Rd *WHIT* RG2 .... 73 K5
Stokeford Cl *BRAK* RG12 .... 100 C3
Stoken La *HTWY* RG27 .... 148 E3
Stoke Row Rd *HEN* RG9 .... 29 F3
Stokes Cl *STHA* RG19 .... 107 K7
Stokes Vw *GOR/PANG* RG8 .... 40 B7
Stonea Cl *EARL* RG6 .... 75 F6
Stone Copse *NTHA* RG18 .... 64 D7
Stoneham Cl *TLHT* RG30 .... 56 B7
Stonehaven Dr *WODY* RG5 .... 59 K7
Stone St *TLHT* RG30 .... 56 C4
Stoney Cl *YTLY* GU46 .... 135 J5
Stoneyfield *THLE* RG7 .... 88 D1
Stoney La *NWBY* RG14 .... 84 C1
  STHA RG19 .... 85 K4
Stoney Rd *BNFD* RG42 .... 10 C2
Stookes Wy *YTLY* GU46 .... 135 G5
Stour Cl *TLHT* RG30 .... 56 B5
Stour Rd *DEAN* RG23 .... 174 A3
Stow Rd *HEN* RG9 .... 31 J3
St Patrick's Br *WAR/TWY* RG10 .... 45 J6
Strachey Cl *GOR/PANG* RG8 .... 54 B2
The Straight Mile
  WAR/TWY RG10 .... 61 J5
Strand Wy *EARL* RG6 .... 74 E5
Stratfield *BRAK* RG12 .... 99 F6
Stratfield Av *WAR/TWY* RG10 .... 126 E2
Stratfield Rd *BSTK* RG21 .... 160 C3
Stratfield Saye Rd *TADY* RG26 .... 129 H4
Stratford Wy *CALC* RG31 .... 55 F7
Stratheden Pl *READ* RG1 .... 2 F5
Strathmore Dr *WAR/TWY* RG10 .... 59 K1
Strathy Cl *TLHT* RG30 .... 56 C5
Stratton Gdns *WHIT* RG2 .... 73 K5
Stratton Rd *BSTK* RG21 .... 176 A2
Strauss Rd *KEMP* RG22 .... 175 H4
Stravinsky Rd *KEMP* RG22 .... 176 A4
Strawberry Flds *TADY* RG26 .... 129 C6
Strawberry Hl *BNFD* RG42 .... 80 B4
  NWBY RG14 .... 12 D2
Streamside *FLET* GU13 .... 167 H3
Streatley Hl *GOR/PANG* RG8 .... 24 A5
Street End *HTWY* RG27 .... 150 C6
The Street *CHAM* RG24 .... 161 H5
  FLET GU13 .... 166 E6
  HTWY RG27 .... 147 H5
  ODIM RG29 .... 179 J1
  TADY RG26 .... 128 E7
  THLE RG7 .... 70 A1
  THLE RG7 .... 108 D1
  THLE RG7 .... 111 G3
  THLE RG7 .... 113 K2
Stretton Cl *THLE* RG7 .... 68 D5
Strokins Rd *KSCL* RG20 .... 124 A6
Stroud Cl *CHAM* RG24 .... 161 F1
Stroud La *HTWY* RG27 .... 166 D6
Stroudley Rd *CHAM* RG24 .... 161 F4
Strouds Meadow *NTHA* RG18 .... 65 H7
The Strouds *THLE* RG7 .... 88 C1
Stuart Cl *THLE* RG7 .... 43 J7
Stuart Rd *NWBY* RG14 .... 103 F2
Stubbs Rd *BSTK* RG21 .... 176 D2
Studland Cl *WHIT* RG2 .... 73 K7
Stukeley Rd *BSTK* RG21 .... 14 B7
Sturbridge Cl *EARL* RG6 .... 9 M9
Sturges Rd *EWKG* RG40 .... 97 H2
Suck's La *GOR/PANG* RG8 .... 52 A3
Suffolk Cl *WWKG* RG41 .... 96 C1
Suffolk Combe *BNFD* RG42 .... 80 C5
Suffolk Rd *TLHT* RG30 .... 2 A7
  TLHT RG30 .... 56 D6
Sulham La *GOR/PANG* RG8 .... 54 D1
Sulhamstead Hl *THLE* RG7 .... 90 B1
Sulhamstead Rd *THLE* RG7 .... 90 C3
Sullivan Rd *KEMP* RG22 .... 175 K3
Summer Down La *DEAN* RG23 .... 157 H6
Summerfield Cl *WWKG* RG41 .... 76 E5
Summerfield Ri *GOR/PANG* RG8 .... 25 C4
Summerfields *CHAM* RG24 .... 145 H6
Summit Cl *EWKG* RG40 .... 116 E2
Sunderland Cl *WODY* RG5 .... 60 A5
Sunderland Pl *NTHA* RG18 .... 85 H3
Sundew Cl *EWKG* RG40 .... 77 K7
Sundial Cl *TLHT* RG30 .... 56 B7
Sunflower Cl *KEMP* RG22 .... 175 F5
Sun Gdns *THLE* RG7 .... 91 F6
Sun La *THLE* RG7 .... 113 J6
Sunley Cl *NWBY* RG14 .... 103 G2
Sunnybank *ASC* SL5 .... 101 K2
Sunny Md *DEAN* RG23 .... 174 A4
Sunnyside *FLET* GU13 .... 167 H1
Sun St *READ* RG1 .... 4 B6
Surley Rw *CAV/SC* RG4 .... 43 H7
Surrey Ct *BNFD* RG42 .... 80 C5
Surrey Rd *WHIT* RG2 .... 7 K4
Sussex Gdns *FARN* GU14 .... 151 J6
  WODY RG5 .... 59 H6
Sussex La *THLE* RG7 .... 93 K6
Sutcliffe Av *EARL* RG6 .... 75 G3
Sutherland Cha *ASC* SL5 .... 81 H7
Sutherland Gv *CALC* RG31 .... 71 K2
Sutherlands *NWBY* RG14 .... 103 H1
Sutherlands Av *READ* RG1 .... 7 M2
Sutton Cl *BSTK* RG21 .... 14 E1
  NWBY RG14 .... 83 G2
Suttons Park Av *EARL* RG6 .... 4 E5
  READ RG1 .... 4 D4
Swains Cl *EWKG* RG40 .... 97 G1
Swains Rd *TADY* RG26 .... 126 E1
Swainstone Rd *WHIT* RG2 .... 7 K2
Swaledale *BRAK* RG12 .... 99 H3

Swaledale Gdns *FARN* GU14 .... 151 J6
Swallow Cl *CALC* RG31 .... 55 H7
  KEMP RG22 .... 174 E4
  YTLY GU46 .... 135 G3
Swallowfield Dr *WHIT* RG2 .... 93 J1
Swallow Field Gdns *THLE* RG7 .... 70 C2
Swallowfield Rd *THLE* RG7 .... 114 D2
Swallow Wy *WWKG* RG41 .... 96 D2
Swancote Gn *BRAK* RG12 .... 10 E9
Swan Ct *HTWY* RG27 .... 149 L4
Swan Dr *THLE* RG7 .... 88 E4
Swan Ms *ODIM* RG29 .... 164 B7
Swanmore Cl *EARL* RG6 .... 75 H5
Swan Pl *READ* RG1 .... 3 H7
Swans Ct *WAR/TWY* RG10 .... 60 C7
Swansea Rd *READ* RG1 .... 3 G3
Swansea Ter *CALC* RG31 .... 55 J4
Swanston Fld *GOR/PANG* RG8 .... 40 C5
Swanston St *KSCL* RG20 .... 139 K5
Swan Wy *FLET* GU13 .... 166 E4
Swedish Houses *TADY* RG26 .... 127 F2
Sweetbriar *CWTH* RG45 .... 118 B1
Sweet Briar Dr *CALC* RG31 .... 71 H2
Sweetzer's Piece *THLE* RG7 .... 110 D2
Swepstone Cl *EARL* RG6 .... 9 M8
Swift Cl *WWKG* RG41 .... 96 D2
Swinbrook Cl *CALC* RG31 .... 55 J2
Swing Swang La *CHAM* RG24 .... 161 G4
Swinley Rd *ASC* SL5 .... 101 F2
Swiss Cottage Cl *CALC* RG31 .... 55 H5
Swithin Cha *BNFD* RG42 .... 80 B5
Sycamore Cl *TLHT* RG30 .... 91 G2
  WODY RG5 .... 9 M2
Sycamore Crs *FLET* GU13 .... 167 F5
Sycamore Dr *WAR/TWY* RG10 .... 46 C7
Sycamore Ri *BRAK* RG12 .... 11 K5
  NWBY RG14 .... 84 B1
Sycamore Rd *WHIT* RG2 .... 8 C7
Sycamore Wk *DEAN* RG23 .... 159 J4
The Sydings *NWBY* RG14 .... 83 G2
Sydney Cl *CWTH* RG45 .... 118 D1
Sylvan Rdg *SHST* GU47 .... 118 B7
Sylvanus *BRAK* RG12 .... 99 G5
Sylvan Wy *FLET* GU13 .... 167 G6
Sylverns Ct *BNFD* RG42 .... 80 A5
Sylvester Cl *NWBY* RG14 .... 83 H2
  WAR/TWY RG10 .... 76 C3
Symondson Ms *BNFD* RG42 .... 78 D2
Sympson Rd *TADY* RG26 .... 109 G7

T

Tadham Pl *STHA* RG19 .... 85 H5
Tadley Common Rd *TADY* RG26 .... 109 F7
Tadley Hl *TADY* RG26 .... 127 F2
Tadpole La *NFNM* GU10 .... 183 J3
Taff Wy *TLHT* RG30 .... 56 B6
Tag La *WAR/TWY* RG10 .... 47 F3
Talbot Cl *NWBY* RG14 .... 83 H2
Talbot Ct *READ* RG1 .... 3 G7
Talbot Wy *CALC* RG31 .... 55 H2
Talfourd Av *EARL* RG6 .... 9 G2
Talisman Cl *CWTH* RG45 .... 117 J3
Tallis Gdns *KEMP* RG22 .... 175 K3
Tallis La *TLHT* RG30 .... 6 A3
Talmey Cl *CHAM* RG24 .... 145 F7
Tamar Dr *DEAN* RG23 .... 174 A3
Tamar Gdns *WHIT* RG2 .... 7 M6
Tamarind Wy *EARL* RG6 .... 8 F9
Tamarisk Av *WHIT* RG2 .... 8 C9
Tamarisk Cl *KEMP* RG22 .... 175 H7
Tamarisk Ct *NTHA* RG18 .... 86 A3
Tamarisk Ri *EWKG* RG40 .... 77 H7
Tamar Wy *WWKG* RG41 .... 96 D1
Tamworth *BRAK* RG12 .... 100 A5
Tamworth Cl *EARL* RG6 .... 9 M9
Tamworth Dr *FARN* GU14 .... 117 F1
Tanglewood *EWKG* RG40 .... 117 F1
Tangley Dr *WWKG* RG41 .... 97 G3
Tangway *CHAM* RG24 .... 145 G6
Tanhouse La *WWKG* RG41 .... 97 F2
Tanners Cl *THLE* RG7 .... 90 E6
Tanners La *CAV/SC* RG4 .... 43 G4
Tanners Wy *DEAN* RG23 .... 174 A2
Tape La *WAR/TWY* RG10 .... 60 E5
Taplin's Farm La *HTWY* RG27 .... 149 K7
Target Hl *BNFD* RG42 .... 80 A5
Targett Ct *WWKG* RG41 .... 76 A4
Tarlton Ct *TLHT* RG30 .... 55 K7
Tarnbrook Wy *BRAK* RG12 .... 100 B5
Tarn La *NWBY* RG14 .... 12 C9
Tarragon Cl *EARL* RG6 .... 8 F9
Tarragon Wy *THLE* RG7 .... 91 G4
Tarrant Gn *BNFD* RG42 .... 79 K5
Tasmania Cl *CHAM* RG24 .... 160 D1
Tattersall Cl *EWKG* RG40 .... 97 K2
Taverner Cl *BSTK* RG21 .... 15 J1
Tavistock Rd *FLET* GU13 .... 166 E3
  WHIT RG2 .... 7 K6
Tawfield *BRAK* RG12 .... 99 F5
Taylor Dr *TADY* RG26 .... 129 H7
Tay Rd *TLHT* RG30 .... 56 B6
Tazewell Ct *READ* RG1 .... 2 E9
Teal Crs *KEMP* RG22 .... 174 E5
Tebbit Cl *BRAK* RG12 .... 11 J4
Telford Crs *WODY* RG5 .... 59 J4
Temple Pl *READ* RG1 .... 3 H8
Temple Wy *BNFD* RG42 .... 79 F6
Templeton Gdns *WHIT* RG2 .... 7 J9
Tenaplas Dr *GOR/PANG* RG8 .... 38 C7
Tenby Av *CAV/SC* RG4 .... 44 A7
Tennyson Rd *NTHA* RG18 .... 85 H3
  WODY RG5 .... 75 H7
Tennyson Wy *KEMP* RG22 .... 175 K1
Teresa V *BNFD* RG42 .... 80 B4
Tern Cl *TLHT* RG30 .... 56 B6
Terrace Rd North *BNFD* RG42 .... 78 D3
Terrace Rd South *BNFD* RG42 .... 78 D4
The Terrace *CWTH* RG45 .... 118 C5
  EWKG RG40 .... 97 G1
Tesimond Dr *YTLY* GU46 .... 135 F4
Tessa Rd *READ* RG1 .... 3 G2
Test Cl *TLHT* RG30 .... 56 B5
Test Wy *BSTK* RG21 .... 15 J5
Teviot Rd *TLHT* RG30 .... 55 K6

Tewkesbury Cl CHAM RG24 160 C2
Thackham's La HTWY RG27 148 E5
The Thakerays STHA RG19 85 J5 8
Thames Av GOR/PANG RG8 40 C6
READ RG1 3 H2
Thames Ct BSTK RG21 15 J4
READ RG1 2 D3
Thames Dr WAR/TWY RG10 45 J6
Thames Pth GOR/PANG RG8 24 E7
GOR/PANG RG8 39 K3
GOR/PANG RG8 41 H7
HEN RG9 19 F7
HEN RG9 32 A5
READ RG1 57 F3
Thames Reach GOR/PANG RG8 55 J1
Thames Rd GOR/PANG RG8 24 E5
NTHA RG18 85 G2
Thames Side HEN RG9 31 H1
Thames Side Prom READ RG1 2 F1
Thames St CAV/SC RG4 59 G1
Thanington Wy EARL RG6 9 J8
Theale Rd TLHT RG30 91 G1
Theobald Dr CALC RG31 55 J1
Thetford Ms CAV/SC RG4 44 A6 2
Thicket Rd TLHT RG30 55 K5
Third St STHA RG19 104 E3
Thirlmere Av TLHT RG30 56 A4
Thirlmere Crs FLET GU13 167 F6 4
Thirtover NTHA RG18 65 G5
Thistledown CALC RG31 55 H4 5
Thistleton Wy EARL RG6 75 H4
Thomas Dr BNFD RG42 80 B5 16
Thomas La EWKG RG40 96 D7
Thompson Cl NTHA RG18 48 E7 4
Thompson Dr STHA RG19 85 K5 2
Thomson Wk CALC RG31 71 K2
Thornbers Wy WAR/TWY RG10 46 A7
Thornbridge Rd WHIT RG2 73 J6
Thornbury Cl CWTH RG45 118 C3
Thorne Cl CWTH RG45 118 B1 3
WWKG RG41 96 C4
Thorneley Rd KSCL RG20 124 A7 5
Thorney Cl EARL RG6 75 H4
Thornfield STHA RG19 105 J5 1
Thornford Rd STHA RG19 105 J6
Thornhill BRAK RG12 11 L8
Thornhill Wy CHAM RG24 145 H6
Thorn La READ RG1 3 J6
Thorn St READ RG1 3 G6
Thornton Ms TLHT RG30 56 D5 3
Thorp Cl BNFD RG42 78 D3 2
Thorpe Cl WWKG RG41 97 F4
Thrale Ms TLHT RG30 56 C5
Three Acre Rd NWBY RG14 83 J7
Three Castles Pth ASC SL5 101 F1
HTWY RG27 133 K4
HTWY RG27 135 F2
ODIM RG29 164 A7
ODIM RG29 179 J2
OVTN RG25 178 D3
Three Firs Wy THLE RG7 90 D6
Three Gables La GOR/PANG RG8 24 D4
Threshers Cnr FARN GU14 151 K6 3
Threshfield BRAK RG12 10 C9
Throgmorton Rd YTLY GU46 135 F4
Thrush Cl THLE RG7 91 G4
Thumwood CHAM RG24 145 G7 4
Thurlestone Gdns WHIT RG2 7 L7
Thurnscoe Cl EARL RG6 74 C6 6
Thurso Cl TLHT RG30 56 B5
Thurston Pl BSTK RG21 176 A3
Thyme Cl CHAM RG24 145 H6
EARL RG6 74 C5
Tiberius Cl DEAN RG23 159 H4
Tickenor Dr EWKG RG40 116 E1
Tickhill Cl EARL RG6 74 C7 3
Tidmarsh La GOR/PANG RG8 53 K3
Tidmarsh Rd GOR/PANG RG8 54 B1
Tidmarsh St TLHT RG30 56 C5
Tidmore La GOR/PANG RG8 26 E2
Tiffany Cl WWKG RG41 96 C1
Tiger Cl WODY RG5 60 A6
Tigerseye Cl WWKG RG41 76 C7 7
Tilbury Cl CAV/SC RG4 57 K2
Tilebarn Cl HEN RG9 31 F2
Tilehurst La BNFD RG42 78 E3
Tilehurst Rd READ RG1 2 D7
TLHT RG30 2 A7
TLHT RG30 56 C7
Tilling Cl CALC RG31 55 G3
Tilney Wy EARL RG6 74 C6 7
Timberlake Rd BSTK RG21 14 E5
Timberley Pl CWTH RG45 117 K4 2
Timline Gn BRAK RG12 80 C7
Tindal Cl YTLY GU46 135 J3
Tinsley Cl EARL RG6 74 C6
Tintagel Cl DEAN RG23 159 H5
Tintagel Rd EWKG RG40 97 F7
Tintern Cl CHAM RG24 160 A3
Tintern Crs READ RG1 6 E2
Tinwell Cl EARL RG6 75 H4
Tippet Gdns KEMP RG22 176 A4
Tippett Ri WHIT RG2 7 J1
Tippings La WODY RG5 59 K4
Tippits Md BNFD RG42 78 E7
Tiptree Cl EARL RG6 74 C6 8
Titchfield Cl TADY RG26 127 F2 3
Tithebarn Gv CALC RG31 72 A2 4
Tithe Meadow KEMP RG22 175 H7 2
Tiverton Cl WODY RG5 59 H4
Tiverton Rd DEAN RG23 159 H6
Tobago Cl CHAM RG24 160 C2
Tocker Gdns BNFD RG42 79 J4 3
Tofrek Ter TLHT RG30 56 D6
Tokers Green La CAV/SC RG4 42 E3
Tollgate Cl DEAN RG23 174 A1
Tollway CHAM RG24 145 H7
Tomlin Cl STHA RG19 85 K5 3
Tomlins Cl TADY RG26 126 E2
Tomlinson Dr EWKG RG40 117 F2
Topaz Cl WWKG RG41 76 D7
Top Common BRAK RG12 80 A5
Tope Rd WHIT RG2 95 J7
The Topiary CHAM RG24 161 H3
Torcross Gv CALC RG31 71 G2
Torrington Rd WHIT RG2 7 M8
Toseland Wy EARL RG6 75 H3
Totale Ri BNFD RG42 79 J4 4
Totnes Rd WHIT RG2 7 M8
Tottenham Cl TADY RG26 129 G5
Tottenham Wk SHST GU47 118 E7
Totterdown THLE RG7 90 E6
Totters La HTWY RG27 164 E2
Toutley Cl WWKG RG41 76 D5
Toutley Rd WWKG RG41 77 F5
Tower Cl CAV/SC RG4 43 K5
Towers Dr CWTH RG45 118 C4
Town Mill La WHCH RG28 169 J7
Townsend Cl BRAK RG12 11 M9
BSTK RG21 14 B6
Townsend Rd GOR/PANG RG8 24 D4
GOR/PANG RG8 37 F1
Trafalgar Cl WWKG RG41 96 D1 19
Trafalgar Ct TLHT RG30 2 B9
Trafford Rd READ RG1 2 D3
Tredegar Rd CAV/SC RG4 43 G7
Tree Cl TLHT RG30 55 J5 6
Treeton Cl EARL RG6 74 C6 9
Trefoil Cl EWKG RG40 77 K7
HTWY RG27 149 H3
Trefoil Dro NTHA RG18 86 A3
Treforgan CAV/SC RG4 43 G7 1
Trelawney Dr CALC RG31 55 G4
Trelleck Rd READ RG1 6 F2
Trellis Dr CHAM RG24 161 H3
Trent Cl WWKG RG41 76 D7
Trent Crs NTHA RG18 85 G2
Trent Wy BSTK RG21 15 K5
Tresham Crs YTLY GU46 135 F3 2
Trevelyan BRAK RG12 99 F5
The Triangle NWBY RG14 104 A1
Trindledown BNFD RG42 79 H5
Tring Rd CALC RG31 55 H2
Trinidad Cl CHAM RG24 160 C2
Trinity SHST GU47 119 F6
Trinity Ct THLE RG7 70 C3 3
Trinity Pl READ RG1 2 F6
Triumph Cl WODY RG5 75 J1 10
Trotwood Cl SHST GU47 119 F6 5
Troutbeck Cl WAR/TWY RG10 46 C6
Trout Cl EARL RG6 5 G4
Trout Wk NWBY RG14 84 A2
Trowe's La THLE RG7 112 E4
THLE RG7 114 A3
Trumbull Rd BNFD RG42 79 H5
Trust Cl HTWY RG27 163 J2 4
Trust Cnr HEN RG9 31 H3
Trusthorpe Cl EARL RG6 75 H4
Tubb's La KSCL RG20 120 C3
TADY RG26 143 F2
Tudor Av KSCL RG20 48 B1
Tudor Cl EWKG RG40 98 A2
Tudor Dr YTLY GU46 135 J4 4
Tudor Rd NWBY RG14 12 F7
READ RG1 3 G4
Tudor Wy FLET GU13 167 H7
Tulip Cl KEMP RG22 175 F5
Tuns La HEN RG9 31 H1
Tunworth Ms TADY RG26 127 F1
Tunworth Rd OVTN RG25 162 B7
OVTN RG25 178 A3
Tupsley Rd READ RG1 6 E2
Turbary Gdns TADY RG26 108 E7
Turk's La THLE RG7 110 E4
Turmeric Cl EARL RG6 8 F9
Turnberry BRAK RG12 99 F4
Turnbridge Cl EARL RG6 74 E6
Turner Cl BSTK RG21 15 L7
Turners Dr STHA RG19 85 K4
Turner's Green La HTWY RG27 150 D6
The Turnery STHA RG19 85 H4 3
Turnfields STHA RG19 85 J4
Turnpike Rd BNFD RG42 78 E7
NTHA RG18 84 D3
NWBY RG14 13 M1
Turnpike Wy DEAN RG23 173 K2
Turnstone Cl WWKG RG41 75 K3
Turnstone End YTLY GU46 135 G3 3
Tuscan Cl TLHT RG30 55 K5
Tuxford Ms TLHT RG30 56 C6 4
Tweedsmuir Cl KEMP RG22 159 G7
Tweseldown Rd FLET GU13 167 J7
Twin Oaks CAV/SC RG4 43 J6
Twisell Thorne FLET GU13 167 F7
Two Gate La OVTN RG25 171 J5
Two Gate Meadow OVTN RG25 171 J4
Two Rivers Wy NWBY RG14 13 M3
Two Tree Hl HEN RG9 30 E3
Twycross Rd EWKG RG40 77 K7
Twyford Rd EWKG RG40 77 G6
WAR/TWY RG10 47 K6
Tyberton Pl READ RG1 6 E2
Tydehams NWBY RG14 103 H1
Tyfield CHAM RG24 143 K7
Tyler Cl CAV/SC RG4 43 F7
Tyler Dr WHIT RG2 115 H1
Tyle Rd TLHT RG30 55 J5 7
Tyler's La THLE RG7 66 C4
Tylers Pl TLHT RG30 56 A5 8
Tylney La HTWY RG27 163 G2
Tylorstown CAV/SC RG4 43 G6
Tyne Wy NTHA RG18 85 G2
Tytherton BRAK RG12 11 H4

U

Uffcott Cl EARL RG6 74 C6 10
Uffington Cl CALC RG31 55 H5
Uffington Dr BRAK RG12 11 M7
Ullswater BRAK RG12 99 F5
Ullswater Cl STHA RG19 85 F4
Ullswater Dr CALC RG31 55 J2
Ulster Cl CAV/SC RG4 44 A7
Underwood BRAK RG12 99 F4
Underwood Rd TLHT RG30 72 A2
Union Cl SHST GU47 119 F6
Union La KSCL RG20 124 A4
Union Rd THLE RG7 69 F3
Unity Cl CAV/SC RG4 43 J6
Upavon Dr READ RG1 6 D1
Upavon Gdns BRAK RG12 100 C3
Upfallow CHAM RG24 161 H4
Uplands Rd CAV/SC RG4 43 F7
Upper Broadmoor Rd
CWTH RG45 118 E3
Upper Chestnut Dr BSTK RG21 14 A8
Upper Crown St READ RG1 3 K8
Upper Farm Rd DEAN RG23 173 K4
Upper Meadow Rd WHIT RG2 8 A7
Upper Red Cross Rd
GOR/PANG RG8 25 F4
Upper Redlands Rd READ RG1 8 B1
Upper Sherborne Rd
BSTK RG21 160 B4
Upper St FLET GU13 167 G2
Upper Warren Av CAV/SC RG4 56 D2
Upper Woodcote Rd
CAV/SC RG4 42 E7
Uppingham Dr WODY RG5 59 J4
Uppingham Gdns CAV/SC RG4 44 A6 3
Upron Field Cl KEMP RG22 175 G5
Upshire Gdns BRAK RG12 100 C2
Upton Cl HEN RG9 31 H2
Upton Crs BSTK RG21 160 B4
Upton Grey Rd OVTN RG25 179 G3
Upton Rd TLHT RG30 56 B6
Urquhart Rd STHA RG19 85 J6
Usk Rd TLHT RG30 56 A7

V

Vachel Rd READ RG1 3 G5
Vale Crs TLHT RG30 55 K4
Valentia Rd TLHT RG30 2 B5
Valentine Cl WHIT RG2 74 B5
Valentine Crs CAV/SC RG4 57 K1
The Vale DEAN RG23 173 K3
Vale Vw WAR/TWY RG10 60 A1
Vale View Dr THLE RG7 112 E3
Valley Cl CAV/SC RG4 57 H1
GOR/PANG RG8 25 F5 3
Valley Crs WWKG RG41 77 F6
Valley Rd HEN RG9 30 E3
NWBY RG14 12 A9
NWBY RG14 83 G7
THLE RG7 91 F4
Valley Wy TADY RG26 109 H7
Valmeade Cl HTWY RG27 164 A2 7
Valon Rd WHIT RG2 95 H6
Valpy St READ RG1 3 J5
Vanburgh Gdns KEMP RG22 175 G5
Van Dyck Cl BSTK RG21 15 L8
Vandyke BRAK RG12 99 F4
Vanlore Wy CALC RG31 71 H1 8
Vanners La KSCL RG20 102 A3
Vastern Rd READ RG1 3 H3
Vauxhall Dr WODY RG5 59 J7
Velmead Cl FLET GU13 167 J4
Velmead Rd FLET GU13 167 H4
Venetia Cl CAV/SC RG4 43 K5
Venning Rd WHIT RG2 95 J7
Ventnor Rd CALC RG31 55 J4 4
Verbena Cl WWKG RG41 75 K3
Verdi Cl KEMP RG22 175 J4
Verey Cl WAR/TWY RG10 60 E2
Vermont Woods EWKG RG40 116 D1
The Verne FLET GU13 167 H6
Verney Ms TLHT RG30 56 D6
Vernon Crs WHIT RG2 73 J7
Vernon Dr ASC SL5 81 G7
Veronica Cl KEMP RG22 175 F5
Veronica Dr FLET GU13 166 E6
Vespasian Gdns CHAM RG24 159 H3
Vetch Flds HTWY RG27 164 B2
Viables La BSTK RG21 176 C3
Vicarage Cl EWKG RG40 116 E2 2
Vicarage Gdns ASC SL5 101 K3 1
FLET GU13 167 G7
Vicarage Hl HTWY RG27 149 J5
Vicarage La HTWY RG27 147 J1
NTHA RG18 65 H6
YTLY GU46 135 H2
Vicarage Rd HEN RG9 31 H3
WHIT RG2 7 M2
YTLY GU46 135 H2
Vicarage Wood Wy
CALC RG31 55 G4 2
Victoria Gdns NWBY RG14 12 F2
Victoria Hill Rd FLET GU13 167 F2
Victoria Rd ASC SL5 101 K3
CALC RG31 55 J5
CAV/SC RG4 57 H2
FLET GU13 167 F2
SHST GU47 119 F7
THLE RG7 110 E2
WAR/TWY RG10 46 D2
Victoria St BSTK RG21 14 E6
READ RG1 4 A7
Victor Pl THLE RG7 87 K5
Victor Rd STHA RG19 85 K4
Victor Wy WODY RG5 59 K6
Victory Rbt BSTK RG21 14 D4
Vigo La YTLY GU46 135 H4
Viking BRAK RG12 99 F3
Village Cl WHIT RG2 93 J1 3
The Village EWKG RG40 116 D5
Village Wy YTLY GU46 135 J2
Villiers Md WWKG RG41 97 F1
Villiers Wy NWBY RG14 103 F2
Vincent Cl WODY RG5 59 J7
Vincent Ri BRAK RG12 11 L5
Vincent Rd NTHA RG18 85 K3
Vine Crs TLHT RG30 72 B2
The Vines WWKG RG41 96 B4
Vine Tree Cl TADY RG26 127 G2
Vinns La OVTN RG25 171 G5
Viola Cft BNFD RG42 80 C6 3
Violet Cl KEMP RG22 175 F5
Violet Gv NTHA RG18 85 K2
Violet La TADY RG26 125 K3
Virginia Wy TLHT RG30 72 C1
Viscount Wy WODY RG5 59 J6
Vivaldi Cl KEMP RG22 175 K5
Vivian Cl FLET GU13 167 J5
Voller Dr CALC RG31 55 H7
Volunteer Rd THLE RG7 70 C3
Vulcan Cl WODY RG5 60 A4
Vyne Meadow CHAM RG24 144 A6
Vyne Rd BSTK RG21 14 E2
CHAM RG24 144 A6

W

Wade Rd CHAM RG24 161 F3
Wadham SHST GU47 119 G7
Wagbullock Ri BRAK RG12 99 K4 3
Wagner Cl KEMP RG22 175 K4
Wagon La HTWY RG27 164 A1
Wagtail Cl WAR/TWY RG10 60 D1
Waingels Rd WODY RG5 59 K3
Wakeford Cl TADY RG26 109 H7 2
Wakefords Copse FLET GU13 183 J1
Wakefords Pk FLET GU13 183 J1
Wakemans GOR/PANG RG8 53 G1
Walbury BRAK RG12 11 M8
Waldeck St WHIT RG2 7 J1
Walden Av WHIT RG2 95 F4
Waldron Hl BRAK RG12 80 C6
Walker Cl GOR/PANG RG8 26 D2 2
Walkers Pl TLHT RG30 56 D6 5
Wallace Cl WODY RG5 75 G1
Wallcroft Cl BNFD RG42 79 F5 4
The Walled Gdn WAR/TWY RG10 46 C2
Waller Ct CAV/SC RG4 57 J3 1
Waller Dr NWBY RG14 84 D2
Wallingford Cl BRAK RG12 11 M8
Wallingford Rd GOR/PANG RG8 24 D3
KSCL RG20 21 K6
Wallins Copse CHAM RG24 161 G1 4
Wallis Dr TADY RG26 129 J7
Wallis Rd BSTK RG21 14 E8
Wall La THLE RG7 110 B6
Wallner Wy EWKG RG40 97 J2
Wallop Dr KEMP RG22 175 F6
Walmer Cl CWTH RG45 118 D3
TLHT RG30 56 B7 2
Walmer Rd WODY RG5 59 J4
Walnut Cl CAV/SC RG4 29 F6
WWKG RG41 96 E2 9
YTLY GU46 135 J5
Walnut Tree Cl WAR/TWY RG10 46 D6
Walnut Tree Ct
GOR/PANG RG8 25 F5 4
Walnut Wy TLHT RG30 55 J5
Walrus Cl WODY RG5 60 A6
Walsh Av BNFD RG42 80 B5
Walter Rd WWKG RG41 76 D6
Walters Cl NTHA RG18 65 H6
Waltham Cl SHST GU47 118 E7 9
Waltham Ct OVTN RG25 171 J4 1
Waltham La OVTN RG25 172 A7
Waltham Rd OVTN RG25 171 J5
WAR/TWY RG10 47 G7
WAR/TWY RG10 60 D1
Walton Av HEN RG9 31 H3
Walton Cl WODY RG5 5 M6
Walton Dr ASC SL5 81 J6
Walton Wy NWBY RG14 13 J1
Wandhope Wy CALC RG31 55 H3
Wansey Gdns NWBY RG14 84 C2
Wanstraw Gv BRAK RG12 100 B5 7
Wantage Cl BRAK RG12 11 L9
Wantage Rd GOR/PANG RG8 24 C2
TLHT RG30 56 D6
Warbler Cl CALC RG31 55 G7 4
Warbler Dr EARL RG6 9 K9
Warbleton Rd CHAM RG24 145 H7 5
Warblington Cl TADY RG26 127 F2
Warborough Av CALC RG31 55 G6
Warbreck Dr CALC RG31 55 G2
Warbrook La HTWY RG27 133 K1
Ward Cl EWKG RG40 77 J6
Wardle Av CALC RG31 55 J4
Wards Stone Pk BRAK RG12 100 B5 8
Wareham Rd BRAK RG12 100 C3
Warehouse Rd STHA RG19 104 E3
Warfield Rd BNFD RG42 79 K4
Warfield St BNFD RG42 79 K3
Wargrave Hl WAR/TWY RG10 46 C2
Wargrave Rd HEN RG9 31 K3
WAR/TWY RG10 46 C5
Waring Cl EARL RG6 75 F6 13
The Warings THLE RG7 68 D7
Warley Ri CALC RG31 55 G1
Warnford Rd TLHT RG30 56 A6
Warnham La KSCL RG20 35 G2
Warnsham Cl EARL RG6 74 E5
Warren Cl FLET GU13 167 J4
HTWY RG27 149 J5
THLE RG7 91 F5
Warren Cnr NFNM GU10 183 H5
Warren Down BNFD RG42 79 F6 2
Warren House Rd EWKG RG40 77 J6
Warren La EWKG RG40 116 C3
Warren Rd NWBY RG14 103 G2
WODY RG5 59 G4
Warren Rw ASC SL5 81 G7
Warren Row Rd WAR/TWY RG10 32 E4
WAR/TWY RG10 33 K7
The Warren CAV/SC RG4 56 D2
READ RG1 57 G3
TADY RG26 126 D1
Warton Rd BSTK RG21 15 G2
Warwick BRAK RG12 100 B5
Warwick Dr NWBY RG14 13 H8
Warwick Rd DEAN RG23 159 H5
WHIT RG2 7 L3
Wasdale Cl SHST GU47 118 E6
Wash Brook HTWY RG27 163 K1 8
Washington Gdns EWKG RG40 97 F7
Washington Rd CAV/SC RG4 57 J3
Wash Water KSCL RG20 102 D5
Wasing La THLE RG7 108 A2
Watch La WHCH RG28 170 B3
Water End La CHAM RG24 162 C4
Waterford Wy EWKG RG40 97 H1 3
Waterham Rd BRAK RG12 99 J4
Wateridge Rd BSTK RG21 160 D3
Water La STHA RG19 104 B1
Waterlily Cl BSTK RG21 15 K5
Waterloo Av DEAN RG23 159 H4
Waterloo Crs EWKG RG40 97 K3
Waterloo Ri WHIT RG2 7 J3
Waterloo Rd CWTH RG45 118 B4
EWKG RG40 97 K3
WHIT RG2 7 J2
Waterman Pl READ RG1 3 G2
Waterman's Rd HEN RG9 31 H3
Watermans Wy WAR/TWY RG10 46 B3
Water Rede FLET GU13 183 F1
Water Ridges DEAN RG23 174 A4
Water Rd TLHT RG30 56 C6
Watersfield Cl EARL RG6 74 E5 4
Waterside Ct FARN GU14 151 J7
Waterside Dr GOR/PANG RG8 41 J7
THLE RG7 70 E3
Waterside Gdns READ RG1 3 H7
Watersplash La BNFD RG42 79 J4
Water St NTHA RG18 36 A6
Water Wy BSTK RG21 15 K4
Watery La FLET GU13 183 F1
Watling End KEMP RG22 175 G5
Watlington St READ RG1 3 L6
Watmore La WWKG RG41 76 C3
Watson Wy DEAN RG23 159 J4
Wavell Cl KEMP RG22 175 K2
WHIT RG2 74 C5
Waverley BRAK RG12 99 F3 1
Waverley Av BSTK RG21 176 B2
FLET GU13 151 G7
Waverley Cl ODIM RG29 180 E1
Waverley Rd TLHT RG30 56 C6
The Waverleys NTHA RG18 85 J3 1
Waverley Wy EWKG RG40 96 D6
Waybrook Crs READ RG1 4 E9
Wayfarer's Wk KSCL RG20 139 G4
Wayland Cl BRAK RG12 100 C2
Waylands THLE RG7 69 F2
Waylen St READ RG1 2 F6
Wayside Gn GOR/PANG RG8 26 D3
GOR/PANG RG8 26 D3 2
Wayside Rd DEAN RG23 159 G6
Wealden Wy TLHT RG30 55 K5
Weald Ri TLHT RG30 56 A3
Weatherby Gdns HTWY RG27 149 J4 5
Weavers Wy WAR/TWY RG10 60 C1
Webb Cl BNFD RG42 79 F5
CHAM RG24 161 F1
Webb Ct EWKG RG40 77 K6
Webbs Acre STHA RG19 86 A5
Webbs La THLE RG7 68 E7
Wedderburn Cl WWKG RG41 76 C4
Wedgewood Wy TLHT RG30 56 A4 5
Wedman's La HTWY RG27 147 J3
Weighbridge Rw READ RG1 2 F3
Weir Cl CALC RG31 72 A2 5
Weir Rd HTWY RG27 149 G6
Welbeck BRAK RG12 99 F3
Welby Crs WWKG RG41 76 A5
Weldale St READ RG1 2 F5
Weldon Cl FLET GU13 167 J6
Welford Rd WODY RG5 59 K5
Welland Cl CALC RG31 55 H4
Wella Rd KEMP RG22 176 A2
Weller Dr EWKG RG40 115 K2
Weller's La BNFD RG42 79 K1
Wellesley Dr CWTH RG45 117 K3
Wellfield Cl CALC RG31 55 H6 3
Well House La HTWY RG27 114 E5
Wellhouse La NTHA RG18 49 J7
Wellington Av FLET GU13 167 J1
WHIT RG2 8 B4
Wellington Cl NWBY RG14 84 B2 3
Wellington Crs TADY RG26 108 A7
Wellington Dr BRAK RG12 11 K9
Wellington Gdns THLE RG7 68 C5
Wellingtonia Av EWKG RG40 117 G4
Wellington Rd CWTH RG45 118 D4
EWKG RG40 97 G1
Wellington Ter DEAN RG23 159 H4
Wellmans Meadow KSCL RG20 123 K6
Well Meadow NWBY RG14 84 A2
Well Rd NFNM GU10 182 D6
Well St KSCL RG20 121 K3
Welsh La THLE RG7 113 H6
Welshman's Rd THLE RG7 110 A3
Welton Ct BSTK RG21 14 C4
Welwick Cl EARL RG6 75 H4 12
Wendan Rd NWBY RG14 12 D9
Wendover Wy TLHT RG30 55 J6
Wenlock Edge WAR/TWY RG10 60 A1
Wenlock Wy STHA RG19 85 J5 7
Wensley Cl WAR/TWY RG10 46 C7
Wensley Dr FLET GU13 151 H7 8
Wensley Rd READ RG1 6 E2
Wentworth Av ASC SL5 81 F7
WHIT RG2 74 A6 2
Wentworth Cl CWTH RG45 118 A2
YTLY GU46 135 J4 5
Wentworth Ct NWBY RG14 13 G7
Wentworth Wy ASC SL5 81 F7
Wescott Rd EWKG RG40 97 J1
Wessex Av ODIM RG29 180 C3
Wessex Cl BSTK RG21 14 C9
Wessex Crs ODIM RG29 180 C3
Wessex Dr ODIM RG29 180 C3
Wessex Gdns WAR/TWY RG10 60 D2
Westbourne Ter TLHT RG30 56 D6
West Brook Cl DEAN RG23 174 A4
Westbrook Gdns BRAK RG12 11 H2
Westbrook Rd TLHT RG30 56 D4 3
Westbury Cl CWTH RG45 118 C2
FLET GU13 167 K3
Westbury La GOR/PANG RG8 41 F6
West Chiltern GOR/PANG RG8 26 D3 3
Westcombe Cl BRAK RG12 100 A5
Westcote Rd TLHT RG30 2 A8
Westcotts Gn BNFD RG42 80 A5
West Ct CAV/SC RG4 59 H3
Westdean Ct BSTK RG21 14 B6
Westdeane Ct BSTK RG21 14 B6
Westdene Cresent CAV/SC RG4 57 F1
West Dr CALC RG31 71 K1
CAV/SC RG4 59 G4
West End TADY RG26 143 J5
West End La BNFD RG42 79 J3
West End Rd THLE RG7 110 D3
Westerdale STHA RG19 85 H4
Western Av HEN RG9 31 H3
NWBY RG14 12 E1
WODY RG5 59 G5
Western Elms Av TLHT RG30 2 C7

Western End NWBY RG14 ...... 12 A6 ⊡
Western La ODIM RG29 ...... 180 C2
Western Oaks CALC RG31 ...... 55 K3
Western Rd BNFD RG42 ...... 79 F6
　BRAK RG12 ...... 10 A3
　HEN RG9 ...... 31 H3
　READ RG1 ...... 2 C8
Western Wy KEMP RG22 ...... 175 J2
West Field Cl TADY RG26 ...... 127 G1
Westfield Crs HEN RG9 ...... 46 A1
　NTHA RG18 ...... 85 G3
Westfield Rd BSTK RG21 ...... 15 H9
　NTHA RG18 ...... 85 F2
　WWKG RG41 ...... 76 A4
Westfields KSCL RG20 ...... 21 J7
Westfield Wy NWBY RG14 ...... 12 A6
Westgate Rd NWBY RG14 ...... 12 A6
West Gn YTLY GU46 ...... 135 J2
West Green Rd HTWY RG27 ...... 148 E4
West Ham Cl KEMP RG22 ...... 159 H7
West Ham La KEMP RG22 ...... 159 G7
Westhatch La BNFD RG42 ...... 79 K2
West HI READ RG1 ...... 3 J9
Westland NTHA RG18 ...... 85 G3 ⊡
Westlands Rd NWBY RG14 ...... 12 F9
West La HEN RG9 ...... 31 G1 ⊡
Westleigh Dr CAV/SC RG4 ...... 29 H7
Westlyn Rd TADY RG26 ...... 109 H7
Westmead Dr NWBY RG14 ...... 83 J7
West Mills NWBY RG14 ...... 12 D4
Westminster Cl FLET GU13 ...... 167 H1 ⊡
　KEMP RG22 ...... 175 G5 ⊡
Westminster Wy EARL RG6 ...... 9 L9
Westmorland La WWKG RG41 ...... 96 C1 ⊡
Westmorland Dr BNFD RG42 ...... 80 C4
Westonbirt Dr CAV/SC RG4 ...... 57 F2 ⊡
Weston's KSCL RG20 ...... 34 C4
Westover Rd FLET GU13 ...... 167 J2
Westray Cl BSTK RG21 ...... 15 J1 ⊡
Westridge KSCL RG20 ...... 120 B4
Westridge Av GOR/PANG RG8 ...... 41 H7 ⊡
West Rd EWKG RG40 ...... 98 D5
　HEN RG9 ...... 28 C1 ⊡
Westside Cl KEMP RG22 ...... 175 J1 ⊡
West St HEN RG9 ...... 31 G1 ⊡
　KSCL RG20 ...... 121 H4
　NWBY RG14 ...... 12 D3
　ODIM RG29 ...... 180 B2
　READ RG1 ...... 3 G5
　TADY RG26 ...... 127 G1
Westview Dr WAR/TWY RG10 ...... 46 C6
Westward Rd WWKG RG41 ...... 76 E7
Westway GOR/PANG RG8 ...... 25 F3 ⊡
Westwood Gln CALC RG31 ...... 55 H5
Westwood Rd CALC RG31 ...... 55 J4
　NWBY RG14 ...... 13 H9
Westwood Rw CALC RG31 ...... 55 H3
Wetherby Cl CAV/SC RG4 ...... 43 K6
Weybridge Md YTLY GU46 ...... 135 K2
Weybrook Ct TADY RG26 ...... 143 J6
Weycrofts BNFD RG42 ...... 79 G5
Weyhill Cl TADY RG26 ...... 126 E2
Weysprings Cl BSTK RG21 ...... 15 J4
Whaley Rd EWKG RG40 ...... 77 J6
Wharfedale Rd WWKG RG41 ...... 75 K3
Wharfe La HEN RG9 ...... 31 H1
Wharf Rd NWBY RG14 ...... 12 F4
Wharfside THLE RG7 ...... 89 F4
Wharf St NWBY RG14 ...... 12 E4
Whatley Gn BRAK RG12 ...... 99 J4 ⊡
Wheatfields Rd WHIT RG2 ...... 94 B2
Wheatlands La CALC RG31 ...... 71 K2
Wheatlands La NWBY RG14 ...... 102 E2
Wheatley Cl WHIT RG2 ...... 74 B5
Wheble Dr WODY RG5 ...... 59 G5
Wheeler Cl THLE RG7 ...... 91 G4 ⊡
Wheeler Ct CALC RG31 ...... 55 K4
Wheeler HI HTWY RG27 ...... 164 B2
Wheelers Green Wy STHA RG19 ...... 85 K5
Wheelton Cl EARL RG6 ...... 75 H3 ⊡
Whinchat Ct HTWY RG27 ...... 149 H3
Whin Holt FLET GU13 ...... 167 H5
Whistler Cl BSTK RG21 ...... 15 J8
Whistlers La THLE RG7 ...... 110 A7
Whistley Cl BRAK RG12 ...... 11 L6
Whitby Dr READ RG1 ...... 7 M1
Whitby Gn CAV/SC RG4 ...... 44 A6
Whitchurch Rd GOR/PANG RG8 ...... 40 C6
Whitebeam Cl WWKG RG41 ...... 96 E4
White City CWTH RG45 ...... 118 E3
White Cl NTHA RG18 ...... 128 C1
Whitedown Rd TADY RG26 ...... 126 C1
Whitegates La EARL RG6 ...... 5 H6
Whitehall Dr WHIT RG2 ...... 95 H7
Whiteham Cl THLE RG7 ...... 70 D2 ⊡
White Hart La BSTK RG21 ...... 15 G6
　TADY RG26 ...... 142 D2
Whitehead Cl CHAM RG24 ...... 161 G4 ⊡
White HI GOR/PANG RG8 ...... 38 A6
　HEN RG9 ...... 30 D6
　HEN RG9 ...... 31 K1

　KSCL RG20 ...... 121 G7
　KSCL RG20 ...... 122 E6
Whitehills Gn GOR/PANG RG8 ...... 25 F5
White Horse La EWKG RG40 ...... 116 B3
White House Cl THLE RG7 ...... 175 J2
White House Gdns YTLY GU46 ...... 135 H2 ⊡
Whitehouse Rd GOR/PANG RG8 ...... 26 D3
Whiteknights Rd EARL RG6 ...... 9 H3
Whitelands Dr ASC SL5 ...... 81 G6
Whitelands Rd NTHA RG18 ...... 85 H3
White La HEN RG9 ...... 16 B3
　OVTN RG25 ...... 179 C2
　TADY RG26 ...... 157 F5
White Lion Wy YTLY GU46 ...... 135 J2
White Lodge Cl CALC RG31 ...... 55 G2
Whitemoor La GOR/PANG RG8 ...... 38 B7
Whitenights Rd READ RG1 ...... 8 K2 ⊡
Whites Cl HTWY RG27 ...... 163 J2 ⊡
White's HI THLE RG7 ...... 90 D3
White's La THLE RG7 ...... 68 E6
Whitestone Cl EARL RG6 ...... 75 H3 ⊡
Whitestones KEMP RG22 ...... 175 H6 ⊡
Whitewalls Cl KSCL RG20 ...... 21 J6
Whitewater Ri HTWY RG27 ...... 164 B1 ⊡
Whitewater Rd ODIM RG29 ...... 164 B7
Whitewell Cl WHIT RG2 ...... 95 H5 ⊡
Whitewood CHAM RG24 ...... 145 G7
Whitley Park La WHIT RG2 ...... 8 A3
Whitley Rd YTLY GU46 ...... 135 J5
Whitley St READ RG1 ...... 7 K1
Whitley Wood La WHIT RG2 ...... 73 K7
Whitley Wood Rd WHIT RG2 ...... 74 B5 ⊡
　WHIT RG2 ...... 93 J1
Whitmarsh La CHAM RG24 ...... 145 J7
Whitney Rd CHAM RG24 ...... 15 L1
Whitstone Gdns WHIT RG2 ...... 7 L9
Whittle Cl EWKG RG40 ...... 116 D1
　SHST GU47 ...... 118 B7 ⊡
Whitton Cl EARL RG6 ...... 75 G4
Whitton Rd BRAK RG12 ...... 100 C1
Whitworth Rd WHIT RG2 ...... 115 K1
Whynstones Rd ASC SL5 ...... 101 K3
Wickers Cl WHIT RG2 ...... 94 C3 ⊡
Wickford Wy EARL RG6 ...... 74 C6 ⊡⊡
Wickham Cl FLET GU13 ...... 167 F6
　TADY RG26 ...... 126 E1
Wickham Pl FLET GU13 ...... 167 F5
Wickham Rd EARL RG6 ...... 75 H5
　FLET GU13 ......
Wickham V BRAK RG12 ...... 99 F4 ⊡
Wick Hill La EWKG RG40 ...... 117 F3
Wicklow Cl KEMP RG22 ...... 175 G1
Wick's Gn BNFD RG42 ...... 78 C3
Wicks La WAR/TWY RG10 ...... 61 K3
Widmore La CAV/SC RG4 ...... 29 H5
Widmore Rd KEMP RG22 ...... 175 H2 ⊡
Wield Ct EARL RG6 ...... 75 H5 ⊡
Wiggett Gv BNFD RG42 ...... 78 D4
Wights Wk KEMP RG22 ...... 175 G5 ⊡
Wigmore La THLE RG7 ...... 70 B4
　TLHT RG30 ...... 56 C4 ⊡
Wigmore Rd TADY RG26 ...... 108 C7
Wilberforce Wy BRAK RG12 ...... 100 A3 ⊡
Wild Briar EWKG RG40 ...... 116 E1
Wild Cl EARL RG6 ...... 75 F6 ⊡⊡
Wildcroft Dr EWKG RG40 ...... 97 F6
Wilder Av GOR/PANG RG8 ...... 40 D7 ⊡
Wilderness Ct EARL RG6 ...... 9 G5
Wilderness Rd EARL RG6 ...... 8 E6
Wilders Cl BNFD RG42 ...... 79 H5
Wild Herons HTWY RG27 ...... 164 B2 ⊡
Wildmoor La HTWY RG27 ...... 145 K4
Wildridings Rd BRAK RG12 ...... 10 D5
Wildwood Gdns YTLY GU46 ...... 135 H5
Wilfred Wy STHA RG19 ...... 86 A4
William Cl STHA RG19 ...... 85 J5
William Sim Wd BNFD RG42 ...... 80 E4
William St READ RG1 ...... 2 E5
Williams Wy FLET GU13 ...... 167 K2
Willis Cl NTHA RG18 ...... 65 G3
Willoughby Rd BRAK RG12 ...... 10 A6
Willoughby Wy DEAN RG23 ...... 159 J5
Willow Cl NWBY RG14 ...... 12 D8
　TLHT RG30 ...... 91 G2
Willowdale EWKG RG40 ...... 96 E7 ⊡
Willow Dr BRAK RG12 ...... 11 H2
　WAR/TWY RG10 ...... 46 C6
Willowford YTLY GU46 ...... 135 J3
Willow Gdns CALC RG31 ...... 55 G3 ⊡
　WHIT RG2 ...... 8 B9
Willowherb Cl EWKG RG40 ...... 77 K7
Willow La HEN RG9 ...... 32 B7
Willowmead Cl NWBY RG14 ...... 103 F3
Willow Rd KSCL RG20 ...... 104 E6
　TADY RG26 ...... 126 E1
Willowside WODY RG5 ...... 59 H4
The Willows READ RG1 ...... 3 H1
Willow St READ RG1 ...... 3 G9
Willow Tree Gld CALC RG31 ...... 71 H2 ⊡⊡
Willow Wy DEAN RG23 ...... 159 J4
　HTWY RG27 ...... 146 A1
　SHST GU47 ...... 118 A7

Wilmington Cl WODY RG5 ...... 59 H5
Wilmot Cl BNFD RG42 ...... 78 D4 ⊡
Wilmott Wy DEAN RG23 ...... 159 J5
Wilsford Cl WHIT RG2 ...... 74 B7
Wilson Av HEN RG9 ...... 31 H3
Wilson Cl KSCL RG20 ...... 21 K7
Wilson Ct WWKG RG41 ...... 76 A5 ⊡
Wilson Rd WWKG RG41 ...... 76 A5 ⊡
Wilstrode Av BNFD RG42 ...... 79 G5
Wilton Pl BSTK RG21 ...... 14 B5
Wilton Rd TLHT RG30 ...... 56 D5
Wiltshire Av CWTH RG45 ...... 118 C2
Wiltshire Dr EWKG RG40 ...... 77 J7
Wiltshire Gv BNFD RG42 ...... 80 C4
Wiltshire Rd EWKG RG40 ...... 77 H6
　EWKG RG40 ...... 97 H1
Wilwood Rd BNFD RG42 ...... 79 F5 ⊡
Wilwyne Cl CAV/SC RG4 ...... 57 K2
Wimblington Dr EARL RG6 ...... 74 E6
Wimborne Gdns TLHT RG30 ...... 56 B4 ⊡
Wimbushes EWKG RG40 ...... 116 C2
Wincanton Rd WHIT RG2 ...... 73 K7
Winch Cl BNFD RG42 ...... 78 D3 ⊡
Winchcombe Cl FLET GU13 ...... 167 H2
Winchcombe Rd BSTK RG21 ...... 14 C6
　NWBY RG14 ...... 12 F5
　WAR/TWY RG10 ...... 60 D2
Winchester Rd BSTK RG21 ...... 14 B9
　KEMP RG22 ...... 175 J3
　KSCL RG20 ...... 139 K3
　READ RG1 ...... 7 K4
Winchester St BSTK RG21 ...... 14 E6
　BSTK RG21 ...... 171 J4
Winchfield Ct HTWY RG27 ...... 166 B2 ⊡
Winchgrove Rd BNFD RG42 ...... 79 H5
Wincroft Rd CAV/SC RG4 ...... 43 F7
Windermere Av KEMP RG22 ...... 175 F2
Windermere Cl WWKG RG41 ...... 76 B3 ⊡
Windermere Rd WHIT RG2 ...... 8 A5
Windermere Wy STHA RG19 ...... 85 F4
Windlesham Rd BNFD RG42 ...... 10 B1
Windmill Av WWKG RG41 ...... 76 D7
Windmill Cnr THLE RG7 ...... 111 F2
Windmill La THLE RG7 ...... 87 H2
Windmill Rd BNFD RG42 ...... 10 B1
　THLE RG7 ...... 111 F2
Windrush Wy TLHT RG30 ...... 56 C6 ⊡
Windsor Gdns KEMP RG22 ...... 175 F6
Windsor Ride ASC SL5 ...... 100 E3
　BFOR GU20 ...... 100 B6
　EWKG RG40 ...... 117 F1
Windsor Ri NWBY RG14 ...... 13 J9
Windsor Rd ASC SL5 ...... 81 J7
Windsor Wy CALC RG31 ...... 71 G2 ⊡
Wingate Rd WODY RG5 ...... 59 H7
Wingrove Rd TLHT RG30 ...... 56 D7
Winkfield BNFD RG42 ...... 80 E3
Winkfield Cl WWKG RG41 ...... 97 G4
Winkfield Rd ASC SL5 ...... 81 K4
Winklebury Wy DEAN RG23 ...... 159 J4
Winkworth La THLE RG7 ...... 109 F6
Winnersh Ga WWKG RG41 ...... 76 C4
Winnersh Gv WWKG RG41 ...... 76 B5
Winscombe BRAK RG12 ...... 99 F3
Winser Dr TLHT RG30 ...... 6 A3
Winston Av TADY RG26 ...... 127 G2
Winston Cl THLE RG7 ...... 94 A5
Winston Wy STHA RG19 ...... 84 E3
Winterberry Wy CAV/SC RG4 ...... 43 H6
Winterbourne Rd KSCL RG20 ...... 62 B2
Winterthur Wy BSTK RG21 ...... 14 D4
Winterton Dr NWBY RG14 ...... 83 G2
Winton Crs YTLY GU46 ...... 135 J4
Winton Rd WHIT RG2 ...... 74 B5
Wintringham Wy GOR/PANG RG8 ...... 41 J7
Wise's Firs THLE RG7 ...... 90 C4
Wispington Cl EARL RG6 ...... 75 G4
Wistaria La YTLY GU46 ...... 135 H4
Wisteria Cl WWKG RG41 ...... 96 E2 ⊡
Wiston Ter READ RG1 ...... 3 J5
Witan Ct WHCH RG28 ...... 169 G6
Witcham Cl EARL RG6 ...... 75 G6 ⊡
Wither Rd DEAN RG23 ...... 173 K2
Withybed Wy NTHA RG18 ...... 85 K2
Withy Cl CALC RG31 ...... 71 H1
The Withys NTHA RG18 ...... 51 F4
Wittenham Av CALC RG31 ...... 55 G5
Wittenham Cl GOR/PANG RG8 ...... 26 E3 ⊡⊡
Wittenham Rd BRAK RG12 ...... 80 C6
Woburn Cl CAV/SC RG4 ...... 57 F1
Wokefield Rw THLE RG7 ...... 91 J7
Wokingham Rd BNFD RG42 ...... 10 E2
　CWTH RG45 ...... 117 K5
　EARL RG6 ...... 4 D7
　HEN RG9 ...... 9 K3
　WAR/TWY RG10 ...... 60 E5
Wolseley St READ RG1 ...... 3 G9
Wolsey Rd READ RG1 ...... 3 H1
Wolsingham Wy STHA RG19 ...... 85 J5 ⊡
Wolverton La TADY RG26 ...... 141 G1

Wolverton Rd TADY RG26 ...... 125 H4
Wondesford Dl BNFD RG42 ...... 78 D2
Woodbine Cl EARL RG6 ...... 9 M9
　EARL RG6 ...... 75 F5 ⊡
Woodbine La KSCL RG20 ...... 103 J7
Woodbourne Cl YTLY GU46 ...... 135 J3 ⊡
Woodbridge Rd CALC RG31 ...... 55 G7 ⊡
Woodbury Rd KEMP RG22 ...... 175 G6
Wood Cl KEMP RG22 ...... 175 G6
Woodcock Ct THLE RG7 ...... 93 H3
Woodcote Gn FLET GU13 ...... 166 E3
Woodcote Pl ASC SL5 ...... 81 J6
Woodcote Rd CAV/SC RG4 ...... 57 F1
Woodcote Wy CAV/SC RG4 ...... 42 E7
Wood End CWTH RG45 ...... 118 A4
Woodenhill BRAK RG12 ...... 99 F5
Woodfield Wy THLE RG7 ...... 70 D2 ⊡
Woodford Cl CAV/SC RG4 ...... 57 F1
Woodford Gn BRAK RG12 ...... 100 C2
Woodgarston Dr KEMP RG22 ...... 175 F6
Woodgate FARN GU14 ...... 151 K7 ⊡
Wood Gn GOR/PANG RG8 ...... 26 D3 ⊡
Woodgreen Cl TLHT RG30 ...... 2 C7
Woodhouse La STHA RG19 ...... 107 F5
Woodhouse St BNFD RG42 ...... 79 F5 ⊡
Woodhurst La WWKG RG41 ...... 76 E5 ⊡
Woodland Av WWKG RG41 ...... 76 D6
Woodland Crs BNFD RG42 ...... 79 K5
Woodland Dr TADY RG26 ...... 129 J7
　TLHT RG30 ...... 55 J6
Woodland Ri FLET GU13 ...... 167 F6
Woodlands CHAM RG24 ...... 145 H6 ⊡
　CWTH RG45 ...... 118 C5
　FLET GU13 ...... 167 G1
　KSCL RG20 ...... 120 D2
　OVTN RG25 ...... 171 H4
　YTLY GU46 ...... 135 J6
Woodlands Av EARL RG6 ...... 5 K7
　THLE RG7 ...... 91 F4
　WODY RG5 ...... 59 G6
Woodlands Cl ASC SL5 ...... 101 J4
　NTHA RG18 ...... 64 C1
Woodlands Ct SHST GU47 ...... 119 G6
Woodlands Gv CAV/SC RG4 ...... 58 A1
Woodlands Ride ASC SL5 ...... 101 J4
Woodlands Rd CAV/SC RG4 ...... 29 F5
　HEN RG9 ...... 31 H5
　TADY RG26 ...... 108 A7
The Woodlands WWKG RG41 ...... 96 C3
Wood La CAV/SC RG4 ...... 28 C7
　CAV/SC RG4 ...... 42 D1
　FLET GU13 ...... 167 K2
　GOR/PANG RG8 ...... 26 C3
　HTWY RG27 ...... 163 F6
　THLE RG7 ...... 113 F3
　WHIT RG2 ...... 95 J5
Wood Lane Cl CAV/SC RG4 ...... 29 G6
Woodleigh FLET GU13 ...... 167 H3
Woodley Gn WODY RG5 ...... 59 J5
Woodman Cl WHIT RG2 ...... 93 K1 ⊡
Woodmancott Cl BRAK RG12 ...... 100 C3
Woodman's La THLE RG7 ...... 90 E4
Woodmere BRAK RG12 ...... 11 L8
Woodmere Cl EARL RG6 ...... 9 J7
Woodmere Cft KEMP RG22 ...... 174 E5
Wood Moor EWKG RG40 ...... 116 E6
Woodpecker Cl KEMP RG22 ...... 174 E4
　NFNM GU10 ...... 183 J4 ⊡
　WAR/TWY RG10 ...... 60 D2
Wood Rdg NWBY RG14 ...... 103 H1
Woodridge Cl BRAK RG12 ...... 11 G6
Woodroffe Dr KEMP RG22 ...... 175 H3
Woodrow Dr EWKG RG40 ...... 97 K1
Woodsend Cl EARL RG6 ...... 74 B6
Woodside NTHA RG18 ...... 65 H5
　NWBY RG14 ...... 103 G1
Woodside Cl EWKG RG40 ...... 96 D7 ⊡
　THLE RG7 ...... 86 D2
　THLE RG7 ...... 111 F2 ⊡
Woodside Dr NTHA RG18 ...... 49 G7
Woodside Gdns CHAM RG24 ...... 145 G6
　FLET GU13 ...... 167 K1
Woodside La CAV/SC RG4 ...... 28 D6
Woodside Wy WHIT RG2 ...... 74 A7
Woods La OVTN RG25 ...... 176 A5
Woods Rd CAV/SC RG4 ...... 58 A1
Woodstock St READ RG1 ...... 4 B6
Woodview Rd GOR/PANG RG8 ...... 40 C7 ⊡
Woodward Cl WWKG RG41 ...... 76 C6
Woodwaye WODY RG5 ...... 59 G6
Woodyer Cl WODY RG5 ...... 75 H1
Woolacombe Dr EARL RG6 ...... 8 D8
Wooldridge Crs ODIM RG29 ...... 180 B4
Woolford Cl BNFD RG42 ...... 80 E5
Woolford Wy DEAN RG23 ...... 159 J5
Woolhampton HI THLE RG7 ...... 85 H3
Woolhampton Wy BRAK RG12 ...... 11 K9
Woolton Lodge Gdns KSCL RG20 ...... 102 C6 ⊡
Woosehill WWKG RG41 ...... 76 E7
　WWKG RG41 ...... 96 D1

Woosehill La WWKG RG41 ...... 96 E1
Wootton Cl CALC RG31 ...... 55 H5 ⊡
Wootton Rd HEN RG9 ...... 31 F3
Worcester Av KEMP RG22 ...... 175 G4
Worcester Cl TLHT RG30 ...... 72 B1
Worcestershire Lea BNFD RG42 ...... 80 C5 ⊡
Wordsworth BRAK RG12 ...... 99 G3
Wordsworth Av YTLY GU46 ...... 135 G5
Wordsworth Cl CHAM RG24 ...... 160 D3
Wordsworth Rd NTHA RG18 ...... 85 H3 ⊡
Worlds End HI BRAK RG12 ...... 100 C4
Wormersley Rd STHA RG19 ...... 104 C1
Worrall Wy EARL RG6 ...... 74 C6
Worsley Pl THLE RG7 ...... 70 D3
Worting Rd BSTK RG21 ...... 14 B6
　DEAN RG23 ...... 158 D7
　KEMP RG22 ...... 159 J7
Worton Dr WHIT RG2 ...... 73 H6
Wote St BSTK RG21 ...... 14 F6
Wrekin Cl KEMP RG22 ...... 175 G1
Wren Cl THLE RG7 ...... 91 G4 ⊡
　WWKG RG41 ...... 96 D2
　YTLY GU46 ...... 135 G3 ⊡
Wrenfield Dr CAV/SC RG4 ...... 43 G7
Wrenswood Cl WHIT RG2 ...... 93 J1
Wroxham BRAK RG12 ...... 10 A9
Wroxham Rd WODY RG5 ...... 59 G5
Wurford Dr STHA RG19 ...... 86 A4
Wychcotes READ RG1 ...... 57 G3
Wychelm Rd WHIT RG2 ...... 94 B2
Wychwood Av BRAK RG12 ...... 100 C2
Wychwood Cl EARL RG6 ...... 8 F7
Wychwood Crs EARL RG6 ...... 8 F6
Wye Cl TLHT RG30 ...... 56 A7
Wyfold La CAV/SC RG4 ...... 28 B4
　HEN RG9 ...... 29 F3
Wykeham Ct ODIM RG29 ...... 180 C4
Wykeham Dr DEAN RG23 ...... 159 F7
Wykeham Rd EARL RG6 ...... 5 G8
Wylam BRAK RG12 ...... 10 B9
Wyld Court HI NTHA RG18 ...... 36 C7
Wyncote Cl WHIT RG2 ...... 8 E9
　WHIT RG2 ...... 74 C5
Wyndale Cl HEN RG9 ...... 31 H2
Wyndham Cl YTLY GU46 ...... 135 J2
Wyndham Crs WODY RG5 ...... 5 M4
　WODY RG5 ...... 59 G4
Wyndham Rd NWBY RG14 ...... 84 C2
Wynford Cl TLHT RG30 ...... 72 D2 ⊡
Wynne Gdns FLET GU13 ...... 167 J6
Wyre Ct CALC RG31 ...... 55 H2
Wyresdale BRAK RG12 ...... 100 C5 ⊡
Wythemede BNFD RG42 ...... 78 C4 ⊡
Wyvern Cl BRAK RG12 ...... 10 D7

Y

Yale Cl SHST GU47 ...... 119 G6
Yardley BRAK RG12 ...... 99 G3
Yarnold Cl EWKG RG40 ...... 78 A7 ⊡
Yarnton Cl CAV/SC RG4 ...... 43 K6
Yates Copse NTHA RG18 ...... 84 D2
Yattendon La NTHA RG18 ...... 51 H4
Yattendon Rd NTHA RG18 ...... 49 H6
Yellowhammer Rd KEMP RG22 ...... 174 E6
Yelverton Rd WHIT RG2 ...... 7 L6
Yeomans HTWY RG27 ...... 134 D2
Yeomans La KSCL RG20 ...... 103 K7
Yeovil Rd SHST GU47 ...... 119 F7
Yew Cl KSCL RG20 ...... 124 B7
　WWKG RG41 ...... 96 E2
Yew Ga NWBY RG14 ...... 83 J1
Yewhurst Cl WAR/TWY RG10 ...... 46 B6
Yew La READ RG1 ...... 6 E3
Yew Tree Cl DEAN RG23 ...... 174 A4
　TADY RG26 ...... 108 E2
Yew Tree Ct GOR/PANG RG8 ...... 25 F5 ⊡
Yew Tree Ri CALC RG31 ...... 71 H1
Yew Tree Stables KSCL RG20 ...... 21 K7
Yield Hall La READ RG1 ...... 3 J6
Yield Hall Pl READ RG1 ...... 3 J6
Yoreham Cl EARL RG6 ...... 75 H5 ⊡
York Cl KEMP RG22 ...... 175 G4
　NWBY RG14 ...... 13 G6
York La HTWY RG27 ...... 149 H5
York Rd BNFD RG42 ...... 78 E3
　HEN RG9 ...... 31 G1
　NWBY RG14 ...... 13 G6
　READ RG1 ...... 3 H1
Yorkshire Pl BNFD RG42 ...... 80 B5 ⊡
Young Crs STHA RG19 ...... 13 M9

Z

Zinnia Cl KEMP RG22 ...... 175 F6
　WWKG RG41 ...... 76 C7 ⊡
Zinzan St READ RG1 ...... 2 F6

Index - featured places

The AA-Fanum House
　BSTK RG21 ...... 15 K3
The Abbey School
　READ RG1 ...... 3 L9
Acre Business Park
　WHIT RG2 ...... 73 J6
Addington School
　WODY RG5 ...... 59 J7
AFC Newbury Football Ground
　NWBY RG14 ...... 13 G3
Aldermaston C of E School
　THLE RG7 ...... 108 C1
Alfred Sutton Primary School
　EARL RG6 ...... 4 F9
All Saints C of E Junior School
　FLET GU13 ...... 166 E3
All Saints Infants School
　READ RG1 ...... 2 D7
Ambulance Station
　READ RG1 ...... 2 F5

Animal Care College
　ASC SL5 ...... 101 K1
The Anvil Concert Hall
　BSTK RG21 ...... 14 E4
Arborfield C of E School
　WHIT RG2 ...... 95 M4
Arcade Gallery
　GOR/PANG RG8 ...... 24 E5
The Argyle Clinic
　READ RG1 ...... 2 D6
The Ark School
　THLE RG7 ...... 89 J6
Arlington Business Park
　BRAK RG12 ...... 11 G3
Art Gallery
　HEN RG9 ...... 31 H1
The Art Gallery
　READ RG1 ...... 3 H1
Arthur Hill Memorial Swimming Baths
　READ RG1 ...... 4 B7

Ascot Heath Junior School
　ASC SL5 ...... 81 H5
Ashford Hill Primary School
　STHA RG19 ...... 107 F7
AshMead School
　WHIT RG2 ...... 7 L9
Auction Market
　READ RG1 ...... 2 F4
The Avenue School
　READ RG1 ...... 7 L3
Badgemore CP School
　HEN RG9 ...... 31 H1
Bartley Wood Business Park
　HTWY RG27 ...... 164 B3
Basildon House
　GOR/PANG RG8 ...... 39 H3
Basildon School
　GOR/PANG RG8 ...... 38 D6
Basing County Infants School
　CHAM RG24 ...... 161 J5

Basingstoke Business Centre
　KEMP RG22 ...... 175 K2
Basingstoke College of Technology
　BSTK RG21 ...... 14 C5
Basingstoke County Court
　BSTK RG21 ...... 15 H4
Basingstoke & Deane Borough Council
　CHAM RG24 ...... 161 F3
Basingstoke Ice Rink
　KEMP RG22 ...... 159 J6
Basingstoke & North Hants Cricket Club
　BSTK RG21 ...... 14 E8
Basingstoke Rugby Club
　KEMP RG22 ...... 175 G3
Basingstoke Sports Centre
　BSTK RG21 ...... 14 E4

Basingstoke Town Football Club
　KEMP RG22 ...... 175 G2
Battle Farm Trading Estate
　TLHT RG30 ...... 2 A3
Battle Primary School
　TLHT RG30 ...... 2 A6
Bearwood College
　WWKG RG41 ...... 76 A1
Bearwood Primary School
　WWKG RG41 ...... 76 A6
Beech Down County Primary School
　KEMP RG22 ...... 175 J4
Beechwood County Junior & Infant School
　WODY RG5 ...... 59 H6
Beedon Primary School
　KSCL RG20 ...... 34 C4
The Bell Surgery
　HEN RG9 ...... 31 G1

Benham Park
  KSCL RG20 .... 82 D3
Berkshire Business Centre
  STHA RG19 .... 86 B5
Berkshire County Council
  NWBY RG14 .... 12 E7
Berkshire County Council
  NWBY RG14 .... 12 B8
Berkshire County Council
  NWBY RG14 .... 12 D3
Berkshire County Council
  READ RG1 .... 3 K6
The Berkshire Golf Club
  ASC SL5 .... 101 F2
Bilton Industrial Estate
  CHAM RG24 .... 160 E2
Bilton Industrial Estate
  CHAM RG24 .... 161 F2
Binfield Primary School
  BNFD RG42 .... 78 D4
Binfield Surgery
  BNFD RG42 .... 78 D3
Birch Copse Primary School
  CALC RG31 .... 55 H5
Birch Hill Medical Centre
  BRAK RG12 .... 99 J5
Birch Hill Primary School
  BRAK RG12 .... 99 K6
Bishop Challoner RC Secondary
  School
  KEMP RG22 .... 175 H1
Bishopswood Co Junior School
  TADY RG26 .... 126 E1
Bishopwood Co Infant School
  TADY RG26 .... 126 E2
Blakes Lock Museum
  READ RG1 .... 4 A5
Blands Infant School
  THLE RG7 .... 90 E5
Blue Mountain Golf Club
  & Conference Centre
  BNFD RG42 .... 78 E4
Boathouse Surgery
  GOR/PANG RG8 .... 24 E5
Bohun Gallery
  HEN RG9 .... 31 H2
Borocourt Hospital
  CAV/SC RG4 .... 28 B2
Boundary House Surgery
  BRAK RG12 .... 11 H4
Bracknell Business Centre
  BRAK RG12 .... 10 B4
Bracknell College
  BRAK RG12 .... 11 G1
Bracknell College
  BRAK RG12 .... 11 H4
Bracknell Forest
  Borough Council
  BRAK RG12 .... 11 G3
Bracknell Rugby Football Club
  BRAK RG12 .... 11 M4
Bracknell Sports Centre
  BRAK RG12 .... 99 K3
Bracknell Town Council
  BRAK RG12 .... 10 F3
Bracknell Town Football Club
  BRAK RG12 .... 11 H4
Bradfield C of E Primary School
  THLE RG7 .... 68 E4
Bradfield College
  THLE RG7 .... 53 F7
Brakenhale School
  BRAK RG12 .... 10 F8
Bramley C of E Primary School
  TADY RG26 .... 129 G5
Brickfields Industrial Park
  BRAK RG12 .... 10 C4
Brick Kiln Industrial Estate
  TADY RG26 .... 109 F7
Brighton Hill
  Community School
  KEMP RG22 .... 175 J3
Brimpton School
  THLE RG7 .... 107 G2
Broadmoor County
  Primary School
  CWTH RG45 .... 118 E4
Broadmoor Hospital
  CWTH RG45 .... 118 E4
Brockhurst Preparatory School
  NTHA RG18 .... 66 A2
Brookfields School
  CALC RG31 .... 55 H2
Brookside Business Centre
  THLE RG7 .... 114 A2
The Brookside Group Practice
  EARL RG6 .... 75 G3
Bucklebury C of E
  Primary School
  THLE RG7 .... 86 D1
Building Design School
  WHIT RG2 .... 94 C3
The Bulmershe School
  WODY RG5 .... 5 M6
Burdwood Surgery
  STHA RG19 .... 85 K5
Burghclere CP School
  KSCL RG20 .... 121 K3
Burghfield Aqua Sports Club
  TLHT RG30 .... 72 B5
Burghfield Health Centre
  THLE RG7 .... 91 G4
Burma Hills Surgery
  EWKG RG40 .... 77 J7
Burnham Copse Junior School
  TADY RG26 .... 108 D7
Burnside Surgery
  FLET GU13 .... 167 H2
Buryfields Infant School
  ODIM RG29 .... 180 D2
Bus Depot
  READ RG1 .... 2 F4
The Business Centre
  BSTK RG21 .... 15 G5
The Business Centre
  THLE RG7 .... 107 G2
The Business Centre
  WWKG RG41 .... 97 F3
Calcot Junior and Infant School
  CALC RG31 .... 71 G2
Calleva Roman Antiquity
  and Museum
  THLE RG7 .... 110 A7
Calthorpe Park School
  FLET GU13 .... 166 D3
Castle Hill Clinic
  READ RG1 .... 2 E7
Castle Hill Junior School
  DEAN RG23 .... 159 G6
Castle Industrial Park
  NWBY RG14 .... 84 B2
Castle Royle Golf Club
  WAR/TWY RG10 .... 47 J2
Castle School
  NWBY RG14 .... 83 J1

Caversham Park Primary School
  CAV/SC RG4 .... 44 B6
Caversham Primary School
  CAV/SC RG4 .... 57 H2
Cedar Park School
  WAR/TWY RG10 .... 46 B7
Cedars School
  THLE RG7 .... 108 D1
Centenary Business Park
  HEN RG9 .... 31 J2
Central Swimming Pool
  READ RG1 .... 2 E5
Century Galleries
  HEN RG9 .... 31 H1
Century Galleries
  HTWY RG27 .... 149 J4
Chalfont Surgery
  EARL RG6 .... 74 D5
Chalkridge School
  KEMP RG22 .... 175 K3
Chapel Hill Surgery
  CALC RG31 .... 55 H5
Chapel Row Surgery
  THLE RG7 .... 67 K6
Charles Kingsley School
  HTWY RG27 .... 134 B1
Chatham Street Surgery
  READ RG1 .... 2 F6
Chiltern Edge Secondary School
  CAV/SC RG4 .... 29 F7
Chineham Park Primary School
  CHAM RG24 .... 160 E3
Christchurch Primary School
  WHIT RG2 .... 7 J2
Christ the King School
  CAV/SC RG4 .... 73 K6
Church Grange & Bramblys
  Grange Health Centre
  BSTK RG21 .... 14 D6
Church Grange Lychpit Surgery
  CHAM RG24 .... 161 G2
Church Hill House Hospital
  BRAK RG12 .... 99 H3
Church of England School
  THLE RG7 .... 88 A3
The Clere Secondary School
  KSCL RG20 .... 121 K2
Cliddesden Primary School
  OVTN RG25 .... 176 B7
Clift Surgery
  TADY RG26 .... 129 F5
Club House
  BRAK RG12 .... 100 A6
Coley Park School
  READ RG1 .... 6 D2
Coley Park School
  READ RG1 .... 6 D1
Coley Primary School
  READ RG1 .... 3 G8
Colleton CP School
  WAR/TWY RG10 .... 60 D2
Comprehensive
  YTLY GU46 .... 135 H5
Compton C of E Primary School
  KSCL RG20 .... 21 K7
Coombe Infants School
  WHIT RG2 .... 95 H4
Court Moor School
  FLET GU13 .... 167 G4
Coxmoor Farm Light
  Industrial Estate
  NFNM GU10 .... 182 C2
Cranbourne School
  ASC SL5 .... 81 K2
Cranbourne Secondary School
  BSTK RG21 .... 14 B9
Crazies Hill Primary School
  WAR/TWY RG10 .... 32 E5
Crondall CP School
  NFNM GU10 .... 182 E6
Crookham C of E
  Infants School
  FLET GU13 .... 167 G7
Crookham County
  Junior School
  FLET GU13 .... 167 J7
Crosfields School
  WHIT RG2 .... 74 B6
Crown Wood CP School
  BRAK RG12 .... 100 A4
Crowthorne Business Centre
  CWTH RG45 .... 118 D1
Crowthorne C of E
  Primary School
  CWTH RG45 .... 118 C3
Curridge CP School
  NTHA RG18 .... 64 C2
Curtain Gallery
  WWKG RG41 .... 76 B5
Danesfield County
  Combined School
  MLW SL7 .... 19 K3
Daneshill East Industrial Estate
  CHAM RG24 .... 15 L2
Daneshill Industrial Estate
  CHAM RG24 .... 15 M1
Daneshill School
  HTWY RG27 .... 131 G5
David Lloyd Sports Centre
  EARL RG6 .... 5 H2
Delwood Hospital
  TLHT RG30 .... 56 D7
Diva Gallery
  ODIM RG29 .... 180 D1
Dogmersfield C of E
  Primary School
  HTWY RG27 .... 166 B4
The Dolphin School
  WAR/TWY RG10 .... 61 F3
Donnington Castle
  NWBY RG14 .... 63 H7
Douai School
  THLE RG7 .... 88 A2
Dove House School
  BSTK RG21 .... 14 F1
Downe House School
  NTHA RG18 .... 65 F3
Downlands Sports Centre
  KSCL RG20 .... 21 J7
The Downs School
  KSCL RG20 .... 21 J7
Downs Way School
  CALC RG31 .... 55 H2
Dryleas Sports Ground
  HEN RG9 .... 17 G7
Duffield Road CP School
  WODY RG5 .... 59 J4
Dunston Park School
  NTHA RG18 .... 85 J3
Eagle House School
  SHST GU47 .... 118 B6
East Barn Surgery
  CHAM RG24 .... 161 G3
East Berkshire Golf Club
  CWTH RG45 .... 117 K3

Eastern Business Centre
  BRAK RG12 .... 11 K4
Eastfield House Surgery
  NWBY RG14 .... 12 E6
Easthampstead Park School
  BRAK RG12 .... 98 E4
Ebony Health Centre
  WAR/TWY RG10 .... 46 C7
Edgebarrow School
  CWTH RG45 .... 118 C5
Edgebarrow Sports Centre
  CWTH RG45 .... 118 D5
Elstree School
  THLE RG7 .... 88 A3
Emmbrook County Junior
  & Infant School
  WWKG RG41 .... 76 E5
The Emmbrook School
  WWKG RG41 .... 76 E6
Emmer Green Clinic
  CAV/SC RG4 .... 43 J7
Emmer Green CP School
  CAV/SC RG4 .... 43 J6
Emmer Green Surgery
  CAV/SC RG4 .... 43 H6
Enborne C of E School
  KSCL RG20 .... 102 B2
Enborne Lodge
  NWBY RG14 .... 102 E3
Englefield Estate Yard
  THLE RG7 .... 70 A1
Englefield School
  THLE RG7 .... 70 A2
English Martyrs RC
  Primary School
  TLHT RG30 .... 56 B6
E P Collier School
  READ RG1 .... 3 G3
Eversley Cricket Club
  HTWY RG27 .... 134 E1
Evingar Industrial Estate
  WHCH RG28 .... 169 G6
Fairfields Primary School
  BSTK RG21 .... 14 E7
Fairview Trading Estate
  HEN RG9 .... 31 J3
Falkland CP School
  NWBY RG14 .... 103 G2
Family Planning Clinic
  READ RG1 .... 3 M8
Farley Hill Primary School
  WHIT RG7 .... 115 F3
Farmhouse Gallery
  KSCL RG20 .... 120 E2
Finchampstead C of E
  Primary School
  EWKG RG40 .... 116 D5
Finchampstead Sports Club
  EWKG RG40 .... 116 D5
Finns Industrial Park
  NFNM GU10 .... 182 C2
Fireplace Gallery
  EWKG RG40 .... 97 H1
FireStation
  READ RG1 .... 3 G3
Fir Tree CP School
  NTHA RG18 .... 84 D3
Fleet Business Park
  FLET GU13 .... 183 J1
Fleet Community Hospital
  FLET GU13 .... 167 F1
Fleet Police Station
  FLET GU13 .... 167 G4
Food Gallery
  READ RG1 .... 4 B6
Football Club
  HEN RG9 .... 31 J3
Forbury Retail Park
  READ RG1 .... 3 L5
The Forest Comprehensive
  School
  WWKG RG41 .... 76 A4
Forest End Medical Centre
  BRAK RG12 .... 99 J4
Fort Hill School
  DEAN RG23 .... 159 H5
Forthill Surgery
  DEAN RG23 .... 159 H5
Fosters Business Park
  HTWY RG27 .... 163 G4
Foxhill Primary School
  BRAK RG12 .... 10 F9
Francis Bailey School
  STHA RG19 .... 85 K4
Friar's Walk Shopping Centre
  READ RG1 .... 3 H5
The Gallery
  CAV/SC RG4 .... 44 E7
Garlands County Junior School
  THLE RG7 .... 91 F4
The Garth Hill School
  BRAK RG12 .... 11 G1
George Palmer Junior School
  WHIT RG2 .... 7 L3
Gillies Health Centre
  KEMP RG22 .... 175 J4
Gillotts School
  HEN RG9 .... 30 E4
Golf Course
  HEN RG9 .... 104 E1
Goring C of E Primary School
  GOR/PANG RG8 .... 25 F4
Goring & Streatley Golf Club
  GOR/PANG RG8 .... 24 B4
Gorse Ride Junior School
  EWKG RG40 .... 116 D1
Grazeley School
  THLE RG7 .... 93 F5
Great Hollands County
  Infant School
  BRAK RG12 .... 99 F3
Great Hollands County
  Junior School
  BRAK RG12 .... 99 F3
Great Hollands Health Centre
  BRAK RG12 .... 99 G4
Great Hollands
  Recreation Centre
  BRAK RG12 .... 99 F6
Greenfields Junior School
  HTWY RG27 .... 149 H5
Greenham Road Retail Park
  NWBY RG14 .... 12 F6
Green Meadows Surgery
  ASC SL5 .... 81 J4
Green Road Surgery
  EARL RG6 .... 4 F9
Gresham Way Industrial Estate
  TLHT RG30 .... 56 B3
Grey House Private School
  HTWY RG27 .... 149 J4
Greys Gallery
  HEN RG9 .... 31 H2
Grimsbury Castle
  NTHA RG18 .... 65 H1

Grovelands Surgery
  TLHT RG30 .... 56 C5
Gun Street Gallery
  READ RG1 .... 3 J6
Hackwood Ho
  OVTN RG25 .... 176 E4
The Hampshire Clinic
  CHAM RG24 .... 15 M2
Hampshire County Council
  BSTK RG21 .... 14 F5
Hampshire County
  Council - Basing House
  CHAM RG24 .... 161 H5
Hampshire County
  Council - Chute House
  BSTK RG21 .... 14 E4
Hampstead Norreys
  Primary School
  NTHA RG18 .... 36 A7
Harmans Water Infant
  & Junior School
  BRAK RG12 .... 11 L9
Harriet Costello School
  BSTK RG21 .... 15 H6
Hart Sports Centre
  FLET GU13 .... 166 D3
The Hart Surgery
  HEN RG9 .... 31 G1
Hassocks Wood
  Industrial Estate
  CHAM RG24 .... 161 F4
Hatch Ride Primary School
  CWTH RG45 .... 118 C1
Hatch Warren County
  Infant School
  KEMP RG22 .... 175 H5
Hatch Warren County
  Junior School
  KEMP RG22 .... 175 H5
Hatch Warren Retail Park
  KEMP RG22 .... 175 F6
Hatch Warren Surgery
  KEMP RG22 .... 175 F6
Hawkedon Primary School
  EARL RG6 .... 75 H4
Hawthorns Primary School
  WWKG RG41 .... 76 D7
The Hawthorns School
  KEMP RG22 .... 175 H3
Haymarket Theatre
  BSTK RG21 .... 14 E6
Headmaster Bradfield College
  THLE RG7 .... 53 F7
The Health Centre
  WHIT RG2 .... 8 D6
Heatherwood Hospital
  ASC SL5 .... 101 H1
Heathfield School
  ASC SL5 .... 80 E7
Heath Hill Surgery
  CWTH RG45 .... 118 C4
Hemdean House School
  CAV/SC RG4 .... 57 H2
The Henley College
  HEN RG9 .... 31 F2
Henley District Indoor
  Sports Centre
  HEN RG9 .... 30 E4
Henley Golf Club
  HEN RG9 .... 31 G5
Henley Town Football Club
  HEN RG9 .... 31 J3
Hermitage Primary School
  NTHA RG18 .... 49 G5
Hernes Estate
  HEN RG9 .... 30 C3
Heron Industrial Estate
  THLE RG7 .... 93 H7
The Hexagon
  READ RG1 .... 3 G6
Highclere Castle
  KSCL RG20 .... 120 C7
Highdown School
  CAV/SC RG4 .... 43 H7
Highwood Primary School
  WODY RG5 .... 5 M8
The Hill Primary School
  CAV/SC RG4 .... 43 K7
Hillside Primary School
  EARL RG6 .... 74 C6
H M Prison
  READ RG1 .... 3 L5
Hollyspring Junior
  & Infants School
  BRAK RG12 .... 11 L3
Hollywood Bowl
  BRAK RG12 .... 10 E3
Holme Grange School
  EWKG RG40 .... 98 A4
Holmwood Health Centre
  TADY RG26 .... 108 D7
The Holt School
  WWKG RG41 .... 77 G2
Home Farm School
  THLE RG7 .... 88 A4
Hook County Junior School
  HTWY RG27 .... 164 A2
Hook Infant School
  HTWY RG27 .... 164 A2
Horris Hill Preparatory School
  KSCL RG20 .... 103 H5
Houndmills Industrial Estate
  BSTK RG21 .... 159 K4
Humphries Industrial Estate
  BRAK RG12 .... 11 G8
The Hurst Community School
  TADY RG26 .... 108 A7
Ian Walker Odiham Gallery
  ODIM RG29 .... 180 D1
Ibis Sports Club
  CAV/SC RG4 .... 56 C3
Inhurst House School
  STHA RG19 .... 107 K7
John Hunt of Everest
  Community School
  CHAM RG24 .... 160 D2
John Rankin County
  Infants School
  NWBY RG14 .... 83 G3
John Rankin Junior
  NWBY RG14 .... 83 G3
The Junior School
  GOR/PANG RG8 .... 39 J7
Katesgrove Primary School
  READ RG1 .... 3 H8
Keep Hatch County
  Junior School
  EWKG RG40 .... 77 J7
Kempshott County
  Infant School
  KEMP RG22 .... 175 F4
Kempshott County
  Junior School
  KEMP RG22 .... 175 F4
Kendrick Girls School
  READ RG1 .... 3 K7

Kennet Secondary School
  STHA RG19 .... 85 K4
Kennet Surgery
  READ RG1 .... 4 D6
Kennet Valley Primary School
  TLHT RG30 .... 72 A2
Kenton Theatre
  HEN RG9 .... 31 H1
Kidmore End Primary School
  CAV/SC RG4 .... 42 E1
Kingsclere Health Centre
  KSCL RG20 .... 124 A7
Kingsclere Primary School
  KSCL RG20 .... 124 A7
Kings Furlong Infant School
  BSTK RG21 .... 14 A8
Kings Furlong Junior School
  BSTK RG21 .... 14 B8
Kings School
  BSTK RG21 .... 14 D6
Laffords Industrial Estate
  THLE RG7 .... 71 F4
Lambrook Haileybury School
  BNFD RG42 .... 80 D3
Lambs Farm Business Park
  THLE RG7 .... 93 H7
Lambs Lane CP School
  THLE RG7 .... 93 H7
Lambwood Industrial Estate
  THLE RG7 .... 92 D6
Langtree Secondary School
  GOR/PANG RG8 .... 26 E3
Lavender Golf Club
  ASC SL5 .... 101 F1
Leighton Park School
  WHIT RG2 .... 8 C4
Leighton Park School
  WHIT RG2 .... 8 D6
The Licensed Victuallers School
  ASC SL5 .... 81 F7
Limington House School
  KEMP RG22 .... 175 J1
Loddon Business Centre
  CHAM RG24 .... 15 M1
Loddon County Infants School
  EARL RG6 .... 75 G3
Loddon County Junior School
  EARL RG6 .... 75 G3
The Loddon Vale Practice
  WODY RG5 .... 59 K6
Loddon Valley Leisure Centre
  EARL RG6 .... 74 D5
London Road School
  ODIM RG29 .... 180 D1
Long Barn Lane Surgery
  WHIT RG2 .... 7 K5
Longfellow Parade Clinic
  CHAM RG24 .... 160 D3
Long Lane Primary School
  GOR/PANG RG8 .... 55 G1
Longshot Industrial Estate
  BRAK RG12 .... 99 F1
Luckley Oakfield School
  WWKG RG41 .... 97 G4
Ludgrove Preparatory School
  EWKG RG40 .... 97 J4
Madejski Stadium
  WHIT RG2 .... 73 G6
Maiden Erlegh School
  EARL RG6 .... 9 K4
The Malls/The Walks
  Shopping Centre
  BSTK RG21 .... 14 F4
Manor County School
  TLHT RG30 .... 72 B2
Manorfield Infant School
  KEMP RG22 .... 175 K5
Mansbridge House School
  READ RG1 .... 4 E8
MapledurhamHouse
  CAV/SC RG4 .... 41 K6
Maple Ridge School
  BSTK RG21 .... 14 E1
Marnel Infant & Junior Schools
  CHAM RG24 .... 160 D2
Marsh Farm Business Centre
  NFNM GU10 .... 182 E3
Mary Hare Grammar School
  NWBY RG14 .... 63 J3
Mayhill County Junior School
  ODIM RG29 .... 180 D2
May's Bounty
  BSTK RG21 .... 14 E8
Meadow Vale CP School
  BNFD RG42 .... 10 B1
Meadway
  Comprehensive School
  TLHT RG30 .... 56 A6
Meadway Sports Centre
  TLHT RG30 .... 56 A7
Melrose Surgery
  READ RG1 .... 3 M7
Merton County Junior School
  CHAM RG24 .... 160 B3
Micklands CP School
  CAV/SC RG4 .... 58 A1
The Micro Centre
  WHIT RG2 .... 7 H6
Milestone Transport Museum
  KEMP RG22 .... 159 H6
The Mill at Sonning
  CAV/SC RG4 .... 59 F1
Mill Ride Golf Club
  ASC SL5 .... 81 G6
Milman Road Health Centre
  WHIT RG2 .... 7 K2
Moorlands Primary School
  TLHT RG30 .... 55 K6
Morland School
  TADY RG26 .... 126 E2
Mortimer Surgery
  THLE RG7 .... 110 E2
Mulberry Business Park
  WWKG RG41 .... 97 F3
Murrell Green Business Park
  HTWY RG27 .... 164 D1
The Museum
  of Berkshire Aviation
  WODY RG5 .... 60 A7
The Natural Health Centre
  NWBY RG14 .... 103 G2
Newbold College
  BNFD RG42 .... 78 E5
Newbold School
  BNFD RG42 .... 78 E5
Newbury Business Park
  NWBY RG14 .... 13 J2
Newbury College of Further
  Education
  NWBY RG14 .... 12 C1
Newbury District Council
  NWBY RG14 .... 13 G6
Newbury District Council
  WHCH RG28 .... 169 H6
Newbury District Hospital
  NWBY RG14 .... 12 D7

Newbury District Museum & Tourist Information Centre *NWBY* RG14 ... 12 F4
Newbury Retail Park *NWBY* RG14 ... 104 A1
Newbury Rugby Football Club *NWBY* RG14 ... 103 J2
Newbury Town Council *NWBY* RG14 ... 12 F4
The New Chineham Surgery *CHAM* RG24 ... 161 G1
New Greenham Park Leisure Centre *STHA* RG19 ... 105 H4
Newlands CP School *YTLY* GU46 ... 135 H4
New Scotland Hill CP School *SHST* GU47 ... 118 B6
Newtown Junior & Infant School *READ* RG1 ... 4 B5
Nimrod Industrial Estate *WHIT* RG2 ... 7 J2
Northcroft Surgery *NWBY* RG14 ... 12 D4
North Hampshire Hospital *CHAM* RG24 ... 159 K3
North Hants Golf Club *FARN* GU14 ... 151 H6
The Norton Practice *READ* RG1 ... 3 L7
Oaklands Business Centre *WWKG* RG41 ... 97 F4
Oaklands County Junior & Infant School *CWTH* RG45 ... 118 B2
Oakley C of E Junior School *DEAN* RG23 ... 173 K3
Oakley County Infant School *DEAN* RG23 ... 173 K3
Oak Park Golf Club *NFNM* GU10 ... 183 F6
Oakridge County Junior School *BSTK* RG21 ... 160 B4
Oakwood School *HTWY* RG27 ... 149 J5
Odiham Castle *ODIM* RG29 ... 164 A7
Odiham Cottage Hospital *ODIM* RG29 ... 180 D2
The Odiham Health Centre *ODIM* RG29 ... 180 C1
Old Art Gallery *EWKG* RG40 ... 98 A5
Old Basing Surgery *CHAM* RG24 ... 161 J6
Oracle Shopping Centre *READ* RG1 ... 3 J6
The Oratory Preparatory School *GOR/PANG* RG8 ... 26 C7
The Oratory School *GOR/PANG* RG8 ... 27 F3
Osborn Way Industrial Estate *HTWY* RG27 ... 163 K3
Our Ladys Preparatory School *CWTH* RG45 ... 118 B5
Overbridge Surgery *KEMP* RG22 ... 159 K7
Overton C of E Primary School *OVTN* RG25 ... 171 G3
Overton Gallery *OVTN* RG25 ... 171 H4
Overton Surgery *OVTN* RG25 ... 171 J4
Owlsmoor Primary School *SHST* GU47 ... 119 F7
Oxford Rd Surgery *READ* RG1 ... 3 G6
Oxford Road Primary School *READ* RG1 ... 2 D6
Paddock Road Industrial Estate *CAV/SC* RG4 ... 4 A2
Paddock Road Industrial Estate *CAV/SC* RG4 ... 4 A1
Padworth College *THLE* RG7 ... 89 H6
Palmer C of E Junior School *EWKG* RG40 ... 77 J7
Pangbourne College *GOR/PANG* RG8 ... 53 J2
Pangbourne Infants School *GOR/PANG* RG8 ... 40 D7
Pangbourne Medical Centre *GOR/PANG* RG8 ... 40 B6
Papplewick School *ASC* SL5 ... 81 J6
Park House School *NWBY* RG14 ... 103 H2
Park Lane Primary School *CALC* RG31 ... 55 H5
Parkside Business Centre *WODY* RG5 ... 59 H5
Park View Infant School *KEMP* RG22 ... 175 H2
Park View Junior School *KEMP* RG22 ... 175 H1
Parsons Down Infant School *STHA* RG19 ... 85 G4
Parsons Down Junior School *STHA* RG19 ... 85 H4
Peppard C of E School *HEN* RG9 ... 29 H3
Perborough Castle *KSCL* RG20 ... 35 K4
Phoenix Business Park *BRAK* RG12 ... 78 D7
Phoenix Plaza Bowling Alley *EWKG* RG40 ... 97 G2
Physiotherapy Surgery *GOR/PANG* RG8 ... 40 C6
The Piggott C of E School *WAR/TWY* RG10 ... 46 B4
The Pines Junior & Infant School *BRAK* RG12 ... 99 H5
Pinewood Leisure Centre *EWKG* RG40 ... 98 C7
Pipers Industrial Estate *STHA* RG19 ... 86 A6
P M S Health Centre *READ* RG1 ... 3 L9
Polehampton County Infant School *WAR/TWY* RG10 ... 46 C7
Polehampton Junior School *WAR/TWY* RG10 ... 46 C6
Presentation College *TLHT* RG30 ... 6 A1

Princess Marina College *EWKG* RG40 ... 95 J7
Priors Court School *NTHA* RG18 ... 48 C5
The Priory Primary School *TADY* RG26 ... 143 G1
Progress Theatre *READ* RG1 ... 7 M2
Prospect Foot Clinic *CAV/SC* RG4 ... 57 H2
Prospect School *TLHT* RG30 ... 72 B1
Purley C of E School *GOR/PANG* RG8 ... 41 H7
Queen Annes School *CAV/SC* RG4 ... 57 J2
Queen Marys College *BSTK* RG21 ... 14 F9
Raceview Business Centre *NWBY* RG14 ... 13 H5
Radstock CP School *EARL* RG6 ... 9 J8
Ranelagh School *BRAK* RG12 ... 11 G5
Ranikhet Primary School *TLHT* RG30 ... 56 B5
Reading Adult College *TLHT* RG30 ... 56 D5
Reading Adult & Community College *READ* RG1 ... 3 H1
Reading Blue Coat School *CAV/SC* RG4 ... 59 F2
Reading Borough Council *READ* RG1 ... 3 G7
Reading Business Centre *READ* RG1 ... 3 K7
Reading Clinic *READ* RG1 ... 3 M7
Reading College *READ* RG1 ... 4 B6
Reading College of Technology *READ* RG1 ... 4 F9
Reading County Court *READ* RG1 ... 3 K5
Reading Girls School *WHIT* RG2 ... 7 M5
Reading Retail Park *TLHT* RG30 ... 56 C4
Reading School *READ* RG1 ... 4 A8
Reading Superbowl *CALC* RG31 ... 71 F2
Reading University *READ* RG1 ... 9 H3
Redfields Industrial Estate *FLET* GU13 ... 183 G1
Redfields Industrial Park *FLET* GU13 ... 183 F2
Redlands Primary School *READ* RG1 ... 8 C1
Red Shute Hill Industrial Estate *NTHA* RG18 ... 65 F1
Register Office *READ* RG1 ... 2 F8
Reme Museum *EWKG* RG40 ... 95 K7
Retail Park *NWBY* RG14 ... 13 K3
Retail Park *READ* RG1 ... 3 M5
Richard Aldworth Community School *KEMP* RG22 ... 175 J2
Richmond Surgery *FLET* GU13 ... 167 G5
Ridge House School *NTHA* RG18 ... 65 J4
Rivermead CP School *WODY* RG5 ... 59 J7
Rivermead Leisure Centre *READ* RG1 ... 2 E1
Riverpark Industrial Estate *NWBY* RG14 ... 13 J3
The River & Rowing Museum at Henley *HEN* RG9 ... 31 J2
Robert Cort Industrial Estate *WHIT* RG2 ... 7 J2
Robert Mays School *ODIM* RG29 ... 180 B1
Robert Piggott C of E Infant School *WAR/TWY* RG10 ... 46 D3
Robert Piggott C of E Junior School *WAR/TWY* RG10 ... 46 C3
Rosedale Clinic *READ* RG1 ... 8 A1
Royal Ascot Golf Club *ASC* SL5 ... 81 K7
Royal Berkshire & Battle Hospital *TLHT* RG30 ... 2 B5
Royal Berkshire Hospital *READ* RG1 ... 3 M8
Ruckstall County Primary School *BSTK* RG21 ... 15 J8
Rupert House School *HEN* RG9 ... 17 H1
Russell Street Surgery *READ* RG1 ... 2 F7
Ryeish Green Comprehensive School *THLE* RG7 ... 93 J3
Sacred Heart RC School *HEN* RG9 ... 31 G2
St Andrews School *GOR/PANG* RG8 ... 53 F4
St Annes Catholic Primary School *KEMP* RG22 ... 175 J1
St Annes RC Primary School *CAV/SC* RG4 ... 57 J3
St Bartholomews *NWBY* RG14 ... 12 B7
St Bartholomews School *NWBY* RG14 ... 12 B8
St Bedes Catholic Primary School *CHAM* RG24 ... 160 B2
St Crispins Secondary School *EWKG* RG40 ... 97 K1
St Crispins Sports Centre *EWKG* RG40 ... 97 K1
St Dominic Savio RC Primary School *WODY* RG5 ... 59 G1

St Edwards School *TLHT* RG30 ... 2 C7
St Finians School *NTHA* RG18 ... 65 J6
St Francis RC School *ASC* SL5 ... 101 K4
St Gabriels School *KSCL* RG20 ... 104 A2
St Johns C of E School *READ* RG1 ... 3 M7
St Johns School *BSTK* RG21 ... 14 D9
St Johns School *NWBY* RG14 ... 12 D9
St Johns School *THLE* RG7 ... 111 F3
St Josephs Convent School *READ* RG1 ... 8 C1
St Josephs RC Primary School *BRAK* RG12 ... 11 J4
St Josephs RC Primary School *NWBY* RG14 ... 13 H1
St Margaret Clitherow Primary School *BRAK* RG12 ... 99 G5
St Marks C of E School *NTHA* RG18 ... 65 H5
St Marks Primary School *KEMP* RG22 ... 175 G6
St Martins RC Primary School *CAV/SC* RG4 ... 44 B6
St Marys All Saints C of E Primary School *READ* RG1 ... 6 D2
St Marys C of E Junior School *CHAM* RG24 ... 161 J5
St Marys C of E Junior School *NTHA* RG18 ... 85 J3
St Marys C of E Primary School *BNFD* RG42 ... 80 E3
St Marys Preparatory School *HEN* RG9 ... 31 H3
St Marys Primary School *TLHT* RG30 ... 91 H1
St Marys School *THLE* RG7 ... 111 J3
St Michaels C of E Primary School *SHST* GU47 ... 135 K1
St Michaels School *BRAK* RG12 ... 99 H3
St Michaels Primary School *TLHT* RG30 ... 56 B7
St Michaels School *KSCL* RG20 ... 121 J3
St Neots Preparatory School *HTWY* RG27 ... 133 H1
St Nicholas C of E Primary School *WAR/TWY* RG10 ... 60 E5
St Nicholas C of E School *NWBY* RG14 ... 12 D6
St Nicholas School *NFNM* GU10 ... 183 F2
St Pauls C of E Junior School *WWKG* RG41 ... 97 F1
St Pauls RC Primary School *CALC* RG31 ... 55 H6
St Peter C of E School *EARL* RG6 ... 9 J2
St Peters GM C of E School *YTLY* GU46 ... 135 J3
St Sebastians Primary School *EWKG* RG40 ... 97 K7
St Teresa RC Primary School *EWKG* RG40 ... 97 J2
St Thomas Infant School *KSCL* RG20 ... 120 B1
Sandford Springs Golf Club *TADY* RG26 ... 124 D7
Sandleford Hospital *NWBY* RG14 ... 83 K7
Sandmartins Golf Club *EWKG* RG40 ... 97 G6
Sandy Lane County Infant School *BNFD* RG42 ... 79 K5
Saxonwood School for the Handicapped *DEAN* RG23 ... 159 G3
Shaw-cum-donnington School *NWBY* RG14 ... 83 K1
Sherborne St. John Primary School *CHAM* RG24 ... 143 K6
Shinfield C of E Junior School *WHIT* RG2 ... 94 C3
Shinfield Infant School *WHIT* RG2 ... 94 B3
Shiplake C of E Primary School *HEN* RG9 ... 45 H2
Shiplake College *HEN* RG9 ... 45 J3
Showcase Cinemas Reading *WHIT* RG2 ... 75 J2
Shute End Medical Practice *WWKG* RG41 ... 97 G1
Silchester Primary School *THLE* RG7 ... 110 A7
Sindlesham School *WWKG* RG41 ... 75 J7
Skimped Hill Health Centre *BRAK* RG12 ... 10 F3
Sonning Church of England Primary School *CAV/SC* RG4 ... 59 G2
Sonning Common CP School *CAV/SC* RG4 ... 29 G6
Sonning Common Health Centre *CAV/SC* RG4 ... 29 G6
Southcote Clinic *TLHT* RG30 ... 72 D2
Southcote CP School *TLHT* RG30 ... 72 D2
Southfields Special School *EWKG* RG40 ... 97 J3
South Ham Medical Centre *KEMP* RG22 ... 175 H1
Southlake County Junior School *WODY* RG5 ... 75 G1
Southlake Primary School *WODY* RG5 ... 75 H1
South Reading Leisure Centre *WHIT* RG2 ... 7 M9
21 South Street Arts Centrel *READ* RG1 ... 3 K7
Speenhamland CP School *NWBY* RG14 ... 12 D1

Springfield Primary School *CALC* RG31 ... 55 G6
Spurcroft Primary School *STHA* RG19 ... 85 J5
Stadium Industrial Estate *TLHT* RG30 ... 56 C4
Station Industrial Estate *FLET* GU13 ... 151 J7
Station Industrial Estate *WWKG* RG41 ... 97 G1
Sterling Industrial Estate *NWBY* RG14 ... 13 G5
Stockcross School *KSCL* RG20 ... 82 B1
Strathfield Saye *THLE* RG7 ... 130 E2
Streatley School *GOR/PANG* RG8 ... 24 C5
Surrey Hampshire Borders NHS Trust *BSTK* RG21 ... 15 G5
Suttons Business Park *EARL* RG6 ... 5 C4
Suttons Business Park *READ* RG1 ... 4 D5
Swallowfield Medical Practice *THLE* RG7 ... 113 K1
Swallowfield Park *THLE* RG7 ... 94 B7
Swinley CP School *ASC* SL5 ... 101 K3
Swinley Forest Golf Club *ASC* SL5 ... 101 J5
Tadley CP School *TADY* RG26 ... 127 F3
Tadley Police Station *TADY* RG26 ... 108 E7
Tavistock County Infant School *FLET* GU13 ... 166 E3
Tavistock Industrial Estate *WAR/TWY* RG10 ... 46 E7
Temple *READ* RG1 ... 3 H7
Tempus Business Centre *BSTK* RG21 ... 14 A1
Tennis Club *FLET* GU13 ... 183 G1
Thames Gallery *HEN* RG9 ... 31 H1
Thameside School *READ* RG1 ... 3 J1
Thatcham Bowling Club *NTHA* RG18 ... 85 J3
Thatcham Health Centre *NTHA* RG18 ... 85 H3
Thatcham Town Council *NTHA* RG18 ... 85 H3
Thatcham Town Football Club *STHA* RG19 ... 86 A7
Theale C of E Primary School *THLE* RG7 ... 70 C3
Theale Green School *THLE* RG7 ... 70 C3
Theale Medical Centre *THLE* RG7 ... 70 C3
Theatre & Arts Centre *WHIT* RG2 ... 74 A7
THMaes Valley Business Park *EARL* RG6 ... 5 H2
Thorneycroft Industrial Estate *BSTK* RG21 ... 14 A6
Thorngrove School *KSCL* RG20 ... 120 B2
Tilehurst Medical Centre *TLHT* RG30 ... 55 K5
Tilehurst Parish Council *CALC* RG31 ... 71 G1
Tilehurst Village Surgery *CALC* RG31 ... 55 J5
Toutley Industrial Estate *EWKG* RG40 ... 76 E4
Town Hall & Museum *READ* RG1 ... 3 J5
Townlands Hospital *HEN* RG9 ... 31 F1
Trinity Primary School *HEN* RG9 ... 31 H2
Trinity School *NWBY* RG14 ... 84 A2
Tunworth Ho *OVTN* RG25 ... 178 A4
Tweseldown Infant School *FLET* GU13 ... 167 J7
Twyford Business Park *WAR/TWY* RG10 ... 60 C1
Twyford Health Centre *WAR/TWY* RG10 ... 46 D7
Tylney Park Golf Club *HTWY* RG27 ... 147 G6
U C I Cinema *BRAK* RG12 ... 10 E3
Ufton Nervet Parochial Primary School *THLE* RG7 ... 90 B3
University Health Centre *WODY* RG5 ... 59 H6
University of Reading *WHIT* RG2 ... 8 B3
University of Reading *EARL* RG6 ... 5 K8
University of Reading *EARL* RG6 ... 8 E4
University of Reading *EARL* RG6 ... 3 L8
University of Reading *READ* RG1 ... 8 C1
University of Reading *READ* RG1 ... 8 A3
Upcroft Primary School *CAV/SC* RG4 ... 56 A5
Upton Grey Ho *OVTN* RG25 ... 178 D6
Valley Road Primary School *HEN* RG9 ... 31 F3
Viables Industrial Estate *KEMP* RG22 ... 176 B3
Vickers Business Centre *CHAM* RG24 ... 159 K3
Waingels Copse School *WODY* RG5 ... 59 K3
Walter County Infant School *WWKG* RG41 ... 97 F1
Warfield C of E Controlled Primary School *BNFD* RG42 ... 80 B5
Watermill Theatre *STHA* RG19 ... 104 D3
Watermill Theatre & Restaurant *KSCL* RG20 ... 62 E7

Waverley School *EWKG* RG40 ... 96 E6
Welfare Clinic *TLHT* RG30 ... 55 J5
Wellington Business Park *CWTH* RG45 ... 117 K4
Wellington College *CWTH* RG45 ... 118 B5
Wellington Industrial Estate *THLE* RG7 ... 93 H6
Wellington Sports Centre *CWTH* RG45 ... 118 A4
Wescott County Infants School *EWKG* RG40 ... 97 J1
Wessex Bowl *KEMP* RG22 ... 159 H6
Wessex Downs Golf Club *THLE* RG7 ... 88 B3
West Berkshire Council *NWBY* RG14 ... 12 D5
West Berkshire District Council *NWBY* RG14 ... 12 E5
West Berkshire District Council *NWBY* RG14 ... 12 E4
West Berkshire District Council *NWBY* RG14 ... 13 G2
West Berkshire District Council *NWBY* RG14 ... 70 D3
Westende County Junior School *EWKG* RG40 ... 97 J1
Western Elms Surgery *READ* RG1 ... 2 C6
Westfield County Junior School *YTLY* GU46 ... 135 G4
The West Street Practice *HEN* RG9 ... 31 G1
Westwood Farm County Junior School *CALC* RG31 ... 55 H2
Westwood Road Health Centre *CALC* RG31 ... 55 J4
Whitchurch Medical Centre *WHCH* RG28 ... 169 G7
Whitchurch Primary School *GOR/PANG* RG8 ... 40 D5
White County Infants School *EWKG* RG40 ... 77 J7
White Hart Gallery *OVTN* RG25 ... 171 H4
White House School *WWKG* RG41 ... 97 F4
Whiteknights CP School *EARL* RG6 ... 8 E8
Whitelands Park CP School *NTHA* RG18 ... 85 H2
Whitewater C of E Primary School *HTWY* RG27 ... 147 H5
Whitley Park School *WHIT* RG2 ... 7 K8
Whitley Villa Surgery *READ* RG1 ... 7 L1
Whitley Wood Surgery *WHIT* RG2 ... 73 J7
Wildridings CP School *BRAK* RG12 ... 10 C8
Willink Leisure Centre *THLE* RG7 ... 90 E5
Willink School *THLE* RG7 ... 90 E5
Willis Museum *BSTK* RG21 ... 14 F6
Willowdene Play School *CHAM* RG24 ... 161 G1
Wilson Junior & Infant School *TLHT* RG30 ... 56 D6
Winchcombe CP School *NWBY* RG14 ... 83 K2
Winchcombe Junior School *NWBY* RG14 ... 12 E1
Winkbury Infant School *DEAN* RG23 ... 159 J5
Winklebury Junior School *DEAN* RG23 ... 159 J5
Winklebury Medical Centre *DEAN* RG23 ... 159 H5
Winnersh CP School *WWKG* RG41 ... 76 C3
Winterbourne House Clinic *READ* RG1 ... 2 C6
Wokingham Child Guidance Clinic *EWKG* RG40 ... 97 G1
Wokingham Cricket Club *WWKG* RG40 ... 97 G2
Wokingham Hospital *WWKG* RG41 ... 97 F1
Wokingham Theatre *EWKG* RG40 ... 77 G6
Wokingham Town Council *EWKG* RG40 ... 97 H1
Woodcote CP School *GOR/PANG* RG8 ... 26 D2
Woodley Centre Surgery *WODY* RG5 ... 59 H6
Woodley C of E Primary School *WODY* RG5 ... 60 A5
Woodley Park Estate *WODY* RG5 ... 59 G5
Woodley Town Council *WODY* RG5 ... 59 H5
Woodside Business Park *WHIT* RG2 ... 73 J7
Woolton Hill County Junior School *KSCL* RG20 ... 120 B2
Wooshill Surgery *WWKG* RG41 ... 76 E7
Worting County Infant School *DEAN* RG23 ... 159 F7
Worting County Junior School *KEMP* RG22 ... 159 G7
Yateley County Infant School *YTLY* GU46 ... 135 J3
Yateley Health Centre *YTLY* GU46 ... 135 J3
Yateley Manor Preparatory School *YTLY* GU46 ... 135 J2
Yateley School *YTLY* GU46 ... 135 H4
Yattendon C of E Primary School *NTHA* RG18 ... 51 F3
Youngs Industrial Estate *THLE* RG7 ... 108 C4

Page 31

G3
1 Cromwell Cl

Page 41

J7
2 Lilac Cl
3 Park Wk

Page 43

H7
1 Pinetree Ct

Page 55

K2
1 Ferndale Cl
2 Oak Tree Copse
3 Overlanders End

K4
1 Brendon Cl
2 Dudley Ms
3 Hirstwood
4 Hornsea Cl
5 Larissa Cl

K5
1 Dalton Cl
2 Halcyon Ter
3 Lemart Cl
4 Midwinter Cl

K6
1 Cadogan Cl
2 Hollicombe Cl
3 Hursley Cl
4 Ogmore Cl
5 St Michael's Rd

Page 70

D2
1 Chestnut Cl
2 Ellerton Cl
3 Kathleen Sanders Ct
4 North Wk
5 The Orchard
6 Swallow Field Gdns
7 Whiteham Cl
8 Woodfield Wy

Page 71

G2
1 Bamford Pl
2 Caistor Cl
3 Camden Pl
4 Charlville Dr
5 Glamis Wy
6 Hatfield Ct
7 Lennox Cl
8 Marlborough Wy
9 Sandringham Wy
10 Silbury Cl
11 Windsor Wy

Page 75

F5
1 Bourn Cl
2 Elford Cl
3 Fordham Wy
4 Martins St
5 St Clements Cl
6 Sturbridge Cl
7 Tamworth Cl
8 Woodbine Cl

F6
1 Bassett Cl
2 Bottisham Cl
3 Ebborn Sq
4 Gregory Cl
5 Harlton Cl
6 Irvine Wy
7 Ledran Cl
8 Littington Cl
9 Manea Cl
10 Porter Cl
11 Soham Cl
12 Stonea Cl
13 Waring Cl
14 Wild Cl

H4
1 Barholm Cl
2 Barkwith Cl
3 Burniston Cl
4 Dunholme Cl
5 Flamborough Cl
6 Forndon Cl
7 Hengrave Cl
8 Marfleet Cl
9 Sawtry Cl
10 Skeffling Cl
11 Stilton Cl
12 Welwick Cl

Page 80

B5
1 All Saints Rl
2 Augustine Wk
3 Barley Mead
4 Bartholomew Pl
5 Benedict Cn
6 Bernadine Cl
7 Burnthouse Gdns
8 Caesars Ga
9 Cleopatra Pl
10 Cressida Cha
11 Jig's La South
12 Ormathwaites Cnr
13 Rachaels Lake Vw
14 Shakespeare Wy
15 Swithin Cha
16 Thomas Dr
17 Yorkshire Pl

C5
1 Juliet Gdns
2 Julius Hl
3 Northumberland Cl
4 Shakespeare Wy
5 Shropshire Gdns
6 Suffolk Combe
7 Surrey Ct
8 Worcestershire Lea

C6
1 Beswick Gdns
2 Drummond Cl
3 Plantagenet Pk
4 Romeo Hl
5 Viola Cft

Page 85

J5
1 Cairngorm Rd
2 Danvers Cl
3 Glenmore Cl
4 Porlock Cl
5 Snowdon Cl
6 The Thakerays
7 Wenlock Wy
8 Wolsingham Wy

Page 91

F4
1 Horseshoe Crs

G5
1 Burdock Cl
2 Field Cl

H4
1 St Mary's Wy

Page 93

J4
1 Pursers Farm

Page 95

H5
1 Anderson Crs
2 Brants Cl
3 Chamberlain's Gdns
4 Harts Cl
5 Whitewell Cl

Page 96

C1
1 Cornwall Cl
2 Cumberland Wy
3 Rembrandt Cl
4 Riding Wy
5 Somerset Cl
6 Spencer Cl
7 Suffolk Cl
8 Westmorland Cl

D1
1 Agincourt Cl
2 Bedfordshire Wy
3 Blenheim Cl
4 Cambridgeshire Cl
5 Crecy Cl
6 Derwent Cl
7 Dieppe Cl
8 Dunkirk Cl
9 Fleet Cl
10 Jutland Cl
11 Kesteven Wy
12 Lalande Cl
13 Mercury Av
14 Minden Cl
15 Mons Cl
16 Neptune Cl
17 Phoenix Cl
18 Saturn Cl
19 Trafalgar Cl

E7
1 Burchett Coppice
2 Burnt Oak
3 Charlton Cl
4 Dodsells Well
5 Elgarth Dr
6 Jerrymoor Hl
7 Willowdale

Page 97

G1
1 Alderman Willey Cl
2 Bell House Gdns
3 Bird Ms
4 The Terrace

Page 100

B5
1 Burn Moor Cha
2 Cabin Moss
3 Higher Alham
4 Kilmington Cl
5 Mallowdale Rd
6 Pyegrove Cha
7 Wanstraw Gv
8 Wards Stone Pk

Page 118

E7
1 Cherry Tree Cl
2 Faversham Rd
3 Hailsham Cl
4 Helksham Cl
5 Hormer Cl
6 Hornbeam Cl
7 Magnolia Cl
8 Okingham Cl
9 Waltham Cl

Page 129

H7
1 Beech Cl

J7
1 Oaklea Gdns

Page 145

G7
1 Birchwood
2 Larchwood
3 Martins Wd
4 Thurnwood

Page 149

H4
1 Hartford Ct
2 Peel Ct

Page 160

B7
1 Devonshire Pl

E2
1 Crockford La

E6
1 Buckby La
2 The Butty
3 Colne Wy
4 Duddon Wy
5 Hamble Ct
6 Medway Ct
7 Ribble Wy
8 Roding Cl
9 Rothay Ct
10 Severn Wy
11 Thames Ct
12 Trent Wy
13 Weysprings Cl

Page 161

G3
1 Bracken Bank
2 Clover Fld
3 Crofters Meadow
4 Dragonfly Dr

Page 163

K1
1 Broad Leaze
2 Chalky Copse
3 Elms Rd
4 Ferndale Gdns
5 Hatchgate Mead
6 John Morgan Cl
7 Nursery Cl
8 Reading Rd
9 Wash Brook

Page 175

F5
1 Berewyk Cl
2 Bunting Ms
3 Sunflower Cl